THE BEST OF BOTH WORLDS

THE BEST OF BOTH WORLDS

An autobiography by

Colonel Brindley Boon

Edited and abridged by Cyril Wood from articles which
first appeared in *The Musician* 1981/84

World of Brass
The Salvation Army Trading Company Limited
66-78 Denington Road, Denington Industrial Estate
Wellingborough, Northants NN8 2QH

ISBN 978-0-85412-798-6

COLONEL BRINDLEY BOON

Colonel Brindley Boon, who became a Salvation Army officer in 1950, is internationally known as a journalist, songwriter and composer of vocal and brass band music. He has 150 published works to his credit.

The colonel's appointments included editorship of *The Musician* (1955-1961, 1965-1966); the Canadian edition of *The War Cry* (1962); and the *International War Cry* (1972-1976). He was Editor-in-Chief at International Headquarters (1973-1977) and retired officially from active service in 1979 after serving as Chief Executive Officer for the 1978 International Congress.

From 1966 to 1972 Colonel Boon served as National Secretary for Bands and Songster Brigades in the British Territory, during which time he was also a member of the Song Book Council. In retirement he gave much valued assistance to the International Music Editorial Department and, as Chairman, to the 1985 International Youth Congress.

The author was a member of the International Staff Band (1952-1960), with which he visited The Netherlands, Switzerland, the USA and Canada. He was promoted to Glory in March 2009.

By the same author:

Play The Music, Play!
Sing The Happy Song!
ISB
Miss Duff (play)

From THE GENERAL

Just a little to give to ~ buy something for your wife as a token of thanks for letting you come away with me at Easter. In haste, AO.

Above: Personal message to Second Lieutenant Brindley Boon
from General Albert Orsborn

Contents

		Page
Foreword		
Chapter 1	Jubilee at Wembley	1
Chapter 2	Tongs and Toy Trumpets	7
Chapter 3	A Matter of Heritage	13
Chapter 4	Another Tree and More Branches	25
Chapter 5	Growing Up in London	33
Chapter 6	Salad Days	41
Chapter 7	Mysterious Ways	51
Chapter 8	Into the Depths and Out Again	63
Chapter 9	Broadening Horizons	75
Chapter 10	The Calm Before the Storm	87
Chapter 11	Pressing On Regardless	99
Chapter 12	Towards the Stars	115
Chapter 13	Picking Up the Pieces	137
Chapter 14	In Double Harness	149
Chapter 15	The Eleventh Hour	165
Chapter 16	Where the Curfew Still Tolls	181

Chapter 17   With Notebook and Biro   195

Chapter 18   My Worlds Converge   207

Chapter 19   Reporter At Large   219

Chapter 20   Some Special Assignments   237

Chapter 21   Behind a Baritone   249

Chapter 22   New World Interlude   271

Chapter 23   The Salt of the Earth   287

Chapter 24   Keyboard Reflections   313

Chapter 25   Words and Music   317

Chapter 26   Where We Came In   337

Chapter 27   And Now Hallelujah...!   351

Chapter 28   Epilogue   359

Index   361

Foreword

Brindley Boon was one of my heroes. He knew that. I told him. We had that sort of relationship after more than three decades of shared soldiership at Croydon Citadel in South London, during which I followed in his footsteps in a number of editorial appointments, including my present one. I was always grateful for his advice – and occasional admonition, always offered kindly. 'Remember the tone, Charles, remember the tone,' he told me when my enthusiasm for editorial licence took me, in his opinion, a little too far when editing one of the UK weeklies in my comparative youth.

The truth is, Colonel Brindley Boon was the best Salvation Army journalist our movement has ever produced. And we've produced some very good ones. During his active service he was an outstanding reporter, writer, interviewer and editor. And he always had a phenomenal memory – even at the age of 95.

Brindley Boon had an inquiring and perceptive mind, impeccable judgment, warm heart, mischievous sense of humour and boundless love for the Army. No one ever pulled wool over his eyes but in recording our Movement's history he occasionally turned a blind eye for the sake of the Army and the Lord he loved. After a lifetime of taking the closest interest in the minutiae of Army life he knew a hundred secrets, and took most of them to Heaven with him.

Some, though, can be told, and are to be found in these memoirs, *The Best of Both Worlds*, much of which was previously published in *The Musician* and *Salvationist*, but some of which has never previously seen the light of day.

For example, if you haven't read the story before, read Brindley's eyewitness account of the visit of Chalk Farm Band's ground-breaking and highly controversial visit to Rome, where the band visited the Vatican and sang The Founder's Song in the presence of the Pope, receiving his personal blessing. The visit was international dynamite at the time, and the subject of urgent telephone calls between Brindley and General Frederick Coutts. One red hot topic was whether or not the Pope touched the flag when he blessed the band! Read Brindley's account and discover all!

The title *The Best of Both Worlds* refers to the fact that Brindley's active officership – after just one year as a corps officer – was divided between editorial and music appointments. These saw him serving as Editor of *The War Cry* in both Britain and Canada, as Editor of *The Musician* and the youth magazine *Vanguard*, and as Editor-in-Chief at International Headquarters at a time when IHQ had responsibility for the weekly publications of the then British Territory, and also as National Secretary for Bands and Songster Brigades in the British Territory.

This music appointment was phenomenally influential in the life of the territory, particularly in the spiritual life of Britain's tens of thousands of musicians, who were so involved at the very heart of the territory's activities. As National Secretary Brindley Boon was known to practically every Salvationist, and was a much loved and respected figure. As a songwriter and composer, his words and music were heard week by week both in festivals and in regular Sunday worship, as they still are. His classic song of commitment, 'I Would Be Thy Holy Temple' alone will guarantee him a place forever in the corporate memory of English-speaking Salvationists throughout the world.

The Salvation Army's mission has been well described as threefold: to save souls, grow saints and serve suffering humanity. But that excellent description doesn't fully acknowledge the unique nurturing provision the Army makes to those who find their lifelong spiritual home within its ranks – which represents a priceless fourth dimension to its ministry.

Today, Salvationists still make The Salvation Army their spiritual home, but there was a period in the history of the Movement – which might now have passed – when Salvationists joined up hook, line and sinker. The Army was their whole life. It was their family, their social life, their nationality, their identity.

The Best of Both Worlds is about The Salvation Army which was made up of such people, of whom Brindley Boon was the exemplar. When he joined The Salvation Army he became not just a member of it, but an integral, organic part of it. *The Best of Both Worlds* is more than his memories – it is the story of a Movement from which he was inseparable. It's not hard to fathom why. His love for it shines through every page.

Charles King
Lieut-Colonel
Editor-in-Chief and Literary Secretary
International Headquarters

Chapter 1

Jubilee at Wembley

THE 1978 International Congress was drawing to its close. It was Saturday 8 July with one day to go. It had been an exciting day, with non-stop music presented in the Conference Centre auditorium and the smaller Avon and Severn Theatres. There were sporting competitions in the great stadium and the arena and the march past round the famous cup final pitch and it all culminated in a service of thanksgiving.

But the day was by no means over. The musical *The Blood Of The Lamb* was to be presented in the auditorium and the needs of Salvationist youth and their friends were to be catered for in 'Rhythm Rendezvous' programmes to be featured in the two theatres. In addition, the massive arena was to be the scene of a 'Meet the Composers' festival, in which composers and songwriters of international repute were to conduct their own instrumental or vocal works and take part in other ways.

The festival was something of an anniversary occasion for, 50 years previously, on Wednesday 15 February 1928, the Army's most famous composers' festival had taken place at Clapton Congress Hall, when the guests of honour were the Duke and Duchess of York (later King George VI and Queen Elizabeth). This was the first time that royalty had graced such a Salvationist event with their presence and the young couple – they had been married but five years – were quickly at home, 'fixing bayonets' to sing the refrain of the opening song and clapping their hands to accompany the chorus,

And above the rest this note shall swell,
My Jesus has done all things well.

1

The distinguished visitors shared a beautifully decorated royal box erected in the seating area under the clock – opposite the entrance in those days – with General and Mrs Bramwell Booth, the setting providing a study in crimson and gold which, with the mass of uniforms, combined to complete the Army colours.

In his speech the duke said, 'The music of The Salvation Army is symbolic of the spirit which animates that great organisation. It is martial! It is cheering! And, best of all, it is inspiring!'

Six bands took part – the International Staff Band, Chalk Farm, Regent Hall, Clapton Congress Hall, Penge and Cambridge Heath – along with a party of singers from the International Training Garrison.

The royal couple remained for two hours, a part of the festival was broadcast over the new wireless system and the proceedings concluded with the playing of 'Man Of Sorrows' – vividly illustrated by a series of lantern slides – by the massed bands. There have been many subsequent composers' festivals throughout the Army world, but surely never one like that.

The organisers of the 1978 International Congress, therefore, considered that Clapton epic event to be worthy of special commemoration and so it was that no fewer than 20 composers and songwriters were introduced to the capacity audience of 10,000 and overseas delegates were given the opportunity of seeing and hearing a number of British bands in action for the only time during the congress.

General Arnold Brown, himself a composer of band music and a songwriter, called it 'a night never to be forgotten'. He read a message from Queen Elizabeth the Queen Mother who remembered the earlier festival she attended with her late husband and had a special greeting for Eric Ball, the sole-surviving composer-participant of the 1928 festival. It was an historic occasion and one which proved worthy of the description given it by the international *War Cry*: 'An unrepeatable gathering'.

I was honoured to be invited by my colleagues to conduct the 1,000-voice congress chorus in the selection, 'Into The Presence Of The King', my first through setting, published almost 40 years before.

2

The story of the song goes back to May 1937, the month of the coronation of King George VI and his consort. The souvenir edition of *The War Cry* published to mark that historic event contained music of a 'song without words' by Adjutant Eric Ball to which readers were invited to provide words. The majestic and stirring music immediately caught my attention. I decided to try my hand and wrote three verses and a refrain under the title 'Hail To The King!' Although I did not secure first prize I did receive an 'honourable mention'.

Realising that my words would probably never be published to Eric Ball's music, I decided to write my own musical setting and make it a full-length songster piece. The inspiration for the introduction, and incidentally for the title, came one day when I opened my morning paper and saw a picture of Gracie Fields entering Buckingham Palace to receive her CBE medal. The caption announced, 'Gracie passes into the presence of the king'.

That was it! My song was based upon the ultimate coronation of the King of kings, with the blood-washed throng of victorious warriors passing into his presence to receive the triumphant 'Well done!' From then on I knew where I was going; I forwarded my completed selection to Brigadier Bram Coles, Head of the International Music Editorial Department (who predicted it would 'prove useful') and awaited events. The composition was eventually published in *The Musical Salvationist* for September 1938 – even before the prize-winning words and Eric Ball's music appeared in print!

So – here I was, a little more than a month from my 65th birthday, retirement on the horizon, sitting with other Salvationist writers, similarly honoured, in the body of the Wembley Arena waiting for my name to be called and my item to be announced.

There was little tension. For me, all the many months of planning were nearing their end. The anxious times were but memories; the hours of poring over seating plans of a dozen halls; visits to St Paul's Cathedral, Westminster Abbey, the City Temple and Buckingham Palace; endless excursions to Wembley for lengthy discussions about the multitude of events to be held there; reporting progress to the various planning councils and sub-councils at International

Headquarters; countless interviews with the General and Chief of the Staff; the incessant correspondence with territorial commanders and their appointed representatives around the world; preparing programmes, song sheets and other relevant material; making tour arrangements for overseas music sections; delicate negotiations with Scotland Yard, the City of London police authorities and the Greater London Authority concerning traffic concessions, parking facilities, processions and open-air rallies – all such multifarious interests that had occupied my waking hours and haunted my fitful sleep were now at an end. I felt perfectly relaxed and could settle down to enjoy and appreciate the final music festival of the ten hectic days.

This was truly an international offering. Erik Silfverberg, Stanley Ditmer, Terry Camsey and Richard Holz were among those sharing the honours with their British counterparts. I was mindful of the importance of the occasion to Salvation Army history. No other international congress had included such a musical recognition and, frankly, I wondered what I was doing there. I reviewed my years of service as an Army musician and journalist and thanked God – and my leaders – for permitting me to enjoy the best of both worlds. This was undoubtedly the highlight of my career.

Lieut-Colonel Ray Steadman-Allen who, fittingly, acted as compère on this night of nights, introduced my item and added a few kind words, referring to me as one who had been part of the London music scene for 'more than 40 years'. And then I found myself making the long, so long journey from my allotted seat in the arena to the specially prepared rostrum on the massive constructed platform.

The experience was unreal. It was like I have always imagined going out to bat in a test match at the Oval or Lord's might be. I could only imagine.

When I accepted the baton offered me by the courteous Major Ray Bowes my dream was over. There was the International Staff Band, instruments poised awaiting my down beat. Away above them and stretching as far as the eye could discern was the veritable army of neatly clad, blue-uniformed songsters from all parts of the British Territory.

4

They were there at considerable cost to themselves in terms of time and money. Many had travelled long distances. All were responsible for the cost of travelling and accommodation during their busy weekend in London. I gained a new respect for them in that moment. They did, in fact, comprise the fourth such chorus of 1,000 voices to function since the royal opening nine days before.

Two bars of brilliant brass and we were well and truly launched into 'Into The Presence Of The King'. The task in hand had to be concentrated upon. This was no time for flights of fancy or excessive bouts of nostalgia. But I must confess to allowing my thoughts to wander slightly to ask myself, 'What am I doing here? Where did all this begin?'

Chapter 2

Tongs and Toy Trumpets

I WAS two years of age. One morning my mother missed me. Her frantic calls and house-searching drew a blank, but the sight of the front door ajar gave her a clue. For the first time in my young life I had decided to explore the big world outside for myself.

Mother ran into the street. I was nowhere to be seen. Enquiries of neighbours did not help very much. She collected the key, closed the door and hurriedly made her way to the next road. Her fears were quite unfounded. I was perfectly safe and happy, calmly marching down the middle of the street playing a 'trombone', a pair of tongs which I had evidently removed from their place beside the sitting room grate.

Come to think of it, those implements, which seem to have been driven into oblivion by electric switches, gas buttons and central heating thermostats, were not unlike miniature trombones and I can imagine myself manipulating the prongs as slides and seeking to make a sound with my mouth comparable with the tone provided by the trombone section of our band at Willesden Green.

It was wartime. My father was away serving in the forces, his absences between leaves highlighted by the frequent arrival of delightfully humorous postcards, which my mother read to me, taking the trouble – where necessary – to explain the point of the caption printed under the picture. I loved those postcards – and, through them, my absent father – and kept them well into adulthood.

Soon after my debut as a 'trombonist', Mother and I were making one of our regular visits to nearby Gladstone Park, the crowning glory of which was Dollis Hill House and the adjacent rose gardens, which were always a picture to behold. During the First World War the house

7

was taken over as a military hospital for wounded soldiers returned from the Western Front and, on this particular afternoon, the recuperating patients were enjoying tea on the lawn. There was evidently plenty going on to interest my mother while I was just happy to play with a ball on the grass.

After a time, a photographer approached us and my mother was asked, 'Can I borrow your little girl for a few moments?' Older readers, and those who have studied contemporary pictures, will know that fond parents in that era did clothe their precious sons in dresses and other paraphernalia, to such an extent that it really was difficult to distinguish between the juvenile sexes.

I was duly carted off, lifted on to a tea table and given a tenor horn to hold. Acting upon instructions, I attempted to produce a note and, while the blue-uniformed 'Tommies' cheered their encouragement, the camera recorded the scene for posterity.

The next morning the picture appeared in *The Daily Sketch*, bearing the telltale caption, 'Her Turn'. The press cutting has remained in our family ever since and an inscription on the reverse side of a glossy, black-and-white print, in my father's handwriting, states 'Brindley, aged two'.

What few recollections I have of those days are still vividly alive in my memory. I can, for instance, clearly remember being in the park with my mother and paternal grandmother, who was staying with us for a few days, when a German Zeppelin went over. It was a Saturday morning in 1917. We could not believe our eyes and were too amazed even to think of taking cover. Fortunately, no damage was done and thousands of Londoners shared the experience.

Not quite so vivid are memories of air raids. The coal cellar under the stairs was our shelter on these occasions – my mother cleaned it out for just this purpose – and the Tate family from next door joined us. There were two boys and a girl. I liked their company and we played snakes and ladders and other parlour games. Together we also learned to read and tell the time.

When, just after the war, Cynthia Tate, the daughter, died after contracting diphtheria, it was my first experience of that deep sense of loss which accompanies the passing of one I had known closely. It was thought right and proper that the children in the road should attend the funeral service in the local church and so I was introduced to 'There's A Friend For Little Children Above The Bright Blue Sky'. The thought worried me for a long time.

Air raid warnings I cannot remember. 'All Clears' I can, possibly because immediately we received the message we would dash out into the street and cheer like mad, whatever the hour. The good news was spread by a policeman, mounted on a bicycle, blowing a whistle and wearing an 'All Clear' card round his neck.

Regent Hall was the central corps of the North London Division in those days. All the big meetings were held there and a bus took us from our High Road direct to Oxford Circus. The fare was threepence (old money) for my mother and nothing for me. My father was with the Royal Army Service Corps at Grove Park, near Bromley, and sometimes on a Sunday we three would meet at the 'Rink' in the afternoon, attend the meeting, share sandwiches and a flask of tea in Hyde Park, listen to the band at the 'open-air', follow the march to the hall and stay for part of the meeting before Dad saw us off on the No 8 bus for home and left for his barracks. I liked those days.

My 'Rink' hero was, without a doubt, Bandmaster 'Bert' Twitchin. He could do anything: conduct the band, play the cornet, accompany at the piano, play the cornet and accompany himself at the piano at the same time, and lead the prayer meeting. He was the songster leader as well. I sat and watched and hoped that I would be able to do some of those things when I grew up.

Once or twice an air raid cut the meeting short and the congregation was invited to take shelter in the passages under the platform. This was a great experience, for it not only brought me into proximity to the bandsmen, whom I revered as gods from another planet, but also enabled me to strike up casual acquaintance with the bandmaster's son, 'Young Bert', as he was called. We chased each other in and out of the underground warrens which were Regent Hall corridors and side rooms, with the speed and breathlessness of scared rabbits facing their judgment day.

We must have had prior warning that the war was going to end. On Monday 11 November 1918 – I had celebrated my fifth birthday just three months previously – we left home in what seemed to be the middle of the night and made our early journey to Regent Hall. Crowds were already lining Oxford Street but my mother and I managed to squeeze into a small vacant space on the opposite side of the road. Everyone was cheering, singing and waving flags. Mother bought me a flag from a street vendor and I joined in the rejoicing without knowing what it was all about. Presently I saw Bandmaster Twitchin pushing his way through the throng in a stalwart effort to enter the hall. Mrs Twitchin was with him and his son was perched on his sturdy shoulders. Something was in the air!

On the stroke of 11 o'clock, I learned afterwards, the cheering of the crowd was punctuated by the sound of music as the band marched from the hall into Oxford Street playing 'Rule, Britannia!', with the bandmaster and his cornet leading the way. We were soon walking in the middle of that famous thoroughfare, mingling with the thousands who formed a procession to follow the band into Regent Street, round Piccadilly Circus, down Haymarket to Trafalgar Square and along The Mall to Buckingham Palace.

This was not one of the band's many command performances. It was just one of those touches of inspiration that makes life so interesting and worthwhile. On reaching the palace the band could not get anywhere near the gates because of the masses of people. Then it started to rain and it took all the bandsmen's time and patience to re-form into ranks and return to Regent Hall.

On the following Sunday the band was invited to play in the forecourt of Buckingham Palace, but this time marched through the thronged West End with police escort. My father must have been on leave that day for I remember him taking me and trying to explain on the journey what the coming of peace would mean to the world.

It was during the period of the First World War that I became aware of Salvation Army life and service. Corps officers had a tremendous influence on my young life and, as 'specials' were invariably billeted at our home, I became acquainted with many who, in later years, became leaders in our Movement.

Captains and lieutenants seem to flit in and out of my childhood memories with amazing rapidity. Mind you, I think the success of any officer stationed at our corps at that time was, with my mother, determined by his or her tolerance of my disturbing the meetings by frequent outbursts on my toy trumpet.

When my musical prowess began to take shape and I started to take an interest in band instruments and the marches and selections the band played, my parents bought me a trumpet which had four 'valves' and boasted of no particular system of note progression. To play a scale was a work of art and I was not very proficient in seeking to solve the mysteries of creating recognisable melodies. However, this did not deter me from sitting next to my father in the band and joining in, with indescribable tonal colouring, in such pieces as ''Neath The Flag' and 'Eventide'.

I was not aware of the frequent crises which flared up over this indiscretion when the bandmaster was confronted by some bandsmen who objected to the auxiliary assistance from a slip of a boy who could not even blow a trumpet in tune! A compromise was reached. I was allowed to sit next to my father, but on the understanding that not a sound would escape from my 'cornet' when the band was playing. There were times when I forgot this condition of service but, in the main, it was a rewarding recompense just to sit with the band.

Chapter 3

A Matter of Heritage

ON the bookshelf of my childhood home there was an old brown volume with a red label bearing the title *Life Of Brindley*. These were three of the first words I came to read and I will never forget the awe that came over me when my mother, for good or ill, explained that this was a book in which all my misdeeds were recorded.

This threat had a profound effect upon me and, I am sure, deterred me from yielding to many boyhood temptations. To disobey an order and see my mother reaching to record the fact for eternity was a gruesome experience, just as it brought a sense of unspeakable relief when, in response to my tearful pleadings, she would accept my apology, close the book and return it to its rightful place beyond my reach. How was I to know she was only kidding?

There came a wonderful day, however, when, my mother out of the room, I managed to climb on to a chair, open the glass doors of the bookcase and remove the telltale 'diary' to remind myself of all my misdemeanours. I then discovered the truth and kept it to myself for some time.

This was the biography of my illustrious ancestor, James Brindley, with the name of my grandfather inscribed on the flyleaf. The book eventually passed into my possession.

Born in Thornsett, Derbyshire, James had no more than a smattering of the three 'Rs', never could write more than his name and roughly scrawl down the figures of a simple sum. However, he was a rare genius of a mechanic and seemed to be able to do anything: mend a broken machine; invent a new one; or pump a mine by methods crazily original but marvellously effective.

When he died in 1771 at the age of 56 he had given England 365 miles of canals and left a system of inland waterways which should have put the country ahead of nearly all other countries in the world, had not selfish interests been allowed to render his work very largely useless.

I have not succeeded in tracing my family tree directly back to that first Brindley, but I do know that, somewhere along the line, a John Boon married a great-granddaughter of the great man and that they named their eldest son John Brindley Boon to perpetuate the two surnames.

That first owner of the second Christian name was born in the first decade of the 19th century and was married in 1839 to Sara Salt. Six years later a son, William Brindley Boon, was born to them at Burslem, Staffordshire, and he became my grandfather.

John Boon, in addition to managing his own business, was superintendent of the local fire brigade. He was a Wesleyan – a born leader and a good man. His wife, according to their second son, 'was good and loveable; her voice was music'. After the family had lived for some time in Oxford, a domestic disaster made it necessary for William Brindley Boon and his brother John to seek employment elsewhere and they found work in Manchester.

Having lost his situation through a whirlwind of passion, young Will, as his family called him, took a position in Cleckheaton, Yorkshire, at a ridiculous salary, borrowed ten shillings to go with and never looked back. He became manager of a drapery business and, after a while, decided to open a business on his own account. He took a shop in a good situation and soon had one of the best businesses in the town.

By this time he had married a devout church woman and when he attended any place of religion at all he accompanied her to her services. Her death after two years of marriage, leaving him with one child, affected him deeply and it was the thought of the life and influence of his departed partner that led to his conversion.

He joined the Independent Methodists and preached his first sermon at Hunsworth, in the open air, to a group of colliers who sat on a wall and listened. He married again – Annis Fielding was the woman's name – and was elected a member of the local board of the town and spent much time and labour in seeking to right the grievances of the poor.

A new chapel was to be built, costing £1,200, and somebody was required to draw plans. He knew nothing about such skills but, after days and weeks of toil, learnt how and did it.

There must have been some indication, in those days, of his interest in music and leanings towards composition. When the United Free Gospel Churches decided to have a new hymn book, William Boon was appointed, with two others, to select and present *Tunes For Worship*, a companion to the words-only version of another production.

He entered into this task with typical prayerful enthusiasm, supplying three new hymn tunes – 'New Jerusalem', 'Grasmere' and 'Victory' – and arranging three others.

When The Salvation Army made its first appearance in Heckmondwike, just down the road from Cleckheaton, rumours of riot and bloodshed came up the valley and William Boon's heart went out to the two lasses in charge. He decided to lend a hand. He found the town all upset. There might have been a fire. The streets were crowded and everyone was discussing the Army. He went to the barracks. Guarding the door was a young woman with flushed face and tangled hair, wearing an enormous bonnet.

She saw him coming and declared: 'There's nobody else coming into this barracks tonight, and I don't care who you are!' the bonnet punctuating each emphasis. He mildly insisted on going in – but she made a sudden pounce on him and he found himself at the bottom of the steps leading to the hall. From this he gathered that The Salvation Army was quite capable of taking care of itself – that night, at any rate – and went home.

Soon afterwards General William Booth was announced to be in Heckmondwike and the undaunted Boon went down the valley to hear him. He attended all the meetings. At night the crowd surged in and broke up everything. But he had heard the General tell of his East

End of London struggles and victories and the young man's heart went out towards him and The Salvation Army.

Conflicting thoughts began to worry him. A revival of religion took place in his soul and he spent some days alone with God on the moors. He saw more of the Salvationists and was convinced that they were his people.

One morning, walking between Heckmondwike and Cleckheaton, he had received the divine assurance, 'I will be with you', and his mind was made up. He wrote to the General offering himself for full-time service and, soon afterwards, William Booth broke his journey to conduct a campaign in the north-west at Rochdale to meet his latest candidate for officership. The interview took place on the railway station, the two men walking up and down and exchanging points of view. The General boarded the next train. William Boon returned across the Pennines to his home.

His was not an easy decision to reach. There were so many matters to be finalised and the General had not been too encouraging in his attitude. (Boon was later to learn that this was not unusual in such circumstances.) But there must be no going back. He would become a Salvationist and enter fully into Army service.

The business was sold by auction, the sale taking more than a fortnight, so great was the stock. Then, leaving his wife and four children with her mother, he packed a few belongings and arrived at International Headquarters on Monday 1 January 1883. The building was a hive of activity. Any New Year's Day carried an aroma of excitement, but this day possessed more than most.

The General warmly welcomed the newcomer and was full of the day's battle news. He had received a telegram from Staff Officer Hanna Ouchterlony in Sweden reporting the successful launching of Army work in that country. 'Great victory! Hall full! Nine souls! Town all wondering! Hallelujah!'

A cable had arrived from Major Frederick Tucker in India giving news of the beginnings of operations in Calcutta: 'Great crowds in town hall; good order; perfect attention; finance good; Hallelujah!' William Booth was no doubt delighted with this news, especially after the contemptuous way in which his pioneer officers had been received by the authorities of Bombay only two months before.

After a prayer and a handshake, the somewhat bewildered recruit was handed over to Major Frank Smith, who had recently been appointed in charge of the London Division at its headquarters at 20 Charing Cross Road, virtually in Trafalgar Square itself. William Brindley Boon was appointed to assist the major, and the multifarious duties of the former master draper included coal-carrying, fire-lighting, sweeping, dusting, window cleaning, addressing and writing letters, entering returns, leading meetings and marches, inspecting and reporting on buildings and dealing with any other business which unexpectedly came to hand.

A month after starting his new life his first report, published in *The War Cry* of 24 February, graphically described what he called 'The Battle of Trafalgar Square'. It began:

The great Nelson's order, when in the thick of the fight, was 'Nail your colours to the mast'. For the past few days he has looked down upon the flag of a people whose motto is the same. The Blood and Fire emblem has been floating over our West End office. Thousands in the square, after smashing the platform of Mr Bradlaugh, advanced on No: 20 to pay their respects to The Salvation Army.

Charles Bradlaugh was, of course, the atheist who caused a sensation when he refused to take the oath when taking his place in Parliament for the first time as a member.

The 'Battle of Trafalgar Square' raged fast and furiously for some time, the small staff being determined to shut up shop and replace the gates of the building in position as the mob fought to get into the premises. How Major Smith and his helpers managed to stand their ground despite physical attack and howling abuse makes fascinating reading. The feature revealed the reporter as a good newspaperman with an acute sense of humour. This and similar reports and experiences revealed that the circumspect Mr Boon, Independent Methodist, had indeed become a Blood and Fire Salvationist!

After he had been in London for three months Captain Boon (exactly when the rank was conferred is not known) sent for his wife and family and took a house in Hammersmith. Some three months later he was summoned to the office of the Chief of the Staff (Bramwell Booth) who 'handed me the villages of England'. At that time no more than eight outposts were being run but, by dint of writing and worrying, praying and travelling, more than 200 outposts were opened by the first year.

Promoted to Staff Captain and appointed to the office of the Chief of the Staff, William Boon served as private secretary during an eventful period of Army history, including the famous 'Maiden Tribute' case when W. T. Stead and Bramwell Booth were required to stand trial at the Old Bailey.

Early in 1886 William Brindley Boon's appointment as field secretary, with the rank of major, was announced, this marking his third anniversary as a Salvationist. At the first International Congress in that year Major Boon was responsible for the participation of 'the field' in all the major events, himself supporting the General and Chief of the Staff in the many meetings held in the Great Western Hall and other centres. Tribute was paid to his organising ability and flair for detail.

The War Cry dated 24 August 1889 announced that W. Brindley Boon, now a colonel after six years' service, had been appointed 'chief secretary to Commandant Herbert Booth for affairs in the United Kingdom'. He was the first to hold such a position and was introduced as the forerunner of all succeeding chief secretaries.

This new Booth/Boon partnership marked the beginning of what became known as National Headquarters in the British Territory. Herbert Booth was, in essence, the first British Commissioner and a separate headquarters, known as the Home Office at International Headquarters, was established at 179 Queen Victoria Street, close to Blackfriars Station. The officers and employees who served on this new headquarters were called 'Home-lot' and the premises remained the nerve centre of Army activity in the British Isles until April 1893 when *The War Cry*, under the heading 'Flitted', gave the news that the Home Office had moved to 101 Queen Victoria Street.

About this time, at the General's insistence, the chief secretary began to use his second Christian name when signing letters and documents. 'William Boon' and 'William Booth' were almost identical and led to confusion. Additional embarrassment was caused through 'W.B.B.' being the initials of both the Chief of the Staff and the chief secretary. From that time on it was Bramwell Booth and W. Brindley Boon!

Colonel Boon remained as chief secretary for five years and, in April 1894, he was appointed to succeed Commissioner John Carleton in the oversight of the International Trade Department, which in those days included responsibility for Army papers and magazines. All seemed set for greater responsibility and further signs of confidence on the part of his leaders. The colonel was still under 50 years of age and had been an officer for merely 13 years.

But, in August of that year, having been in his new appointment a few months, he resigned his commission 'to the General's great regret', to devote himself to the advancement of various social and political reforms. The announcement, with the explanation, was published in what my family has come to regard as the 'Resignation *Cry*' and repeated in *The Officer* magazine, with a leading article based upon the misguided decision taken.

I shall never know what made him take that step, which appeared to be quite out of character. His children certainly never discussed it. From correspondence it is equally apparent that neither William Booth nor Bramwell could understand the sudden decision.

The family moved to Derby, which became the focus of Brindley Boon's new activity. It was not long, however, before he became thoroughly disillusioned with his newly embraced political dogma and realised how mistaken he had been.

In *The Officer* for May 1897 it was announced: 'We understand that Mr Boon is to recommence his Army career as an officer in charge of a corps, and we can assure him that his old comrades will rejoice over his return the more because of his readiness to share the difficulties and burden of the Field.'

Then followed copies of correspondence which passed between the Founder and my grandfather and it is obvious from these letters that

Bramwell Booth played an important part in the negotiations which resulted in the former colonel returning to the ranks. The Chief of the Staff wrote with tenderness and affection his letter of 30 April 1897, stating, 'May God direct you and make all this work for His glory in every way.'

And so the former colonel, pioneer chief secretary and later international secretary for trade was reaccepted as an officer with the rank of adjutant and appointed in charge of Dover Corps. He quickly settled in to his new surroundings and once again made the headlines when Dover, under his command, became the first corps to form a young people's legion, a new section inaugurated that year.

After six months, farewell orders took him, with his patient and loving wife and family, to Southsea, which corps he commanded with energy and compassion until, in May 1898, he was appointed to the Editorial Department, International Headquarters, as subeditor of both *The Officer* and *Local Officer*. Promotion to Staff Captain quickly followed. The fact that he had held that rank some 16 years before did not seem to worry him, nor that at one time he had been head of that department.

A review of the Editorial Department published in *The War Cry* in November 1900 referred to Staff Captain Boon as 'a happy, sociable creature, always ready to lend a book, a pen, hunt up a reference, or a frugal lunch'.

After some years he was transferred to the Staff Department, which proved to be his last appointment. The junior clerks and office boys then working at International Headquarters became his special responsibility and one of these young charges, Albert Orsborn, graciously spared space for a reference to him in his autobiography *The House Of My Pilgrimage*.

* * * * *

In 1898, when the family returned to London, Major and Mrs Boon and their children became involved in the life of the corps at East Finchley. Later came a move to Willesden Green and the new, developing area of Cricklewood where my grandfather served as corps sergeant-major and also as corps organist. His musical ability and organ-playing prowess extended to headquarters where, for some time, he presented new songs, in manuscript form, to the International Music Board.

In this way he was associated with many of the musical giants of those days. There is no doubt that, when his office duties were over for the day, he delighted in taking an active share in the corps fighting and would invariably be the first at the open-air stand. If there was a delay in starting, instead of standing about, he would make for the nearest public house (if there was one nearby) to talk to the men there about salvation, regardless of the kind of reception he might receive.

On the way home from the meetings he would pause to conduct a one-man open-air meeting outside the Spotted Dog, the Crown, or the Case is Altered, or some other well-known hostelry. Someone who knew him in those days told me that, on such occasions, to hear him give out the verses of 'A Charge To Keep I Have' before he sang them, unaccompanied, was like discovering this well-known song for the first time.

Major Boon's death, a month after his 65th birthday, came as a 'stunning surprise'. It was on 17 July 1910 when, after being taken ill while on a short walk, he was seized with double pneumonia and was promoted to Glory within 36 hours.

This man of unfailing courtesy and good humour, of rigid discipline and genial personality, was given a warrior's funeral. The service, held on a Saturday afternoon at Tottenham Citadel, was conducted by Commissioner David Rees who, four years later, was to lose his life in *The Empress Of Ireland* tragedy. Among the many tributes paid was a message from the Chief of the Staff Bramwell Booth, who described Major Boon as 'a lover of souls – a man of real conviction about eternal things and a happy servant of the Cross'.

The procession to Abney Park Cemetery was headed by the International Staff and Cadets' Bands, which played alternately. There he shares a communal grave with such Army notables as Commissioner James Dowdle, Commissioner Edward Higgins (father

21

of General Edward Higgins) and others, while just across the path rest his beloved leaders, William and Bramwell Booth, and George Scott Railton, after whom he named one of his sons. He is in good company.

Each of my father's four brothers, as well as himself, served as Army bandsmen at one time or another, at East Finchley, Willesden Green or St Albans, and when their mother died towards the end of 1919, having realised her ambition to see all her boys return safely from the war, they insisted on walking behind her coffin to its burial ground as a tribute to 'Little Mum'. Annis Boon's last resting place is St Albans Cemetery.

My father Alfred Railton, one of twin boys born to Field Secretary and Mrs Major Boon on 22 December 1886, had a keen appreciation of music without being an expert. However, there was an occasion when my mother had left me the front-door key to let myself into the house (she was going out for an hour or so) and my father had come home early from the office.

He did not hear my approach for he was busy meandering across the keys of the American organ, which had a cherished place in the corner of our sitting room. He was experimenting with harmonic cadences, but it all made sense. I did not know that he could even play the instrument. When he became aware of my presence he abruptly ceased. I never heard him play again. The experience was a mystery – and still is!

After attending schools in Barnet, Derby, Dover, Southsea and East Finchley, in 1903 my father became an office boy at International Headquarters. Serving with him in a similar capacity of responsibility were such noted future Army leaders as Albert Orsborn, John Evan Smith, Joseph Smith and William Alex Ebbs – all of them destined to become commissioners.

Later Alf Boon was promoted to the exalted position of junior clerk and, as such, became responsible for the training of each battalion of office boys as it joined the staff – a kind of house prefect.

My father became busily involved with the 1904 International Congress. With other juniors employed in what was then known as the Foreign Office, he was required to meet delegates at London termini, carry their luggage, call a cab, tip the driver and ensure they were fixed up with a billet. He seems to have missed most of the congress meetings because of this behind-the-scenes activity. When the great event was over, it was the same process in reverse.

In those days, a headquarters employee of a certain length of service and within a certain age bracket was required to face the matter of officership. A responsible representative of the Staff Department would interview each prospective candidate and tactfully explain that if the young man had no desire to enter the training garrison, there was really no future for him 'on the building'.

Major Brindley Boon was the 'responsible representative' and his duty it was to interview his son. Although so many of his friends had taken the way to Clapton and fuller service, my father felt that this was not the direction he was destined to take – and said so. My grandfather was naturally disappointed at this decision and sought to counsel Alfred, to no avail. There was no alternative other than for my father to accept the inevitable ultimatum and find other employment.

Although we never discussed the matter I always felt that my father lived to regret his decision. He had many gifts, was a capable meeting leader, an able exponent of the word of God and a fine Christian.

A lover of travel and always relishing the challenge of seeing new scenery and meeting people, he would have enjoyed the ever-changing adventure provided by Army officership. Instead, he spent the rest of his life in the Willesden district of north-west London – 46 years in the same road – and fell in love and married Sara Butler, an attractive songster.

They were married in August 1910, a month after the sudden passing of my grandfather, who was to have conducted the wedding ceremony. Later that year my father was asked to organise a carolling party at nearby Harlesden Corps, in whose district my parents set up home as newly-weds, and this group evolved into that corps' first songster brigade. My father has been given the credit for being the pioneer leader of this section, but he was never commissioned.

He was also corps correspondent and reports from his pen appeared in *The War Cry* with efficient rapidity. In this way Willesden Green Corps was kept in the news. Everything he did was done conscientiously and well.

Chapter 4

Another Tree and More Branches

MY two grandfathers were totally different characters, yet both shared common ingredients in that they loved their Lord and delighted to serve him in the ranks of The Salvation Army.

Jack Butler was a son of Willesden, where he lived all his days as his parents and grandparents had done before him. Born in 1863 in a cottage a few yards from where the Salvation Army hall stood, he had little if any schooling and could never read or write. He started work on a farm when he was seven, taking the place of his brother 'Mick', who became a notorious prizefighter.

He was a birdminder at first and was then entrusted with the task of driving horses, ploughing land and milking cows. He first drove a pair of horses at the age of 12 and used to drive to London twice a day. One of his regular duties was to harness three horses ready for the ploughs, which meant standing in the manger to do so. Thus began Grandfather Butler's devotion to horses, which lasted all his life.

The development of industry in the district, together with the building of new housing estates, saw the increase in coal trading. At 15, Jack saw his future in this business and after working for two or three firms, driving the horses and delivering sacks of fuel, he began, at 19, in the employ of Eli Beckett and Company. He remained with the firm until his death 54 years later.

At 18, he married 17-year-old Sarah Verrinder, also Willesden-born and bred, whose antecedents had come from France generations before. The Butlers had 16 children, of whom 13 survived into adulthood. My mother was the third in the long line.

Jack had not been brought up under Christian influences, and in his tenderest years was initiated into the habits of drinking, swearing, fighting and gambling. Rabbit coursing was a passion with him and by the time he reached manhood he was widely feared as the terror of the neighbourhood.

When The Salvation Army 'opened fire' in Willesden he was not a bit impressed. He didn't like this 'new religion' or those who preached it. What right had they to interfere with the public traffic? That meant his horse and coal trolley.

He proceeded to put a stop to the Army's little game. Observing the march approaching, he deliberately pulled his van across the street and so obstructed its passage.

In the skirmish that followed one of the Salvationists was knocked down and almost trampled on by the frightened horse. Jack was worried. An earlier confrontation with the Army, when he had driven his trolley through an open-air ring, had led to his appearance before the magistrate and a speedy conviction. This incident could lead to even more serious trouble.

To his amazement and utter relief, the Salvationists did not call the police or take other drastic action. They simply knelt in the street and prayed for Jack's salvation, the injured comrade leading them.

Opposition and hostility gave way to admiration and respect and the following Sunday found Jack Butler at an Army meeting. A new light had penetrated his dark soul and the reflection revealed what he had been and, equally, what he could be by the grace of God. He turned his back on his old life and threw in his lot with the Salvationists.

William Esson, the corps bandmaster who had been commissioned a few weeks before, took an interest in the convert and patiently taught him to beat the drum and to count musical time. He was soon playing out and remained the drummer for 35 years, then relinquishing his bandsmanship to become corps colour sergeant, which commission he held until he passed away.

Bandmaster Esson was a musician of above-average ability and Willesden Green Band began to earn a reputation that led to invitations to take part in important Army functions. One of these was the first Crystal Palace Day in July 1890, held to celebrate the

Movement's 25th anniversary. Jack Butler was with the band and drove the horse coach which conveyed the bandsmen to the other side of London. They left at 7.30 am for the long journey and on the way were joined by other companies of Salvationists travelling by similar means until there was quite a convoy.

The bandstands, erected in the Palace grounds, were each devoted to different branches of Army work and each band, as it played, was under promise to get good collections! Following the great march past, in which all bands paraded, the instrumentalists made their way to the salvation tent for a little refreshment, free of charge. This took the form of a bottle of aerated water and a bun.

In his 'Notes on the CP', published in *The War Cry*, Herbert Booth wrote, 'This year it has been decided to arrange the entire force of bands in order of their instruments. When complete, this band, the largest the world has ever seen, will march to the Palace, entering by the orchestral entrance. They will then take their places in the same order on the orchestra.'

The plan to form the participants into one band in instrumental order proved too ambitious. The instruction was subsequently cancelled and the bands were required to form up and march to the Palace in their individual order.

The Central Transept, scene of the night festival, was radiant with colour. The sun-like balls of electric light illuminated the vast arena, which, with the delicately formed galleries, must have accommodated 12,000 people.

The galleries themselves were ablaze with vivid jets of diverse colours, beautifully arranged in the shapes of stars, suns, comets and arrows, and when the full light was thrown upon the opening paean of praise there were tears of joy.

Thanks to the advance in public illumination, it was a spectacle such as never had been seen before, and Jack Butler had certainly never seen such a demonstration of Christian witness or Salvationist pageantry. The memory of that day never left him and he delighted, in later years, to enthral his grandchildren as he relived the experience.

Three months later, he was again with the band when it played at the funeral of the Army Mother at Abney Park Cemetery and in the preceding long march from Victoria Embankment. The procession was due to move off at 12 noon, but thick fog from the River Thames caused a delay of an hour. Instead of arriving at the cemetery at 2 pm, the march eventually arrived at 4 o'clock. The bands simply marched into the fog and out again.

Willesden Green Band claims to have been one of the first to undertake 'specialing' engagements. The Diamond Jubilee Anniversary of Queen Victoria's accession to the throne was to be marked by a public holiday and, when Bandmaster Esson heard that the Metropolitan Railway was to run a special excursion train from Baker Street to Chesham – to which country area the line had been recently extended – it was decided that the band should undertake this momentous journey and provide music for the benefit of the holidaymakers.

The enterprising band secretary, 'Teddy' Wiggins (uncle of Lieut-Commissioner Arch Wiggins), was responsible for the arrangements and secured a party ticket at reduced rates for the 60 bandsmen and other corps comrades who wished to make the trip. That was in 1897!

Early in 1954, I conducted weekend meetings at Willesden Green and in the Saturday night festival Bandmaster Esson – a sprightly veteran – had the duty to express appreciation to the participants. I had been promoted to captain the previous day and the bandmaster said something like this: 'I remember the captain's grandfather, Colonel Brindley Boon; I remember his uncle, Colonel Herbert Boon; he will have to get his skates on if I am to see a third Colonel Boon.' He was then 84!

'Bill' Esson did live to see the day and, when I called to see him soon after my 'elevation', his amazing memory rolled back the years as he reminded me of my heritage and thanked God for sparing him to enjoy such a long life. Shortly afterwards I was honoured to conduct his funeral – a month before his 103rd birthday.

I have *The Oxford Book Of English Verse* by which to remember him. It was given to him on his 88th birthday and it was his family's wish that I should have it. We had discussed many of the contents in various conversations we had.

Grandfather Butler was a hearty gospel singer. Possessed of a pleasant, tuneful voice, he had the gift of swaying a congregation who loved to hear him sing, especially in a Sunday afternoon praise meeting. His solo was invariably a testimony and, although he could not read, a touch of inborn genius enabled him to memorise song after song.

I cannot remember hearing him sing many songs, but his favourites he used over and over again with telling effect and much inspiration. From hearing him sing the chorus on numerous occasions I learned:

> *I cannot read Latin, I know,*
> *And Greek I don't understand.*
> *But one thing I know, my heart's white as snow,*
> *I'm washed in the Blood of the Lamb.*

On other occasions he would burst forth with:

> *We once lived on dry bread and what we could get*
> *And when we had nothing we hardly dared fret;*
> *But now we have bread and nice treacle each day,*
> *Salvation for Salvation, hurrah!*

His day was generally a busy one: up before six, brushing the horse; harnessing it to the trolley; travelling to the railway sidings which served as a wharf for loading the coal; a morning's hawking coal round the district with a short break for lunch; reloading and another round of distribution, sometimes including orders for factories or schools; and, when all the day's demands had been met, releasing the horse from its shafts, another wash-down of beast and cart and a clean-up of the stable. Only when the horse was comfortably housed for the night would my grandfather allow himself the privilege of eating a cooked meal.

This ritual over, the tired but contented workman would enjoy a doze in the kitchen armchair beside the carefully blackleaded grate. My grandmother knew that this routine was essential to her man's wellbeing and would find a duty to perform in another part of the home.

The slumber would not last long and the end of the refreshing but necessary recuperation would be heralded by the sonorous sounds of one of my grandfather's solos coming from the darkened room, the gas mantle remaining unlit.

It was into such a setting that I once gatecrashed when I was about seven. I had not heard grandfather sing the song before and so I tiptoed out of the kitchen and paused to listen at the other side of the door.

I was petrified! The solo contained a frightening sentiment that I had not experienced before and I was scared out of my young life. The last line of the chorus haunted me for years – 'That's how my angel mother died'. It was my first glimpse of eternity and I hated the prospect.

How Jack Butler could memorise so many songs and sing them so sincerely and effectively continues to baffle me. But I have to admit that I appreciate them more in my adult years than when I first heard them!

Grandfather loved the poor and became their friend, giving thousands of pounds of credit to people who could not afford to pay for their coal. At the end of the week he tried to remember those who had not settled their bills and, with a cousin, I would visit the addresses Grandfather had given us. Many paid up, grateful for Jack's kindly indulgence. Many never did. Others whom he had not remembered brought the money round when they collected their wages on a Friday night. His generosity kept him poor.

I came to know Grandfather best when I spent two weeks with him 'on the job' during the General Strike of 1926. I was 12 and on holiday from school. A message left at my home requested that I should report for duty at the coal wharf at 7 o'clock the next morning ready to help Grandfather.

I could not possibly imagine what help I could give. I had seen him more than once climb on to the cart, lift two hundredweight of coke on his back and take a hundredweight sack in one arm and deliver them to a grateful customer – but how could I possibly compete with such strength?

Early the next morning I soon learned the role I was to play. Street hawking by coalmen had been suspended for the duration of the emergency and deliveries were confined to private orders for essential industries. My grandfather was provided with a list of firms to be served in this way but, because of his inability to read, was at a complete loss to know their destination. This was when he thought of me and I respected the compliment.

From the list I read out the name and address of the next call and so we built up an effective working arrangement. Sometimes I was permitted to take the reins and guide the horse. At other times I was treated to some of his boyhood memories, especially when we rode along highways he remembered when they were but twisting lanes.

His rapport with the many people we passed enthralled me. Everyone seemed to know him and I found delight in basking in the glory of his popularity.

Horses were a passion with him. He tended them like children and they knew and loved him in return. Whit Monday, which marked the annual London Cart Horse Parade held in Regent's Park, was a red-letter day in the Butler household. Competition was fierce and there were scores of entries. My grandfather had first paraded a horse and cart in 1891 and over the years had a number of first- and second-prize medals to his credit.

For us grandchildren there were few days to compare with this. There were too many of us to attend this colourful, 12-hour event with any degree of regularity but we were allowed to take our turn. I went only twice, both occasions being before I was ten.

When the horse-drawn cart eventually gave way to the motor-driven trolley Jack Butler seemed to lose heart for the job. Although two of my cousins continued to assist him in the business and became his drivers, things were never the same. Jack, in fact, died in the cab of his lorry, between his 'mates', when they were returning from a day's last load.

It was two days after Easter 1935. For three days before the funeral Jack lay in 'state'. There was a constant stream of visitors to the firm's offices, opposite the Willesden Green Salvation Army hall. *The Willesden Chronicle* reported: 'They came to look for the last time upon the face of this simple, hard-working, golden-hearted man who was the friend of all men.'

On the day of the funeral shops were closed and the busy traffic was halted while the procession crossed the road and entered the Army hall, which had been filled long before the service was due to begin. Local policemen had sent a wreath and marched in the procession. Two of their number, mounted on horseback, led the march to the cemetery and guarded the entrance.

In the funeral service Jack Butler's favourite songs were sung and my father, who had married Jack Butler's second daughter 25 years before, paid worthy tribute to 'one of the greatest of God's gentlemen', concluding with words with which everyone present agreed: 'What he has done about this district will live for ever. His memory will never fade.' I was privileged to 'preside' at the organ.

The Daily Express estimated that 2,500 people attended. The cemetery gates had to be closed as 'Happy Jack' was borne to his last resting place on the staunch shoulders of four of his old Salvationist pals.

Chapter 5

Growing Up in London

TO say that I was brought up on Salvation Army words and music is a gross understatement. I positively flourished on them and could claim to know most of the popular songs of the day before I reached my sixth birthday.

My mother inherited her father's memory and his pleasant voice. Her singing often lulled me to sleep and, when I was old enough to take an interest in things around me, it was her songs that fascinated me.

The International Congress of 1914 was in the recent past and among my earliest memories are those of her humming some of the melodies featured in that event.

My mother had been a member of the first songster brigade at Willesden Green and remembered when the only accompaniment for the singing was supplied by the euphonium of Songster Leader Tom Bloomfield, who would play each part in turn until the notation was thoroughly memorised.

The songster leader had the gift of being able to spot a 'winner' in a current issue of *The Musical Salvationist* and each songster was expected to secure a copy of this periodical and learn the songs before the next practice. This was how my mother came to try them out on me and I was certainly richer for the experience.

The years of the First World War seemed to abound with the advent of new songs. March 1915 saw the publication of 'In Him Abiding' by Ensign Albert Orsborn and Assistant Cadet Sergeant-Major Wilfred Kitching. This, and 'You Can Tell Out The Sweet Story' from the pen of a new writer, Captain Sidney Cox of Canada, became part of my mother's repertoire, as did 'I Love Him Better Every Day' and 'In My Heart A Song Is Ringing', published in 1916 and 1917 respectively.

I was especially moved by songs of spiritual appeal. Maybe I have recollections of people making their way to the penitent form, often in tears, as they were sung. My favourites of this kind were 'Coming This Way', 'Someone' and 'Have Thy Way, Lord'.

About this time I made my first appearance as a performer on an Army platform. The war was still on and my item was a recitation, 'Daddy's Deputy'. It began with the line, 'My daddy is a soldier brave'. The rest is mercifully forgotten. How was I to know that my father's bravery consisted of sitting at a desk in a Royal Army Service Corps depot in Bromley dealing with complaints from soldiers' wives?

Shortly afterwards, Gypsy Nell, a prominent 'special' of the day, spent a weekend at our corps. On the Monday, for her heart-rending lecture, a tent was erected at the side of the platform and I was invited to recline therein while a soloist offstage sadly whined, 'Into a tent where a gypsy boy lay'. Thus I made my dramatic debut. Not even a walk-on part. But I was on the bottom rung of the ladder!

The war over, my father, with other corps servicemen, returned home and to the band and life took on a normality I had not known before.

By the time my sister Thelma was born in 1921 the war years for me were quite forgotten. At this time my father was the band secretary and my mother was involved in many corps activities.

It was decided that Thelma should be duly dedicated under the Army flag.

My arrival, seven years before, had not been marked by such ceremony. I was christened in the ancient font of the 13th-century parish church. I suspect that my mother was influenced by her traditional background. Her forebears on both sides had been christened there and she was determined that I would not be an exception.

But my parents' consciences must have caught up with them for, on the last Sunday of March 1921, the Commanding Officer (Adjutant Bertram Marriott) officiated at the double dedication of the Boon children. The announcement in the Gazette column of *The*

Bandsman And Songster a few weeks later must have given the impression that we were twins!

The ceremony was in the morning. In the afternoon my sister nearly met an untimely end when severe winds whipped the pram out of my mother's grasp, overturned it and sent Thelma rolling down the hill like a discarded bundle of family washing.

The bandsmen, who were marching by on their way to the hall, broke ranks and hurried to the rescue, led by my out-of-breath father. The frightened, screaming baby was safely retrieved, apparently none the worse for the ordeal.

In those days, immediately following the end of the war, sectional 'specialing' was quite a feature. Evening engagements were frequent, as if everyone wanted to make up for the lost years.

When Wandsworth Band gave a festival at our corps, its Commanding Officer (Ensign Wilfred Kitching) came too and conducted the united bands in his march 'Bridgwater'. He was the first composer I ever saw. My eyes rarely left him.

Engagements at corps farther afield were always important. One such visit to Harrow was something of a corps outing. We met at Dollis Hill Station (on the old Metropolitan Line from Baker Street to Rickmansworth), caught the same train and from the moment we pulled out of the station began to sing a medley of Army songs and choruses. 'Cheer Up, Comrades, There's Nothing To Worry About' gave way to 'We're On The Homeward Trail', to be followed by 'I Was Wandering In The Wilderness' and 'I Love Him Better Every Day'.

More than 30 years later my son John came home from a local scouting display singing a chorus he had learned during the show. 'We're On The Scouting Trail' was a blatant parody of Arnott's popular refrain, but I held my peace.

'It's a great tune, Dad,' volunteered my son, 'and good words. You ought to get it for the Army.' Get it for the Army! I wasted no time in informing John that the Army had it first and that Bandmaster Gullidge had included it in his prize-winning march, 'The Heaven-Bound Throng'. The lad seemed quite crestfallen and disillusioned. Maybe I should have kept quiet.

To return to that corps excursion. We alighted at Harrow-on-the-Hill and walked across the fields to the built-up area in which the Army hall was situated. We continued to sing and the march-time songs we used helped us to keep in step and ensured a brisk rate of progress.

The hall reached, wives, children and girlfriends entered the gas-lit building, occupied the best available seats and filled the hall with happy conversation while the band led a half-hour open-air meeting in the road outside.

When the festival was over, visitors were requested to remain in their seats until refreshments were brought – without charge. The welcome biscuits and tea fortified us for the long journey home. Today it would take no more than 15 minutes by car.

We returned home the way we had come, lending a hand with the instruments and continuing to sing our favourites. To a seven-year-old Army boy this kind of outing was a real adventure, and if the bandmaster spoke to me or gave me his baton to carry, I felt twice my age and quite grown up.

In the early 1920s my father began to organise a series of festivals to help restore the band fund, which had diminished considerably while the men were away at war. His earlier headquarters office-boy association with Major Bramwell Taylor resulted in the major bringing Wood Green Band for an evening festival. He was the bandmaster.

The assembly hall of a local school was hired and I remember the disappointment when the confined stage space meant that the band had to be seated on the floor of the hall, level with the audience.

The chairman, invited because he could be depended upon to put a pound note in the collection, did not arrive and I was most impressed when it was announced that the bandmaster's wife would substitute for him.

This provided me with my first glimpse of Mrs Major Phillis Taylor, stately, gracious and charming. She was the eldest daughter of the Chief of the Staff (later General) and Mrs Commissioner Edward J. Higgins and much later was to become the wife of General Albert Orsborn.

36

After the festival my father introduced me to the major, who was then the editor of *The Bandsman And Songster*. He *looked* a leader and instantly appealed to me. Little did I dream in that moment that one day I, too, would edit the Army's paper for its musicians, by that time renamed *The Musician*.

On another occasion, Chalk Farm Band and its legendary bandmaster, A. W. Punchard, were the visitors. The same school hall was hired, with the same disastrous viewing frustration. As the hall was the largest in the vicinity it was impossible to make an alternative arrangement.

The only memory I have of that evening is my father's reaction to the expenses charged by the band, considered by him to be an exorbitant amount which left the band fund severely in the red. By the time I became songster leader at Chalk Farm and worked closely with the great A.W.P. the incident was forgotten. Or, at least, never mentioned.

The periodic visits of Territorial Band Inspector Edward Hill were treated with tremendous respect by the bandsmen. Instruments were required to be cleaned, inside and out, polish was liberally applied and the men, properly uniformed, had to be at the practice in good time. This was an inspection in the true sense of the word and the rehearsal instruction, a 'lecture' on the observance of regulations and the spiritual epilogue were accepted with a deep sense of privilege and sincerity.

On one such visit my father was not well enough to attend and it was my great joy to take his flugelhorn, suitably cleaned and tied up in the green baize bag provided with the instrument. Only the cornets had leather cases.

That night I was permitted to stay for part of the practice, on the understanding that I sat quietly out of sight in a darkened portion of the hall. In that way, for the first time, I heard the lilting melodies of Ensign Bramwell Coles's new 'Undaunted' march and the thrilling, rapidly played passages of Brigadier Arthur Goldsmith's latest 'test piece', 'The Banner Of Liberty'.

I shall never forget that experience, or the influence of the dynamic personality of Ted Hill. I never saw him again. He was promoted to

Glory in 1925, after tirelessly and lovingly serving the interests of the bandsmen of the British Territory for 18 years. His successor was Bandmaster Edward Saywell, of Gillingham.

The final decade of the pre-radio age was an exciting time for a boy to grow up. It was the pre-homework era as well and I became involved in the life of the corps.

There was junior activity most nights. Monday saw the weekly magic lantern show, for which the darkened hall was packed with noisy youngsters who yelled their delight or disapproval as the mood took them. The pioneer movies, of which General Orsborn writes in his autobiography, had come and gone by this time and in their place less exciting literature was illustrated by a series of slides, not always coloured.

By this means I was introduced to such sob-stuff classics as *Christie's Old Organ* and *Jessica's First Prayer*. It was all pretty tame, but relieved the boredom of staying at home and playing Ludo or 'I Spy'.

Other weekly events were held in the interests of the singing company, band of love and the newly inaugurated life-saving chums. I attended all of them, being a full member of the first two and serving as 'mascot' for the chums, being too young to be officially recognised.

My debut on the Regent Hall platform was at a united chum demonstration. Being the youngest and smallest of our group, I was given the responsibility of sitting on the back of a human donkey – two older boys appropriately covered by the necessary animal skin – while we all sang: 'Come along, Neddy, gee-up old thing', or words to that effect. Other versions allowed 'girl' or 'boy' to be substituted for 'thing' according to the chosen sex of the donkey.

I was never a young people's band member, and consequently missed the opportunity of learning to play a brass instrument in my formative years. This was due to no lack of enthusiasm on my part.

My father had very definite ideas about the ideals of Army bandsmanship and strongly objected to junior bands, on the grounds that they encouraged boys to play out before they were old enough to know the real meaning of conversion. One Decision Sunday I ran home excitedly to report that I had 'been out the front'. It made no difference. He did not relent.

I went to a church school, not because my parents had any particular allegiance to St Andrew's, Willesden, but simply because it was the nearest school to where we lived. At first I was not aware of any religious pressure.

The headmaster, Robert Kent, was a balding, rotund, severe person who appeared to lose his temper at the slightest provocation and to wield his cane ferociously with frightening regularity. Such outbursts were usually witnessed by the whole school and were obviously intended as a deterrent. We came and went in fear of him – and for our lives.

The only touch of religious influence about the school was the morning assembly. Mr Kent took this ritual seriously and mingled his intimidating leadership of hymns and prayers with a terrifying tirade of complaints, not hesitating, in the 'hallowed' atmosphere, to make a public example.

That could be why 'When Morning Gilds The Skies' and the tune 'Ellacombe', frequently used on such mornings, hold unhappy memories for me and why I still go nervously cold when I hear them.

But school life suddenly changed. The tyrant retired and in his place we welcomed quite a different character named Harry Williams. His coming heralded an era of extreme happiness.

We quickly began to live up to our name as a church school. Morning assemblies became meaningful and memorable. Harry Williams was an exemplary churchman who filled our minds with good Christian teaching, healthy patriotism and a code of high moral conduct. He believed that Parry's setting of William Blake's 'Jerusalem' would one day become the national anthem, and if every school function began with 'God Save The King' it invariably concluded with 'And did those feet in ancient times'.

Not only did the school take on a new lease of life, but also our Alma Mater began to change as well. Suddenly it dawned upon us that its 'Church of England' designation was being supplanted by 'Anglo-Catholic'. The priests were now 'fathers', and when the angelus bell began to toll at noon each day we had to stop whatever we were doing and spring to attention beside our desks.

Each Wednesday morning, upon arriving at school, we paraded and were marched to the church for mass. The school choir was robed impressively in surplices and cassocks to perform the musical honours, while the headmaster, similarly robed, played the organ and led the choir. Others were enlisted for incense-swinging duties and assisting the officiating priest.

This high church ceremonial was very different from my Salvationist background but I did not mind. It at least planted the seed of ecumenism within me and taught me my first lesson in religious tolerance.

I graduated to the choir and all went well until my mother found out about my 'popish' misdemeanours. A strongly worded letter to the headmaster made it perfectly clear that I was forbidden to take part in any more celebrations of mass, or any other function to do with the church. Looking back I am surprised that I was permitted even to remain at the school. The headmaster, however, agreed to the request of my irate parent and, each Wednesday, I was given class work to do instead of attending mass.

To Harry Williams's lasting credit he never took it out on me or caused me to suffer the slightest embarrassment. In fact, my vocal services were enlisted each Armistice Day to augment the choir as, again attired in surplices and cassocks, it did duty at the annual remembrance service held at the war memorial outside our local bus garage.

Sara Boon – Brindley's mother

Alfred Boon – Brindley's father

Brindley in school cricket team (2nd row, far right)

The Men's Social Work Band (Brindley is 3rd from the right, second row)

Chapter 6

Salad Days

I HAD begun to take piano lessons after my sixth birthday. My teacher, a one-time professor of the Royal Academy of Music, was quite elderly and of German extraction, and had been a brilliant concert pianist in her time. She gave me a thorough grounding in the rudiments of theory and instilled into me the basic laws of harmony even before I progressed very far beyond the realm of five-finger exercises.

After I had been learning for two years she considered me ready for my first exam – of the Associated Board of the Royal Schools of Music. This consisted of playing a set piece, performing from sight and negotiating an aural test with reasonable accuracy. I passed and have a certificate dated November 1922 to prove it. That was the Primary Division and the exams of the Elementary, Lower and Higher Divisions were passed at annual intervals.

My reward for passing the first exam was a bicycle. Fairy cycles had not yet come on the market, so this two-wheeled vehicle was a miniature of an adult's cycle. It was also a Christmas present and my father, mounted on his iron-framed steed, took me for my first long-distance ride.

We rode to Harrow and back, a distance of some ten miles, and on our return journey Dad pointed out, across the fields, a huge edifice being erected on the skyline. He told me it was Wembley Stadium, which was being built in connection with the British Empire Exhibition to be held in two years' time. The famous twin towers were already completed and looked magnificent.

Four months later, on 28 April, I cycled again to Wembley, this time on my own, to watch the thousands making their frenzied way

41

into the new stadium to watch the first Football Association Cup Final to be held there. Bolton Wanderers and West Ham were the teams. How the out-of-hand spectators broke through the barriers and spilled over on to the pitch, thus holding up the game several times and bringing fame to a certain white police horse, is now history. I was fortunate not to have my bike smashed up in the rush and managed to reach home unscathed. More than 50 years later I sat in the office of the Wembley Stadium manager to discuss the possibilities of The Salvation Army taking over that famous venue for a field day during the International Congress. The impressive view from his window was of that 'sacred' area of turf. A huge framed picture on the wall showed the pitch being invaded at the first cup final, with the white horse and its rider prominent in the foreground.

Wembley figures very much in my boyhood memories. On Empire Day, 1924, we assembled in the school hall to hear King George V open the British Empire Exhibition. This was the BBC's first public broadcast. I had never heard of wireless before and could hardly believe that the voice coming from the 'gramophone horn' was authentic and being heard all over London. It must be a recording, I concluded, until it was proved otherwise.

I attended the exhibition on two occasions with school parties. I remember the lofty buildings housing exhibits from Australia and Canada, the Salvation Army pavilion, the reconstructed old London Bridge, the boating pool and other landmarks, to say nothing of the amusement park. One night I returned with my parents to see the International Rodeo and Torchlight Tattoo in the stadium and got thoroughly chilled as we sat on the stone steps between spectacular presentations.

As my piano prowess developed I was invited to play to the class at school every Friday afternoon for the final period. This gave me a chance to rehearse my exam pieces. After a while I was appointed to play for the hymns at morning assembly.

One day I was sent to buy some manuscript paper and given a hymn to copy out. This was my first experience of four-part music writing and I did not find it easy. It was Dr Ralph Vaughan Williams's tune 'Monk's Gate', set to John Bunyan's words, 'Who would true valour see'. The hymn soon became a school favourite.

On Empire Day parents were invited to attend a parade held in the playground. Seating was provided and each class made its own contribution to the entertainment. School singing was a feature, for Harry Williams was a first-class musician and an able teacher and conductor. I learned much from his full-chord pianoforte playing. I was usually at the piano on such occasions and thus became acquainted with 'God Bless The Prince Of Wales', 'The Minstrel Boy', 'Loch Lomond' and other popular national songs.

The ever-resourceful Mr Williams had the bright idea of putting on a comic opera, and hardly was the suggestion made than we were learning the songs, rehearsing the dialogue, painting the scenery and selling the tickets.

The production was *The Mandarin*, a kind of Chinese version of *The Mikado*. I was given the part of the principal girl, 'Yung-shi' the Mandarin's daughter, and was described in a local newspaper report as a boy with a pleasing voice.

So successful was the venture that the idea was repeated the following year. This time it was *The Dogs Of Devon*, set on Plymouth Hoe with Queen Elizabeth I, Sir Francis Drake, a squad of beefeaters and a Spanish villain among the characters. Once again I was principal girl, but by this time my voice had started to break and some of the songs needed to be transposed.

Theatricals, too, attracted my attention. This was no doubt heightened by school visits to the old Metropolitan Music Hall in Edgware Road, long since demolished, and the Willesden Hippodrome. In these strongholds of Edwardian variety and drama I saw Russell Thorndike as Scrooge in *A Christmas Carol*, in which Sir Ben Greet was brilliant, if frightening, as 'The ghost of Christmas past'. In this way I was also introduced to Shakespeare's plays, particularly *Julius Caesar* and *A Midsummer Night's Dream*.

Russell Thorndike was a brother of Dame Sybil Thorndike and the author of the *Dr Syn* series of detective stories. He was better known for this literary work than as an actor and producer, although his all-round brilliance certainly enhanced the dramatic stage of my boyhood.

One summer holiday was spent at West Newton, a village adjoining the royal estate at Sandringham. We stayed in the home of Will and Lily Dye. Many of the Dye family had been in the royal employ since King Edward VII, as Prince of Wales, had bought Sandringham House as his country residence. 'Uncle' Will was on the gardening staff and his wife gave domestic help when it was required. They were on speaking terms with Queen Alexandra, then in her 80s, and with her daughter, Queen Maud of Norway, whose English home was at nearby Appleton House, where she had been born.

All this impressed me greatly. At ten years of age I was developing a passion for history. This experience came just at the right time.

I gazed with awe upon toys played with by the then Crown Prince Olaf, Queen Maud's son, and was horrified when Bobby Dye, son of our hosts, came running home with a golf ball he had 'found' on the course during a game the Prince of Wales (later Edward VIII) had been enjoying up to then!

One day I was returning along a quiet lane from Sandringham to West Newton with some young friends, when a large car approached from the opposite direction.

'The Queen,' someone announced. There was no excitement or panic. For them this was an everyday happening – but not for a bewildered London lad.

As the car passed, with Queen Alexandra and her faithful lady-in-waiting in the back, my country 'cousins' charmingly curtsied as to the manner born while I, completely taken by surprise, pressed my tummy in, bowed awkwardly and tried to curtsy at the same time. The result was disastrous, but by the time I picked myself up the car was a distance along the lane. Thus I had my only glimpse of Queen Alexandra, with her gracious smile and friendly wave of the hand. She died the following year.

My love of sport – mostly cricket and football – highlighted my schooldays. When I started at St Andrew's our cricketing hero at the school was Frank Tarrant, a good-looking curly-headed boy in his last year. His ability as a batsman was already legendary in the district. The cream-coloured shirt he wore for matches enhanced his undoubted charisma.

Frank's father had played for Victoria State in Australia in the early days of the century and had moved to England to qualify for Middlesex, taking up residence in the Willesden area. Here young Frank – he was given his father's name – was born. Left-handed and gifted with enormous biceps, he could hit a cricket ball higher than anyone I had ever seen, and it was customary for us junior pupils to arrive at school half an hour early just to see him bat in one of the improvised games organised, with a tennis ball, in the playground.

The 'wicket' was a chalk-marked jutting of the wall which separated the playground from the adjacent woodyard. Over the wall was out of bounds so if a batsman hit the ball in that direction it was 'six and out'. On the other side of the road, facing the school, was a highly built local telephone exchange. It was the ambition of every boy to hit the ball sufficiently hard and high for it to clear the top floor, land in 'no man's land' beyond and hopefully be lost for ever. This won the batsman six good runs (not out) and the lasting adulation of his mates. Frank Tarrant was one of the few to gain such fame.

It was a cause of real regret when Tarrant disappeared from the scene before the end of term without warning or a chance to say goodbye. Playing days over, his father secured a coaching job in India and took the family to Bombay.

During Easter school holidays Gamage's store arranged a cricket week, engaging professionals to advertise the firm's sportswear and equipment, sign autographs and give tuition to interested youngsters. For me a day at Gamage's was an annual fixture for some years and thus I came into close contact with such giants of the game as Herbert Sutcliffe, Walter Hammond, Harold Larwood, George Geary and Fred Root. The last two were distinguished slow bowlers and every schoolboy wanted to grip the ball as they did. The cricket week gave us a wonderful opportunity to talk to them and try to learn the art. Some were successful.

The thought of making a fool of myself in the nets in front of gaping onlookers did not appeal to my sensitive nature. I did, however, allow myself the luxury of putting on pads and gloves, taking a Gamage's 'Superior' bat and being bowled at by the great Larwood. He was the fastest bowler in the world at that time and had not yet become involved in the 'bodyline' controversy which ended his international career.

Larwood was neither at his fastest nor his best when I faced him on that matting wicket and in front of those heavily wired store windows. Hammond was at hand to correct my cross-bat stance and weakness for playing back, but I am afraid little real progress was made. But what did it matter? I had 'played' against Larwood and been 'coached' by Hammond – even if my future record on the field gave little indication of the fact.

On such occasions I always walked from Holborn to Fleet Street and paused at No 59. This was a sports outfitters with the magic words, JACK HOBBS, blazoned across the shopfront. 'Sir Jack', as he afterwards became, was possibly the greatest batsman in the history of the game and it was a pulse-racing experience out of the cricket season to glance into his shop in the hope of seeing him.

One day I plucked up enough courage to enter to get his autograph, only to find that the hero behind the counter was, in fact, his brother, who managed the business. The remarkable likeness fooled me. He was kind enough to tell me when Jack would be in, and I duly obtained his autograph to go with the others I had acquired at Gamage's.

From time to time I saw these personalities, and others, performing mighty deeds at Lord's. Like my father and grandfather, I was something of a loner and never tired of my own company. A day in the sun at Lord's was something to be cherished. Armed with sandwiches and a bottle of grapefruit drink, I would pay my shilling at the turnstile, resist the temptation to pay an extra threepence on a 'soft seat', find a vantage point high on the terrace at the Nursery End facing the lovely pavilion and settle down for the next seven hours, moving only to parade before the players' dressing room to watch my heroes return from lunch and tea.

On such a day I saw Jack Hobbs, playing for Surrey, score 266 not out, and almost regretted that I did not play truant from school next day to see him reach 316 not out.

As I approached my 14th birthday, my parents began to show concern for my future. I was not so concerned. Schooling was such fun and I was developing with my music and sport. Reports show that history was by far my most successful subject, with essay-writing and music following closely behind. Science and art were a complete failure.

I cannot remember the time when I did not want to be a journalist. On those days at Lord's I spent the time reporting the game as it progressed. On the way home I would buy an evening paper and compare my account with the published version of some noted sports correspondent.

My father did not dismiss out of hand the idea that I should become a newspaper reporter, but he felt that I should have wider spheres of interest from which to choose. One thing was certain in his mind. There was no future for me in music, at least so far as wage-earning was concerned. It was his decision, therefore, that I should take a two-year commercial course at the well-known and respected establishment of Clark's College. I enrolled at the Cricklewood Branch.

But my music was not entirely neglected. There were college concerts and breaking-up parties, at which I was invited to sing as well as provide piano accompaniments for other soloists.

A song I performed at this time proved to be quite popular. It was 'Those Girls At The School At The End Of The Street'. In it I told the story of a lovesick swain who tried to make a hit with a number of girls attending a nearby school. His attempts at 'chatting up' were rebuffed and the refrain to each verse took the form of a spoken rejection given in the dialect or language of the recipient of the tender wooing. Thus was I initiated into the art of dialect mimicry. Scottish, Irish, Welsh and German girls were represented in this way and the song proved a 'hoot'.

Prior to this, when I had been learning the piano for about a year, I was invited to play my first solo at a young people's festival at the corps. The night arrived, my item was announced and nervously I made my self-conscious way to the platform. It was an ordeal for an eight-year-old. I moved quickly towards the piano. It was locked. The incident was too much for me. I burst into tears and ran from the hall in utter confusion. My mother followed and tried to console me, declaring that the piano had been locked deliberately. She there and then vowed that I would never go to the 'juniors' again and that she and my father would likewise sever their association with the corps. That incident and its outcome could have altered the whole course of my life. It did for a time.

With my parents withdrawing from Army service the pattern of my life changed. I did not attend any place of worship regularly until a door-to-door recruitment campaign resulted in my sister and me being sent to the Wesleyan Methodist Sunday school in Cricklewood. I was made welcome and soon felt completely at home. My musical talent was quickly unearthed and before long I found myself Sunday school pianist and performing on programmes to do with the Junior Wesley Guild.

Inter-church rallies provided me with a yet wider platform of usefulness and Saturday excursions to Westminster Central Hall, the home of London Methodism, gave me the opportunity of listening to such speakers as Leslie Weatherhead – then an up-and-coming minister in his 30s. His preaching captivated me and, when he complimented me upon my accompaniment after a Young Methodists' meeting, my admiration was even greater!

As the years passed I was entrusted with playing the church organ for Sunday school anniversary services. This was a high privilege and the organist gave up precious time instructing me in the art of keynote technique, pedal manipulation and couplet negotiation.

When my voice broke and settled to its committed register, I was asked to join the church choir – on bass. I had reached the advanced age of 15! Accepted into church membership, I began to share the fellowship of adults for the first time. In fact, my two worlds of church and school were good to me with plenty of music and sport thrown in. My cup of happiness was overflowing. I hated the thought of my life ever being disturbed.

But with all the joys of those happy 1920s, my links with the Army were not entirely broken. There was the periodical visit to Judd Street, with the inevitable purchase of Triumph Tea from the ebullient and 'Hallelujah'-filled Major Charles Coller, the occasional visit to Regent Hall for a special event, a field day at the Crystal Palace, or a day off school to attend the funeral of an Army leader.

Major Coller intrigued me with his warm personality and friendly interest in the hobbies of a passing schoolboy, but I did not know him then as the writer of 'Make The World With Music Ring', 'Unto Thee, O Saviour-King' and a host of other songs. That appreciation and respect came later, after he had passed to his reward and I had missed the opportunity of thanking him.

When Commander Evangeline Booth, on one of her rare visits from the USA, was announced to lead Sunday meetings at Clapton Congress Hall, mother decided that the family would go. This meant leaving home after an early lunch and taking our places in the queue in Linscott Road while the afternoon meeting was still in progress.

As the hall emptied, the waiting crowd slowly moved into the building to claim their seats and eventually it was our turn to enter the fine old hall, descend the steps and be shown to seats high in the section facing the platform. I cannot remember anything about that meeting except the stifling atmosphere created by the congregation (which overflowed until it filled all available standing space and packed the open doorways) and the commanding eloquence of the speaker. It was not what she said, but the dramatic and compelling way she said it which captivated me and impressed itself upon my young mind. The commander was supported by the Chief of the Staff and other commissioners. I was certainly not aware of the mounting tension which, two years later, was to culminate in an historic drama in which such leaders were to take prominent roles.

An Army funeral was always a great affair. We would leave in the morning, allowing ourselves time to cross London and arrive at Clapton Congress Hall in good time for the service. The parade of personalities fascinated me and I would spend the time, before and during the service, 'pinning' names to faces.

We would leave the service a little before the end and take up good positions along the kerb of Linscott Road. When the cortège passed and General Bramwell, Chief of the Staff Higgins, British Commissioner Hurren and other leaders followed in sad procession, I was required to salute. The older I got the more difficult the ritual was to maintain, but it went on for a few years, beginning with Commissioner John Lawley's funeral in 1922.

My last attendance in this way, as a 'conscripted' mourner, was in 1929, the funeral of Lieut-Commissioner William Haines who, as vice-president of the first High Council, had been promoted to Glory from Sunbury Court a few days previously. I seemed to feel the full impact of the crisis as the group of leaders marched slowly by, bearing the weight of anxiety which, on the morrow, would need to be translated into a decision which would affect the Army for all time.

They were all there: Higgins leading the way with Evangeline Booth from the USA at his side, Hurren of Britain, Yamamuro of Japan, Rich and Maxwell from Canada, Larsson from Norway, the saintly Brengle and the rest. What a parade! It had taken a funeral to enable me to see them all in the same place at the same time.

Chapter 7

Mysterious Ways

MY family had one permanent link with the Army during those years of 'exile' – through the Assurance Society. Agents frequently called at our home and one of them built our first 'cat's whisker' wireless set.

One day the superintendent made a special visit. It had nothing to do with possible new business. He was merely looking for lodgings for an agent who was transferring to the district. My mother agreed to take the young man into our home until he found somewhere else to live. He stayed with us until he was married two years later.

'Joe' Nicholson came from Edmonton and was attracted to the Army through the life-saving scouts. He was 21 and an enthusiastic bandsman when we first knew him. His prowess on the cricket field instantly appealed to me and he was soon established as 'big brother'.

The year 1929 proved to be one of the most momentous of my life. It was only a few weeks old when 'Joe', who by now was the deputy bandmaster at Child's Hill, asked me if I would help the songster brigade by playing the organ for its song at the divisional Self-Denial ingathering. The regular organist, who had served the brigade for some years, was no longer available and, in a quandary, the songster leader asked 'Joe' if he had any ideas regarding a substitute.

He thought of the lad at his 'digs' and promised to explore the possibility. The suggestion appealed to me, my parents raised no objection and I duly turned up at the next practice to rehearse the vocal march 'Our Flag'.

I cannot remember much about the practice, apart from the hearty singing and the friendliness of the songsters. Herbert Spencer, who was also the bandmaster, impressed me as being an able leader. The instrument I played was an American organ type, with stiff pedals and a limited range of stops. The platform position required me to sit side on to the brigade and to follow the leader's manoeuvres with the aid of a mirror.

The ingathering was held in the Mildmay Conference Hall, recently acquired by the Army, and I arrived wearing the only 'uniform' I possessed: pinstriped trousers, black jacket, stiff collar and school tie. This time there was no American organ. A small portable instrument, borrowed from another brigade, had to be collected when our item was announced and returned immediately afterwards. I was far more nervous helping to carry the precious organ, which threatened to collapse beneath my shaking hands, than I was in accompanying the song.

The following week I went with my family to the cadets' Self-Denial festival at Clapton. Here I heard Erik Leidzén's song, 'We're Sure Of Victory', for the first time and was intrigued by the cry of 'Where?' in the chorus which came from a different window in the old Congress Hall each time it was shouted. It was a touch of imaginative production.

My friend 'Joe' soon had another request to make. Child's Hill Band was visiting a small corps in Kent for the Easter weekend. Would I go along to accompany the instrumental and vocal incidental items and play in the band?

'Joe' persuaded me I could manage it. I appreciated his mark of confidence, which quality I was sadly lacking. A flugelhorn and set of second cornet music were loaned me and I started to attend practices. My knowledge of the rudiments of music enabled me to work out the fingering, and that of the more difficult pieces I pencilled in on the copy.

There was the question of uniform. I was still singing in the Methodist church choir and had no intention of becoming a 'regular' Salvationist. One of the bandsmen, Will Straughan, came to my rescue by loaning me a spare tunic, resplendent with the band's old trimmings, a pattern discarded a year or two before. Another bandsman provided an old band cap. My mother confirmed her approval of what was happening by treating me to a pair of blue trousers, which were more or less a match with the tunic. Thus clad, I accompanied the band on its Easter campaign.

There was no piano at the corps we visited, so I had to be content with a rather wheezy harmonium on which to play for 'The Larboard Watch', 'Excelsior', 'Anchors Aweigh' and other popular cornet duets of the day.

My flugelhorn-cum-second cornet contribution was by no means a failure. A few naturals which should have been accidentals and one or two wrong entries did not spoil my enjoyment of the experience, even if my unfortunate errors did cause some eyebrows around the band to be raised. Not all the 'blobs' were my fault. How was I to know that when the band played 'American Melodies' it always started at Letter A and not at the beginning?

'Joe' and I billeted in a nearby village with a fruit farmer and his wife. They were not Salvationists but we invited the son of the house, a lad of my own age, to attend on the Sunday night. In the prayer meeting I found myself moved by an overwhelming impulse to express my feelings to the Lord. As if propelled by a power beyond myself, I stood to my feet and prayed in public for the first time in my life. That was a great spiritual victory – a victory not only over myself and an inherent shyness but also over a frightening and embarrassing stammer that had taunted me since childhood.

While I prayed, the young man from our billet made his way to the penitent form to dedicate his life for Salvation Army service. Rightly or wrongly, I regarded him as my first convert – my first soul for Christ.

There is a sequel to that incident which has to be told at this point. Twenty-one years afterwards, my wife and I, standing on the platform of the Royal Albert Hall on commissioning day, heard ourselves appointed to Sandwich, the very corps where I had spent my first 'specialing' weekend with Child's Hill Band and where I had gained my first spiritual victory.

When we arrived at the station, who should be there to meet us but my 'convert', now the corps bandmaster. In that moment the seal of God's approval was placed upon our dedication and decision to become officers. We had no further doubts.

After my return to London at the end of that Easter campaign, Bandmaster Spencer lost no time in contacting me. Should I not become a Salvationist? In a fatherly way he spoke of my value to the Kingdom of God and the Army, and the needs of the corps. I appreciated his kindly interest but I had already made up my mind. In that prayer meeting at Sandwich I felt 'at home' and realised that the Army was where I belonged.

A letter to the Methodist minister and the choir secretary explained the position. They were puzzled by the news, but were gracious enough to wish me 'all the best'. The choir secretary went so far as to foresee a 'possible promising musical future'. In this unplanned way I signed the articles of war, was sworn-in as a soldier and became a bandsman and the songster organist at Child's Hill Corps.

Bandmaster Spencer did much to encourage me. As songster leader he made a brigade organist out of me, and I am grateful that he saw some potential usefulness in a boy of 15. I took notice of what he said, and learned much from his teaching methods and musical application. Long afterwards I discovered that he was severely reprimanded for permitting a non-Salvationist to play for his songster brigade at that ingathering, for dressing me up in uniform to go to Sandwich and permitting me to play with the band.

He seemed to have no regrets about this breach of regulation and I often wonder what my future might have been had he not taken such a daring step. I was not so well acquainted with restrictive rulings.

Although our ways parted when he transferred to Hendon, we remained in contact. When he heard my wife and I were to enter the training college, he was the first to express his joy and to donate a contribution to our collecting card. I was able to pay a personal tribute when honoured to conduct 'Bert' Spencer's funeral service in 1980. He was 86 years of age.

Will Straughan, who loaned me my first tunic, became a lifelong friend. A candidate for officership when I first met him, he entered the training college in 1930 and the following year was appointed as a lieutenant to Chipping Norton. When Will's captain went on furlough that summer I spent a week as his 'lieutenant', having my first taste of a corps officer's life and taking part in the meetings.

All through the years my wife and I kept in touch with Will and Olive Straughan, sharing holidays and enjoying friendship of mutual benefit. It was a sad day for me when, in September 1980, I conducted his funeral at Branksome, near Bournemouth, and told of our earlier associations. Brigadier Straughan was 'a good sort' who meant much to me.

'Joe' Nicholson, who started it all when he came to share our home and suggested I might be 'borrowed', remained in the employ of The Salvation Army Assurance Society until his retirement, when he settled in New Zealand with members of his family.

* * * * *

Having returned to the Army fold, I plunged into activity as if to redeem the years. On 10 April I went with my father to William Booth's '100th birthday celebrations' held in the Royal Albert Hall. It was the first time I had been inside this magnificent building. Our seats were high in the balcony.

Far, far below I saw the bands of the Salvation Army Assurance Society and Men's Social Work and the International Staff Band, like clockwork models wound up and ready for action. When they played massed for the Pageant of Army Progress, it was a gorgeous sound, the like of which I had never heard before. In the Albert Hall distance certainly lends enchantment. Some of the pageant remains photographed on my memory – the parade of the survivors of 1865 impressed me greatly.

The guest of honour was Prime Minister Stanley Baldwin, whose brilliant speech winged its way to all parts of the hall. I heard every word. Messages from the Founder's daughters, Evangeline and Lucy, were read, the British Commissioner (Commissioner Samuel Hurren) spoke and the address was given by General Edward Higgins.

The Founder's Centenary Celebrations, as they were called, were held at the Crystal Palace in July of that year. With Bandmaster

Spencer I attended the evening festival in the Central Transept and positively thrilled to the playing of the bands. Earlier, our songster brigade had been part of the united chorus. On duty at the grand organ was a teenage bandsman from Regent Hall, Philip Catelinet, a brilliant musician and promising composer who had recently joined the staff of the International Music Editorial Department.

Two weeks before the celebrations were held, hundreds of Salvationists, one Monday morning, mustered along the Thames Embankment between Blackfriars and Charing Cross Bridges for General Bramwell Booth's funeral procession. There were said to be 3,450 of them, with 20 bands and a multitude of white-ribboned banners. Thousands more people on the pavements made the route along Queen Victoria Street to the Mansion House quite impassable. Older Salvationists had seen nothing like this since William Booth's promotion to Glory 17 years before. Those of a newer generation, like me, born since the Founder's death, were experiencing something that we had only heard about.

The General's car had been converted into an open funeral carriage, with the motto of the Companion of Honour (to which the beloved leader had been appointed by His Majesty King George V only a month before) boldly inscribed on either side: 'In action faithful. In honour clear.'

As the procession reached International Headquarters a halt was made to allow the carriage to join it and for members of the late General's family, headed by his widow, to follow on foot. The clock on St Paul's Cathedral tolled the noon hour and the procession moved off again. It took 45 minutes for the marching Salvationists to pass headquarters. All other traffic was stopped. Thousands crowded the steps of the Royal Exchange and the adjoining thoroughfares as the citizens of London paid their own silent tribute to one of the city's greatest adopted sons. It was fitting that the Mayor and Mayoress of Halifax, the birthplace of Bramwell Booth, should be riding in the procession.

It was estimated that 10,000 people were admitted to Abney Park Cemetery that sparkling summer afternoon – the first arrivals having taken up vantage positions hours before while the procession was forming up four miles away. Battalions of police lined the cemetery approaches and controlled the marching masses as they proudly escorted the earthly remains of their beloved leader to their last resting place.

Two weeks later I left school. Clark's had kept their advertised promise and found me a job. I was engaged as an office boy at a finance house in Regent Street on a month's trial at a salary of £1 per week. 'If your work is then satisfactory,' said the letter confirming my employment, 'we shall be pleased to take you on our permanent staff when your salary will be paid monthly.' I 'made it' and at the end of the trial period received an increase to £4. 6s. 8d per month! The firm's main interest was car hire purchase, with the new popular Austin Seven the main attraction.

At the end of the year I accompanied our lieutenant, Bernard Bax, for a weekend 'specialing' to Buntingford, Hertfordshire, which corps was without officers. The lieutenant was a 'live wire' and able euphonium soloist. We contributed items to the Saturday night programme and on the Sunday morning I delivered my first sermon – based on all the experience of my 16 years!

I was grateful to the lieutenant of those days for helping me to develop this public side of my life. When he farewelled to take command of Stevenage Corps he invited me there for a weekend. The hall was down a country lane. Imagine my horror when I arrived to see myself billed as 'The boy preacher'!

My Army life developed considerably. I was moved from solo horn to euphonium and immediately took to the part. A new Triumph De Luxe pedal organ with six levers replaced the old American model and, before long, I was entrusted with the leadership of the male voice party and started appearing in programmes as an elocutionist. Musical monologues appealed to me most and as there was no other pianist available in the corps I started to accompany myself.

Poems published in *The Bandsman And Songster* were utilised in this way. Pounding the piano background as I went along was, I suppose, my first attempt at musical composition, although nothing was committed to paper.

I shall never forget the first young people's councils I attended. Conducted by General Edward Higgins, they were held in the Clapton Congress Hall and the youth of all five London divisions were included. More than 2,500 delegates crowded into the old building and, after the morning session, it became apparent that more had attended than were expected. A ticket, secured well in advance, entitled a delegate to be present at the three sessions of councils and to partake of lunch and tea. As the hungry crowd made its eager way out of the hall towards the Temple at the back it gradually dawned on us that there would not be enough food and drink to go round. Full marks to the organisers who ingeniously met the emergency! Delegates from the two divisions nearest to Clapton would have the 'privilege', in turn, of missing one of the meals. How they decided on the order of 'batting' I shall never know, but the cold truth is that young people of the North London Division missed their lunch and instead were marched off behind an energetic concertina-playing divisional young people's secretary to hold open-air meetings in the near vicinity.

We were rewarded by being the first in the queue for tea while the East London delegates evangelised the district on empty stomachs. It was many years before I again attended young people's councils.

I had been persuaded to attend the councils by a young songster in whom I had begun to show more than a passing interest. I had first become aware of her at that momentous ingathering meeting at Mildmay.

It took me most of the year of 1929 to pluck up courage to speak to her, let alone ask her out. Eventually it happened and she accepted my invitation. Our first 'date' was a Monday evening visit to Regent Hall for a harvest festival demonstration.

I cannot remember anything about the meeting or the ride home on top of an open bus complete with a mackintosh cover which, neatly contained at the back of the seat in front, could be unrolled and fastened to two studs inserted on the top of one's own seat. This ingenious, if primitive, covering was partial protection against the rain or wind as one travelled through London's dimly lit streets towards the suburbs. But the ice had been broken. That was the beginning of a romance that lasted more than 60 years.

Nina Hart, who came from an old Child's Hill Salvationist family, had recently left school when I first knew her and was employed by a firm of court dressmakers in the West End's famous Carnaby Street. Always gifted with her fingers, this was the work she had always wanted to do. Her second name was Dorcas – the Bible character of that name was also a needlewoman!

The dressmaking firm was situated within minutes of the office where I worked, so we were able to see each other quite regularly apart from at the corps. Lunch often consisted of an apple and a walk round the stores. When there was something special on at the Rink we spoiled ourselves, went into a teashop and partook of a cheese roll or, if it was payday, egg and chips. We discovered the Army together as we attended all the big London 'dos' and watched the adverts in *The Bandsman And Songster* to decide where we could go 'this Saturday'. Activity in our busy corps occupied much of our time as well.

After serving as deputy songster leader for a short while I was requested to accept the leadership of the brigade. I was still under 18. Nina was commissioned young people's singing company leader at the same time and I became her organist.

As a young songster leader I was fortunate to have as my songster sergeant a veteran retired officer named Commandant Frances Raper. She had been one of the great women officers of the Army. What a sergeant she was! A leader of immense spiritual strength and influence, she was fearless in her dealings with what she called 'shortcomings'. Many times she would take my arm and walk me gently along the road, counselling me with wisdom and lovingly, but firmly, correcting those impetuosities of youth of which I was only too aware.

At times the dear commandant exasperated me by breathing in the middle of words, not carrying phrases over to the next bar or preceding words like 'Army' and 'am' with an aspirate. But she was a gem of transparent Christianity who reflected sheer goodness in her radiant personality. I was happy to know such a person in the days of my youth.

One of my great frustrations was that I could never call upon the services of a regular organist. For an away engagement I had to borrow, which created rehearsal problems. At the corps there was no alternative but to turn the organ round so that I sat at the keyboard facing the brigade, conducting with hand waves where possible and at other times nodding-in the parts required.

The songsters were trained to this unorthodox method of leadership and responded magnificently. When at national songster festivals I saw George Phillips, of Bristol Staple Hill, and other leaders conduct in this way I knew I was in good company.

In May 1933 I was at Clapton for the farewell of the Musical Troopers who were leaving on a 500-mile 'tramp for God'. This group of 30 instrumentalists consisted of newly commissioned lieutenants of the Torchbearers Session. It was said there were not enough corps in the British Territory for the new officers to 'occupy' and that this arrangement for the summer months would help to ease the situation. Times have changed!

My main memory of the evening is of seeing and hearing the Army's first bandsman, Fred W. Fry, for the first time. I managed to secure his autograph. In December 1891 he had been the first bandmaster of the International Staff Band and, 13 years before that, with his father and two brothers, had formed the first band.

That summer the Queen's Hall, Langham Place, at the north end of Regent Street, was used for an Army national event for the first time. Seven bands took part (where did they seat them all?) and to hear such pieces as 'Good Old Army', 'A Soul's Triumph' and 'The King Of Kings' made it a magical evening.

One cornet soloist made an unprogrammed appearance that night. He was white-bearded, 75-year-old Trumpeter Sheard who, with his ancient cornet, treated us to some melodies from the past. Arthur Sheard, as a young lieutenant, had been appointed the General's Trumpeter – the only person to hold that office – and, 50 years before, had accompanied William Booth to the opening of Regent Hall. He was left in London to form the first band at the corps and one of the pioneer instrumentalists was eight-year-old 'Bert' Twitchin. Sheard became the boy's hero and mentor.

It was an historic moment at the Queen's Hall, therefore, when the trumpeter's 'protégé' was called to his side and master and pupil delighted the excited crowd with an unaccompanied, impromptu duet based on the tune 'Canaan'.

They played it once, 'H.W-.T.' providing an unorthodox second part. The repeat was a 'riot'. Sheard prepared to play variations on the melody, mentally rearranging as he went, with quavers and semiquavers added as inspiration took him. His partner did likewise with the underpart, the embellishment of triple-tonguing enhancing the presentation. This unexpected item 'brought the house down'.

The festival was a tremendous success and became an annual event until the outbreak of the Second World War when, sadly, the lovely hall, home of Sir Henry Wood's Promenade Concerts for so long, was destroyed in an air raid in 1941.

Chapter 8

Into the Depths and Out Again

WITHOUT warning my world was shattered. At the office a new accountancy machine (the word 'computer' had not then been invented) was installed which, it was promised, could do the work of five clerks. Four would have to go. I was one of them.

To find myself caught up in the great economic depression of the 1930s was a frightening experience. I had been out of work a month when 1934 dawned and one of my new year resolutions was to find a job as quickly as possible. I was confident it would not take long. However, it was not that easy. Twice a week I made my way to the labour exchange to see if there was 'anything doing' and to sign for my dole money. If I remember rightly this was less than a pound a week.

Occasionally there were vacancies and I would hopefully walk to the address supplied, sometimes a few yards and at other times a distance of anything up to four miles. Invariably the job had been taken, or my qualifications and experience were not thought adequate. To have turned down an interview would have meant one's instant withdrawal from unemployment benefit. For five months I was a reluctant participant in this humiliating charade.

Fortunately, my Army interest did not wane. Despite the personal depression and frustration caused by my descent into the depths of despair, I was still finding plenty of variety in my young life.

One day my self-imposed round of job-hunting took me to Queen Victoria Street and my first sight of International Headquarters. It was an impressive building, the big, bold brass lettering and mammoth Army flag surmounting the centre of the massive structure leaving no one in any possible doubt as to the identity of the premises.

I managed to secure interviews with Colonel Onslow Edwin, Staff Secretary at International Headquarters, and Lieut-Colonel Railton Howard of the Assurance Society. Both were courteous and kind. Both regretted there were no vacancies. Both promised to make a note of my name and address.

When I heard that a local Assurance Society agency was becoming available I lost no time in applying for the vacancy, only to be told that unemployed people could not be considered. I thought this strange reasoning.

I suppose it was the ambition of most Army boys of that era to get into a headquarters band. Membership of these groups was strictly confined to officers and employees in the various headquarters' buildings, and it was strongly rumoured that securing work at these establishments depended upon one's ability to pass an instrumental audition.

When I was informed rather secretively that there was a vacancy in the accounts department of Salvationist Publishing and Supplies, Limited, I was immediately interested. I had misgivings, though, when I was told that applicants were required to play the soprano cornet, but I decided to try my hand.

Some time before, the depletion of the band at Child's Hill had necessitated my moving from euphonium to cornet, and this had brought its own quota of experience in blowing hard and keeping the little band going. We were limited to *Second Series* music. I had never even held a soprano. As for playing one... but I desperately wanted a job.

An interview was arranged and I duly arrived at Judd Street to be auditioned by the Salvationist Publishing and Supplies bandmaster, Captain Eric Ball. There was a puzzled expression on his face as he smiled, greeted me and said, 'I didn't know you played soprano.' 'I don't,' I replied, honestly enough, 'but I want a job.'

Eric handed me the instrument and asked me to play anything I liked. I selected 'Rockingham' in the normal key, commencing on 'C' for the soprano. 'Put it up a fourth,' said Captain Ball when I had finished. This took me up to top 'F' and I shall never forget the pained look on the face of the 'examiner' as I struggled to reach that lofty, hitherto unexplored pinnacle. Sight-reading from the captain's *air varié* 'The Old Wells' followed and then the soprano solo from 'The King Of Kings'.

What an ordeal! I did not expect to hear anything more – and was not disappointed. When, some weeks later, I saw and heard Victor Nelson, of Regent Hall, the successful applicant, playing so delightfully at the Associated Headquarters Festival, I realised what a narrow escape I had had. Or was it so narrow?

I first met Eric Ball when I had the temerity to invite Southall 1 Songster Brigade to give a festival at Child's Hill. This was one of the leading London brigades and the name of its leader, Sam Hooper, was already a household word throughout the Army musical world. Captain Ball was the organist and featured on the programme as a soloist on that instrument – we had no piano – as well as providing accompaniment to the songster leader's bass solo.

The date of that event, Wednesday 29 November 1933, is indelibly impressed on my mind. Not only was it the first songster festival I had organised (and by no means the last!) but also, on the Thursday, I had joined the ranks of the unemployed. I tried not to let that dreaded prospect spoil my enjoyment of the fine festival, which I had asked my own brigade to regard as a demonstration of 'how to do it'.

Over refreshments I had my first conversation with Eric Ball. I had heard many of his public utterances and come under the spell of his incomparable music, but this experience was different. I was immediately impressed by his knowledge, ability to express himself in simple but sincere terms and, most of all, his Christian humility.

Neither of us could have visualised the occasion, 45 years hence, when I would be honoured to preside over his 75th birthday tribute festival in the Poole Arts Centre.

The chairman for the Southall Brigade's festival was Staff-Captain Arch R. Wiggins, Editor of *The Bandsman And Songster*, who had known my parents since, as a teenager, he began attending meetings at Harlesden. He became my champion in those dark days.

When I had been out of work for five months a telegram arrived asking me to ring the *Bandsman And Songster* office. I eagerly did so.

The editor was not there but his assistant, Staff-Bandsman Charles Watts, knew what the message was all about and filled me in with the details of a vacancy in the accounts department of the Men's Social Work Headquarters. Lieut-Colonel Arthur Goldsmith, the Financial Secretary, was looking for a journal clerk who could 'bump up' the cornet section of the Men's Social Work Headquarters Band, of which he was the renowned conductor.

A few days later found me on the second floor of 110 Middlesex Street waiting to see the colonel. He came in after the midday band practice, saw me, beamed, shook my hand and commented on my resemblance to my Uncle Herbert, with whom he had played in the Junior Staff Band and, later, the ISB.

The colonel was another of my boyhood heroes and, as I followed him into his office, it seemed like a dream as I sat answering his questions. He was generous enough to say that my humble first effort at composing 'showed promise' and 'signs of maturity'. He was perfectly frank concerning his need in the band and felt that my experience of sustained stamina in a small band could help bolster his cornet team. Mercifully I was spared an audition.

The accountant was called in and the deal was settled. My seemingly endless nightmare was at an end. I was in work again.

The following Monday I began my new career as a Salvation Army employee at a salary of 35 shillings a week. Uniform, including a cap, was required to be worn every day to and from the office and duty with the headquarters band was to take priority over all corps commitments.

Among my colleagues in the department, who soon made me feel at home, was Charles Skinner, a young bandsman who travelled in from Bishop's Stortford every day. We instantly formed a friendship that lasted until the sad day, 43 years later, when I paid tribute at his funeral service.

The creditors' section of the accounts department was divided into alphabetical sections and I joined the G-M section. On my first day I was handed a number of invoices to be entered. An item on one of these simply stated '12 dozen Polish'. This was duly entered as '144 tins of polish' and carried out to what I assumed to be the correct column. It was not until the end of the month that my grave error was discovered. How was I to know that the bald statement on the invoice signified '12 dozen Polish eggs', or that David Greig, the well-known provision merchants, did not supply polish?

The Governor of the Men's Social Work in Great Britain and Ireland at that time was Commissioner George Langdon. One day, soon after my arrival, I came face to face with the commissioner on the narrow staircase and, not having suddenly met a leading officer in such close proximity before, I was completely nonplussed as to how to deal with the emergency. I merely hurried by, mumbling, 'Good morning, Guv'nor' as I passed. Some lessons are learned the hard way on an Army headquarters.

The banding side of my new life instantly appealed to me. My ambition was realised at long last. I was issued with a tunic and sent, with an order, to Judd Street to obtain a cap of suitable size. This was of the braided peak and red-piping variety, complete with white-lettered name ribbon, black chinstrap and ensign's badge.

While I was there I was measured for a model 'C' overcoat and black-braided trousers, both part of the band uniform. These were a personal responsibility and, for the privilege of wearing them, half a crown was deducted from my weekly wages until they were paid for.

In those days a record was kept of the number of meetings attended by employees. We were expected to fill in a weekly 'score sheet' which was signed by the departmental head and passed on for 'higher scrutiny'. I cannot remember whether officers were included.

A fair average aggregation was six on Sunday and four during the week. None of us would think twice about including open-air and indoor meetings in the Sunday record but we could not agree as to the matter of practices. Were they meetings or not?

The difference of opinion led to heated arguments as we shouted to each other across the crowded office. The accountant sat in solitary state in her inner sanctum with the door open, offering advice from time to time, or interrupting with a reprimand when the atmosphere became too highly charged. The adjudged culprit was named and, from within, ordered to apologise to his offended comrade. There would then be silence and the inevitable follow-up: 'Have you done it?' How could one disobey such an instruction when surrounded by a cloud of witnesses who looked on and made facetious signs – well out of view of 'The Brig'?

A break was made each day at 12 noon for a 15-minute prayer meeting. This was held in the Accounts Department, which meant no escape for those who worked within its boarded confines.

The Chief Secretary (Colonel Gerald Freeman) was the presiding genius and controlled everything from his 'vantage point' behind one of the many Dickensian desks which adorned the office. The colonel appointed 'Mr Skinner' as the daily organist and, when I arrived on the scene, I was 'deputed to be his deputy' – as the colonel gleefully announced, always appreciative of his own wit. On the occasions when Mr Skinner was absent, Colonel Freeman loved to declare to the assembled host, 'Mr Boon will play the toon.'

When we knelt to pray the chief secretary would descend to a crouching position on hands and knees. This enabled him, if there was a lull in the requested prayerful response, to crawl rapidly across the room and prompt some poor, unsuspecting, reluctant comrade! This was accomplished by a sharp dig in the ribs, a 'gentle' slap on the back or a painful pinch. Often the audible involuntary reaction, 'Oh!', became the beginning of one's invocation, 'O Lord...'.

The organist, being nearer to hand than anyone else, had more than his fair share of 'promptings'. Both Charles and I preferred to carry out the musical duties when the colonel was off the building.

Prayers over, a meal was served in the two dining rooms situated in the basement – one for officers, the other for employees, separated by a closed partition. This arrangement was not a shock to me. I was used to seeing 'Gentlemen' and 'Players' take the field by different gates and change in different dressing rooms at Lord's.

All was going well. My cup of happiness was filled to overflowing. I had passed through the slough of despond and there was everything to live for.

On the last day of May 1934, Nina and I travelled across London to attend the Clapton Congress Hall central holiness meeting to see and hear the Maréchale, eldest daughter of the Founder and Catherine Booth. It was a musical occasion. Clapton Congress Hall Band, conducted by its bandmaster, Staff-Captain Albert Jakeway, took part, as did the East London Chorus, led by Adjutant Ernest Rance. The meeting concluded with the congregation singing the guest of honour's well-loved song, 'O Lamb Of God, Thou Wonderful Sin-Bearer'. This was my first and only glimpse of this remarkable leader, whose voice was still vibrant and youthful, and whose speaking that night was so challenging. I was pleased to have made the effort.

After lunch the next day, I collected my cornet from the band room and went into practice as usual. We started to play and, to my horror, I could not produce a sound. My lip muscles had gone and my embouchure was non-effective. The air was escaping from the side of my mouth without making contact with the mouthpiece.

Realising something of my discomfort and state of panic, Lieut-Colonel Goldsmith took one look at me and ordered me off to see a nearby doctor.

Dr Joseph Parry was a police medical adviser with a reputation for unedited candour and forthright diagnosis. After giving me one or two simple exercises, such as clenching my teeth and closing my left eye, he exclaimed, 'Good Lor', boy, you've got paralysis!' He scribbled out a note to be taken immediately to the London Hospital in Whitechapel Road, where it was arranged for me to see a specialist the following Monday.

It was the first day of June. My little world, which had known so much joy during the past month, was again shattered.

On the way home to break the news to my loved ones, I sought calmly to assess the position. It did not take me long to confirm that the left side of my face was indeed paralysed and that my eye was permanently open to receive dust and other foreign objects from which one would normally recoil.

I was still two months away from my 21st birthday. What future could there possibly be? That weekend I spent in bed, alone with my thoughts, refusing to have anything to do with even my nearest and dearest. In this way, between bouts of fitful sleep, I steeled myself against whatever shocks might be awaiting me on the Monday.

Arriving at the hospital in good time, I was placed in the keeping of Russell Brain, a Harley Street specialist in nervous diseases and the hospital's consultant on such matters. He gave me a thorough examination, witnessed by a dozen or so medical students, and then, in the privacy of his room, calmly informed me that I had Bell's Palsy, a complaint of which I had never heard.

To me, my case seemed even more hopeless. Facial paralysis would have been bad enough, but this...?

'But you're young enough and healthy enough to take it,' went on Mr Brain. 'Leave yourself in my hands, trust me and we'll get that silly old face straight again.' In that moment my fears went and a comforting assurance that all would be well took their place.

An hour later I began a course of massage and electrical treatment which took me to the hospital every morning – Monday to Friday – for six months. After the initial shock my sense of humour returned and I made capital out of the ludicrous situation of being able to laugh on one side of my face while the other side remained serious.

I shall always be grateful for Russell Brain's interest in me and his tender handling of my case. I was evidently a rare specimen of guinea pig, for whenever the brilliant specialist, not then 40 years of age, reviewed my progress he was accompanied by a bodyguard of young men desirous of learning all they could about nervous maladies. Becoming an expert in this particular realm of medical research, Mr Brain was later knighted and, at the time of his death, had been a baron for some years.

My days on cornet were over. There was to be no more playing for me that year. This deprived me of being with the band at the Crystal Palace Day in June and at other engagements. However, by the time 1 November arrived I had recovered sufficiently to be with the band at the Royal Albert Hall for the retirement meeting of General and Mrs Edward Higgins, and to accompany it as a non-playing member to High Wycombe that weekend.

The Albert Hall event provided me with a close-up view of the Duke and Duchess of York (later King George VI and Queen Elizabeth), as they mounted the platform to pay their tribute to the farewelling leaders, and of a number of other leading public figures of the day, including General (later Field Marshall) Jan Smuts who, in a speech, described the gathering as 'a royal ending to a great career'.

A few months before, Lieut-Colonel Goldsmith had relinquished the conductorship of the MSW Band because of the continuing illness of his wife. This was a great disappointment to us all. Leonard Bloomfield, a gifted organiser and keen bandsman, who had served as bandmaster for some years with the colonel as instructor, now added the musical direction of the band to his administrative duties and Adjutant Rance was appointed deputy bandmaster.

The tour of southern prisons by the MSW Band was an annual event and it was with a sense of adventure that I set out with the band on my first experience of this kind. It meant leaving London on the Saturday, having lunch at a restaurant in Winchester and giving a programme in the local prison. It was then on to Portsmouth, a hurried tea at the citadel and a programme in Portsmouth Prison, followed by a festival in the hall.

Early next morning we caught the first ferry across to the Isle of Wight, disembarked at Ryde and then travelled by coach to Camphill Borstal where a service was shared with the grey-uniformed young men.

At Camphill, the first Sunday morning in each month was allotted to the farewell service for those whose sentences were completed and who were to be released during the next few days. The Governor, Mr C. A. Joyce, had written a hymn to be sung on such occasions and this was pasted in the front cover of the hymn books. As our visit invariably fell on the same Sunday each year, we became familiar with the words and, accompanied by the organ, found deep satisfaction in blending our voices with those of the lads in confession and dedication of the future. Mr Joyce's sincerity shone through all his dealings.

An afternoon programme in Parkhurst was always a highlight. Seven hundred hard-boiled, long-sentence prisoners in the care of seven warders was a formidable sight, especially when there was sometimes a doubt about the reception accorded to the items. Perhaps the most terrifying experience was when the vocal party sang 'Keep In Step'. The words and melody of this song had been written by Alf Vickery, a member of our band, some years previously but this particular arrangement had been set to Rachmaninoff's 'Prelude In C Sharp Minor'. Can the result be imagined?

To fit the majestic music, the words, 'Keep in step – O, keep in', were required to be repeated time and time again, with the basses plumbing the depths in grovelling abjection and the top tenors soaring into the heavens with intricate harmonic meanderings. How we came to venture forth into such an inescapable situation I shall never know. The longer the piece lasted the louder was 'the bird'. The louder 'the bird' the more worried became the warders, who left their seats to parade ominously among the audience. There was a sigh of utter relief, shared by singers and victims alike, when our classical sorties came to an end.

My other abiding memory of 1934 is of attending the welcome to General Evangeline Booth at the Royal Albert Hall when the MSW Band was again on duty. I was still not playing an instrument but my treatment had ended and there was every prospect of my resuming active service in the new year.

As I walked around the outside of the vast building I saw the lone figure of a shortish, well-dressed Salvationist with a neatly trimmed moustache. He was studying the ticket in his hand, looking at the door and obviously trying to find his way in. As it was obvious he was a stranger I asked if I could be of help and immediately recognised the man from a photograph. It was Bandmaster Erik Leidzén, of the USA, composer superlative and songwriter extraordinary. He was not impressed with the location of the ticket he showed me and suggested that he might come with me. Somehow we managed to evade the usually eagle eye of the man on guard at the artists' door and I was proud to take him under my wing for the rest of the evening.

In this unexpected way I made the acquaintance of Erik Leidzén for the first time. It was the beginning of a fellowship of shared correspondence and occasional contacts on both sides of the Atlantic (once in Sweden) that was to last for nearly 30 years.

A few weeks before his death in 1962 we 'specialed' together at Danforth (now Agincourt) Citadel Corps, in Toronto – he the gifted, challenging speaker and I leading the meeting and having the honour to introduce him. Dear Erik! He looked a film star in Army uniform the first time I saw him.

Chapter 9

Broadening Horizons

IT was good to be playing a brass instrument again. This time I was on euphonium. The Men's Social Work Headquarters Band began 1935 'under new management'. Adjutant Leonard Bloomfield, after a brief period of leadership, had been appointed to Newcastle upon Tyne. His deputy, Adjutant Ernest Rance, was the new bandmaster. Among other officials announced was Bandsman Charles Skinner (songmaster). This designation was the inspiration of the Chief Secretary (Colonel Gerald Freeman), who was nothing if not original. 'Songmaster' Skinner's responsibilities were to conduct the full band and to lead the vocal octet, which was re-formed under his direction.

It was a busy life, full of thrilling interest. None of us would have wished it to be otherwise. There was plenty of variety in our banding. Hostel meetings, prison programmes, corps visits, week-night festivals and participation in national events in the Royal Albert Hall, Westminster Central Hall, Clapton Congress Hall and Regent Hall were all part of our crammed engagement calendar.

As young Salvationists we were given an early insight into many facets of Army life and service, as well as a working knowledge of a caring ministry that was so dear to the hearts of William and Catherine Booth.

Because of such hitherto unknown opportunities, I suppose it is natural that I should remember the happenings of that particular year so vividly. At reasonable intervals the band accompanied the commissioner or chief secretary on Sunday visits to London hostels. Three meetings – at Spa Road, Bermondsey, Victoria Home, Whitechapel, and Blackfriars – constituted a typical day.

The headquarters' one and only stores van, driven by George Usher, my mate on euphonium, conveyed the instruments. We were required to make our own way. There was always plenty of time for us to walk from one place to another.

Weekend 'specialing' with the band took me to many new parts and certainly enlarged 'my coast'. The Sunday morning march through the quiet main street of Chippenham and festivals in the Neald Hall come readily to mind. At Worthing we were generously given the Monday off to enjoy a little relaxation. We decided that we could spend the time in no better way than playing cricket. None of your improvised stuff on the sands – or pebbles; this game would have a touch of class. Our luggage included an assortment of flannels, shirts and sweaters, and we managed to borrow gear from Regent Hall Band.

Upon arrival on the Saturday afternoon the self-appointed cricket committee, armed with a map of the town with parks and sports grounds clearly marked, did some diligent exploring. After several fruitless enquiries we came to a beautiful stretch of green where, it was said, Sussex county teams had played. I am sure it was the impressive pavilion and the lengthy walk to the wicket which appealed to us more than the actual playing area.

When we asked a stern-looking park keeper for permission to play there on Monday afternoon he did not respond with too much enthusiasm. In fact, he did not hesitate to inform us that only the town hall could give such approval.

After further explanations on our part the light dawned. He had thought we wanted to give a band concert! To play cricket was another matter. Of course we could have the ground – and the pavilion. Free of charge.

We took advantage of the sea air on the Monday morning and turned up at Homefield Park for the match in the afternoon. We changed in the dressing rooms like real professionals. Colonel Freeman, our worthy patron, appointed himself as scorer and produced an open penknife to keep his pencil sharpened. Wearing a mixture of 'regimentals' – his word – and mufti he unwittingly appeared in the guise of a trendsetter.

Another Monday memory is of returning from Bristol Bedminster, where we asked our band 'locals' to persuade the coach driver to return to London via the mighty Cheddar Gorge. Most of us had not been there before. But we had not realised that the route would take us so much out of our way. There were some red faces, quickly conceived excuses and severe tickings off when we arrived at our Middlesex Street headquarters, three hours late.

When we went to Newport, Isle of Wight, the chairman on Sunday afternoon was Sir Dan Godfrey, former director of the Bournemouth Symphony Orchestra and that town's musical adviser. He conducted the band in the 'Hallelujah' Chorus and in his gracious remarks revealed that, through The Salvation Army, his son had been led to God.

The Newport commanding officer was Adjutant Burnal Webb, whose three-year-old daughter Joy seemed intrigued and highly amused by the band's playing of the unusual 'The Salvation Army Patrol'.

The visit to Manchester was unforgettable. We travelled up on the night train, leaving Euston at midnight on the Friday, and so sleeping berths were booked – four to a compartment. After breakfast at Francis Street Hostel, we were taken by coach to Lewis's famous store where, on a stage in the spacious restaurant, we played and sang to a host of customers as they partook of morning coffee.

The impromptu concert was a lengthy affair. The shoppers, many of them Salvationists who came solely to hear the band, took time over refreshments and received the items with great enthusiasm. The management was delighted with the success of the venture and let the band play on. The professional orchestra waiting in the wings to take our place, as arranged, was not enthusiastic about our prolonged appearance. I remember feeling sorry for them.

Their leader, short, swarthy, sleek-haired and immaculately groomed, had not yet become famous. Neither had his orchestra. They were billed that day as Joe Loss and his band.

Lewis's entertained us to lunch and after an hour or two's free time we made our way to the BBC's studios in Piccadilly for the band's first broadcast – over the North Regional wavelength. It was a nerve-racking experience, but the charming announcer, David Potter, who later became a skilled and well-known producer of radio drama, put us at ease. The programme included two marches, 'Heaven-Bound Throng' and 'Montreal Citadel', a horn solo and three short pieces from the works of Wagner. As there was time to spare, the hymn tune 'Deep Harmony' was added.

During the evening festival in Manchester Temple a telegram arrived from Riga, Latvia. The enthusiastic, ever-thoughtful musician/officer-in-charge of that isolated outpost of the Army's 'empire', Major Alfred Lockyer, succeeded in picking up the broadcast and wired his congratulations. That gesture meant a great deal to us.

Sunday's activities included a morning meeting at Francis Street Hostel, an afternoon programme at Strangeways Prison and an evening salvation meeting in the Temple. I was to return to Manchester many times but wonder if any subsequent visit ever captured the pioneering excitement of that first venture.

Participation in the Associated Headquarters festival was a dream come true. This was the musical highlight of the year. To play in a headquarters band at this annual event was the height of every London Army boy's ambition. Here I was, then, at the festival making my nervous debut as a performer.

That night the winners of the 1934 International Band Music Competition were announced and the first prize compositions played.

The prize-winning composition in our section was 'Room' and the writer, to our surprised delight, was the flugelhorn player in the International Staff Band, sitting but a few yards away – Adjutant Harold Zealley. After the announcement and the avalanche of congratulatory applause, we sought to do justice to the selection. We were interested to learn that the third place in that particular section went to our own bandmaster, Adjutant Rance, with 'The Call Of The Cross'.

When 'Songmaster' Skinner farewelled to enter the training college he was succeeded in that role by Stuart Holden Beaumont, who was named after the Rev Stuart Holden, Vicar of St Paul's, Portman Square.

He was the band's able principal cornetist for seven years. For some time he was my billeting partner and when he left us to take an executive appointment with a London business house, I became the vocal leader and remained so until the band ceased to exist at the beginning of the Second World War.

By the time I took over the responsibility for the band's singing, Colonel Freeman had retired and the title 'songmaster' had been mercifully dropped.

I was appearing regularly on programmes as an elocutionist. Musical monologues became superseded by character studies, chiefly, I think, because pianos were not always situated in the ideal position for me to accompany myself and be seen and heard by the audience.

Bransby Williams was all the rage at the time. His Dickensian recitals on radio proved immensely popular and crowds were being lured to music halls to witness his 'top of the bill' performances. It did not take long for me to become an ardent fan. The idea of impersonations appealed to me. I even went a step or two further by giving items involving more than one character. Being in the middle of a festival prevented dressing up for the parts, of course, but with disguised voice, facial expression and a variety of stances I did my best to create this illusion.

'Scrooge' was my first experiment. I re-scripted the opening chapter of *A Christmas Carol* to allow for a conversation between Ebenezer Scrooge and his nephew, who had called at his uncle's office to pay the compliments of the season, and then a brief altercation about a day off and the cost thereof between Scrooge and his clerk, Bob Cratchit.

'Scrooge' appeared on MSW Band programmes on and off for a number of years. Long-term prisoners in such places as Parkhurst, Broadmoor, Maidstone, Leicester and Chelmsford came to expect it and requested its inclusion if it was not on the programme.

When Barking Corps put on *A Christmas Carol* to run for a week, I was invited to appear as Scrooge. I had always 'fancied' the part since I saw Russell Thorndike cast in the role at the Metropolitan, Edgware Road. The idea of performing in costume was an added attraction.

The production was excellent, the scenery magnificent. Rehearsals went well and we came to the opening night. The first scene was important. The curtain operators had been well briefed. The dialogue would end. The silence should not be hurried.

Bob Cratchit would climb down from the lofty stool of his high desk, put on his scarf and hat and scurry into the night. Scrooge, too, would prepare to leave for home, taking time to put on his coat, wind his lengthy muffler round his neck, apply his silk top hat, snuff out the candle which, standing precariously on his desk, provided the office's only illumination and exit unsmilingly into the street. All very dramatic.

The instructions were perfectly clear. The curtain was not to be lowered until the candle was extinguished. Unfortunately, Scrooge took longer over his closing drama than had been anticipated. While members of the audience were able to witness the silent antics of the old miser, those offstage, not being able to see a thing, were not so appreciative. In fact, the curtain operator thought that Scrooge had availed himself of another exit and forgotten to put out the candle.

The result was that the flimsy curtain – which fell in two folds either side of the stage, meeting in the middle – when released, passed through the flame of the still-lit candle and proceeded on its way alight. The audience shrieked, arresting the attention of Scrooge, who had to abandon his much-prepared exit and, with his precious silk hat, assist alarmed stagehands to put out the flames. It was a nasty moment.

The rest of the performance proceeded without incident, minus curtains of course, but a new pair had been secured by the next night and the week's presentation was a great success. I never again was asked to take part in a Charles Dickens masterpiece, although I have a lasting affection for *A Christmas Carol* – and Scrooge.

In the late summer of 1935 a new member was added to the Accountants' Department and joined the band. He was conspicuous by the red tunic he wore for office use. This bore the inscription 'Palmerston North Band'.

His name was Walter Stanley Cottrill and he had just arrived from New Zealand with his parents. He introduced us to a delightful Maori melody which he had brought from New Zealand. It went to the words 'How wonderful it is to walk with God'. I arranged it for the vocal party and it became a great favourite on the social band programmes.

Some years later Gracie Fields, after a visit to the Antipodes, gave it a special place in her concerts as 'Now Is The Hour'. After the Second World War it was included in the Army's chorus book with the words 'Search me, O God', the music designated as a Maori melody. Some time later the music was claimed to have been composed by Clement Scott, the owners of the copyright being Keith Prowse and Co, Ltd. Subsequent reprints of the chorus book noted the correction and a fee was required for its inclusion. But there are those who still believe that the tune is a Maori melody beyond the reach of copyright restrictions.

Erstwhile banding colleagues of Stan Cottrill felt very proud when much later General Arnold Brown appointed him his Chief of the Staff.

*　*　*　*　*

We loved General Evangeline Booth, and the Men's Social Work Band welcomed every opportunity to give its musical support. For me it was a continuation of earlier heroine worship, but now a little closer.

Every Christmas Day during her term of office, when she was not out of the country, the General visited Men's Social Work establishments in the London area. Traditionally, those of the Women's Social Work were so honoured on Boxing Day. It was customary for a group of instrumentalists to accompany the General on these visits and I was appointed leader of these 'seasonal serenaders', as Colonel Freeman dubbed us. We were all unmarried.

We would have to reach the first port of call (usually Victoria Home) in time to play a number of carols before the General's arrival. There would then be more music before her Christmas message and we would hurry on to the next stop, possibly Spa Road, to repeat the ritual.

Christmas dinner at Spa Road with the men – and the General – was always memorable. The fact that it was also her birthday added greatly to the festivities. After the meal, with all the trimmings, she would send for 'young Boon' and, after exchanging a few words of good-humoured banter, present me with large boxes of chocolates for the 'band boys'. 'For your sweethearts and mothers, remember!' she would mischievously chuckle across the yard.

And then it was on to Blackfriars and finally the Great Western Hostel where, when the Great Western Hall was a thriving centre of corps evangelism on that same site, she had been the fearless girl captain. The General was never lost for memories there.

With London's public transport coming to a halt at 4 pm I cannot imagine how long it must have taken us all to reach our homes. From Marylebone to Willesden Green was a long and lonely walk, I remember, relieved now and again by a reveller who had lost his way and welcomed a Salvationist's company for a while. One of our number managed to borrow his father's car on such occasions and carry out a taxi service for those living south of the Thames. Private transport was rare indeed.

The General's lecture, 'The World's Greatest Romance' – later changed to 'The Romance Of The Salvation Army' – took Britain by storm.

Announced to give this for the first time in the Royal Albert Hall, she asked for a male chorus to give support at intervals in the script. The International Staff Band and the bands of the Men's Social Work Headquarters and Salvationist Publishing and Supplies, Limited, formed the nucleus of the group and other available personnel were added to build up the required avalanche of sound.

We did not receive any copies of the songs until the day, when we were excused duty from work. A full day in this loveliest of halls was not to be treated lightly.

In the morning the songs, produced in manuscript and distributed upon arrival, were rehearsed and the seating formation was decided.

After lunch the General arrived for a rehearsal, patiently testing the acoustics and repeating the parts of the lecture affecting the singing background over and over again until she was satisfied. 'It's important,' she kept saying.

At one point she sent the British Commissioner (Commissioner Charles Rich) up to the topmost gallery to listen. When she eventually saw him in position she asked, 'Rich, can you hear me?' There was no answer.

She tried again, this time raising her voice a little: 'Rich, I love you!' 'Thank you, General,' was the instant reply. The chorus exploded. Turning to us, she roguishly commented, 'Ah, I thought he would hear that. You men are all the same.'

In the evening, while the packed audience sat rigidly under the spell of her incomparable oratory, the General stood for more than an hour, her personal flag clasped in her hand, every inflection of the voice and gesture of the hand heavy with meaning. With only the occasional dramatic, well-timed pause to interrupt the amazing flow of language, and without a note to prompt her, she unfolded the glorious Salvation Army story, touching upon every facet of its complex structure with a knowledge and skill that few in the Movement could have possessed.

And the male chorus sat intent, waiting for the familiar upbeat of Colonel Railton Howard to stir us into action with 'O Boundless Salvation!', 'Bowed Beneath A Garden Shade', 'Sun Of My Soul' or 'Rescue The Perishing'. Evangeline Booth was her father's daughter. His mantle of dramatic presentation had descended upon her, and she too learned to use it to the glory of God. Her lovely smile, flourish of the hand and affectionate incline of the head towards the 'gentlemen of the chorus' as she left the platform amid the lingering cheers in which we joined as loudly the rest, was all the reward we wanted for a long, tiring, often frustrating day.

How I came to be a member of a smaller group which travelled to various centres to give similar support to the General I shall never know. Colonel Ernest Wellman was in charge, I remember, and several staff bandsmen were included. We came to know the lecture almost by heart, also the theatrical 'business' that went with it. The General knew this and teased us about it at rehearsal.

For certain events a composite band from the Associated Headquarters was formed, usually under the bandmastership of

Colonel George Fuller. I sometimes found myself in this august company and loved every minute of the fellowship. One such event was an outing of 1,500 children and 500 mothers from the London slums to Boxmoor, Hertfordshire.

This excursion was inaugurated by General Evangeline in the first summer of her leadership and continued through the six years until her retirement. Names of the 2,000 'lucky people' were submitted by officers of what were then known as the London slum posts, later happily renamed goodwill centres.

The outing invariably took place on a Friday. The mothers and children made their way to the Victoria Embankment, between Blackfriars and Waterloo Bridges, where at 8 am they boarded 55 motor coaches.

The first year, the General arranged for the Lord Mayor of London to take the salute outside National Headquarters, on the opposite side of Queen Victoria Street to International Headquarters, as the motorcade drove by, yellow, red and blue balloons dangling from the windows.

They were a noisy crowd. Some sang 'For he's a jolly good Lord Mayor', others 'We want everybody to be 'appy'. They were going to enjoy themselves. For some unknown reason the band played 'The Farmer's Boy' as we passed. Could it have been because we were to spend a day in the country? This was the first time I had been required to play 'mounted' and I am afraid my efforts were not too successful. But I was not alone in my shortcoming, I was relieved to notice.

The guests were provided with a meal upon arrival and then followed an afternoon of fun and frolics. A Punch and Judy show, penny-on-the-mat (without charge), organised games, sweet scrambles, races, the highest of high teas and a present parade were all there for the taking, and each child was given a new penny to spend and a stick of rock to take home. The General entered into the fun, starring particularly in 'Ring-a-ring o' roses'.

The band played almost non-stop all day, being required to improvise (without permission of the music board) in such 'classics' as 'Knees Up, Mother Brown' and 'The Farmer's In His Den'.

General Eva always had a friendly word for the bandsmen on such days, and a specially warm greeting for Colonel Fuller, who as a boy had played in her band at Marylebone.

It was a thrill for me to be invited to accompany Tottenham Citadel Band on an Eastertide visit to Middlesbrough and North Shields – as guest elocutionist and to play the piano for the violin soloist, Ernest Hill.

It was a great weekend. After a Good Friday morning visit to Redcar, with its magnificent stretch of sand, afternoon and evening meetings were held at Middlesbrough Citadel and, on the Sunday, we travelled on to Newcastle, where we boarded a local train to North Shields. Regent Hall Band was at Newcastle Temple that weekend, I believe, with another band from the south at Sunderland Citadel. I remember being somewhat amazed at the appeal of brass bands in this north-east corner of England.

The Saturday festival was presided over by Mrs George Marshall. She and her composer husband were to celebrate their 17th wedding anniversary the next day. Being aware of this, Band Secretary George Dilloway thoughtfully arranged for the chairperson to be presented with a beautiful bouquet of flowers from the Tottenham men to mark the occasion.

On the Monday, George Marshall himself attended the final festival, having been lovingly pushed in his wheelchair by friends from his South Shields home to the Tyne ferry and then, the river having been crossed, conveyed in the guard's van of a train to North Shields.

That night George heard his selection 'Behold The Man!' for the first time. He wept unashamedly at the impact and was deeply appreciative of the help given the congregation to understand the music and its message as the band secretary, section by section, held up printed cards of explanation.

George Marshall was one of my boyhood heroes. I was nurtured on his story of courage and dedication. I thrilled to the warm, harmonious cadences of his music.

At the end of that festival at North Shields I met my hero for the first time. Bandmaster Marshall had recognised my name when he saw it on the programme and asked to see me. Major Thomas Dennis, our leader for the weekend, took me into the anteroom where I received a beaming smile and warm, firm handshake.

It was not a conversation between strangers. In a fatherly fashion he had something to say about my humble efforts at songwriting, gave me advice on a possible line of future study and made quizzical comments on the humour of the character study he had listened to in the programme.

And then came the challenge. Fixing my gaze with his own penetrating brown orbs of challenge, he said: 'Sonny! Give all you have to the Lord. He wants to use you.'

The memory of that encounter became one of the inspirations of my life.

Chapter 10

The Calm Before the Storm

THE carefree late 1930s were thrilling years. Changes at headquarters took old friends from us and brought new ones in their place. The fellowship of the Men's Social Work Headquarters Band continued to add its quota to our wealth of experience.

The sorrow that came upon Adjutant and Mrs Ernest Rance when it was discovered that their baby son Richard was sightless led to the adjutant relinquishing the bandmastership of the band. The courageous way in which the stricken parents faced the tragedy won our admiration and our hearts of love went out to them in brotherly sympathy. *The Bandsman And Songster* announced: 'Adjutant and Mrs Rance are perfectly resigned to the inevitable and are making arrangements to give the little fellow such special training as will be necessary to one who will never be able to see.'

I am always reminded of that closely knit banding fraternity and circle of prayer whenever I hear Richard Rance's tune 'Worcester' ('Depth Of Mercy') played or sung. Although sad circumstances took the adjutant from our immediate banding fraternity, he remained an integral part of that undiminished fellowship.

When it was announced that Major Leonard Bloomfield was to return as bandmaster and Colonel Arthur Goldsmith as leader and instructor, we prepared to welcome 'the old firm'. The colonel was soon in his stride with rehearsals.

As the annual Isle of Wight prison tour loomed up, the bandmaster made it known to me that he wished to 'fill in' the programmes, especially for secular meetings. The withdrawal of Ernest Rance and his concertina had left a gap that would be difficult to fill. Did I play an accordion? I did not. Would I be prepared to learn? I would 'have a go', but was not too keen.

This rather negative conversation led to my being sent to the showrooms of a firm of musical instrument manufacturers to purchase an accordion of my choice. The cash in my pocket, supplied personally by the generous bandmaster, ruled out too elaborate an instrument, but I thought I had been wise in my selection and returned in triumph with what looked like an outsize typewriter and a case to match.

This was Wednesday. The first festival was in Winchester Prison on Saturday afternoon and I was on the programme, items two and 12. I had three days to master the accordion and to learn two pieces. I almost worked my fingers to the bone that night. The keyboard presented no problem; it was the same as the piano. The chording of the left-hand buttons created a far greater difficulty. I knew what chords I wanted but could not find them. Then I had a brainwave. I would get a large mirror to help me. This should solve the problem. I could now see a reflection of the buttons and, having established the position of 'C', it was reasonably easy to work from there through the various keys and chord progressions.

After a while a medley of popular song tunes began to emerge and this would be my first item. The second would be just a simple melody, presented twice, with the left hand taking the air the second time, with tremolo, right-hand accompaniment.

So far, so good. The recital began to take shape and at last the moment arrived when I felt confident enough to rehearse without the aid of the looking glass.

I turned away and faced the blank wall. But I had reckoned without the phenomenon of reverse direction. I had memorised all the moves all right, but now found myself going up instead of down and moving to the left instead of right. The result was complete chaos. My nerves were in shreds. What could I do? There was now barely two days to go and my name was on the programme.

There was nothing else for it. I just had to forget the mirror and start all over again, feeling my way and relying upon my memory to get me through.

I had kept the purchase of the accordion and my rehearsal ordeal a secret from my band colleagues, which meant that it was a most interested audience behind me as well as in front when I proceeded to strap the accordion on and stepped forward to make my debut in this new role. The lads, like the Winchester inmates, were kind to me and even joined in singing 'My Bonnie Lies Over The Ocean' and 'When Irish Eyes Are Smiling' to help me on. I was playing the Army words, of course!

This was the beginning of a new music ministry, which lasted to the outbreak of war.

As I was still required to give my monologues, accompany at the piano and lead the singing of the band and the vocal party, I was kept rather busy. The programme was an embarrassing sight, consisting of 'Band, Boon, Band', as my 'friends' constantly reminded me!

* * * * *

When the fury of the Spanish Civil War was at its height, Britain, with other nations, was asked to take a number of Basque refugee children, many of whom had been rendered orphans through the conflict.

The Salvation Army came to the rescue and a large number of these sad victims were housed on the Clapton premises. Brigadier and Mrs John Martin, assisted by Major Stanley Hannam, recently returned from service in South America and experts in the Spanish language, were placed in charge of this work. A feature of the busy programme was the nightly entertainment for the youngsters. The social work band's instrumental party was invited to assist and we spent many evenings at Clapton, not only playing special arrangements of music the children were likely to know, but also sharing games with them in the grounds.

Another crop of evacuees was placed in the Army's care at Hadleigh Farm Colony in Essex, where we spent a Saturday entertaining them with our music and playing football with them on the famous slopes of the castle grounds.

Sunbury Court in Middlesex was then a Men's Social Work eventide home, and had been for some years, since the fine old house had ceased to be used as an international staff college.

Men whose past interests covered multitudes of trades and professions spent retirement hours playing carpet bowls in the sun lounge or billiards in the games room, strolling through the lovely grounds or on the nearby river bank, or, in less energetic vein, devouring a good book in the well-stocked library.

When Charles Skinner went into the training college, I was 'promoted' to do a stocktake at these premises each 1 April in connection with the end of the financial year. This meant an all-day trip, even if the checking and accounting took considerably less time. There was then no bus service from Kingston. Visitors were required to travel by train from Waterloo to Sunbury and walk across the fields and along the lanes to the Court.

My duties consisted of checking the contents of the food store against the items listed on the stock sheet. Such a deviation from routine was always welcome. Other members of the Accountants' Department had similar responsibilities at other institutions.

I developed a warm affection for Sunbury. Visits by musical parties became a regular feature, Saturday afternoons being a popular time for such events. Programmes were often preceded by a hired rowing-boat trip on the peaceful waters of the River Thames.

We felt somewhat robbed when it was made known that General Evangeline Booth had decided that Sunbury Court and its lovely grounds should become a national youth centre and that the residents of our beloved eventide home should be moved to premises in London. There is, however, one Sunbury occasion that stands out in my memory. It was at the time of the Munich crisis of 1938. The social work band was required to be on duty on Saturday 1 October for the benefit of students taking the practical test in connection with the bandmasters' correspondence course.

The news all that week had been black. We half expected the Sunbury date to be cancelled. As we opened our newspapers before leaving home we were greeted with the large-print front-page announcement, 'IT IS PEACE'. How relieved we were! The reprieve was to last for less than a year.

Events at Regent Hall and Chalk Farm continued to attract me. Bandmasters Herbert Twitchin and A. W. Punchard ('A.W.P.') both possessed a gift for securing chairmen with 'names' and this went a long way to ensuring a full house.

Colonel Fred Hawkes had his retirement festival of appreciation at Regent Hall. This was an impressive tribute to the man and his music, in which the 'Rink' Band and Harrow Songster Brigade presented pieces composed or arranged by the colonel.

It was worth going to hear two captain members of the International Music Editorial Department, Eric Ball and Phil Catelinet, play the 'Vesper Hymn' and 'The Warrior' marches as pianoforte duets. Colonel Hawkes had been a member of the department for 44 years, and its head for more than half that time. But the welcome of the evening was reserved for two colleagues of the past – the Army's first bandsman, Fred W. Fry, close on 80 years of age, and Caleb Burgess. The crowd spontaneously stood to them. Both had served as bandmaster of the International Staff Band, and the latter was the last bandmaster of the Household Troops Band, of which Colonel Hawkes had been a member.

On the homeward journey I found myself seated on the top of a bus near to Major Bramwell Coles. He was on one side of the gangway, I the other. He had recently arrived from the chills of Canada, where he had been stationed for 11 years, and the first thing I noticed from my close-up view was his long, winter uniform coat, trimmed with astrakhan collar and cuffs.

When the conductor collected the fares the coin the major offered somehow slipped from his grasp. There was no accompanying 'tinkle' on the floor. It just vanished into thin air. I saw it happen and promptly assisted the conductor and the embarrassed passenger in their search. All to no avail. Did it disappear into the hidden recesses of the cuffs? I shall never know.

'It was only a penny,' said Major Coles, producing another one. Which serves as a reminder of what it cost to travel on a General omnibus from Oxford Circus to Baker Street station in those far-off days.

In this stranger-than-fiction way I made my first acquaintance with yet another boyhood hero, a man who was to encourage me tremendously in the years to come.

The social work band was invited to visit Newcastle upon Tyne for the 1938 New Year festivals. With an eye open for the unusual, the bandmaster arranged for a watchnight festival to be given at Royston, Yorkshire, on the way up.

Leaving our Middlesex Street headquarters in the mid-afternoon of New Year's Eve, the coach should have been at its destination in good time for the programme, which was announced to begin at 11 pm. But the planners had reckoned without fog!

Having become lost and reduced to a crawl somewhere near Pontefract, we eventually arrived at Royston barely in time to welcome in the New Year. The hall was filled and the band went through its advertised programme, pausing after the opening march for a devotional period as a nearby clock struck midnight and then carrying on with the festival.

This ended at 1.30 am! The final piece was 'Discipleship' and, as we came to the reiterated phrases to which, for private consumption, Colonel Goldsmith had put the words 'I wish I could go home', the music was played with real conviction. Even the colonel saw the joke.

At 7 o'clock that morning, after a few hours' rest, we were at the hall ready to continue the journey northward. On the return trip, two days later, the band again stopped at Royston to provide an afternoon festival for miners who had just come off the morning shift. Again the hall was crowded.

* * * * *

That summer Nina and I were married in the Child's Hill hall that had been our spiritual home for so long. Lieut-Commissioner Alfred Barnett conducted the ceremony and Major Eva Fouracre sang a wedding song (words by her friend, Major Doris Rendell) that I had

92

written a little while before for the marriage of her niece, 'Dot', to Will James at Regent Hall. Captain Bernard Topley, an office colleague, was at the organ.

My salary at that time was £2 17s 6d per week, of which 24 shillings went on rent for our three-room flat. My wife was earning almost twice my princely sum, so we managed to survive on pooled resources until a comparatively substantial increase in my salary brought 'improved conditions'.

Settling in a new district, we transferred to Chalk Farm Corps, where we received the warmest of welcomes and were soon made to feel completely at home.

The songster leader was Herbert Little, whom I remembered from when he served in a similar capacity at Holloway. It was not long before he insisted on relinquishing his duties and my taking over. The character and spirit of the man was further revealed when he agreed to become my deputy songster leader. This arrangement happily prevailed, with mutual respect and affection, until he transferred to Hemel Hempstead during the war years.

Retired Songster Leader Edward Souter was a member of the brigade and he, too, was a source of encouragement and a tower of strength to me as I did my best to adapt myself to the manifold ramifications of a famous larger corps. The great 'A.W.P.' was in his heyday. He had become bandmaster in 1894 and had served as national bandmaster since 1921. It is no exaggeration to say that A.W.P. *was* Chalk Farm Corps in those days. He was a power to be reckoned with. The bandmaster immediately became my mentor and never ceased to interest himself in all aspects of my life, even to the extent of leaving me a typewriter in his will.

The social work band's only overseas trip took place at Easter 1939 when Paris was visited for the weekend.

There was one big disappointment. A week before, the band had spent the Saturday and Sunday at Thornton Heath and, as he was returning home after the campaign, Colonel Goldsmith was knocked down by a car outside London Bridge station. He was taken to Guy's Hospital where it was found he had sustained a fractured leg.

This unfortunate accident prevented the colonel from being with the band in Paris, but the bandsmen rallied round in their customary manner and the venture was a great success.

The only mishap was that, upon disembarkation at Calais, we boarded a train for Paris while our instruments were loaded on to a transcontinental express bound for Istanbul – together with a restaurant car containing our much-overdue meal!

We were relieved to learn, upon arriving at the French capital, that the express, Turkey-bound, had been halted at an unscheduled stop and that the instruments had been re-routed to Paris. It was not until we had commenced our first festival, in the Paris Central Corps hall, that they eventually reached us.

It was a full and exciting weekend. The itinerary included a visit to Versailles, a broadcast from Poste Parisien, festivals in the Tuileries Gardens and the Luxembourg Gardens, a Sunday morning service in the British Methodist Church, a meeting in La Cité de Refuge and a Monday morning pilgrimage to the Arc de Triomphe and the laying of a wreath on the Tomb of the Unknown Soldier. Participation in a field day at Morfonde and the final festival in the Palais de la Femme completed the campaign. We billeted together at the Palais de Peuple.

The Governor of the Men's Social Work (Lieut-Commissioner John Lewis) led the campaign and for translation purposes we were in the capable hands of Adjutant Francis Evans, then editor of *En Avant!*, the French edition of *The War Cry*.

Another officer we met for the first time on that trip, and who served us so well in many different ways, was Major Arthur Best, then the Territorial Financial Secretary.

I had been at Regent Hall some eight years before, when Arthur Best farewelled from the International Staff Band with the euphonium solo 'Land Beyond The Blue', before leaving with his wife for service in Japan. The Army wheel had turned once again and here he was in Paris, 'catching up', he said, on some of the new music as he heard it played that weekend.

This man of God and his charming wife walked straight into our hearts. So very soon they were to be interned in Germany and Austria 'for the duration'. Returning to London after the war, Lieut-Colonel Best was never to regain his full measure of health and was promoted to Glory while serving as Staff Secretary of The Salvation Army Assurance Society, on Boxing Day 1947.

A few days after returning from France the band was at Clapton Congress Hall taking part in a festival to honour our greatly loved Colonel Goldsmith.

The bands joining us were from Clapton Congress Hall and Chalk Farm, with vocal support from Southend Citadel Singing Company and soloists Major Eva Fouracre and Songster Harry Kniveton.

All the items on the programme were composed by Colonel Goldsmith and it was a tremendous thrill to hear and take part in such massed band items as 'Marching Onward', 'Rockingham', 'Showers Of Blessing' and 'Memories Of The Masters' and to hear individual sections play such 'A. G.' classics as 'Conquering Faith', 'The Cleansing Current', 'Following The Lord', 'My Guide' and 'Battle Strains'.

The guest of honour was there, with his leg encased in plaster. But this encumbrance did not prevent him from standing up, within three weeks of the accident, to conduct the massed bands on this his 'benefit night'.

He received an ovation 'fit for heroes' as he rose to speak. He summed up his long record of exemplary music-making when he said, 'I have never written a selection without having the Army and its demands always in mind. I always ask myself, "Is this suitable for Salvation Army requirements?"'

Another event of that spring of 1939 was the national youth festival at the Royal Albert Hall, with the stirring pageant, 'Wake Up, Britannia!', written and presented by Major Alfred Gilliard, the brilliant young editor of *The War Cry*.

I can still feel the shattering impact of his effective finale, with its youthful host in national costume and the sweet, complacent loveliness of a well-cast 'Britannia', disturbed almost to distraction when 'the enemy' invades her peaceful domain to steal her children's affection and loyalty. It was all so horribly prophetic.

The masterly background of Adjutant Eric Ball on the grand organ – the last time I was to hear him perform on that gigantic instrument – added poignancy to the drama and enhanced the challenge.

But, I have to confess, my interest that night was at times diverted to the Publicity Box, as it was known. This was traditionally situated next to the Royal Box, which was easily distinguishable by the golden crown above it. (Until January 1936 a box on the other side of the auditorium sported the Prince of Wales's feathers.)

The Publicity Box was usually reserved for VIPs, with impressive entries and exits presided over by General Evangeline Booth's personal publicity secretary. On that April evening, the box was occupied by Sybil Thorndike, her husband (Lewis Casson), playwright George Bernard Shaw and the noted film director, Gabriel Pascal.

Shaw's *Major Barbara* was to be made into a film and he had amended the script to suit the celluloid medium. To bring the play up to date he had introduced a new character, 'The General', no doubt influenced by the fact that a woman was now the international leader of The Salvation Army. Sybil Thorndike was to take the part, obviously moulded on Evangeline Booth, and she had come to the Albert Hall, with her escorts, specifically to study the personality and mannerisms of the General as she presided over the festival and delivered her challenging address at the end of the pageant.

After the visit, Bernard Shaw and Gabriel Pascal decided to introduce an Albert Hall scene into the film. This had a ring of authenticity about it.

Salvationists were divided in their reactions. Delight, disgust, shame and flattery proved conflicting emotions. Officially, the Army went along to the extent of co-operating in the Albert Hall sequences, loaning uniforms and providing a group of Regent Hall bandsmen for an open-air scene.

In the Albert Hall 'shots', professional actors were augmented by one or two selected Salvationists, among them Major George Sowton, who was seen leading the prayer meeting, and Assistant Sergeant-Major Phil Catelinet, of Regent Hall.

Rex Harrison looked perfectly at home behind the bass drum at the rear of the band, even if Robert Morley, taking the part of Major Barbara's father, looked less comfortable wearing 'civvies' on the end of the trombone section.

Throughout the summer of 1939 preparations were feverishly being made for the retirement recognition of Evangeline Booth after nearly five years of international leadership.

Earl's Court was booked for Saturday 2 September and it was to be a day of days. Non-stop events from the morning opening were to be climaxed by a concluding pageant of 3,000 characters, and London and provincial bands and songster brigades were invited to take part. Chalk Farm sections were among this number and the brigade was supplied with the special booklet of songs to be rehearsed.

The pageant 'Omnia Vincit Amor', which we were assured meant 'Love conquers all things', was devised by Major Edgar Grinsted, Divisional Commander for Manchester, who was to serve as pageant master, and Brigadier Wilfred Kitching, Divisional Commander for East London, was appointed marshal of the pageant.

The pageant was founded on the General's song 'The World For God', which would be sung at the close of the ceremonial meeting.

It is now Army history that, at the 11th hour, the event was cancelled, owing to the 'uncertainties of the times'. War broke out the next day.

A month later the General said goodbye to officers and soldiers of Britain in a less elaborate gathering at Regent Hall. I was there to see and hear her for the last time and to watch approvingly as she admitted her old friend 'Bert' Twitchin to the Order of the Founder and pinned the medal and ribbon of the Order to his tunic.

By this time we were well and truly in the grip of war, even if the adjective 'phoney' was quickly adopted. Evacuation plans were put into immediate operation; gas masks were issued; calling-up began; normal Army service was considerably curtailed; blackout was introduced.

If it wasn't exactly the end of the world, it was certain that life would never be the same again.

Chapter 11

Pressing On Regardless

'THE day war broke out' was a phrase coined by radio comedian Robb Wilton. Many of his recitals, delivered in the most sardonic voice, began like that and the idea caught on with the listening public.

There are still thousands of people in Britain – Salvationists among them – who remember 'the day war broke out'. Can we ever forget it?

The third day of September was a Sunday. During the week the news of world tension had gone from bad to worse. On the Friday our task of filling sandbags for stacking as a barricade outside the Men's Social Work Headquarters was interrupted from time to time to allow crocodile lines of mothers and children to pass.

They were the first of the army of evacuees, bound for 'somewhere in the country'. Gas masks in cardboard boxes carried on their backs and large-written name tags hanging round their necks told their own lamentable story.

When we went to bed on the Saturday night there was a strong feeling that something was 'in the wind'. A thunderstorm in the early hours of the morning did not ease the tension. At first we thought that this was 'it'. Was it gunfire? Had someone cheated and started the war without our being officially notified?

We tried to treat that Sunday as normally as possible. We hoped for the best, but feared the worst, and somehow had the intuition to know what the Prime Minister was going to say when he broadcast at 11 o'clock. This was the nonchalant atmosphere engendered by all and sundry as we entered the Chalk Farm hall for the holiness meeting.

Our commanding officer, Adjutant Wesley Rich, was not there. He was one of the 300 officers and 200 cadets alerted to stand by to assist with the evacuation of 600,000 women and children from the vulnerable areas of London.

His call-up had come on the Saturday and he had been put in charge of a party which travelled to Downham Market, Norfolk. There the adjutant stayed the night, before returning to London for the evening meeting. Mrs Rich and her 11-day-old baby (the first in memory to be born to Chalk Farm corps officers) were also absent.

I cannot recall who was responsible for the meeting but I do remember that it was during the second song that two veteran comrades came to the platform – one from the band room, the other from the songsters' entrance – to interrupt the proceedings. They had heard the dreaded wail of the air-raid siren and felt it their duty to pass on the warning, which we had certainly not heard.

We did not finish the song. In a hurried but orderly fashion the congregation made its way via the platform to the boiler room beneath and into the make-do 'shelter', which had been pressed into service much earlier than we could have imagined.

It was only then that we became aware that we were at war. The gist of Prime Minister Neville Chamberlain's announcement was conveyed to us by someone who had heard it over the radio and, in our innocence, we quite thought that the reason for the warning siren was an immediate response to the declaration of war. Bombers must be on their way to obliterate London and everyone in it.

Before long the cause of the alarm was identified as a friendly plane, the reassuring level sound of the 'all clear' was heard and the first panic was over.

Did that initial fearful scar ever heal? We had the good sense to lift our hearts in prayer before we dispersed from the boiler room.

There was an immediate reaction from the Army's Associated Headquarters.

International Headquarters moved to the International Training College, Denmark Hill. A skeleton staff of The Salvation Army Assurance Society, with essential records and business requirements, took up residence at 'Rosehill', a premises at Caversham, outside Reading.

The headquarters of the London and Southern Territory shifted to the Evangeline Booth Youth Centre, Sunbury Court; The Salvation Army Fire Insurance Corporation to St Albans; and the Women's Social Work Headquarters from Hackney to 'Rookstone', Hadley Wood (home of the Founder).

Cadets of the Hold Fast Session, who had been in residence at Denmark Hill less than a month, were quickly dispersed: the men to Manchester (Star Hall), Leicester, Liverpool and Leeds; the women to Brighton, Northampton, Nottingham (Notintone Place, the Founder's birthplace), Pontypridd and Glasgow. A remnant remained at Denmark Hill.

It was also announced that the engagements of the International Staff Band, Assurance Songsters and the SP&S Band had been cancelled, but it was pointed out that rumours that the songsters had been disbanded were not true.

Salvationist Publishing and Supplies, Limited, proudly announced that the service at its Judd Street emporium was 'as usual' and that its male members were all carrying their gas masks.

An advert in *The Musician* (16 September 1939) implored, 'Bandsmen on active service, carry your mouthpiece with you. It will be ready when opportunity presents itself and you can "have a blow".' The prices of such utensils were then given: cornet and tenor horn, 9d; baritone, trombone and euphonium, 1s 3d; Eb bombardon and BBb monstre, 1s 6d.

New legislation hurried through Parliament provided for the call-up of men between the ages of 18 and 41. By the end of September Bandmaster Herbert Twitchin was reporting: 'What a complete change outbreak of war has caused at Regent Hall! As it is situated in the heart of London's restricted area, week-night attendances are almost completely cut out. On Sunday we had to finish by 6.45 pm.

'The band has been hit very hard, some of its members being called to military service; others are engaged on national service involving Sunday duties. In addition, there has been dislocation on account of evacuation... senior and young people's bands have united for the time being.... The men have responded admirably and are doing their best to keep the flag flying.'

At Chalk Farm we had a similar situation. By this time Bandmaster Bram Allington had joined the City of Birmingham Police and had been succeeded by Deputy Bandmaster Edgar Cuell as acting bandmaster.

Eddie Cuell had given outstanding service as young people's band leader both at Portsmouth Citadel and Chalk Farm but could not see his way clear to accept the full responsibility of leadership because of his fire service responsibilities which, in wartime, had become even more formidable. Transfer from the Kentish Town station to Wimbledon had not eased the situation but, with Mrs Cuell and their fine Army family, the acting bandmaster made the journey across London whenever possible, disregarding the blackout and braving potential hazards.

Perhaps it was Eddie Cuell's recruitment persuasion that led to five soldiers of the corps enlisting in the Auxiliary Fire Service some time before the war and thus joining two permanent firefighters in giving moral support to the acting bandmaster.

Many Salvationists were becoming involved in Air Raid Precautions. When General Evangeline Booth said farewell to her fellow soldiers of Wimbledon Corps before leaving for the USA and retirement, she wore a conspicuous armlet with a red cross and 'A.R.P.' worked in the same colour, both against a background of grey.

The General's message to her people at the outbreak of hostilities had the familiar oratorical ring: 'The brazen throat of war has been heard throughout the world and the surging billows of sorrow and misery have swept the seven seas.'

Her rallying challenge to the women of the Army a month later was no less dramatic. 'I call the knitting needles into service,' she declared. 'I call the sewing machines into service. I call various commodities into service. I call upon whatever money you can afford to give... I suppose this is the last personal request I shall make of you and I do it with affection and confidence.'

Acting Bandmaster Cuell's leadership of Chalk Farm Band did not last very long. As a sub-officer on the permanent staff of the fire service, he was now on almost continuous duty at brigade headquarters and his corps appearances were, of necessity, becoming more and more infrequent.

He was still deputy bandmaster and it was at his request that A.W.P. came out of retirement and once again took up the reins of leadership 'till the boys come home'.

Augmented by Band Leader Eric Andre and as many of his young people's band boys as had not been evacuated, the band rallied to the baton of their revered bandmaster.

A.W.P., still National Bandmaster, had been Chalk Farm's bandmaster during the Crimean and First World Wars, so this was his third war as the corps bandmaster. No sooner was he in harness again than his restless organising genius sought to combat the lull which had set in since the outbreak of war. He planned a series of 'anti-depression' festivals and summoned the commanding officer, organising secretary, band 'locals' and me (as songster leader) to a meeting to discuss the matter.

It was agreed that there should be an experimental festival and, in his orderly, methodical manner, the bandmaster listed the purposes of this event: (1) to see if people would attend a festival notwithstanding the blackout; (2) to ascertain what success the band, in its present depleted condition, would have in an effort to produce a programme.

The bandmaster claimed success on both points; (1) about 200 people attended, despite the fact that it was raining hard; (2) the band was able to acquit itself in 'true Chalk Farm style' in such pieces as 'Scandinavian Songs', 'The Pilgrim Way' and 'O Rest In The Lord'.

It was intended to keep the festivals going every third Saturday but, in time, this good intention had to be abandoned because of the worsening of wartime conditions.

In fixing dates for the 'people's festivals', as they then were called, Bandmaster Punchard was guided by a paragraph that appeared in *The War Cry*. It said: 'Meeting organisers are finding it beneficial to watch the moon and will do so until the light nights are here. Full moons on the next three months occur on...'

'Go by the moon!' became a password.

My third visit to Regent Hall since the outbreak of war took me to the Sunday afternoon memorial service for Lieut-Colonel Richard Slater. I would not have missed it.

All the songs and choruses used and the band selection, 'The City Of God', had been written by him. They included 'Round Us Flows The Cleansing River', 'Ever Thine', 'The Saviour Chose A Lowly Place' (the first Christmas song written by a Salvationist and sung that afternoon by Regent Hall Songster Brigade), 'By The Blood My Saviour Shed Upon The Tree', 'No! No! Nothing Do I Bring' and 'All I Have I Am Bringing To Thee'.

Bandmaster Twitchin was one of the speakers. It seemed impossible that the bandmaster could remember the then Mr Slater (who had been lecturing against God at the Hall of Science) first attending the Regent Hall in a light-grey suit and, before the meeting had concluded, seeing him surrender to God at the penitent form. Dramatically he pointed to the spot in front of the platform and said, 'That is where it happened.'

'Soon afterwards,' continued the bandmaster, 'this new convert, whom none of us realised was a great musician, entered the band on the 2nd cornet part, but later joined an orchestra we had at the corps. It was then we discovered him to be a master of the violin.'

All this appealed to my mounting sense of Army history. And to think that I had once shaken hands with 'the father of Salvation Army music'!

At the Men's Social Work Headquarters there were signs of change.

When war was declared The Campfield Press was quickly off the mark by issuing some 'Timely Posters', bearing 'cheery messages and suitable prayers for people during wartime'. A series of five posters could be purchased for 2s 6d.

The first set was ordered by Brigadier Percy McLean, our enterprising chaplain on the building, for display on the sandbags with which the building was fortified. Passers-by frequently stopped to note the encouraging messages.

The headquarters band continued to function, albeit in a very limited way. Corps engagements had been cancelled, in keeping with the policy of other headquarters groups.

Our leaders soon became ARP-conscious. No doubt inspired by government-issued literature, emergency plans were drawn up and we were given a list of duties in the event of an incendiary bomb attack. A list of such responsibilities was pinned on a noticeboard for all to behold. The first line naively announced, 'To deal with bomb – Brigadier Bell'.

Now, the good Brigadier George Robert Bell (later a Lieut-Commissioner) was a man of many parts, as efficient and as conscientious as they come. But to expect him to meet unaided the full measure of his responsibility was surely to tax his skill to its utmost! Even he would need help with so formidable a task.

I was given a lesser responsibility. This was to run to the nearest fire station and alert the personnel there to the emergency when our headquarters became engulfed in flames. I was flattered to think that my fame as a speedy winger on the football field had spread sufficiently for me to be entrusted with such a job.

When all the duties had become known and the magnitude of the undertaking began to sink in, it was decided to have a full-scale exercise. There were to be no half-measures about this 'dummy run'.

I dressed up in steel helmet, overalls, gas mask, fireproof trousers and gumboots. At the given signal I would take off to the fire station at full speed, deliver my appeal for help and return. The operation would be timed.

Sensing something unusual was brewing, a crowd quickly gathered outside headquarters to witness the spectacle. This included men from the Middlesex Street Hostel and residents of Liverpool House, the Army's hotel on the other side of us (which later became a blitz victim with heavy loss of life), and workers from the clothing factory on the opposite side of the road, who took time off to fill the verandas between the floors.

This was to be my big moment. This errand of mercy – the dash down Petticoat Lane, along Wentworth Street to the fire station, the rapid delivery of the message in clear, concise terms and the return journey at the same breakneck pace would establish me as the right man for the job.

The command 'Go!' rang out like a pistol shot. I was off like a greyhound, loud cheers ringing in my ears. Twenty yards brought me to the farther end of Liverpool House where I missed the kerb and went sprawling in the middle of the road.

After what seemed an age I was conscious of friendly hands trying to lift me to my feet and became aware that the encouraging cheers had given way to hoots of derisive laughter.

My helmet went rolling away. The oxygen tube of my gas mask became separated from the face-piece. My grazed elbows were showing helplessly through my torn overalls. My asbestos trousers had parted company with my bleeding legs, sadly belying their advertised recommendation of being foolproof.

That was the only ARP manoeuvre I can remember taking place at Middlesex House, but at least it provided some much-needed practice for those on the building who had been allocated first aid as their amateur fire-fighting service.

I never did discover why a phone call to the fire station could not have saved everyone a great deal of trouble.

New Year's Day 1940 heralded a change in the attitude of London Salvationists. Three months and more had passed and 'nothing had happened'. It was indeed a phoney war. The lull had brought a false sense of security. There was a clamour for a return to normal.

The International Headquarters had returned to Queen Victoria Street and the cadets were back at the training college. In London and the Home Counties the cry was 'Business as usual'.

Although the steady call-up had deprived bands of their manpower, there was a frantic revival of musical parties to provide programmes. This involved a great deal of travelling across the capital and farther afield. Public transport had not felt the full impact of the emergency. That was to come.

I found myself caught up in the new avalanche of activity. At Kilburn, where I gave elocution items, my fellow participants were Songster Lily Cossar (piano), Young People's Band Member Dennis Thorn (trombone and accordion), both of Regent Hall, and James Williams, a youthful cornet soloist who was to make an international name for himself in Army music circles. His father was then Kilburn's bandmaster.

The next week I was in a party consisting of Major Eric Russell (concertina), Songster Winnie Cobley (vocalist) and Bandsmen Cliff Haines (cornet) and Arthur Brown (trombone), which journeyed to Reading Central to take part in a guest night arranged by Organising Secretary Archie Griffiths. What an enthusiast he was!

Another energetic organising secretary, anxious to keep the flag of Army 'entertainment' flying in those days, was Fred Wilkins, of Catford and the Assurance Songsters.

It was Fred who invited me to his corps one Sunday afternoon. There I met Songster Leader Oliver Cooke for the first and only time. His 'I Know A Fount', 'The Lord's Brigade' and 'Come To The Wayside' were familiar to me and I was aware of the host of other compositions that had come from the pen of this veteran vocal composer.

Some days after our encounter Oliver Cooke was given unsought and unwanted publicity in the national daily press, an incident that greatly troubled this loyal Salvationist.

A few weeks earlier, to correspond with the announcement that the butter ration had been reduced to four ounces a week, *The War Cry* published the words and music of a song that the retired songster leader had written. This was entitled 'You Can't Ration Sunshine'.

Although this had a topical flavour it did not really catch on with Army congregations until, without warning, it was broadcast over the radio by Henry Hall and his orchestra. A special arrangement had been prepared and it went well.

The next morning some papers gave prominence to this 'premiere'. One of them published an alleged interview with the songwriter, adding that this 'poor man' was at last likely to make a fortune. The truth is that the composer did not receive any payment and would not agree to any suggestions that he should claim royalties for its performance.

In good faith Henry Hall, who had been a young bandsman in the corps at Nunhead when Oliver Cooke was the songster leader, had seen the song, sensed its topical value and decided to include it in his repertoire.

The writer's acute embarrassment and indignation caused a statement to be made in *The Musician*. It said: 'Retired Songster Leader Oliver Cooke fervently trusts that his innumerable comrades and friends still believe in his salvationism, despite certain reports which have appeared in the press, which are a misrepresentation of the facts, and which have caused both Mrs Cooke and himself considerable pain. He is still a loyal and true Salvationist, intends to remain such, and hopes to write many more songs for the Army.'

If the saying 'press on regardless', coined by forces personnel, had not yet come into general usage, its injunction was certainly being followed at Chalk Farm and numerous other corps in the British Territory.

If Regent Hall was London Salvationists' shop window, then Chalk Farm was certainly the second biggest attraction. Bandmaster Punchard firmly believed that visitors to London, however long or short their stay, would not return home until they had been to both these centres. They must have something to see and hear when they went.

To maintain the mounting interest, it was suggested that I should arrange something 'out of the ordinary' for Easter, involving a goodly number of corps comrades and not only those serving in the musical forces.

This was a challenge. I decided to write and produce what would now be called a musical. Then it was a play with music, a form of presentation at that time still frowned upon by Army authorities.

A few years before, Nina and I had 'discovered' Ivor Novello and his scintillating productions at the Drury Lane Theatre. These had provided the composer of the First World War hit 'Keep The Home Fires Burning' with an opportunity of further developing his outstanding talents. A number of plays with music was the outcome. Ivor wrote the script and composed the music. Some of the lyrics were also his.

Here were acting and singing at their best. A serious plot with plenty of dramatic content was laced with lovely melodies sung by the leading stage vocalists of the day. The result for me was a rewarding form of worthwhile entertainment that I wanted to emulate and transform for Army purposes.

These lavish productions, which ran to full houses for months on end, were memorable spectaculars. I sat spellbound beneath their magic. In the first, *Glamorous Nights*, an invention was introduced that would enable people in one country to watch a state occasion in another simultaneously. This was Jules Verne-ish in its conception. I dismissed the impossible dream from my mind – until television arrived.

Careless Rapture featured an earthquake in a far-off, fictitious musical-comedy land. *Crest Of The Wave* presented a shipwreck and in *The Dancing Years* we were treated to a train crash. The revolving stage at Drury Lane no doubt lent its considerable advantage in creating the illusion, but such spectacles, coupled with the haunting music, whetted my appetite for stagecraft. *Perchance To Dream* and *King's Rhapsody* were yet to come.

The coronation of King George VI and Queen Elizabeth in 1937 gave me my chance. I was songster leader at Child's Hill at that time and saw the possibilities of a 'pageant with music' portraying various 'children of the empire' paying their homage to 'Britannia'.

Special songs were written for the 'children' to sing and I enlisted the help of my friend Major Eva Fouracre, persuading her to appear as the 'Herald of Peace'. She sang appropriate truths and joined a well-known tenor soloist, Arthur Cleaver – a product of our own corps – in a duet, 'The sun never sets on the empire'. It was all very patriotic and summed up the general excitement of those days.

In *Crest Of The Wave* Ivor Novello had introduced a dozen or so male vocalists to sing 'Rose Of England' in front of the curtain. Still thrilling under its impact, I decided to uses a similar chorus in *Children Of The Empire*.

Being short of men at Child's Hill, I recruited some of my ever-obliging colleagues of the social work band and Nina used her ingenious needle-and-thread technique to transform them into 'Defenders of the Realm', temporarily modifying their festival tunics and adding headgear of the hussar variety, in the same patriotic colours with plumage attached.

How magnificent they looked as they paraded in pairs from the back of the hall down a centre aisle singing 'Hail, Britannia!' – a future Chief of the Staff among them!

Earlier my friends, with their instruments, had provided an original overture to complete the Drury Lane plagiarism.

I was in trouble. News of such a break with tradition soon reached the ears of the Divisional Commander, Lieut-Colonel William Armstrong, and then his superiors at the London and Southern Headquarters. Under the threat of having my songster leader's commission withdrawn I was called to give an explanation.

Demonstrations were all right. Services of song, with a narrator's script interspersed with published gems from *The Musical Salvationist*, were quite in order. But to present a pageant on a secular theme, with original music written to suit the scenes, could not be countenanced. In addition, the songs had not been approved by the International Music Board.

In view of my unblemished record I was let off with a caution, but it was not to happen again. I admit I was technically guilty of some of the charges levelled against me and perhaps I should have known better. But I had gone at least some way towards emulating the great Novello!

I wonder if I became the pioneer of Army musicals that day in May 1937? I told Captain John Larsson the story behind the stage at Butlin's after I had congratulated him on the first performance of *Take-Over Bid*, which he had written with Captain John Gowans.

And then, after three years, I decided to put on another musical – this time at Chalk Farm where, ironically enough, *Children Of The Empire* had been given a repeat performance before I was 'hauled over the coals'.

A Comrade Of The Cross was quite different. It was intended to be a thought-provoking play based upon a legend I had read somewhere, that one of the thieves who died with Jesus was the son of Caiaphas, the High Priest. The boy had been stolen by bandits as a child and the plot was centred around his adventurous life and its tragic end. The music was an integral part of the story.

Perhaps the West End theatre stage was influencing me too much at that time but I had no qualms in introducing a gang of outlaws not unlike the robbers in *Chu Chin Chow*.

In the Galilee of New Testament times, as the crowds left their homes to go after Jesus, so these marauders would plunder the houses and carry off all they could find, singing as they went their theme song, 'It's Demas and his band, we're marching through the land'.

Adjutant Rich was Caiaphas, Mrs Rich the wife of Caiaphas and other well-known Chalk Farm personalities entered wholeheartedly into the unusual experience and took prominent parts.

Once again my friends from headquarters rallied round to provide a chorus of Roman soldiers who, in the fashion of *Crest Of The Wave*, paraded in front of the curtain to sing 'Rome, imperial Rome, mistress of the world' while a change of scenery was effected behind.

The production was too ambitious. There were 36 scenes, culminating with Calvary and the Cross. With wartime difficulties and so many of the cast on national service shift duty it was impossible to hold a dress rehearsal for the whole play. I had no idea how long it would take and was in a mild panic when the curtain went up on the opening night.

Just as this was about to happen some well-meaning friend handed me a copy of that night's *Evening News*. On the front page was a photograph of Colonel Booth Davey, Mrs Rich's father, with the announcement that, with other officers on his staff, he was reported missing in France.

Somehow this had to be kept from 'Mrs Caiaphas' until afterwards. Fortunately, later news revealed that the colonel and others had managed to reach a southern port of embarkation and were safe.

The production seemed interminable. When the Roman soldiers were due to appear I went to the officers' room, which had been allotted to them for changing purposes, to warn them to be ready for the grand entry. On the table, neatly piled one on top of the other, were the costumes, the helmets adorning the walls around them. On top of the neat pile was a note bearing the shattering tidings: 'Sorry! Could not wait any longer.'

This meant cutting out five scenes and going straight to the finale. Word was somehow passed to the bewildered cast, who smartly summed up the situation.

When the closing chord died on the notorious Chalk Farm echo, the clock in the hall signified that it was 11.10. There were about 20 people left to express their feeble approval.

I am sure that 'play with music' represented my biggest failure, even if the music board did approve the songs. For the cast, it was somehow rewarding. For me it provided much-needed experience that was to stand me in good stead when I joined the RAF and became caught up with camp entertainment.

The invasion of many countries on the Continent and of Denmark and Norway suddenly changed the whole complexion of the war. Our complacency was jolted overnight.

As we made our way to 'Day with God' meetings at the Queen's Hall, bleak placards announced 'Biggest air attack' and 'The greatest battle in history'.

Dunkirk came and went. There was growing anxiety for the future. The old social work band that I had known was no more.

Many were called up but among those who joined the staff around this time was a 14-year-old lad straight from school, suitably clad in a provided uniform with red piping on the sleeve to denote his 'junior' status. His name was Norman Bearcroft and he was appointed to the Cashier's Department. His brother Bramwell had been on the building for some time, but had left to enlist in the RAF. Bram Bearcroft became a bomb-aimer and, as a flying officer, was killed over Germany in 1944.

I registered for the Royal Air Force in a church hall at West Hendon which had been commandeered for such purposes. That was in April 1940.

My call-up papers came three months later. I was to report at No 2 Recruiting Centre, Cardington, on 22 July. The day before that date, a Sunday, marked my farewell from the corps.

After the afternoon meeting those expected to join the forces in the near future were invited to take tea with the corps officers and census board members. Our wives were included. It was naturally something of a sentimental occasion, threaded with kindly spontaneous speeches.

In the salvation meeting of that last Sunday I spoke my hesitant word of farewell and the congregation was asked to stand as the band sang a verse of 'Saviour, Lead Me Lest I Stray', then the refrain, and Bandmaster Punchard committed me, with a colleague, to the loving care of God.

I went well armed. Commissioner John Lewis, the Men's Social Work Governor, presented me with a copy of *The Soldier's Guide* bearing the signatures of my old bandmaster, Major Leonard Bloomfield, and those of the social work band still remaining on the building.

Bandmaster Punchard handed me a New Testament, suitably inscribed, and Adjutant Rich gave me a newly published *Daily Readings From The Moffat Translation Of The Bible*, which carried on the flyleaf the injunction, 'Be of good courage, play the man', and the Adjutant's signature.

There was every encouragement to 'press on regardless'.

Brindley as Child's Hill Songster Leader

Brindley in RAF uniform

Brindley (in his RAF uniform) conducting a meeting at Chalk Farm Underground station during the Second World War

Production of The Enchanted Castle, *written and composed by Brindley (who played the King)*

Chapter 12

Towards the Stars

THE week I joined the Royal Air Force, recruits were passing through Cardington at the rate of 1,000 a day. Clothing equipment was in short supply. You never saw such a motley crew as our intake.

In lieu of full RAF uniform, I was issued with what pieces of official dress were available plus odds and ends to make do until new supplies arrived. This meant a khaki shirt (no tie) and muffler, peak-style cap (surely an heirloom from the First World War) and no tunic.

The remainder of the issue was authentic and, worn with the augmented gear and civvy suit-coat, did its best to hide the real identity of 'No 1173969, Boon, B. J. R., aircraftman second class under training'.

No time was lost. So anxious were the authorities to enlist us that the 'swearing-in' ceremony was mass-produced. We were herded into a disused airship hangar – was not Cardington the home of the R33, R100 and R101? – a red-faced squadron leader yelled our airman's 'promise' at rifle-shot speed and, responding to his instruction without a second thought, we each raised our right hand to signify our acceptance of the oath we had hardly heard.

What those initial rules and regulations were have long since been forgotten, but I am able to recall the hyena laugh of a delighted NCO as he shut and bolted the door behind him and leered, 'You're in now. Just try to get out!'

This ceremony took less than five minutes. It took five years – and more – to get out!

Trade classification took much longer. Accountancy, administration and similar duties of which I had some knowledge and experience were closed to me because of my youth and fitness. I would have to try some other interest.

On the second day, after breakfast we paraded on the square and were then dismissed to sit on a huge green in front of the orderly room to await the calling of our names over the Tannoy. Coffee break, dinner break and afternoon tea came and went.

At 5.30 my name boomed out. A charming flight lieutenant greeted me. To which branch of the RAF would I be most fitted? Was I an electrician? (I knew that a switch went down and a light came on – that was the limit of my knowledge.) Was I a mechanic? (The extent of this experience was mending a bicycle puncture, and I had a collection of bent forks to prove it.)

Had I done any public speaking? I began to recite my Salvation Army background. He was clearly interested. He rose from his well-padded, comfortable chair to close the door which, up till then, had been left open to let in a welcome cooling breeze. He lowered his voice as he returned. He spoke in confidential tones.

There was a new trade. It was still top secret. He did not know much about it but was looking for likely candidates to be trained. He would test my IQ and general suitability and then...

At that moment another officer entered to collect my man for a game of squash. There was no hesitation. He was ready. He would see me next morning for those tests. The RAF evidently had its priorities.

Next morning, as soon as the orderly room opened, I was there, only to be told that I was expected to follow the previous day's procedure and wait my turn. I sought out my favourite blades of grass and settled down again.

All day I waited and, when the familiar voice announced 'No more today' over the loudspeaker, mustered sufficient courage to make a few enquiries about my fate. To go into a third day was, I felt, asking too much.

A friendly clerk granted me a listening ear. My papers were eventually discovered and from these it was perfectly clear that I had successfully negotiated all the tests, including one on simple electronics, satisfactorily impressed my interviewer and been

116

recommended for training as a radio operator. Why was I wasting their time?

So without even trying I was well and truly in – at the deep end. But my introduction into the 'hush-hush' trade was to wait for some time. First must come the initial physical training, to be followed by a course at radio school.

I spent five days at Cardington being kitted out and, before leaving for an unknown destination, received my first pay. This was 10 shillings to tide me over.

That pay parade was really impressive. We lined up in single file and moved slowly towards the galaxy of accounts officers seated ceremoniously at a long table, all looking extremely smart in their good-quality uniforms and caps. We were required to give the last three digits of our service number, salute smartly, gratefully accept the brown-coloured bank note, salute again, about turn and walk briskly away

I shall never know why I fluffed my line and made '969' '696' but I did. It was in that moment of panic that I recognised the paying officer. He was Pilot Officer Sidney Early, well known to me as the deputy songster leader at Reading Central. I had seen him conduct that brigade in 'Enlistment' at a national songster festival some years before, in the absence through illness of Songster Leader George Andrews, but that memory was of little help to me now.

'Try again,' said a friendly voice, and I am prepared to swear on oath that I saw my comrade Salvationist give me an encouraging wink as I corrected my unfortunate error!

Sid Early and I did not meet again during the war, in which he reached the rank of squadron leader, but afterwards our paths converged on many occasions. He became songster leader and then bandmaster at Reading Central and also served as the highly respected divisional bandmaster for West London. I recalled that Cardington encounter when paying tribute at his memorial service in 1975.

At midnight on the Friday we paraded in the darkness, hoisted our kitbags on our shoulders, lined up, numbered off and set off across the vegetable patches for the local railway station. Here we boarded a waiting train and were soon bound for 'somewhere in England'.

Packed like sardines, we sat bolt upright through the night, hopelessly failing in our valiant attempt to snatch some sleep as the journey progressed. The only clue as to the direction we might be travelling came when we passed through a Leeds station as the longed-for dawn was breaking.

In an atmosphere not far removed from that of a Sunday school outing, our train came to a standstill at 5 am. We crowded excitedly towards the open window to see where we were. It was Morecambe.

We were hurriedly bundled out of the train, paraded on the platform and marched off along the seafront, peeling off as directed to occupy boarding houses, which had shed another load of 'likely lads' the previous day. With 35 others I was deposited in a three-storey billet in Balmoral Road, which was to become my home for three weeks. The motherly landlady, with her domestic staff, was still there and treated us like long-lost sons.

Morecambe seemed swamped by the RAF. We were everywhere. We paraded and marched in the streets. We drilled on the sands and the promenade. We filled the restaurants. We emptied the shops. It was all good for the image of this Lancashire resort.

Although the day raids over London and the south coast had now begun, Morecambe seemed to be quite oblivious of any danger. Those who had been successful in securing summer accommodation in the town were enjoying a holiday in the sun.

The physical training of airmen on the seafront proved a popular attraction. One day our particular squad was subject to a great deal of ridicule and caustic remarks from a group of youthful feminine eyewitnesses.

Corporal Bellamy, our popular instructor, remained calm and aloof from the verbal onslaught and ribald merriment, but at last had had enough. Standing us at ease, he turned to the girls and, addressing them in most uncomplimentary terms, told them that 'these men are going to give their lives for you and all you can do is laugh at them. Aren't you ashamed of yourselves?'

He became our hero. 'Good old Corp!' we murmured, dreaming of the day when we too might become corporals.

I lost no time in finding the Army hall, and regularly attended Sunday night and week-night meetings and practices. Adjutant Catherine Harris was the songster leader and I became her organist.

One Sunday evening we sang 'Let Peace Reign In Your Heart' (words by Doris Rendell) which I had written for that coronation pageant. That thoughtful gesture meant a lot to me.

The small band, led by Bandmaster Neil Price, also occupied my attention and two other RAF boys were happy to lend a hand.

Nina came up for a short holiday and when I met her at the station she immediately carted me off to buy a proper Air Force shirt to replace the khaki garment I was still wearing. (I had been issued with two, but neither matched the collar and tie worn with it.) The new shirt was to be kept for Sundays I was emphatically told. We could not afford two.

At the end of three weeks in the bracing fresh air and lovely summer sunshine we were ready to 'pass on', to use Corporal Bellamy's unfortunate phrase.

Having learned that there were not yet any vacancies at the radio school, I was interested in the news that I was to be posted to Horsham St Faith. The flight sergeant who informed me was such a cockney that it sounded like 'Horsham St Fyth' which, I felt sure, must be in Scotland.

It did not take me long to discover that my destination was, in fact, an aerodrome just outside Norwich. Six of us, all potential radio operators, were involved.

Trying to remember all the pleasant things about Morecambe and doing our best to forget the painful sore-arms legacy we had inherited from numerous vaccinations and inoculations received in the medical quarters, housed in a large room above Burton's (or was it Fifty Shilling Tailors?), we set out for Norwich.

There was no cross-country short cut. We were routed via Euston, across London to Liverpool Street and then on the old

119

LNER line to Norfolk. The short distance between the London termini provided us with our first experience of daylight raids on the capital.

No one at Horsham St Faith knew of our existence. We were not expected, and so late was it that we had to sleep on the floor of an empty, unheated hut with our kitbags for pillows and our greatcoats as blankets.

Next morning we were sorted out and allocated temporary duties until such time as we could begin our technical training. I found myself in charge of the plate-room of the cookhouse. This was my first taste of an automatic washer.

At the first opportunity I made for Norwich Citadel and was immediately made to feel at home. My activity at this corps was short-lived. An invasion scare confined us to barracks for most of our time at Horsham St Faith.

We were told there had been invasion landings at 50 different points along the east coast. The same source caused hurried instruction to be given on how we must meet the threatened attack – without weapons. We were relieved when such rumours were proved to be quite unfounded.

One day a letter arrived at the camp addressed to 'S/Ldr Brindley Boon'. It had been sent to my home and my wife redirected it without thinking of the consequences.

No time was lost in hauling me before the station adjutant who demanded to know what I meant by telling my friends I was a squadron leader. They did not approve of misrepresentation of this kind and I could be in serious trouble.

I opened the letter, read its contents and did my best to explain that I was a songster leader in The Salvation Army and this title had unfortunately been abbreviated!

The 'misrepresentation' was none of my doing and I apologised on behalf of the writer. My explanation was accepted and the troublesome letter handed back to me, but not before the offending abbreviation had been heavily scrawled out and a venomous 'AC2' substituted in its place.

The letter, in fact, was from newly appointed British Commissioner Albert Orsborn, as Chairman of the International Music Board, giving me the news that I had been awarded second prize in the 1939 International Competition for *Second Series* band compositions. My arrangement of 'Still With Thee' was successful in the meditation section.

When the results were announced in *The Musician* I was pleased to see that my friend Charles Skinner had gained two first prizes. My award was worth £2 10s. It was not until later that I realised that the prize took the form of a coupon to be exchanged for goods at SP&S, Ltd. I could have done with the cash. Captain Skinner's 'spoils' amounted to £8!

A letter from Colonel Arthur Goldsmith expressing delight that his 'boys' had done so well was all the reward I needed.

At last the RAF Radio School at Yatesbury, near Calne, Wiltshire, was ready for another intake. It was to be a crash course, condensed to four weeks because of the urgency to train operators in the 'new secret trade'.

We were soon 'in the know'. It transpired that we were in on the ground floor of a bold, exciting experiment afterwards to capture the world's imagination as 'radar'.

That ingenious palindrome of initials was not to come until the Americans' entry into the war. To us it was known as radio direction finding (we were RDF operators), then radiolocation, before its settled description when we became radar operators.

On Sundays I went to Swindon Citadel, as there was a weekly liberty run into town. My first visit was harvest festival, 15 September 1940. A party from Catford was conducting the meetings.

That Sunday went down in history as the climax of the Battle of Britain and marked the end of 'dogfights' in the day skies over England.

Our month's course completed, we were posted to operational stations. It was made quite clear that we were still 'under training' and could not be qualified 'operational' for another six months. The idea of staying put in one place after many wanderings appealed to me, wherever I might be.

Six of us were assigned to the radar station at Foreness Point, Cliftonville, Kent, to relieve the hard-pressed crews which had so valiantly served through the Battle of Britain. We were promised plenty of activity.

Day raids had given place to night conflicts and, when we arrived at Margate station on a lovely moonlit night, the scraps going on in the vast expanse of sky out to sea served as a prelude to 'music' that was to come.

When transport arrived, we quite expected to be taken to Manston, the nearby noted aerodrome. Instead we were to have a seafront billet on what is now known as Palm Bay Avenue. Our quarters were the Godwin Girls' College, where fashionable (renamed) Goodwin Court now stands. The girls, with most of the local inhabitants, had been evacuated.

The whole of Thanet, in fact, was in no man's land. The main defences were 15 miles inland. Houses and streets were practically deserted and one had to possess a permit to enter the town. Military police met every train to examine identification papers and passes. To go into town without wearing a steel helmet and carrying a service gas mask was a chargeable offence.

Our scene of operations was within easy walking distance of our billet. A stroll across the cliffs and we were there.

We found a highly complicated but greatly appreciated duty roster in force, covering the 24 hours a day that the station had to be manned, as well as providing generous free time. By working watches of various lengths – three, four, five and six hours' duration – we were able to cram 42 hours into three-and-a-half days and then have 65 hours' leave. If we had the money we could nip up to London, although things were pretty hot there as well.

They were still early days so far as radar was concerned. The aerials, constantly 'sweeping' out to sea, were operated by an upturned bicycle, the pedals being manipulated by hand to keep the 'Heath Robinson' contraption moving.

The results of such tiring labour were shown on the PPI (Plan Position Indicator), a kind of television set with the coastline marked, to which we kept our eyes glued. What we saw was passed down a phone to the radar unit at Dunkirk (near Canterbury) for transmission to a fighter station.

It all took time and, when there was a high wind, manual control of the pedals could not be maintained and operations needed to be suspended. It was as simple as that.

The RAF Regiment had not yet come into being, which meant that the station was guarded by an efficient military contingent. We were challenged every time we went on duty. As we approached the gate leading to the compound we were confronted with, 'Halt! Who goes there – friend or foe?'

This could be something of a jolting shock, especially in the inky blackness of night with the voice booming from a different direction every time you went on watch.

We would nervously respond 'Friend' (come to think of it, I cannot recall anyone identifying himself as 'Foe'!) and then would come a further test of one's credentials. The guard would hurl a number at us. We were required to give, as our answer, the difference between that number and the day's date. If it was the eighth of the month and the guard shouted 32, our reply would be 24.

This seems a simple method of password, really, but it was not so easy if maths was not your strong subject, or when you found yourself gazing apprehensively down the gleaming barrel of a loaded rifle. I suppose today we would simply take out our pocket calculator and make sure of the answer!

In keeping with other Army corps in the vulnerable south-east, Margate had been sadly affected. Necessary evacuation had robbed the corps of many of its local officers. Only a handful remained to keep the flag flying, but limited activity had done nothing to destroy their faith or dampen their enthusiasm.

The officers, Major Ellen Lupton and Adjutant Frances Moore, led the remnant with courage and utter devotion and set a shining example in faith and steadfastness as they joined in singing their theme chorus: 'Safe am I, safe am I, in the hollow of his hand'.

Both the band and songster brigade were under the leadership of Bandmaster Leslie Brockman. There were five bandsmen left and, with the aid of as many servicemen stationed in the town, the band could average a total of ten on Sundays.

My services were enlisted on euphonium and as organist, and I was asked to form a male voice party which added variety to the meetings.

By this time London was in the front line and my wife had given up our flat in Golders Green to move in with her mother, still living at Child's Hill. When I realised that it would be possible for Nina to be with me at Margate I applied for a permit for her and was given permission to live out. Accommodation in the town was no problem and we obtained two rooms on the Ramsgate Road at a cost of 10 shillings a week. Furnishings, gas and electricity were included.

Nina brought her uniform with her and was a welcome addition to the songster brigade, which numbered 22 and sang nicely.

One morning, when I was on duty, the town was bombed. It was a sneak raid by planes which skimmed over the sea at too low a height to be picked up by our equipment. Much damage was done, mainly in the high street, we were informed.

When I came off watch I cycled down into town to find that the Army hall was one of the 'victims'. The officers were already there and, aided by one or two passers-by, we retrieved what we could from the premises, cleared up the glass and boarded up the gaping holes.

The upstairs hall of memories, approached by an opening between two shops (one of them used as a young people's hall), was never used again. Temporary accommodation was found in a church hall and later the faithful comrades were bombed out of that. Another hall was found and this became the Salvationists' home until the Oddfellows Hall became available for special events. After the war this building became the present citadel.

I had my first week's leave in November 1940. Quite adventurously Nina and I set off from Margate for seven days in London.

Our train was machine-gunned most of the way to Chatham, where the pressure subsided. On arrival at Victoria we saw from placards that Coventry had been blitzed. We looked at each other but remained silent. Nina had a sister who lived, with her husband and two children, on the outskirts of that city. As is usual in such circumstances we imagined the worst but hoped for the best.

We spent the week trying to obtain information, without success. Communications in and out of Coventry had broken down. We acted on the old adage: no news is good news.

It was not until after we returned to Margate that we learned that Winnie, the sister, and her children had been killed when a landmine had fallen on their street. The husband was on night-shift war work and missed the tragedy, although his distraught state confirmed his wish that he had been at home when it happened.

Another sister and *her* two daughters, in another part of the city, were safe.

Having lost her elder brother in Flanders during the bitter fighting of the First World War and her father as an outcome of that conflict, my wife, with her mother, found this additional sorrow hard to bear, especially as an elder daughter of the stricken family had died of tuberculosis a year previously.

Our friends, Captain and Mrs Will Straughan, were stationed at Sandwich, some seven miles away and the scene of my debut as an Army bandsman 11 years before. Constantly subjected to double shelling from across the Straits of Dover, they were in relentless danger, but in addition to their corps duties, which were drastically curtailed because of evacuation, had opened a canteen for servicemen in the little town.

Nina wanted to help and made frequent journeys to assist in this worthy service and several times brought their year-old daughter back with her to stay for a while to relieve the harassed parents.

Towards the end of the year we conducted Sunday meetings at Sandwich, little realising that within ten years we ourselves would be stationed at the corps.

Christmas approached. Having been told that I could regard myself as settled at Foreness until my training was completed, we looked forward to the next three or four months.

125

I went on duty early on Christmas morning to be told that a corporal and I were posted to a place called Sopley on the south coast, not far from Bournemouth. I had never heard of it. My corporal colleague, a Bristolian, was equally ignorant.

All I knew was that I was barely halfway through my 'allotted span' of official training and did not want to move. Being told that my training period was at an end and that I was now qualified to wear my radio operator's 'sparks' was some compensation.

Leaving Nina with Margate friends, I set out with the corporal on the all-day journey to Christchurch, where, in response to a telephone call, transport came to take us on the last stage of our wearying journey. It was not far off midnight when we drew up outside the massive iron gates of a location we were to come to know well as Sopley Park. Our new station was still a mile away.

We were in the New Forest. Sopley turned out to be a delightful, old-world village on the Christchurch-Ringwood road, about four miles from both towns. Bournemouth was some 11 miles away and could be approached by various routes.

The population was no more than 200 and the one general store was run by a family called Berryman. The post office was the front room of a cottage and if three people were waiting to buy stamps the premises were crowded! The arrival of airmen and airwomen brought increased business, but Mrs Harrison, the postmistress, remained as unperturbed as when she had opened up a part of her home for this purpose after the First World War.

The 11th-century village church, built on a mound and towering over a watermill that had been there from the same period; the attractive village inn; scattered thatched cottages augmented by a few modern dwellings; winding lanes and a village hall completed the picturesque scene.

On the moonlit night of our arrival most of this landscape was taken in at one glimpse and somehow I felt I was going to enjoy my first experience of rural life. Is there anything quite like the smell of the country?

There was no communal accommodation. What few personnel who had already arrived were billeted with villagers: two with the squire; two with the vicar; one with farmer Farwell; the CO with a local landowner – and so on.

Warned of our coming, the village policeman, Knight by name, with his bicycle awaited our arrival and, as it was so late, decided to knock up the landlord of the local inn. In this way we spent our first night in Sopley at The Woolpack – a new experience for me.

The proprietor, Andrew Lane, was a bellringer, churchwarden and sacristan at the ancient church across the road and, with his wife, regaled us well into the next day with fascinating stories of village characters and their forebears.

After a breakfast of ham, eggs, new bread, fresh butter and a mug of steaming tea we expressed our thanks to 'mine host' and his gracious lady and made our way some 400 yards along the road to a permanent billet. We borrowed a wheelbarrow in which to convey our kitbags and other personal belongings.

Our new landlady was Annie Button. A charming woman in her mid-40s, she had arrived at Sopley some 20 years previously to teach in the village school. It was not long before she met Charles Button, a young farmer, and they were married. They ran the farm between them, Charlie spending much of his day delivering milk to the outlying areas and Annie feeding and watering the cattle and keeping a friendly eye on the poultry. Chickens had to be shooed off the kitchen table before we could sit down to meals.

Those first days of 1941 were particularly cold and there was a general shortage of fuel. The cottage completely lacked warmth when we arrived. Mrs B. continually apologised for this and, as if to try to keep herself warm by autosuggestion, went around the house singing 'Some day my coal will come', set to a melody from *Snow White And The Seven Dwarfs*, then the rage. Snow White, however, was contemplating the arrival of her prince.

Sopley was the first ground-controlled interception unit. Operations were carried out from a trailer in the middle of a requisitioned field.

There were eight of us in the pioneer team, with necessary maintenance, administration and general duties support. We went 'on the air' between dusk and dawn and worked in co-operation with a night fighter squadron. The advantage over earlier radar stations was that we had direct radio-telephone contact with pilots. In this way they were fed with up-to-date information.

We soon became the eighth wonder of the world. Everyone who was anyone came down to be entertained by the fascinating new 'toy'. Winston Churchill and Clement Attlee (his deputy prime minister); other cabinet ministers; warlords; foreign diplomats; service chiefs; military brass hats – the lot. The crowning glory was the visit of King George VI.

I was the fighter plotter that night. My job was to track the courses and calculate the speeds of friendly and hostile planes on a huge perspex grid reference map and to pass such information to the controller to be included in instructions transmitted to the pilot. The King was given a seat on my right, a curtain separating us.

We had been well briefed. Should the VIP speak to any of us we were to remember that he was there primarily as an RAF officer and we were to address him as 'Sir'. Never 'Your Majesty'!

Imagine my state of panic when, right in the middle of a chase across the southern skies, the curtain was drawn aside and a deep, guttural whisper asked: 'And what are you doing?'

I sprang to my feet, with an action that sent my chinagraph crayon hurtling to the floor, and replied in my best open-air voice, 'Plotting, your Majesty' – as if I were planning to plant a bomb under the throne!

'Oh, are you?' commented the King as he stooped down into the darkness to retrieve the crayon, which he calmly restored to a ledge on the plotting table.

I deserved to be court-martialled for such an indiscretion. Instead I was left with an illustration in humility that has remained with me ever since.

RAF Sopley became a showpiece and a training centre for radar operators. With every new technical development came a fresh intake of personnel of both sexes. That pioneer crew of eight was quickly added to. When I left the station three-and-a-half years later, as Flight

Sergeant in charge of operations, the total strength was more than 200.

Another station pioneer was a radio-telephone operator named Bill Lyon-Shaw.

In civvy street he had been a theatrical producer. Two of his shows were still running at famous London theatres. In our eyes, the fact that he was receiving royalties for such productions put him in an upper financial bracket!

He was a great character, not unlike a younger edition of Charles Laughton. When it was suggested that we should put on a concert in the village hall, Bill was the obvious choice for impresario. I became his musical director and we worked happily together on a revue, *Out Of The Blue*.

The rehearsals were an education and gave me an appreciated insight into professional production. Bill knew all the tricks of the trade, some of which I was pleased to utilise in later years when arranging chorus settings for Army events.

But he could not remember names. A lesser personality would have been embarrassed by this shortcoming, but not Bill. To catch the attention of anyone in the cast he would simply snap his fingers and call 'Sprawston'. There was no one of that name, of course, but when the sound rang out the entire company invariably turned in Bill's direction.

Then, after so effectively gaining everyone's attention, he would point to the person he wished to address and merely say, 'Yes, you!' It never failed. It was always 'Sprawston'.

After the war Bill Lyon-Shaw became a BBC TV producer and when Tyne Tees Television came into being he was appointed its first director.

For that first Sopley production I formed a male voice octet of keen vocalists. Our contributions were a patriotic song, 'The Men Who Fight For England' (a setting to words by Patience Strong published in a daily newspaper and sung by permission of the author), and 'Juanita'.

I moulded the group on Army lines and, as we gathered round the hanging microphone with hands clasped in the custom of the times, we could have been a party of Salvationist bandsmen dressed in another uniform.

* * * * *

For a while our CO at Sopley was Squadron Leader Richard Sharp, a First World War pilot recalled for further service. He was a great traveller and had written several books on his wanderings. One of these was entitled *That Fool Sharp*. One night, during a lull in operations, he told me about it and offered to loan me his copy if I was interested. I accepted his kind offer and embarked on the story of his sheep-farming in New Zealand.

Soon after this I was posted on a week's technical course to Middle Wallop RAF station. A bus took me from Sopley to Salisbury, but the ongoing journey was not so straightforward. The best and quickest means of transport was hitchhiking. This always had to be a patient pursuit.

After a while a car stopped in response to my frantic sign. The man at the wheel was elderly, thickset and heavily moustached. He invited me to jump in beside him and he was soon conversing in an easy, fluent, if gruff, manner. I listened entranced. We were at the gates of Middle Wallop in no time at all and, with a 'good luck' salutation, he drove off into the setting sun.

It was later that night that I missed *That Fool Sharp*. I remembered having it when I gratefully accepted the lift, but it was now lost for ever.

When I returned from the course, I went into Bournemouth at the first opportunity, bent on securing a copy for my CO to replace the one so carelessly left in the car. I was unsuccessful in my search of the bookshops, but one promised to secure a copy from the publishers – if they could be traced.

Within a week I was in possession of such a copy and was able to hand it to Squadron Leader Sharp with the explanation of what had happened. Typically, he said I should not have bothered.

130

Two days later the original copy turned up, wrapped neatly in a brown-paper parcel. Rather puzzled, I opened it and removed a handwritten note from its pages. It simply said:

> 13 Hanover Terrace
> Regent's Park
> NWI

Dear Young Airman,
I take it that you left this book in my car. I secured your name and address from an envelope used as a bookmark.
Why don't you read something decent? Have you never heard of *Kipps*, or *The Invisible Man*, or *The War Of The Worlds*?

> Yours,
> H. G. Wells

I wrote to thank him – still stunned!

As soon as possible after my arrival at Sopley my wife joined me. We obtained a billet with Lord Manners's butler and his wife, Walter and Lilian Kitley. They were active workers in the Ripley village Congregational church.

Their lovely, thatched-roof South Lodge stood at the gate of Avon Tyrrell, the 'big house on the hill' which had been taken over by the military for the duration. Lord and Lady Manners had taken up residence at a smaller home, Tyrrell's Ford – so named, it was said, because Sir Walter Tyrrell, escaping from pursuing forces after he had killed King Rufus in the New Forest, had forded the river at this point.

This happy abode, comfortable and illuminated only by oil lamps, became our home from home. Nina stayed with me until recalled to London to be conscripted for war work in a Finchley Road factory taken over for the making of aircraft components.

As soon as I had a Sunday free from duty we made our way to the Army. We thought there must be a corps in the vicinity of Bournemouth Square and boarded a bus into town. After a while we saw a sign pointing to 'The Salvation Army'. Hurriedly we alighted, followed the indicating arrow and found ourselves at the Boscombe Salvation Army hall.

Travelling the 11 miles to and from meetings presented something of a problem. It meant a cycle ride of four miles (with Nina on the crossbar) to the main-road bus stop. We then hid the bike in the rhododendron bushes by the side of the road and waited for the bus, scheduled to run every hour. Sometimes it was full up. At other times we were more fortunate.

At night it was the same procedure in reverse, but if it was dark we had difficulty in locating our faithful iron steed in the bushes! A torch was often required to help us in our search.

As we rode through the twisting lanes we sang favourite Army choruses, experimenting with close harmony as we went. Our journey would sometimes be disturbed by the thundering sound of forest ponies stampeding towards us. In the dark it was frightening. We would quickly dismount, flatten ourselves against the hedge, drag the cycle after us and remain perfectly still until the danger had passed.

At the end of a busy Sunday we would gather around the piano in the lamplit sitting room of our billet and have an informal 'concert'. This was pure Victoriana, but delightful.

When Nina was recalled to London to undertake war work I became more involved in Boscombe Corps. Bandmaster William Walker had retired from that appointment but, with the call-up of his son-in-law, Bandmaster Sylvester Henning, had returned to temporary leadership, as well as serving as songster leader.

William Walker became a good friend. His name was already known to me as the writer of that popular male voice song, 'Jerusalem', and other worthy contributions to *The Musical Salvationist*, but to meet him in this way and to learn from his deep spirituality and able leadership was a tremendous privilege.

Boscombe Corps suffered a double blow when Bandmaster Henning and Bandmaster Walker were promoted to Glory within a year of each other. The former was killed on active service in India. Our hearts went out in love and sympathy to the young widow and their two lovely little daughters, who grew up to become a credit to their mother and the father they hardly knew.

During that difficult period I was entrusted with the leadership of both band and songster brigade and, together, we sought to keep the flag flying and maintain the vital witness.

Boscombe bandsmen in reserved occupations or too old for military service were always able to provide a balanced nucleus and most Sundays there was an 'invasion' of Salvationist servicemen who were stationed in the vicinity.

Periodic leaves – long and short – usually coincided with some Army event. Early in 1941, soon after my arrival at Sopley, I spent a Sunday at Winchester listening to Rosehill Band for the first time.

I was not disappointed. How could a band with so many stars in its firmament and such an able conductor fail to impress? Did any Army band have such an auspicious start?

I appreciated the opportunity of accompanying the band to Winchester Prison before the afternoon programme in the hall, and of sharing the prisoners' delight in the playing and other items, especially the vocal trio of Lieutenant Ken Nutty, 'Jock' Inglis and Cyril Brisley.

When 'Instruments for Cairo' became a battle cry I was invited to take part in a 'Cairo Night' at Harlesden, arranged to raise money for the appeal. Petty Officer Ray Allen (the 'Steadman-' had not yet been added), one of Harlesden's trombonists, was on leave from the Royal Navy at the time.

In all the activity we did not forsake our comrades at Chalk Farm. The corps's first casualty was one of our youngest songsters, Dorothy Dickens, who met her death when her family shelter received a direct hit. There were others, and when Bandmaster and Mrs Punchard were forced to evacuate their bomb-pounded home at Belsize Park and seek some respite at Reading, Ted Winney took charge of the little band.

Later it became necessary for Ted to have a leg amputated and A.W.P. gallantly resumed leadership again. To see the great man marching from a nearby open-air stand to the hall with a band of seven, carrying his upright frame with the dignified bearing he had shown when heading a procession of 50 men, was an object lesson in fidelity.

By this time there were no mounted policemen to lead the way or foot constables to keep back the crowds on the pavements. Yet the police inspector still saluted the bandmaster and the band flag as the march approached the citadel, as he had done for the past 20 years. Tradition dies hard at Chalk Farm.

The Sunday night meetings on the platform of Chalk Farm Underground Station became a feature of corps life. As night bombing increased, residents were permitted to leave their bedding on covered racks built in the alleyway beside the hall and to collect their precious bundles when they were required. I took part in many such services.

Our son was born in the spring of 1943. Nina was living with her mother at Child's Hill and it was not until I went home on compassionate leave after the birth that I learned, to my sorrow and dismay, that my wife had been very ill. It was broken to me gently that I had nearly lost them both.

The baby was born during an air raid. We named him John Brindley. At least, I did. My wife was still too ill to give much consecutive thought to the matter. I was not then aware that history was repeating itself and that there had been a John Brindley Boon born into our family in 1813, the son of John Boon and Sarah Brindley. Six weeks later Nina was well enough to attend John's dedication ceremony conducted by Colonel Goldsmith.

The last 18 months of my RAF career were spent in Wales. I had never been to the principality in my life, even if my wife had been born in Tredegar.

When I made the long journey by train I quite anticipated a halt at the frontier for my papers to be examined! My destination was a small radar station on the extreme west coast, 70 miles beyond Swansea, and still farther on past Haverfordwest. Ripperston was the name of the site and Talbenny was the nearby parent unit. They called it 'Little England beyond Wales', and not without good reason.

Originally constructed to defend the South Wales docks, the outfit was not now so busy, the danger having passed by March 1944. The main object was how to keep the personnel occupied and happy in such an isolated spot, and it became apparent that that was why I was there.

I quickly found myself entertainments' officer, with responsibility for social events, sports and musical and dramatic productions. Before I arrived, an enterprising NCO had organised a practical interest in a local children's hospital with patients evacuated from premises in Cardiff some time before. Our airmen and WAAFs 'adopted' the youngsters, contributing so much from their pay, sending birthday cards, visiting regularly and providing entertainments from time to time.

This activity became our life. Soon I was in the thick of it. A revue with original songs, sketches and a variety of other items was the first venture, and this was followed by a Christmas pantomime, *Cinderella*. We broke with tradition and had a male prince and female 'Cinders', to the delight of the youngsters. This made it more real for them, especially as we had a galaxy of handsome airmen and beautiful airwomen to choose from!

My portrayal of 'Buttons' undeservedly brought me an avalanche of fan mail from the children. Some of them were too greatly incapacitated even to lift their heads from their pillows, but all the beds were wheeled into the concert hall and we went through our songs, dances and dramatic interludes as though we had 'made' Drury Lane itself.

The costumes were authentically lovely. There was no shortage of money available for this. To be able to cadge a lift on a plane from Talbenny to Croydon and then travel up to London to explore the fascinating hiring showrooms of Fox's in Holborn was a tremendous thrill. To walk round amid the ruffs and crinolines, medieval hats and attractive dresses transported me to another world.

The next production was *The Enchanted Castle*, a fairy story of a beautiful princess held prisoner in a turreted tower by a mad king, her father, to be rescued eventually by a handsome prince. This held the young audience spellbound.

As the scene of the production was Kensington Hospital, it seemed natural that we should call the fairyland kingdom Kensingtonia. This

Ruritanian state had its own national anthem and some dozen other songs were written to complete the musical. I took the part of the 'Mad King'.

Many of the 80 melodies I wrote for RAF productions were later transformed for Salvation Army use, with suitable words added. I make no apology for this – but that is quite another story, belonging to a later chapter.

The nearest corps was Milford Haven. Sunday duty, and the inconvenience of cycling seven miles each way in all kinds of Welsh weather, made my appearances rather infrequent.

On the rare occasions I was able to attend, I was made to feel at home and was pleased to assist in the sections of this little, healthy Pembrokeshire corps.

One day I received a letter from the Divisional Commander (Brigadier Rankin Miller). General and Mrs George Carpenter were coming to St David's for a Sunday. Could I be present to play the organ? There was no corps at this 'smallest city in the world', but the Army's leaders, on holiday in the area, had been invited by the elders of a church to visit that outpost of Britain. I readily agreed and booked the date.

The afternoon meeting was held in Zion Chapel and at night a larger building, the Tabernacle, was taken. The congregation, made up of local worshippers and those from neighbouring villages who had been attracted by the advertisements, was augmented unexpectedly by a large company of RAF men and women from St David's camp. The singing was terrific, often drowning the organ. One hymn was sung in Welsh.

That was in August 1945. The long-awaited demob scheme was under way. Two months later my number came up. I 'signed off' at RAF Uxbridge on Saturday 10 November and, armed with a telltale cardboard box containing my striped demob suit, made my joyous way home.

Chapter 13

Picking Up the Pieces

THERE have been few more frustrating periods in my life than those experienced immediately following my return to civvy street. Life in the RAF was certainly not one I would have chosen, but the years spent in military uniform were not without their happiness and did something for me. They widened my vision without lowering my Salvationist standards. They taught me a lesson in tolerance, and how to respect other people's opinions.

I was quite a different person from the one who had enlisted at Cardington. Loved ones at home and friends at the corps expected me to return unchanged. It could never be, although I did hope that basically I was the same.

Wherein lay my usefulness? My mind was in a turmoil. While my stand as a Salvationist had always been respected – if not totally understood – as my demob number approached, my colleagues were not slow to express the hope that I would not return to my Army life and service.

As I tried to enjoy my 56 days' demob leave I began to sort myself out. There were several courses open to me. With acquired skill in the new and exciting realm of radar, I could continue my RAF service. This did not appeal. Civil aviation was also looking for recruits for ground control duties at an airport being developed at Heathrow.

With such a future recommended, some of us 'old hands' had spent a few days at RAF Honiley, between Coventry and Birmingham, where training was given in the use of the latest ground control approach equipment. This was no doubt an enticement to make commercial flying a career. The idea did not appeal to me.

Of the four controllers who attended from our unit in West Wales, three eventually joined the pioneer staff at Heathrow and gave distinguished service to various airways, one becoming a top executive.

However, the world of entertainment held a distinct appeal. Many influential RAF friends sought to open doors of showbiz glamour.

The musical directorship of the Music For All Club, Cairo, was shortly to become vacant and my name was put forward. Responsibilities at this famous Egyptian centre, well known to British personnel serving in the Middle East, would include organising entertainments, arranging daily concerts and conducting choirs formed from service personnel on leave.

I was interviewed at a Kensington hotel by Flight Lieutenant Clifford Harker, the former director of the club who was in England to be demobbed and had promised to find a successor. He was an eminent church organist in the Midlands and was instantly interested in my background. There were two snags. The job would last only while the British forces were in Egypt, and I would not be able to take my wife and two-year-old son with me. The cordial interview was at an end. After being away from home for nearly six years, I was not prepared for a further separation from Nina, to whom I had been married barely a year when war broke out, and John, who scarcely knew me.

As it happened, in a comparatively short time the exodus of British troops began and my appointment in Cairo would have been short-lived.

One day I received a letter requesting me to attend an audition at some rehearsal rooms in Old Compton Street, off Charing Cross Road. I was rather puzzled but felt that no harm would be done if I showed interest.

Upon arrival, I was required to queue up in the seemingly never-ending line of suspicious-looking characters, all easily identified by their demob suits.

When it was my turn to be interviewed I discovered that an ex-servicemen's revue was about to be launched at a West End theatre, with the prospect of a provincial run at the end of it. A well-meaning RAF colleague had recommended me and it was thought that I had enough experience to assist on the musical and production side of the show. It was to be called *Desert Rats* and, the PR handout announced, was to be presented by a cast that had seen service in the Middle East theatre of war.

As I had never worn a pair of khaki shorts, let alone set eyes on Africa, I suggested that to become involved in such a production would be a gross distortion of the truth. The kindly director of operations, who later became a brilliant producer of BBC variety shows, said he would be prepared to waive the restriction in my case and no one need know of my subterfuge.

I managed to convince him that I was not interested, made my hurried way through the choking haze of tobacco smoke and was relieved to breathe the comparatively pure air of a London fog.

Another contact led me to a famous music-publishing establishment in Tin Pan Alley. Here the proprietor, whose name the firm bore and who was making a fortune as a songwriter under another name, offered me a job as a song plugger. This would mean 'selling' new songs to the public by various means, including nightclub sessions and a number of dubious methods. No doubt someone had to do that kind of work, but it was not for me!

My RAF concert party work in Wales, especially in the occasional broadcasts, had brought me in contact with Mai Jones, a BBC variety producer in Cardiff. She it was who brought my name to the notice of the BBC in London, with the result that I was requested to present myself at Broadcasting House, where I saw Michael Standing, and then at the Aeolian Hall, Bond Street, where Michael North graciously interested himself in a civvy street 'stray'.

This latter Michael had been in the audience at one of our wartime performances when his song 'Lord Of The Air' had been featured by a mixed chorus of airmen and WAAFs.

Both Michaels seemed interested, but there were no vacancies at that moment. They would keep my name before them and let me know. Somehow I felt relieved.

My unsettled state continued throughout my leave. What should have been a happy, relaxed period of rehabilitation with my family and friends became a nightmare of despair. I wanted to pick up the pieces of my old life as soon as possible. At the same time I was looking for a future that would be far removed from the existence I had known before the war.

The crisis came one afternoon when I was on my way to see yet another Charing Cross Road music publisher. I passed through the swing doors, ascertained that the person who was expecting me was on the second floor and began nervously to mount the stairs. The first flight was negotiated without incident. I faced the second.

It was then I became acutely aware of a spiritual tug of war being waged inside me. It had, in fact, been going on for some time, but I would not face up to it.

What was I doing here? I asked myself as I paused for breath before completing the climb. Call it divine intervention, God's leading, his voice or what you will, but I know that in that moment of pause the truth dawned, the light shone and I knew once and for all that I had no place in such surroundings.

I retraced my steps. By the time the street was reached spiritual victory had been won. Never again did such temptation haunt me. From then on all my 'eggs' were in the Army 'basket', although there were still steep mountains to be climbed.

I was suddenly at peace with God, myself and all the world.

Without delay I made it known that I wished to return to employment with the Men's Social Work, if there was a vacancy. The Chief Secretary (Colonel Hugh Muir) saw me and offered me five pounds a week.

Surprisingly, this was music to my ears. Was it not nearly double the salary I was receiving at the outbreak of war? The Devil promptly took the trouble to remind me of the income which might have been mine had I managed to sell some of his songs!

Colonel Muir, always something of a psychologist, quickly summed up the situation and sensed how difficult it was going to be for me to settle down to the 'old life' on headquarters.

On that day in January 1946 he volunteered the opinion that he thought a change would do me some good and proposed that I should become the accountant and cashier at Spa Road, the MSW's well known centre of social activity in Bermondsey. I was thrilled at the prospect of having closer contact with people, and on the following Monday began a happy period of fruitful service. My duties as cashier included paying out salaries to the men and women staffing the plant and settling accounts, as well as preparing weekly profit-and-loss statements for the benefit of the Accountants' Department at headquarters.

My work brought me into contact with the residents, many of whom owed much to the Army and were mindful of the fact. One man, a diligent craftsman, was out on parole from Broadmoor; another was a convicted forger; several were 'lost' to society. I knew them all and shared many beneficial discussions, as well as hilarious moments.

Spa Home, the other establishment on the premises, was under separate management and was being used at the time to house Italian prisoners of war not yet repatriated.

When I joined the staff the officers in charge were Major and Mrs Richard Coates. They were refined, sensitive people who gave themselves wholeheartedly to serve the men entrusted to their tender care. I never knew either of these gentle souls to raise their voices above a normal conversational level, yet they commanded the love and respect of all who lived or worked there. Some of them were tough too.

The Coates children, June and Carl, were very much part of the Spa Road family and were thoroughly spoiled by the staff and the men. It was never quite the same when the youngsters were at school.

The two salvage sales a week were events. These consisted, in the main, of the disposal of clothing which had been donated to the Army and collected by the vans which covered the metropolitan area.

With garments duly sorted and priced, the big wooden gates at the entrance to the yard would be opened and the waiting host would make its rushing way to the salvage warehouse.

This was really Mrs Coates's domain. She could manage the crowd and meet the cockney wit with her matching repartee.

It was my duty to wield a collecting-bag at the end of a long bending cane, not unlike a fishing rod! Mrs Coates would be mounted on a platform and would start perhaps by holding up a pair of trousers and asking who wanted them for 'the old man'. There would be complete silence until the price was given.

'Two shillings!' said Mrs C.

The response would be a forest of hands being raised, accompanied by an excited chorus of 'Major! Major!' Someone in the crowd would be selected as the lucky customer and the rest would lower their hands with the descending lamentation, 'Oh, Major!', on their lips and acute disappointment registered on their faces.

I would then go into action with my 'line and tackle', heave my weapon of war towards the successful buyer, wait for her to insert the money in the bag and then haul in the spoils. When change was required the process was somewhat slowed down.

The ritual would be repeated for anything up to an hour and would end with a number of satisfied customers, delighted with their bargains, and with the Spa Road much-needed coffers considerably swollen.

Jimmy Calderwood was a Spa Road institution – part of the furniture. No one could remember a time when he did not sit in solemn state at the outer end of a desk built for four just inside the door of the 'admin block', an ancient office requiring to be approached gingerly by means of a rickety flight of stairs from the cobbled yard below.

Spa Road was Jimmy's home. Pressed to answer the question as to how long he had been there, he would non-commitally reply, 'Since the year dot,' whimsically peering over the top of his old-fashioned frameless glasses as he spoke.

He was paid a nominal allowance for the work he did and from this was deducted the cost of his board and lodging. He had no complaints and was proud of his humble dwelling.

142

Jimmy was transport manager. He was handed the addresses from which furniture and clothing were to be collected and passed the necessary instructions to the van drivers responsible for the areas of operation. It was an efficient set-up and 'the governor', as the drivers affectionately called him, was at his post of duty from early morning until late at night – seemingly loving every minute of it.

Jimmy Calderwood, who was then well past 80 years of age, was a character from the past. He always wore a brown trilby hat that matched a similarly coloured suit, which was covered by a generously pocketed overall. An overcoat, which had probably fitted him well when he was less frail, hung on a nearby nail, ready to be worn over the overall when the weather was particularly cold while Jimmy hurried across the yard to his beckoning bed. A pair of black mittens, the right one frayed with the constant rubbing of a pen holder – none of your newfangled ballpoint pens for him – completed his 'uniform'.

Jimmy was a Londoner, brought up in the home of elderly grandparents. The grandfather had been born in 1798, when King George III was still on the throne. He vividly remembered the coronations of George IV, William IV and Queen Victoria, and was 27 when George Stephenson's first locomotive made the historic pioneer journey from Darlington to Stockton: carrying six carriages containing flour and coal and one carriage with scared passengers aboard.

The recollections of such incidents were passed on from grandfather to grandson and at mid-morning breaks at Spa Road, Jimmy, when he was in the mood, regaled me with countless stories while we drank tea and munched our sandwiches.

I sat spellbound. It was incredible to me that the memories of two men should span eight reigns and cover so much English history. As I listened it seemed as though the Battles of Trafalgar and Waterloo had been fought only the week before.

My informant, who loved to remind me that he was older than both the nearby Tower Bridge and the Royal Albert Hall, remembered being taken as a boy of eight to the funeral service of Charles Dickens at Westminster Abbey and was in the cheering crowds which greeted the 'soldiers of the Queen, my lad', as they returned from the Boer War.

143

In those fascinating sessions I was introduced to horse-drawn buses, growlers, hansom cabs, bewhiskered 'bobbies', Surrey and all-England personalities of the cricket world performing at Kennington Oval, and the strange goings-on in the gaslit streets of late-Victorian London.

My happy, fulfilling service at Spa Road came to an abrupt end all too soon. A telephone call gave me the news that I was to return to headquarters to continue my pre-war activity in the Accountants' Department. I was puzzled by this unexpected move until I reported for duty the following Monday morning. Then I learned that a songster brigade, already formed on the building for occasional requirements, was to be placed on a permanent footing and that my services were required on the tenor section. It was also rumoured that the band was to start up again. An appointment on headquarters would make it easier for me to attend lunch-hour practices should either idea reach fruition.

However, the band did not materialise although there were times in those early post-war days when a group of instrumentalists was rustled up to do duty at hostel meetings, funerals and special open-air gatherings.

One day the phone rang in my office at Spa Road. The clear, precise voice at the other end of the line belonged to Captain Gladys Moon, sole assistant of Brigadier Arch R. Wiggins, Editor of *The Musician*. Did I intend going to that week's songsters councils and festival at Clapton? If so, the brigadier would like me to report the two events for his paper.

My immediate reaction was to be not particularly interested. They were early days. I was still recovering from the trauma through which I had passed. Big Army meetings, which had meant so much to me in the past, no longer appealed. I was content to concentrate on my work, try to be a good husband and father, and re-establish myself as a songster leader. I had not planned to attend the Clapton event. That phone call, however, shattered my seemingly good intentions.

I was surprised and naturally flattered. True, I had commented upon an International Staff Band festival at Regent Hall for *The Bandsman*

And Songster some ten years before, and had supplied one or two technical articles on organ and pianoforte accompaniments, as well as providing casual reports while in the Forces. I have already said that I cannot remember the time when I did not want to become a journalist. All this led to my reluctant acceptance of the unexpected assignment.

This was the first time for six years that songsters of the London divisions had met in this way. In the tea interval two conversations took place which left me with irremovable memories. Both had vital bearing upon my future.

Major Edward Saywell, an interested mentor since I was 14, asked me if I would be interested in a possible appointment in the Bands Department at National Headquarters. Five minutes after the conclusion of that conversation, on the other side of the same platform, Brigadier Wiggins offered me a job on *The Musician*, 'when things get back to normal'.

My elation on both counts can be imagined. Here my twin worlds of music and journalism converged in one afternoon. Both respected officers had spoken to me 'in the strictest confidence' without knowing of the other's interest. Sensing my curiosity and quiet excitement, both promised to contact me at the appropriate time. I would have to be patient as the proposals were much 'in the air'. They merely wanted to ascertain my reaction.

These things I kept in my heart, patiently respecting the trust placed in me.

To have to report the first London major post-war songster festival after such an ordeal was not easy but, reading my comments after all these years, it is evident that I was genuinely impressed.

On a Wednesday in March of that year (1946), I took an elongated lunch hour to follow Regent Hall Band as it marched from Red Shield House in Buckingham Gate to play at Buckingham Palace at the command of Their Majesties the King and Queen. This was the band's fifth visit and the last under the baton of Bandmaster Herbert Twitchin.

There were 53 in the band that day, 25 of them servicemen wearing uniforms as varied as they were arresting. None was denied special leave for this royal occasion! In the front rank of eight trombonists were two flight lieutenants and, among the cornets, were two officers of similar rank, with their pilot's wings up, while an RASC captain manned one of the euphoniums and a merchant seaman one of the basses. Among those in khaki was the robust figure of Phil Catelinet.

The Regent Hall officers at that time were Major and Mrs Wesley Rich, who have already come into these memoirs. The King asked the major where he had spent the war years and, on hearing that he had been in the vicinity of London, His Majesty exclaimed, 'Then we were pals together!'

The Queen wanted to know about the congregations at Regent Hall and inquired if people were getting converted. Mrs Rich replied with the news of recent converts. Her Majesty answered: 'How wonderful it must be to see lives changed like that!'

London's welcome to the fourth High Council (1946) was held at the Royal Albert Hall. This was the first gathering of international leaders for seven years and it naturally carried a great deal of emotion. A few days later Commissioner Albert Orsborn was elected General.

Early in 1947 the Albert Hall was again taken – this time for the launching of the 'Fighting Faith' campaign. This was the occasion when the General left the morning meeting, in which he had delivered his impressive manifesto, for an audience with the King at Buckingham Palace. He returned to tell the afternoon gathering of His Majesty's interest in, among other matters, the simplicity of the General's uniform.

Recovery at Chalk Farm was slow. Reduced at one time during the war to a mere half-a-dozen players, the band's awakening was nothing short of miraculous.

In 1944 Frank Rawbone, a young engineering executive, transferred from Birmingham to London and, seeing the need, decided to continue his Army banding at Chalk Farm. Frank came from a non-Salvationist background and as a wayward youth became interested in playing the saxophone, which he succeeded in doing in a most able manner, later appearing in divisional and territorial programmes as a soloist on that instrument. After his conversion, he took up the soprano cornet which he played in Birmingham Citadel Band until moving to London.

At Chalk Farm, where the band was still under the fatherly tutorage of A.W.P., he soon became 'deputy bandmaster in charge' and, after a while, was appointed bandmaster. With dedication to a difficult task, much patience and hard work, he built a wartime band of 14 players capable of playing *Festival Series* journals in a proficient manner.

The 'new Farm' became the 'talk of the town' and, as it developed, increasing demands were made upon it. By the spring of 1946 the numbers had increased and the band shared its first partnership festival with Regent Hall for more than six years. By the time another year had passed there were 34 bandsmen and this historic section was once again travelling the length and breadth of the British Territory, delighting all with its captivating interpretations and flexible musicianship. The presence of Brigadier Frederick Coutts as the campaign leader added lustre to the visits.

Although never as busy as the band, the songster brigade had its fair quota of outings. The new music appearing in *The Musical Salvationist* interested and challenged us and we did our best to do it justice. When we crossed London to give a Saturday festival at Penge, *The Musician* reported: 'Chalk Farm Songster Brigade showed itself a highly skilful and well-balanced combination. Rhythm, expression and diction were almost all that could be desired. The leader's interpretation of popular songs was stimulating and at times exciting.'

We were grateful to the anonymous reporter for his kindly, encouraging words.

In my daily employment I was still doing my best to be a good accountant, not always with success. I must confess that those two brief conversations at Clapton more than 18 months before were never far from my mind, even if my hopes did take a dip when Brigadier Wiggins was promoted to lieut-colonel and appointed to Australia as editor-in-chief.

Suddenly the clouds parted and I got a glimpse of the blue sky. My chief secretary at the MSW (Colonel Hugh Muir) told me that a request for my transfer to the *Musician* staff had been received and 'they' would like me to move to International Headquarters as soon as I could be released.

It was sealed and settled on the spot. I commenced work in the Editorial Department in House Eight at the International Training College on Monday 3 November 1947.

The editor, Major Ben Blackwell, explained that *The Musician*, with the lifting of paper restrictions, was to be doubled in size – from 8 to 16 pages – and that he had asked for me as story gatherer and advertisements manager. What that meant I hadn't a clue, but I was going to work for a newspaper, and an Army paper at that. That was all that mattered.

When the news of my move was released the first letter of good wishes I received was from Major Saywell. There was not a mention of our earlier conversation, nor was it ever discussed again. It was, in fact, another nine years before the vacancy he hinted at was filled – and Captain Dean Goffin was brought to London from New Zealand to take up the appointment of national bandmaster, hitherto known as national band inspector.

Chapter 14

In Double Harness

THE Editorial Department was in a state of transition when I joined the staff. Since the end of the war Lieut-Colonel Alfred Gilliard had moved from the editorship of *The War Cry* (after 13 years) and Lieut-Colonel Arch R. Wiggins had become editor-in-chief in Australia after 13 years as editor of *The Musician*. In addition, a few weeks before my arrival, Colonel S. Carvosso Gauntlett, much-loved editor-in-chief and literary secretary, had been appointed territorial commander in Germany and was succeeded by Lieut-Colonel William G. Harris, who had served as editor-in-chief in the USA Eastern Territory some years before.

To find myself, a layman novice journalist, suddenly in the company of some of the Army's literary giants was an overwhelming experience. Here was I, comfortably installed in a little office at Denmark Hill, formerly used as a cadet's bedroom-cum-sitting room, actually being paid for doing the things I had always liked to do as an absorbing hobby. I could not believe it.

The giants were all around me. The editor of *The War Cry* was Brigadier Reginald Woods and his assistant editor was Major Sidney Williams; Lieut-Colonel Catherine Baird was editor of *The Young Soldier*, assisted by Major Bernard Watson, who was also editor of *The Scout And Guard*. Major Ben Blackwell had succeeded Lieut-Colonel Wiggins as editor of *The Musician* and his subeditor was Adjutant William Burrows, who had joined the staff two months before from the command of Kettering Corps.

The Warrior youth magazine was still going, with Lieut-Colonel Madge Unsworth as editor. The colonel also edited *All The World*; her assistant was Captain Gladys Moon. Other members of the editorial staff were Major Albert Kenyon, who brought a wealth of invaluable field experience with him, and Major Mrs Ivy Mawby.

Over the Literary Department 'fence' were Brigadier Frederick Coutts, who was assistant to the literary secretary and edited *The Officer*; Brigadier John Atkinson (*Company Orders*); Major Lily Sampson (*The Demonstrator*) and Miss Catherine Sturgess (*The Salvation Army Year Book*).

Lieut-Colonel Unsworth was the department's oldest inhabitant. She had been a member throughout her officership (35 years) and before that. Her father, Commissioner Isaac Unsworth, had been editor-in-chief some 40 years before, and her mother was a gifted writer, being recognised in the early days by her pen name of 'Mahlah'.

The colonel was of the old school and was delightfully quaint in her dealings with younger editorial assistants and in her approach to her work. Whereas everyone else seemed happy, when making up pages for the printer, to paste galleys to a dummy sheet, Lieut-Colonel Unsworth preferred the Dickensian method of attaching the copy to the page with the aid of pins. I cannot imagine a printers' union of today permitting such a practice!

Cath Sturgess's flair for detail and meticulous workmanship were greatly respected. These gifts, and her encyclopaedic knowledge of The Salvation Army, were ideally suited to editing *The Year Book* which she did efficiently for many years without official recognition because of her non-officer status.

The official photographer was Stanley Chapman, who had succeeded the legendary John Thomas Moyler after the war. This marked the beginning of a new era in Salvation Army camera coverage. Gone was the familiar tripod, antiquated carbide flash and dark, hooded head cover, into which and from which JTM disappeared and emerged from time to time.

Stan was permitted to obtain some new equipment and a well-stocked darkroom was set up next to his office-studio on the third floor of House Eight of the International Training College, which was still the temporary home of several departments of IHQ.

It was in Stan Chapman's office that the lunchtime tea club met. After a meal partaken of in one of the two small dining rooms by the big iron gates on the top avenue at Denmark Hill, members of the club took their china mugs along to Stan's domain and spent half an hour or so drinking his well-brewed beverage while sharing good fellowship and stimulating conversation.

How one joined I never discovered. Nor can I remember being asked for a membership fee or a contribution towards the tea, sugar or milk. All I know is that, on my first day in the department, Ben Blackwell took me along, introduced me to the assembling company and I was 'in', part of a unique fellowship the recollections of which have meant so much to me down the years.

On average, 12 of us managed to crowd into that limited space. There were one or two chairs, characteristically reserved for the ladies, but most of us stood. The exception was Major Blackwell. It seemed part of the ritual that he should occupy the armrest swivel chair which would rhythmically sway from side to side and then down and up as he made one of his logical, clear-minded little speeches or rocked uncontrollably with laughter at some brilliant shaft of wit supplied by Bernard Watson or Stan Chapman. The latter was the punster supreme.

To hear Ben Blackwell laugh was a health-giving sacrament. The sound came from deep down in his stomach and was instantly infectious. His face would wrinkle into a thousand folds as his boyish guffaw reverberated around the room, as if finding it impossible to escape. Soon we were rollicking in chorus, our irresponsible response funnier than the original remark ever was.

I stood quietly in the corner, hopefully out of view, content just to listen. To be in the presence of such people was an education in itself. They were all so different, but each made his or her own distinctive contribution to the discussion. Topics ranged from theology, politics and spiritism to England's chances of winning the Ashes, gardening, music and country life.

It was worth it all just to see these personalities of the pen, each bearing a household name in Army circles, take time off from their heavy workload and relentless concentration and relax in happy abandonment. For them this was unwinding therapy and became a popular and necessary pastime.

I received a warm and generous welcome to the *Musician* team, which Major Blackwell skippered with consummate skill, loving interest and shining example. Ben Blackwell was a craftsman of the finest order. Master of the neatly turned phrase and of descriptive simplicity, anything he wrote was worth reading. He was a gifted and lucid teacher in the art of Salvation Army journalism. This is a realm distinctly different from the general implications of the craft. Although a knowledge of basic English can be obtained from assiduous study, no school of journalism can adequately equip one for Salvation Army editorship.

In secular circles there are experts in every phase of activity. On the editorial side of production there are the reporters, the more senior interviewers, subeditors, galley readers, make-up specialists, proofreaders and editors – all to their separate tasks. The Salvationist editorial assistant has to be all of these.

Sidney Williams and Bernard Watson were among Ben Blackwell's pre-war pupils. After the war, Will Burrows and I were proud to join the 'class' and subsequently to pass such acquired wrinkles and skill on to others, thus ensuring the rich heritage of Salvation Army journalism.

Major Blackwell was blessed with the gift of infinite patience. When I took my first precious pages of copy to him he would instantly pause in whatever he was doing and take time to go through it with me.

One of my first assignments was to write up a short feature announcing the promotion to Glory of General Edward Higgins and give a brief synopsis of his life. I started off by saying: 'Readers will be sorry to learn of the promotion to Glory of General Edward Higgins...'.

The editor stopped reading aloud to give me my first lesson. 'We must never be sorry to learn of the promotion to Glory of a comrade. We must rejoice and be glad. The triumphant life has been lived. The supreme victory has been won. We may be saddened by news of his death, but never by his promotion to Glory.'

Thus I learned my first important lesson in the use of words and phrases as applied to Army life and service. I did not make the same mistake four months later when asked to prepare a tribute after the promotion to Glory of General George Carpenter. Nor have I made the same error since.

Another early lesson had to do with tautology. I allowed a report to go through which said: 'Bandsman Tom Smith was present and played a euphonium solo.'

'Of course he was present,' rebuked the major, 'or he would not have played the solo.'

That day I heard the phrase 'pig on bacon' for the first time.

As a 'news gatherer' I made a weekly visit to the other headquarters, mainly to mingle with the staff and glean titbits of musical information about various corps sections and individuals. I made it the same morning each week, so that in time the good folk at Tottenham Court Road, Vandon Street, Middlesex Street, Mare Street, Judd Street and the one remaining office block being used in Queen Victoria Street knew when to expect me. The IHQ departments at Denmark Hill also received frequent calls. The 'Comrades in Arms' feature (later 'Army People') greatly benefited from this 'round-up'.

The regular calls proved effective, but with further lifting of newsprint restrictions and increase of work in the office the practice was soon discontinued, much to my regret.

It was an unwritten observance that Salvationist editorial assistants did not use their names when writing in their own paper. Initials were all right, as noms de plume. It was Major Blackwell who suggested that I should insert the initial 'J' between my two Bs. His explanation was logical enough. All three of us were 'B.B.' he argued – Ben Blackwell, Bill Burrows and Brindley Boon. So that there should be no confusion, he would become 'H.B.B.', his assistant 'W.B.' and I 'B.J.B.' That abbreviation I have been happy to retain.

My first big assignment as a music critic was the first post-war bandmasters councils festival. This, described by General Albert

Orsborn, who presided, as 'the renaissance of Army music' took place at Clapton Congress Hall, which was packed out.

It was a crush on the platform. On a specially erected structure in front of the main stage sat Harlesden and Bristol Staple Hill Songster Brigades. In the centre of the platform was the International Staff Band, conducted by Major Bernard Adams at a national event for the first time, flanked by the bands of Tottenham Citadel and Rosehill. At the rear, on another and higher built-up platform were Clydebank and Kettering Bands.

When plans for the second national music camp were made I was invited to attend as an instructor. The editor decided that I should wear double harness and provide a day-to-day diary for *The Musician* at the same time. I relished the prospect and the challenge.

The previous year's pioneer event, held at Hadleigh, Essex, had been a great success. When Commissioner John Allan arrived in London to become Chief of the Staff, he brought vibrant memories of music camps held in the USA.

Almost 100 boys attended, sleeping in the far-from-luxurious huts, all of which had seen better days and had been in a state of decline for some years. But it was a beginning and none complained. Nine of the boys became officers, among them Dinsdale Pender, Eric Northwood, David Blackwell, George Church and Idwal Evans. Others became leaders of well known corps sections.

My colleague, Adjutant William Burrows, reported the week's activities and, although I was not involved, I was present at the final Sunday's meetings at Regent Hall and sensed that here was something that had come to stay, even if the music was confined to the *Second Series* Band Journal and the sophisticated age had not yet dawned.

Now in 1948, the Young People's Department at NHQ was turning its thoughts to that year's music camp. The venue presented a problem. As much as Salvationists were sentimentally attached to Hadleigh, it was not the ideal site.

Someone, perhaps half-heartedly, suggested the RAF station at Kenley, Surrey. In no time at all Major G. B. Smith had obtained an interview with a responsible group captain at the Air Ministry and was seated in that worthy officer's office pleading his cause.

Could approximately 100 fine, healthy specimens of Salvationist youth please have permission to take over Kenley Aerodrome for a week's intensive course of cultural studies? 'G.B.' felt it would do the boys good to come into close contact with this noted fighter station, made famous by Battle of Britain heroes. To him it was the ideal setting for such a youth adventure.

The group captain listened politely but did not appear to be terribly impressed. If he did succeed in visualising each camper as a potential RAF recruit he did not betray his enthusiasm. In fact, he curtly regretted that nothing could be done and manoeuvred the conversation towards a close, explaining that he could not give the major any more time as he had to catch a train for Brighton.

'A train, sir?' commented the ever-resourceful Major Smith. 'You cannot travel by train. I will drive you there.' In gambling parlance, this was his trump card.

The persuasive charm of the Salvationist won and soon the two men, proudly attired in their respective uniforms, were heading for the Surrey countryside, the Sussex Downs and the invigorating Brighton breezes.

Details of their conversation on the way have not been left on record. But we do know that, by the time the journey's end was reached, it was all signed, sealed and settled.

On Saturday 14 August at Whyteleaf, a little town nestling in the Surrey hills, a motor van ran a shuttle service from the local railway station to the aerodrome at Kenley, meeting every London train until all 167 students were safely booked in. The RAF had prepared well, even to the extent of posting a sergeant and eight airmen to care for the needs of the boys and their instructors.

The boys quickly settled down, in alphabetical order, in huts named after noted Army musicians: Slater, Coles, Marshall, Goldsmith, Östby, Fuller and Hawkes.

At the first get-together, the station commander (Wing Commander S. Mackenzie) graciously welcomed the students, offering them the freedom of the station while they were his guests. The only stipulation was that they were to keep clear of the airfield. This was still semi-operational and frequently used for planes landing and taking off.

There would appear to have been a breakdown in communications. The authorities had not been informed that the boys would be bringing brass instruments with them, and that they would be playing them for most of each day – and sometimes into the night. It was a surprised company of onlookers, therefore, which, on the Sunday morning, witnessed the mammoth band line up on the parade ground – 15 abreast because there were 15 trombones to accommodate – and march around the square under the leadership of the musical director. There were 66 cornets.

The station commander at Kenley was too trusting. His 'freedom' invitation was abused. The apple trees in the orchard were stripped in record time. When a cue slipped and ripped the beautiful green baize of the billiard table, the Naafi was put out of bounds. The 'last straw' was when a heavily sleeping inmate of one of the huts was removed from his bed and deposited in the middle of the forbidden airfield – still asleep!

In good faith the staff was billeted in the officers' mess. Few of us had enjoyed such privileges before, and there was more than one red face when one of the instructors, a noted composer, came to breakfast wearing his slippers and was promptly dispatched to become 'properly dressed'. I am still wondering how NHQ could afford the mess bills – or if they are still paying!

Kenley was a good idea but too ambitious. The next year we were back at Hadleigh.

We were ill-prepared for the first singing company camp. The idea originated with Songster Leader Muriel Wilson of Nelson, who, after the boys' camp at Hadleigh the previous year, wrote to the British Commissioner suggesting that a similar course might be held for girl singing company members. The enthusiastic Commissioner William Dalziel agreed and the National Young People's Department proceeded to plan.

Songster Leader Wilson (later Mrs Yendell, of Hendon), Senior-Major Mrs Ivy Mawby, Major Wesley Evans, Songster Mrs Winnie Watson, of Hadleigh Temple, and I constituted the technical staff, Mrs Mawby serving as musical director. Upon arrival at Sunbury we quickly evolved a course of study for the week, under the headings of 'Theory of Music' and 'The Art of Singing'. Eighty-five girls attended, including one from Edinburgh and her cousin from Glasgow.

What could we sing? The thoughtful Muriel Wilson had brought some singing company pieces with her and these were augmented by music we were able to borrow from neighbouring corps. Staines, Kingston and Twickenham came readily to our rescue, as they did so often in subsequent years with more substantial requests such as blackboards, easels and organs.

Songster Brenda Fowler, of Regent Hall, was our pianist and, from the very first torrent of sound in the first united rehearsal, we knew that music camps for girls were a good idea and had come to stay. The age compass was 12 to 17, the youthful, tuneful, well-pitched voices giving the singing a spiritually refined effect as well as cultural satisfaction.

Our star unison songs were 'Morning-Tide' ('Nymphs And Shepherds') and 'Through My Window', and we ventured into two parts for 'Such A Lovely World He Made' and 'Now The Day Is Over'. We had to have a camp chorus, of course, and on the spot Mrs Mawby wrote 'Singing We Go' to music left over from one of my RAF productions.

As the week progressed it became apparent that we needed something more ambitious for our end-of-the-week programmes. This necessity led to my hurriedly arranging a Chopin melody (popularly known as 'So Deep Is The Night') as a vocal solo with a three-part chorus backing. Again Mrs Mawby provided the lovely words and 'A Child's Prayer' became our *pièce de résistance*. Winnie Watson was the soloist.

This number was later published under the title of 'If Thou Art Near' and, with Maureen Davey as soloist, was recorded by the London Girl Singers. But it was born at Sunbury in August 1948.

With hindsight I suppose it is safe to conclude that only those interested in singing and with recognised ability would have dared to make the unknown way to Sunbury for that historic week. (The results achieved proved this to be the case.) But there was one young woman from Rugby who, when asked at the initial vocal test what part she sang, calmly replied 'bass'. I smiled benignly and reframed the question. Her reply was the same. I then struck middle C on the piano and asked her to sing it. She promptly pitched a note an octave lower. She *was* a bass singer!

I will refrain from naming this phenomenon for fear the disclosure may bring acute embarrassment to her, her children and possibly grandchildren.

The National Young People's Secretary (Brigadier Kaare Westergaard) and the staff felt that this memorable history-making week should end in worthy fashion. Nina and I persuaded our Chalk Farm comrades to host a weekend visit and we all made our way by bus, train and London's intricate Underground system to Chalk Farm, calling in at a private recording studio in Bond Street and London Zoo on the way.

At the studio we were joined by the British Commissioner who, during the week, had interrupted his furlough to spend an afternoon and evening with us at Sunbury. There must be a number of those unofficial recordings still about providing nostalgic memories for those whose voices are recorded on the old '78'.

Looking back, the spoken prelude was as important as the musical content. It said: 'This is Commissioner Dalziel speaking, introducing a group of young people's singing company members from The Salvation Army's first singing company camp at Sunbury-on-Thames, Middlesex. Here they are, singing their camp chorus, with Songster Leader Muriel Wilson of Nelson conducting. Songster Leader Brindley Boon of Chalk Farm is at the piano.'

'Singing We Go' was followed by 'Morning-Tide' and 'Such A Lovely World He Made' was on the other side. Muriel and I shared the conducting. Pioneers indeed!

All this is bound to bring a smile to the faces of descendants years later, but none shall take the glory from those trailblazers of long ago.

It was after a weekend at Swindon Gorse Hill that I returned on the Monday morning to be greeted by Major Bernard Adams at the front door of the International Training College with the news that my boss, Major Ben Blackwell, had been promoted to Glory on the Sunday.

He had entered hospital a few days before for a minor operation, which was successful. The unexpected embolism which caused his sudden death came as a great shock to us all. He was only 44.

It was Major Blackwell who had taken me to The Campfield Press for the first time, introduced me to the rituals of the press day and helped to get the smell of newsprint into my nostrils. He never failed to thrill to the unique aroma. Neither did I.

Conversation with this logically minded man began as soon as we met at St Pancras Station and took our places in the trundling stopping train to St Albans. They were the days of steam locomotives and, if the wind happened to be blowing from front to back, the carriage windows had to be kept securely shut for fear of being smoked out. There were no well-lit, comfortably heated open-plan coaches.

The journey went all too quickly for me and the conversation would continue as we walked from St Albans Station through the backstreets to the press. Names of side turnings intrigued Ben Blackwell and he noted some of them for characters he was introducing into the plays he was writing for his torchbearer group. That is why Edward Close, Flora Grove and others are *dramatis personae* as well as quiet streets in St Albans.

Our way took us along a narrow, barbed-wire fenced path through a field, the monotonous view suddenly relieved by the sight of a disused railway platform overrun with grass. The single line was still there but seldom, if ever, used.

This was a relic from Victorian days – Salvation Army Halt on the Hatfield-St Albans branch line on the Great Northern system, which served the Army's printing works for so long.

Rumour had it that William Booth and his frock-tunicked entourage sometimes alighted here when returning on a Monday morning from a northern campaign. The General revelled in the opportunity of helping to put *The War Cry* to bed, and in reading what the reporter had to say about him – adding to the copy if necessary!

'Salvation Army Halt' was still shown in the timetable in 1947.

The new editor of *The Musician* was Major Sidney Williams. Like his predecessor he was a skilled editorial craftsman and also an artist with brush, pencil and crayon, as well as words.

For me, life was a round of never-ceasing excitement. The national youth festivals took me to Clapton Congress Hall in a dual capacity – to report the events and conduct the united singing companies.

Other 'double harness' engagements found me at Highgate, for a North London divisional council for bandsmen and songsters and a 'Proclamation Festival' at night, and at Cardiff with the British Commissioner and Brigadier Alfred Lockyer.

I was in Scotland for the 1949 new year celebrations and, as a reporter, I was at Birmingham when the first inter-divisional councils for bandsmen for many years were held in the Kent Street Baths.

When it was announced that the International Staff Band was to visit Holland for Easter, the editor suggested that I should accompany the band as the editorial representative, furnishing *The Musician* with day-to-day coverage and also to report the Easter weekend leadership of the Chief of the Staff for *The War Cry*.

Permission was granted and, with notebook and pencil duly poised, I sailed from Harwich for the Hook of Holland with the band on its first overseas campaign for 23 years.

There were many highlights to report on that first post-war tour. At Rotterdam the band marched through the still bomb-scarred centre to be received at the town hall, and in a great state church gave the first performance, from manuscript copies, of 'Treasures From Tchaikovsky'. On Easter Saturday the band played to Queen Juliana and her daughters at the royal palace at Soestdijk before moving on to the British Airborne Cemetery outside Arnhem. Lieutenant Ray Bowes (one of the band's ex-servicemen) played 'The Last Post' and 'Reveille' and the band played 'O Rest In The Lord'.

The remainder of the period was spent at Utrecht, Hilversum, Almelo, Gröningen and Vlaardingen.

I remember the last day very well. The long journey from north to south included the crossing of the one-time Zuyder Zee along a 20-mile road built on the Aftsluitdijk, a dam separating the North Sea from the Ijsselmeer. A burst tyre halfway across meant a lengthy delay, but when we eventually arrived at Vlaardingen the corps band was still playing in the square, and still wearing the new clogs bought in the band's honour. These were later distributed to the visitors.

A few days after our return from Holland I was required to provide the commentary for the bandmasters councils festival – the first for 11 years to be held in the Royal Albert Hall.

The opportunity to hear the ISB and corps bands from Coventry City, Boscombe, Chalk Farm and Regent Hall caught the imagination and it was worth making the journey just to be present for the British premiere of 'Treasures From Tchaikovsky'.

On the next day, again at Mildmay, I nervously made my debut as a speaker at bandmasters and songster leaders councils. It was an ordeal, I willingly admit. I had provided technical talks in many divisional events, since travelling from the far West Wales to Neath as an airman to take part in Saturday afternoon councils led by Major Edward Saywell. But this, in the presence of The Salvation Army's leaders, many of its musical personalities and 840 sectional leaders of the British Territory, was quite different.

By this time I had a new colleague on *The Musician*. Senior-Captain Burrows and then Senior-Major Kenyon had moved to other papers and Second-Lieutenant Will Pratt had come to join our team from command of Sheerness Corps in Kent. I was entrusted with the responsibility of teaching him some of the editorial know-how that I had learned from Ben Blackwell and Sidney Williams.

Mine was an easy task. The lieutenant was a 'natural' who needed little tuition. We shared lots of fun and fellowship in those days of eager apprenticeship and have remained good friends ever since. When I went off the paper he took over 'Round and About', and 'Observer' became 'Onlooker'. They were his eyes that appeared above the column for so long.

After visiting Cambridge Heath and Boscombe to feature music sections of those corps in the 'Meet the Music Makers' series, I was asked to interview Lieut-Colonel Leonard Woodward who, after 34 years as a missionary in Celebes and 46 years as a Salvation Army officer, had just returned to his homeland to enter retirement.

It was a deeply moving story. Two months before I met him the colonel, during annual congress meetings, had stood with government officials to review a march past which included 15 flute bands and a brass band – a procession in honour of the well-loved, distinguished-looking bearded white man who for so long had been doctor, teacher, friend and spiritual shepherd. There had been no Salvation Army when Leonard Woodward arrived in Celebes.

I was especially interested in the musical side of his ministry and gleaned sufficient detail from the interview to prepare an article which I called 'Twenty Years Of Flute Bands'.

A quarter of a century before, a Menadonese schoolteacher, who taught in one of the schools opened by the colonel, made a flute out of bamboo from the bush. A good player himself, he experimented with his home-made instrument until satisfied with its efficiency. He then sent the boys into the bush to collect bamboo and gave instructions in the making of a flute.

He measured each bamboo cane for length and wind holes, and then left it to the boys. As each instrument was completed it was tested, and destroyed if not up to standard. Work went on until each boy possessed a flute of required merit. The flutes were called 'sulings', some 'small' and others 'great', the difference in size denoting a variation in pitch of an octave.

To complete the feature, the editor suggested that I should have a photograph taken playing one of 'Woodward's woodwinds'. Stan Chapman promptly complied. Neither of us knew that I was holding the flute the wrong way and that it should have gone from the mouth towards the right shoulder!

It was left to a Campfield Press reader to spot the mistake. He sought a second opinion, that of Sam Perry, an expert flautist and fellow employee, who confirmed the error.

It was too late for the feature to be changed or another picture to be substituted, but there was enough time for the caption to be altered to read: 'The writer, uninstructed either in the art of holding or playing the flute, makes a vain attempt to blow a note on one of Lieut-Colonel Woodward's instruments.'

As the article was accredited to 'Observer' few realised my identity. In fact, the New York *Musician* repeated the feature, complete with picture, identifying the writer as 'Senior-Major Ernest Rance'. I am sure he would have known the correct way to hold and blow a bamboo flute!

Participation in the third music camp – there were two at Hadleigh that year – and the second singing company camp at Sunbury completed a busy summer season. The last-named event, possibly as a result of reports of the previous year's successful experiment, attracted more than 100 students.

There was no real let-up in editorial duties, until a Friday in September 1949 when I farewelled from the department to enter the Standard Bearers Session at the training college the next morning.

It was only a few yards' walk across the green at Denmark Hill, but for me it was a much greater step. What was described by General Albert Orsborn as 'God's disturbing call' had caught up with me.

Chapter 15

The Eleventh Hour

SALVATION Army officership always fascinated me. My earliest hero-worshipping was centred upon those good folk, men and women, who were stationed at our corps. Looking back, perhaps through rose-tinted spectacles, they were all lovely people. Instinctively I wanted to be like them.

I came to public work the hard way. It was a constant fight against shyness. The memory of my first testimony has never left me. My father, the band sergeant, was leading a praise meeting and, when all appeals for volunteers to witness had failed, he signalled to me, up till then taking refuge behind my tenor horn, to come to his rescue. I dared not disobey.

A secular ditty at that time declared:

Oh, it ain't goin' to rain no more, no more,
It ain't goin' to rain no more;
So put a penny in the old man's hat,
It ain't goin' to rain no more.

With typical ingenuity someone had converted the words to Army purposes and it became:

Oh, I'm blessedly saved,
I'm sure, I'm sure,
I'm blessedly saved, I'm sure;
I know my sins are all forgiven,
I'm blessedly saved, I'm sure.

This was the chorus which came to me in my panic. With wobbling knees and trembling voice I stood to give my first testimony in song. To my utter horror I heard myself singing:

Oh, I'm blessedly shaved,
I'm sore, I'm sore,
I'm blessedly shaved, I'm sore...

I never did finish. As, only that week, I had been given my first shave, with a cut-throat razor, by our deputy bandmaster, 'Joe' Nicholson, and I was still unable to move my jaw with any degree of freedom, I was able to sing the amended words with feeling – or without it!

My first sermon was preached when I was a 16-year-old corps cadet. It was a Sunday afternoon address and my topic was 'Three Cheers'. Where my text came from or what the 'cheers' were I have long since forgotten, but it was another victory.

Once, in my Methodist Sunday school days, I attended a meeting at Kilburn 1 Corps where a family friend was 'specialing' for the day. In the prayer meeting the corps officer took the trouble to speak to me. On learning of my Methodist interests and something of my Army background, he told my parents, 'I covet sonny for the Army. I think he'll be an officer one day.' At that time the possibility seemed remote, but I have often thought of those prophetic words.

I had not been a Salvationist long before I became aware of a recurring feeling that I should be an officer. Nina and I often discussed the subject. We both sensed a call to full-time service. After we had been 'keeping company' – as they said in those delightful days – for some years and began to plan a married life together, we made our first application.

We tried to make our intentions clear. We were planning to marry and desired to spend our future in the Army as officers. Could there be some understanding that when we were married our application would be considered? This prospect would save us the expense of buying a home. It all seemed logical. But we were asking too much. Our request was rejected.

Married cadets were discouraged in those days. We were advised to apply separately as single candidates. This seemed unreasonable and we declined to act upon the suggestion.

At that time (1937) we had no other thought but to serve as corps officers but, trying to find a solution to the dilemma, we volunteered for other work. Again we were disappointed. In the face of this double blow we went ahead with our marriage plans, spending our meagre savings on furnishing a flat.

Still the call persisted and a year after our wedding we applied a third time. By the time consideration could be given to our request the Second World War had started and as we were both of calling-up age the matter was dropped.

We were reconciled to serving as local officers and making the most of what we considered a second-best future. In fact, we wanted the matter to fade from our minds. We never talked about it. But God had other plans and used good people to fulfil his purposes in our lives.

My editorial colleagues never knew what their exemplary Christianity meant to us, or how the old longing returned. Colonel William Harris led a team of champions of our cause and although by this time – 12 years after our original application – we were both over the regulation age for cadets to enter the training college, he pleaded our case incessantly and with eloquent persuasion.

After many months of correspondence, a period of tension, frustration and considerable heartache – especially as by now there was our son John to think of as well – the miracle happened. The door of hope was prised open at the 11th hour and we were accepted for the next session.

But it wasn't to be as easy as that. There were formalities to be observed. Married candidates were not permitted to sell their homes for two years after entering training. This was a tremendous blow. We needed the money such a sale would bring to buy uniforms and support us while we were in the International Training College. My parents kindly offered to take care of John for the period we were in training. Setback followed disappointment in quick succession until, at long last, thanks to the overwhelming generosity of office colleagues and the faith of other good friends, we received intimation that the way was 'now clear' for us to enter the training college.

It was then panic stations. The session was already six weeks old. The training principal's patience was nearly exhausted. It was made patently clear that if I did not arrive at Denmark Hill by the end of that week the acceptance would be cancelled. It was now or never. There would never be another chance.

What a week! The men's tailoring department at Judd Street made me a cadet's uniform in two days. I worked long into the night to bring my *Musician* features up to date. The hurried goodbyes from the office were sad, but I was deeply thankful for every kindness shown. Second thoughts assured me that I would still be at Denmark Hill and that I was bound to get a glimpse of them all from time to time as they passed along the top avenue to and from the canteen.

During the week I made several trips across the grounds to move the personal belongings I had accumulated during my two years in the department to the little room allocated me in House 6. I was to become a 'single married' until my wife joined me later.

There was no time to farewell from the corps and it was with a heavy heart that I left Nina to collect the £10 required as a contribution towards our training and – I understood – for our lieutenants' uniforms at commissioning. Even £5 per cadet was a lot of money. Educational grants were unknown. Corps comrades, headed by our good friend A.W.P., splendidly came to my wife's aid, although I gathered there was a touch of regret that they were losing a songster leader and a singing company leader, whatever the reason.

On the Saturday morning I made my lone way across London to the International Training College. There was an Edwardian music hall song which perpetuated the termini of one of the first motor-bus routes, No 68. It was called 'From Chalk Farm To Camberwell Green'. That was the route I took that morning, mainly because once my overweight, bulky suitcase had been safely deposited under the stairs I could enjoy the journey until the junction of Denmark Hill and Champion Park was reached. By this time, of course, the original 68 limit had been extended to South Croydon.

I received my baptism of fire that afternoon. My training corps was Hoxton, which local comrades still delighted in calling 'The Grecian'.

As we stood among the market stalls to proclaim the message of salvation we were greeted with a deluge of overripe tomatoes. My new tunic seemed to take the full blast of the salvo. I wondered what had hit me – both literally and figuratively.

The soldiers of the corps were kind-hearted and generous. The Sunday dinners were a joy to behold and to devour the tasty chicken dishes was particularly delightful. I remember the dismay and disappointment I felt when a fellow cadet pointed out to me, in a dingy Hoxton side street, the somewhat dilapidated-looking theatre from which BBC organist Sandy Macpherson every Sunday morning broadcast *The Chapel In The Valley*. And to think of all those chirping birds and other country sounds heard over the air! My simple faith was shaken.

Training days were thrilling. Rationing was still very much with us. Precious clothing coupons were required to be surrendered before our cadets' uniforms could be made. Ration books containing food coupons were placed in the custody of the college authorities and each Saturday morning we paraded in the dining hall to receive our allowance of butter (or margarine) and sugar for the week. We were permitted to keep the sweet coupons. It was part of a daily routine for cadets to carry their bowls of sugar and dishes of margarine (or butter) between their house and meals.

Leaving for training corps on a Wednesday afternoon was a ritual. After a hurried lunch we paraded on the top avenue, in brigades, answered the roll-call, came smartly to attention, left-wheeled and marched determinedly through the gateway into the great world beyond. Each brigade had its own flag and the formidable procession was headed by the Field Training Officer (Major Harry Warren) who, with his faithful concertina, led us into battle to the strains of 'On We March', or some such popular marching chorus.

At the gate the major would jump nimbly to one side, salute the colours as they passed and review his marching troops as they went into action. What an energetic warrior he was! And what a voice he had!

Some brigades turned right up Champion Park; others turned left to follow the road past King's College Hospital and towards Camberwell Green until the respective bus or tram stops were reached. In the first half of the session, when we were at Hoxton, we travelled by the No 35 bus. After the Christmas recess we took a tram to our training corps at Nunhead, although there were times when we marched all the way, I seem to remember.

One of us would be responsible for the 'corps basket', containing our tea. 'Twitchin Pie' was a regular delicacy, but occasionally this was augmented by some luxury such as a tomato or a piece of celery. Yes, the pie inherited its name from the genial bandmaster at Regent Hall who was the managing director of the firm of provision merchants who supplied the tasty morsels.

Those travelling to young people's training corps had the added responsibility of carrying a clothes horse, from behind which puppet shows could be presented. It was not easy to mount the stairs to the top deck of a crowded London bus with such a property tucked underneath your arm!

The weekly Thursday parade to Camberwell Citadel for the central holiness meeting was a much more elaborate affair. The march was headed by a model C-coated party – some half a dozen in number – and other men cadets, carrying battery-powered lamps, would be placed at strategic points in the procession to make sure the cadet bandsmen were able to see their music.

We took the main road. The traffic did not seem to mind crawling to a halt. As a march was ended the concertinas and voices embarked upon a chorus, the happy marching host kept in step by the crisp, echoing taps of the percussionists.

The return route to the college was via the backstreets. At first the band was in 'full cry', but when objections were raised by the residents of the Grove Lane vicinity, the marching aid was reduced to a drum tap. When further complaints made it necessary for this to be discontinued, we marched in silence until the lights of Champion Park and the silhouette of the college came in view. The marching host then began to hum a chorus, which was treated to an artistic crescendo, the whole company taking up the words when the full fortissimo was reached.

As we marched away from Lomond Grove (where the Camberwell hall was situated) and turned left at Peabody Buildings we came almost immediately upon a fried fish shop. There was no sneaking off to give ourselves a treat. The proprietor seemed to know this for, as we passed, he invariably held up two unsuspecting pieces of fish duly battered and all ready to be dropped into the sizzling pan. He knew well how to tempt us at that hour on a Thursday night!

Work section duties had my undivided attention each Friday morning for six weeks at a time. These consisted in turn of scrubbing (and keeping tidy) the office of the cadet sergeant-major (Ray Steadman-Allen), caring for drains, the back stairs and the assembly hall and being dining room server and field stores orderly.

I have memories of work section periods resembling fancy-dress parades. Permission to wear what we wished resulted in a variety of 'costumes'. Many went for the orthodox overalls. Others preferred jeans, with tops to match. There were bandsmen's old-fashioned festival tunics in profusion, while ex-servicemen seized the opportunity to wear out their former proud uniform.

One erstwhile RAF pilot wore his old battledress, his wings and DFC ribbon still adorning the blouse. Other cadets were content to display campaign medals on demob suits. There were khaki jackets in abundance, as well as colourful service berets.

The SSB – which sounded ominously like a secret military task force but really stood for 'Special Service Brigade' – occupied a period of our training. This consisted of Saturday night open-air meetings in Leicester Square and the Soho area, with concentrated late-night 'raids' on theatreland and open-air evangelism in Hyde Park.

This last-named activity at Marble Arch was the devoted responsibility of Major John Tattersall, who kept a fatherly eye on us, leaving us to our own tactical devices but intruding with a wise suggestion or tactful correction. One Sunday I was giving out 'I Must Have The Saviour With Me', aided by a song scroll from which the large crowd could follow the words.

When we had reached the refrain Major Tattersall saw fit to interrupt.

'Just a minute, cadet!' he ordered. 'We're singing "I will go without a murmur". That's not possible, is it? Shouldn't we be singing "I will go although I murmur"?'

Now, I have always had a 'thing' about altering words which songwriters have written and I could not agree that we changed the original sentiment of this song. Some good-humoured banter followed, which interested and entertained the crowd, and we resolved the altercation by shaking hands and the major singing his preferred correction and I staying with the original. He insisted on making it a duet! We lost a good friend when Major Tattersall was promoted to Glory one evening in November 1949, after leading the Hyde Park meeting in the afternoon.

Spiritual days were hallowed occasions, always interesting and full of challenge. They were led, in turn, by the General, the Chief of the Staff (Commissioner John J. Allan) and Training Principal (Commissioner John Bladin). Each, although different, brought his own measure of experience and personality to the task, as well as a compelling sense of stewardship.

On one of these days, conducted by the Chief, the lights went out midway through the afternoon session. It was a bitter winter's day and a power cut was responsible for the power failure. A quantity of candles were quickly secured and placed at various focal points on the platform and, in the semi-darkness, the programme continued.

Commissioner Bladin was a great training principal. To me he was something of a swashbuckling romantic figure. The very name of his home corps in Australia, Korumburra, had an enchanting 'Treasure Island' ring about it. He had seen the world as a Salvation Army officer.

What a wealth of knowledge, experience and deep understanding he was able to bring to the International Training College, especially to sessions containing young men who themselves had so recently tasted the horror of war and travelled the world in its frightening cause.

172

In-Sundays were relaxed treats and very necessary diversions. Colonel William Cooper, Major John Moyse (second side officer), Major Warren and Senior-Captains Geoffrey Dalziel and Gordon Cox were masters of inspiring, challenging confrontation. Old and New Testament characters – infamous as well as famous – came in for more than their fair share of illustrative treatment, but the end product was always the same: we saw ourselves as we really were and wanted to do something about it.

We had most to do with the sectional officers, the two senior-captains. Both Geoffrey Dalziel and Gordon Cox were dynamic leaders. They were front-line fighters who never flinched from the battle's heat and fearlessly led their troops into action, whether it was amid the teeming West End multitudes or in the crowded bar of a country pub, a busy marketplace or the front room of a backslider's home. They set an example, and we would have followed them to the ends of the earth.

I had most to do with Senior-Captain Cox. Always respecting my 'status' as the oldest cadet of the session, he was at the same time uncompromising in the demands he made upon me, especially in field training activities. To be called upon to pray when standing in a street with eight other cadets was not an ordeal. To open my eyes at the end of the prayer only to find that the others had moved on, leaving me to carry out a 'single bombardment' for half an hour, was not so easy. Perhaps it did me no harm.

Only once did I disobey an order from the captain. A party of us were at Gillingham for the weekend and a series of open-air bombardments was held in the busy shopping centre on the Saturday afternoon. I knew we had to be ready for anything, especially when Senior-Captain Cox was about, but my readiness (and willingness) was taxed to the limit when, as we formed up behind the brigade flag to march to the hall (in single file), I was detailed to go into a crowded Woolworths store to announce the meetings. My courage deserted me once I was beyond the swing door. The cadets marched on, singing as they went. I bought a packet of razor blades and caught them up.

When a field day was planned each side was divided, the men going to St Albans or East Grinstead. I was in the half that visited the latter country town. Our coming rather disturbed the peace of the quiet Sussex community. Carried away by a measure of exaggerated enthusiasm, some of our party created signs painted in large whitewashed capital letters showing directions to the hall and times of the meetings.

The enthusiasts were not so sure it was a good idea when puzzled motorists on the main A22 from London to the south coast were suddenly confronted with what they thought to be new road signs and had to leave their cars to carry out a closer scrutiny. Soon this one and only thoroughfare through the town was blocked. The police were sympathetic to our cause but devastating in their condemnation. It took much longer for the 'culprits' to clean away the offending announcements than it had taken to write them!

We spent the morning and afternoon chasing the 'Devil' through the narrow streets. Like the notorious 'Scarlet Pimpernel', we sought him here, there and everywhere, determined to catch him.

It must have been a terrifying experience for the shoppers, some from remote villages, on a quiet Wednesday morning suddenly to encounter 'Old Nick' himself, resplendent in silk satin attire, sprouting horns and a tail and carrying his trident of office. He darted in and out among them, followed by a posse of Salvation Army lads declaring, 'We'll get you before the day is out!' The good folk were glad to take cover in the already crowded shops, and those about to leave the premises were happy to hurry back. It must have been good for business.

At night the easily distinguishable adversary was duly captured and delivered to the open-air ring. The onlookers, as well as the captain, seemed to relish the rare sight of the Devil in chains. Triumphantly he was given a place of honour at the front of the march to the hall and later emerged happily in his uniform to testify!

The end of October found me in a party on a ten-day campaign at Paisley Citadel. Senior-Captain Gordon Cox was in charge and, in the absence of a sergeant, I was appointed orderly. There were ten of us.

We arrived late on a Friday night and went into action early the next morning with an 'advertising' march and bombardment. From then on there was no let-up.

At the initial open-air meeting, near the famous abbey with crowds listening, the captain immediately put me 'on the spot' by announcing that one of the cadets, Johann Wielemaker from Amsterdam, would speak in Dutch and that I would translate his message. I went cold. My knowledge of that language was limited to simple equivalents of 'Yes', 'No', 'Thank you' and 'I need to go to bed', gleaned from my visit with the staff band earlier that year.

The captain seemed to be smiling at my obvious discomfort. There was no need for alarm, he whisperingly assured me. We sang a chorus once or twice while he explained the gimmick to me. It was very simple. Wielemaker would begin by asking the onlookers if any of them spoke Dutch. When there was no response (hopefully!), I would then proceed to give *my* testimony and Wielemaker would interpret *me*, sentence by sentence. But I must remember to have the last word.

No one owned up to speaking or understanding Dutch and so we came through the ordeal. I can still sense the admiring eyes of my unsuspecting and surprised colleagues at their discovery of my linguistic talent.

The Sunday meetings ended with 96 seekers at the mercy seat, and many moving reconciliation scenes. Some of the comrades had not spoken to each other for years. Senior-Captain Cox was anxious to cement these decisions and decided that the following evening's meeting would include a Love Feast.

Early on the Monday morning he took me along to the main street where the two of us engaged in double bombardments. The captain walked in one gutter, I in the other, shouting to each other across the road above the noise of the traffic. The conversation went something like this:

Captain: 'Hallo! What are you selling today?'
Cadet: 'I'm not selling anything. I'm giving it away.'
Captain: 'What is this bargain you're giving away?'

175

Cadet: 'God's free and full salvation. It is offered without money and without price.'

We moved along as we proclaimed the gospel in this way. The street was fairly long. Our ingenuity was severely tested to keep going. At least mine was.

This phase of evangelising the town over, Senior-Captain Cox then sought my help in preparing the Love Feast. Neither of us had experienced such an Army ceremony although we had both heard of it and its effectiveness in early-day salvation warfare. Back at the hall we shut ourselves in the officers' room with a typewriter and reams of paper, not 'coming to ground' until the evening's order of service was finalised and duplicated.

With no precedent to go on, we produced a Cox-Boon ceremony, which seemed to meet the need. To share fellowship with corps comrades as they sought to settle long-standing feuds and to begin again in deeper consecration was a moving, unforgettable experience. Biscuits were broken, offered and accepted. Water was meaningfully sipped and the ordinary tumbler passed on to someone of one's significant choice. No sacrament ever had greater meaning.

The soldiers of Paisley Citadel – and the cadets – made new covenants with each other and with God. The ceremony was sealed with one's signature at the bottom of the personal pledge included on the order of service. My big regret is that I failed to keep a copy of that Love Feast programme.

It was an eventful campaign. A school visit resulted in five of the older boys professing conversion in the classroom, two of them linking up with the Army and joining the young people's band. One brought another school pal and led him to the mercy seat. He too became a YP band member.

The news, a few years later, of the sudden passing of Major Gordon Cox, by then field training officer at the ITC, had a shattering effect upon me – and all of my cadet vintage. He was still under 40.

Once more in residence at Denmark Hill, we moved swiftly towards the session's halfway mark. In the Christmas pageant I was given the part of 'Mr Churl', a Scrooge-like character who lived in a row of terrace houses, the fronts of which were deftly erected on the Camberwell platform. My next-door neighbour was Cadet Ruth Higgins. We seemed to spend precious time in the first part of the production going in and out of our respective homes in the manner of the familiar weather duo.

My first memory of 1950 is of the cadets being conscripted to assist in the great Croydon campaign. Spearheading the seven-day attack were the National Campaigner (Major Thomas Jewkes) and his assistant, Captain Denis Hunter. Divisional and corps officers, headed by the Divisional Commander (Lieut-Colonel William Grottick) and his wife, attended each day and for some of the time we were in the thick of it.

Stage appearances at intervals in cinema matinees, a torchlight procession through the main streets and school visitations were highlights, and the evening evangelistic meetings were enhanced by a divisional youth band, conducted by Major Albert Goldsmith, and a campaign chorus led by Senior-Major Wesley Evans. The campaign resulted in 203 adult seekers – 57 of them non-Salvationists – and 150 children.

Also in that January the International Staff Band conducted a Camberwell central holiness meeting for the first time and how proud we were to fall in behind the band as it led the parade from the college to the citadel! That night I heard Dean Goffin's meditation, 'The Light Of The World', for the first time. It had recently been approved for publication by the International Music Board and was played from manuscript copies. The effect was impressively electrifying.

A BBC *Sunday Half-Hour* community singing programme was broadcast from the women's dining hall and was picked up in places as far distant and as far apart as Singapore, Africa and Scandinavia.

Since Christmas John Snook and I, during free-time periods, had concentrated on learning to play the concertina in the basement of House Seven (the married quarters). At the conclusion of each lesson we went into action, playing our latest pieces as we mounted the back stairs to join our wives and comrades. Handel Everett, who, with his

177

wife Lily, was an expert on the instrument, treated us more kindly than we deserved.

By the time Easter approached, John and I considered ourselves 'ready for the fray' and decided to take our respective 'English' and 'Triumph' models with us to Manchester. Seeing that we were both in the party we could give each other confidence, we thought. Our good intentions were shattered, however, on the first evening of the campaign when Senior-Captain Dalziel decreed that I, with my concertina, would lead a group of local corps comrades through another maze of streets. 'Standard Bearers' certainly learned the hard way.

I know that no one would have appreciated the joke more than Ben Blackwell, whose concertina had been kindly loaned to me for the duration of my training days.

A few weeks before commissioning, Lieut-Colonel Gordon Mitchell invited me to write the session's dedication song. I had already provided a number of songs and choruses for events throughout the training period, including 'There's A Challenge Ringing Out Along The Highway', which we used to march to corps and on other field activity. I had already prepared topical material for the commissioning pageant and the farewell festival. But this was different.

The third floor of House Seven was unoccupied and I remember borrowing the key of one of the rooms and, at odd intervals, shutting myself away amid the stored tables, chairs and washstands, asking the Lord to help me to produce something worthy of the great ceremony. In other words, I put myself in the way of inspiration. 'I Would Be Thy Holy Temple' was the result. I sought to put on paper all that I was feeling in my heart at the moment. The years of disappointment, the struggles, the financial problems – all these negatives were forgotten as I reaffirmed my utter dependence upon God and, still so fearful for the future, desired that nothing should 'stain my commission'.

Two hundred and forty cadets were commissioned and appointed that Friday afternoon, 12 May 1950. In his message (written in the midst of an Australian campaign), the General reminded us: 'You are to carry the lovely Army colours, with their message of salvation and holiness, out into a needy world.'

As in a dream, Nina and I heard the training principal appoint us to Sandwich.

That year the pageant and dedication service, in that order, took place in the evening. The pageant was colourful, with its Mile End Waste scene ('penny-farthings', baked chestnuts stall, flower girls and Victorian policemen all complete), the deep, gruff voice of the Founder played by Major Harry Warren and the Army flag being taken to all parts of the world.

When the beginning of the work on the continent by the Maréchale was enacted, I, as narrator, heard my voice reverberating around the vast auditorium as I declared: 'You see before you the actual flag, sewn together by the Army Mother, held by the great-granddaughter of the Founder.' Fleur Booth (by now the assistant sergeant-major for the next session) received thunderous applause.

At last, 'The Flag Marches On!' From every entrance came the new officers, converging on the aisles and treading purposefully towards the huge stage. Second-Lieutenant Steadman-Allen, also commissioned that afternoon, was at the grand organ, and hundreds of tiny flags fluttered from the great dome, to be eagerly seized by the audience. From the narrator's vantage point I had a grandstand view, and was deeply moved.

'I Dedicate Myself To Thee' had its premiere that night, after which the Chief of the Staff challenged us to 'watch and remember'.

The Saturday farewell festival, at Clapton Congress Hall, brought its usual measure of fun and excitement for the participants.

Once again the Army colours were the focal point of the preliminaries, a tattered, faded banner – the original flag of Poplar (number three) and the oldest surviving corps – being handed down a long line of representative Salvationists as the cadets sang 'See The Colours Go Passing By'. From age to youth, from musician to missionary, from scout to nurse, the flag of truth was handed on.

The festival that followed must have had a predominantly nautical flavour. The male voice party sang a medley of 'Salvation Navy' songs ('converted' words to popular tunes) and I, for the first time for many years, gave 'The Unsinkable Boat' as a monologue, accompanying myself at the piano. The next time I gave this item was at the Standard Bearers' reunion at Catford 25 years later.

Final Sunday meetings at Camberwell, culminating with community singing in front of the flood-lit college tower, were followed by the impressive flag ceremony – we were the 21st session at Denmark Hill – and then packing for pastures new.

Nine happy, hectic months were over. Seven of us left Charing Cross Station for the Canterbury Division. What an invasion!

Chapter 16

Where the Curfew Still Tolls

THE quarters at Sandwich could have been no nearer the hall. They were, in fact, linked by a common wall, the two buildings having been erected many years before by a local grocer, to whose dependants we paid rent.

The hall had been newly decorated and looked a picture of attractive cleanliness when we carried out a tour of inspection soon after our arrival. The green and cream colour scheme brought welcome brightness and a new piano caught my eye and commanded my immediate attention and respect. The old-fashioned 'tortoise' type combustion stove was the remaining relic of the past.

In that moment of discovery we thanked God for our predecessors, Senior-Captain and Mrs William Robinson, whose initiative and hard work with limited financial resources had effected the miracle.

A small room at the rear at the platform was utilised by the bandsmen. The officers' room was the quarters living room, complete with black-leaded range. Our 'bathroom' was a narrow-width 'tub' which hung on the outside wall just inside the back gate. A tearful six-year-old John recoiled from the idea of having his nightly bath 'out there', but felt somewhat happier when assured that the zinc receptacle would be duly installed in front of the living-room fire.

Narrow Loop Street opened at one end to the main Canterbury road and led in the other direction to The Butts, where in medieval times men of the town practised the archery in which English bowmen excelled at Crécy and Agincourt.

It was a street of contrasts. Elizabethan houses, their overhanging upper storey deceiving many a large-vehicle driver who had no alternative but to reverse and seek the safer if longer route of the highway, stood close to the hall. A Tudor cottage standing in the grounds of a farm which was adjacent to a slaughterhouse, an establishment which manufactured plastic products and a pickle factory backing on to a disused tannery completed the picture.

Market day brought great activity to our town of nearly 4,000 inhabitants. Our little street, usually so quiet, resounded to the clop of animals' hooves as, prompted by Bob the well-trained sheepdog and surreptitiously prodded by youthful assistants, bulls, cows, sheep and pigs made their unwilling way past our front door, seeming to be aware of the fate that awaited them.

Some were successful in breaking ranks. It was not unknown for bulls to career into our back garden by way of the side gate. The imprint of many a hoof was left upon my wife's precious plot before the possibly quite friendly creatures were persuaded that they were trespassing and 'went quietly'.

Sandwich is historic. I knew that, of course, but it was not until holidaymakers and overseas tourists began knocking at our door to obtain information about the cottage 'museum piece' next door that I realised how far the interest in one of the ancient cinque ports extended.

There was the Canadian lumberjack, the Australian housewife, the American businessman, the two Swedish youths who worked side by side in a match factory and the New Zealand-born Salvation Army officer who, a week or two later, sailed to take command of a far-off battlefield. With camera and guidebook they, and many like them, invaded our little town and spent an hour or two capturing something of the glory which belonged to Sandwich 500 years ago before it ceased to be the premier port of England.

One day I stood halfway across the toll bridge which linked Sandwich with the Isle of Thanet – vehicles with three or more wheels, whether horse-drawn, pushed or driven were still to be paid for – and gazed upon a scene unique in all Britain. From this spot I could see the places which saw the arrival of Christianity in England and the setting up of the law in these islands.

In a meadow two miles to the north-east, close to the village of Ebbsfleet where English history began with the landing of Hengist and Horsa more than 1,500 years ago, stands a stone cross erected to commemorate the arrival of St Augustine a century and a half later. North-west from the bridge, a mile away, are the ruins of the Roman camp at Richborough (Rutupiae) which, established in AD 43, became the military and civil administrative base for the whole of Britain and remained so for 300 years.

Thus in this quiet corner of the 'Garden of England' the link between church and state was established.

It is not beyond the realms of possibility that some of the Roman soldiers stationed at the original camp had been on overseas duty in Jerusalem on the first Good Friday. This was a thought that was always with me whenever I was in close proximity to Richborough. I liked to think that somewhere in that garrison there may have been a Christian convert who was the first to bring the gospel to these shores.

'You will find little mention of our town in the history of Kent,' a local authority told me. 'We were too busy defending England,' he added, with a twinkle which may have been handed down from an ancestor who, as a boy, watched Thomas à Becket being smuggled away to France and 30 years later greeted Richard Coeur de Lion back from his imprisonment in Austria.

There was probably much in what he said, for the wide expanse of beach, privately owned at Sandwich Bay some three miles from the Guildhall which established the centre of the town, has ever been a focal point for would-be invaders. Five hundred and thirty years ago 4,000 Frenchmen landed, pillaged the town and immediately re-embarked after murdering the mayor and many of the citizens. To this day the Mayor of Sandwich wears a black robe and carries a black wand as a reminder of the events.

A hundred years ago something happened to bring a state of mild panic to the town. The curfew, which for centuries had rung out from the tower of St Peter's Church, was silenced. So strong was the voice of public opinion that after two months the corporation restored the custom which, with the obvious exception of a period during the

Second World War, has been observed ever since. Tradition dies hard in Sandwich.

Many tourists express the wish to see the signpost bearing the strange amalgamation 'Ham Sandwich'. It causes amusement and the visitor cannot refrain from taking a 'snap'. It is a fact that Ham is a little village a mile or two outside the town and may – or may not – be coincidentally named. It was an Earl of Sandwich who gave the town's name to the tasty morsel now so popular. He was such an inveterate gambler, it is alleged, that he could not be persuaded to leave his game for meals. Instead he gave instructions for two slices of bread with meat between them to be brought to him.

We came to know Sandwich and to understand something of its background and tradition. Its winding streets, in which it is not difficult to become lost, fascinated me. Moat Sole, Holy Ghost Alley and Paradise Row were names with a history I was never able to discover.

When at 11 o'clock each night the street lamps were extinguished, I wondered if the shades of the past held a rendezvous at Gallow's Field, where men were burned alive and witches killed, or near the Guestling Stream, where women criminals were drowned, or at the King's Lodging, where stayed the first Queen Elizabeth, and her father (Henry VIII) before her.

We inherited a thriving corps. There were 44 soldiers on the roll, with a few more regular attenders who felt they could not commit themselves to become Salvationists.

The smartly uniformed band and songster brigade numbered 16 and 23 respectively and were a credit to their leaders, Bandmaster Roland Sole and Songster Leader Stanley Kenton, both sons of Kentish soil. These sections were in great demand in the division and could be relied upon to present a worthy programme.

During its first year of marching through England, the Household Troops Band spent two days at Sandwich – Thursday, Friday 11, 12 August 1887. In his diary Trooper Teddy Cork recorded that the men slept on the floor of the hall, which was 'connected with a public house'. The men had been issued with their first suits of uniform two weeks before and were on their way from Ramsgate to Dover.

A year later – 18 August 1888 – the troopers were again in Sandwich and a third visit was paid on Tuesday 27 August 1889, when Field Commissioner (later General) Eva Booth was with them. Accommodation comforts by this time had improved and the campaigners were billeted at the homes of Salvationists. An entry in the diary of Trooper William Cartwright gives the information that the men marched seven miles that day (from Ramsgate) and that he stayed the night with Mr and Mrs Spicer. Those good friends were the grandparents of the corps treasurer of my day, Stanley Spicer.

Sandwich Band enjoyed its palmiest days during the mid-1930s. The opening of the East Kent coalfields meant employment and Yorkshire miners, made redundant because of the devastating depression, were happy to move south for work. Army bandsmen were among them. The Sandwich commanding officer himself hailed from Goldthorpe and lost no time in persuading the comrades from his home corps to sign on with Betteshangser and other collieries in the area.

In a week Sandwich Band went from eight to 40. Brother Leslie Brockman, of Ramsgate, transferred to become bandmaster and his interest and influence were successful in securing the required new instruments. The platform needed to be enlarged.

Several families moved into the town and obtained temporary accommodation with local comrades. For various reasons permanent residency did not materialise, which made it impossible for the happy state of affairs to last long. Overnight the corps reverted to its former strength. Deal, Woolwich and other corps benefited by the exodus.

At the welcome meeting I was introduced to the three responsibilities that, by tradition, went with the CO's job: Eb bass, the collecting box and hall stove. The first two I willingly accepted. The third was left to the tender mercy of my wife, who had always proved so efficient in her methods of dealing with bundles of firewood, buckets of coke and clinker disposal!

On our first Sunday morning at Sandwich my wife went into the 'juniors' while I made my way to the open-air meeting, complete with Eb bass and collecting box. 'Mrs Leff', as she soon became known,

185

could not believe her eyes. Our hall was packed with 108 youngsters, and we soon learned from the faithful young people's sergeant-major, Mrs Doris Cornelius, that this was the usual attendance.

During the war, when the majority of townspeople had been evacuated and shelling from France had made the place a danger zone, the Army was the only Sunday school to remain open and parents availed themselves of these facilities. This meant a build-up of numbers when children returned and younger scholars had joined their elder brothers and sisters to make up the healthy state of affairs we found when we arrived.

The vicar of the remaining Anglican church in the town was not happy about this 'take-over' and called on me from time to time demanding that I should return all those who had been baptised in the Church of England. He did not agree that such a decision should be left to the parents and the children and continued to pay regular visits to the quarters during our stay. None of the youngsters wanted to leave. The vicar and I were not very good friends.

Not that many of the children became senior soldiers. While the parents were quite happy for them to attend the Army Sunday school there was to be no 'taking the bonnet' or other uniform wearing. In fact it seemed a tradition that at 14 or 15 the Army saw them no more.

We were proud of our smartly turned-out singing company. The parents of the 'outside' children seemed to have no objection to uniform skirts, blouses, ties and berets being worn and encouraged membership of the 'junior choir'.

Before we farewelled from the corps a young people's band had been commissioned, thanks to the care and enthusiasm of Bandsman Sid Cornelius, who became band leader. Our son learned to play a cornet during this period and proudly took his place on second cornet at the commissioning. A few months before, the playing of his first tune, 'Onward, Christian Soldiers', was rewarded with a 10 shilling note from his Grandma Hart in fulfilment of a promise she had made before he could even hold a cornet.

Nina's mother was promoted to Glory during our stay at Sandwich. She had taken up residence at St Mildred's Eventide Home, Westgate, some time before our appointment and it was a source of great comfort to my wife to know that her mother's last days were considerably brightened by our close proximity.

That year we succeeded in persuading six singing company members from non-Salvationist homes to accompany us to Sunbury for the national school, of which I was appointed music director for the first time and remained so for most of 20 years. The girls loved their first visit to London and were just as excited to take presents back to their mums as they were to participate in the final joint festival with the boys from Hadleigh at Regent Hall – the first united music camp programme to be given.

Like all officers newly commissioned from the training college, we wanted to turn the world upside down in the least possible time. Although the lovely stretch of beach at Sandwich Bay, some distance from the town, was privately owned, we understood that on Sundays this area was packed with holidaymakers – even at a shilling a time. This, I felt, was where we should be on summer Sunday afternoons.

With the vision of the Army flag firmly implanted in the sands and the band's instruments gleaming brightly in the sunlight, I ascertained that the owner of the beach was the Earl of Guilford and it was to this noble lord that I wrote for the necessary permission. I received a reply from a firm of lawyers, acting as agent for the 16-year-old earl who had succeeded his grandfather some months previously, regretting that permission could not be granted for such a purpose. Propaganda of any kind was out.

Not to be allowed on the beach was a bitter disappointment. But we did seek to evangelise neighbouring villages on Saturday evenings. By this means the inhabitants of Eastry, Ash, Woodnesborough and Worth had the rare opportunity of hearing the gospel message proclaimed by Salvationists.

And while we were busy within the precincts of our isolated cinque port, plenty was happening in the big world beyond. In July 1950, two months after our arrival, our crackling, distorted radio set behaved itself sufficiently to break the news that General Evangeline Booth had been promoted to Glory in her 85th year. Memories of

187

those Christmas days when I had served as her 'bandmaster' came flooding to mind and I felt a sense of personal loss. Distance prevented us from attending the memorial service conducted at Regent Hall by General Orsborn. How I would have loved hearing Harlesden Songster Brigade sing 'Star In The East', Regent Hall Band play 'Streams In The Desert' and Harry Kniveton, of motorcade memory, feature 'I Bring Thee All', and to have joined the congregation in singing 'The World For God' and 'The Wounds Of Christ Are Open'. On this occasion I had to be content to read all about it in the Army's press.

On a Saturday morning in October the postman delivered a letter from the divisional commander informing me that I was due to pray at the beginning of the bandmasters and songster leaders councils festival to be held at the Royal Albert Hall *that evening*. I was not amused. We had a special meeting at the corps and I felt that there should have been longer warning.

As we were not on the phone I had to make my way to the nearest call box (in the marketplace) to make contact with divisional headquarters. Lieut-Colonel Bertie Rolls patiently listened to my protestations before calmly replying: 'I know exactly how you feel, my son, and knew that would be your reaction. I have been fighting it for two weeks, but *they* are adamant. Your name is on the programme. You must go.' My instructions were to hand the special meeting over to my wife, go to London, pray, enjoy the festival and be back in time for the 'open-air' on Sunday morning.

I consulted the timetable. There was no train back on Sunday morning. It would mean catching the afternoon train to Charing Cross, hurrying to the Albert Hall, praying, leaving the platform immediately and rushing to the station in time for the last train to Sandwich (7.15 pm). The fare was £1 6s 6d. It would be a short trip.

Outside the Albert Hall I met my colleague from Deal, Senior-Captain Tom Jones, who, hearing my story, suggested that, as there were some empty seats on the coach from his corps, I should return with them after the festival. How relieved I was, and how I enjoyed the festival I never wanted to attend.

After the festival I learned of the serious illness of Bandmaster A. W. Punchard, who was not expected to recover. At the conclusion of the afternoon session of councils at the Temple, Clapton, the next day, the General announced the bandmaster's promotion to Glory at 3.30 that afternoon.

On the previous Thursday, while ascending stairs at his Hampstead home, he had been overtaken by sudden illness and sustained concussion as a result of the fall. He did not regain consciousness. With so many others who had been closely associated with A.W.P. at the corps, we were saddened by the news of his death. John would miss 'Uncle Punchard', from whom he received a birthday card every year. For as long as he could remember it had been John's responsibility each Mother's Day to take a flower to 'Auntie Punchard' because she had no 'little boy' of her own.

We returned to Chalk Farm for the funeral service led by the British Commissioner (Commissioner William Dalziel). Fifty former Chalk Farm bandsmen formed an avenue of tribute as the earthly remains of their beloved leader were carried from the hall. Headed by Chalk Farm Band, the cortège moved slowly on its way to Hampstead Cemetery, through the pavement-lined backstreets along which the bandmaster had led the band on its march from the Sunday night open-air meeting for over 50 years. At the graveside another large crowd paid silent tribute to the Chalk Farm boy whose name became a household word all over the world and who was laid to rest in beautiful surroundings, near to the last resting place of many of Hampstead's famous sons and daughters. A.W.P., too, was a peer in his realm.

Christmas playing round the picturesque snow-covered Kentish countryside was a delightful experience and our colourful carol service (which coincided with Christmas Eve that year) received a boost when the hall door opened and a party spending the yuletide at the Army's Broadstairs holiday home entered. Their attendance proved a boost for our collection as well!

On Boxing Day we had a funeral. A longed-for daughter of a songster and her husband had been plucked as a flower from their home in early infancy and I had the heartbreaking responsibility of laying the little one to rest in the cemetery of the parish church. As was the custom, the family walked through the quiet streets behind the tiny coffin.

A ceremony we shall never forget was the swearing-in as a Salvation Army soldier of Mrs Cole. She had been bedridden for a long time and when my wife heard of this from neighbours she went along to see her.

Our good friend had been an ardent church worshipper until struck down by illness and now, we discovered, the only religion she experienced was the sound of the Army band playing the old hymn tunes as it marched to the hall each Sunday. Her daughter-in-law erected a large mirror at an angle on the windowsill of her room so that from her bed she could see as well as hear the band. From then on we arranged for the band to halt on its march to play something especially for her.

The visits we paid to Mrs Cole became sacramental. Each week my wife reported on the happenings of the previous Sunday and kept the interested listener up to date with news of people in the corps. She became 'one of us' in no time at all and, in due course, expressed a desire to become a soldier. After much thought and prayer she signed the articles of war and, one day, we took the flag round to her home and carried through the full ceremony as though we were in Regent Hall itself.

As if to complete the picture, our newest soldier asked to try on my wife's bonnet, although she knew she would never wear one. Dear Mrs Cole, whose room had become such a sanctuary, lingered another 12 years. When, after returning from service in Canada, we asked after her, it was to learn that she had been promoted to Glory (she loved the term) while we were on the boat coming home.

We maintained our links with the training college. One weekend, we were visited by Senior-Captain Geoffrey Dalziel and a party of cadets. A pub-raid on the Saturday night resulted in our hall being filled to overflowing and many decisions for Christ at the mercy seat. The conservative complacency of the local populace received something of a jolt during the Saturday afternoon meeting outside the post office in busy King Street, when an overseas cadet announced: 'We are very pleased to wake up your sleepy little town.' He was kindly dealt with. As he became a territorial commander the 'ticking off' could not have done him too much harm.

I was invited to speak at a training college spiritual day and shared some of my Sandwich experiences with cadets of the Ambassadors Session. That morning, as I prepared for the 20-minute walk to the station to catch the first train to London, I could not really understand my wife's anxiety to see me off and for me to get on my way. Some 14 hours later, upon my arrival back at the quarters, all was revealed when Nina happily showed me into the little sitting room, which she had re-papered in my absence. Once again I thanked the dear Lord for providing such a practical helpmate!

Our Chalk Farm comrades did not forsake us. The songsters arranged an outing to the Kentish coast and offered to give an evening festival on their way home, in exchange for one of Nina's renowned teatime repasts. The deal was on and, under the leadership of Deputy Songster Leader Eddie Sizeland who had so loyally served me in that capacity, the brigade held an open-air meeting in the marketplace before presenting an excellent festival in the crowded hall.

Bandmaster Frank Rawbone graciously accepted my invitation to bring Chalk Farm Band for a weekend. We planned to take the visitors to Canterbury hall for the Saturday festival, as this building was larger and more central than our own. This arrangement gave people from a wider area of Kent an opportunity to hear this renowned section. Lieut-Colonel Frederick Coutts accompanied the band as its leader.

The band nearly didn't arrive. It was All Fools' Day and on the Saturday morning someone with a distorted sense of humour informed the coach-hire firm that the trip was cancelled. At the Chalk Farm hall that afternoon all the bandsmen were there but no transport. Urgent phone calls and the discovery of a driver resulted in the journey being made at breakneck speed, I was afterwards told.

The coach eventually came to rest in the narrow Canterbury street, even if considerably late, and the festival proceeded as scheduled. The local Member of Parliament presided.

191

Sunday was a memorable day. It dawned bright and sunny and I sought to take advantage of the lovely morning by taking the band for a 'route march' some distance out of the town to hold open-air meetings on a new housing estate. The venture was a success. People came to their doors. Children crowded into the ring to 'let rip' on a song chosen specially for them. The playing of the band created considerable curiosity and interest.

As we marched proudly back to the town, however, the weather, without warning, completely changed. The heavens opened. My, didn't it rain! There was no shelter. There were no overcoats. There was only one thing for it. The orderly 'route march' became a disorderly 'rout run' as the men, without awaiting instructions and soaked to the skin in seconds, made a beeline for the hall by the quickest possible course. I led the undignified retreating army via a short cut along The Butts, part of the wall that had encircled the town from earliest times.

The quarters (next to the hall you will remember) was quickly transformed into a somewhat cramped dressing (or undressing) room as our friends attempted to dry their clothes (and their skins) in time for the holiness meeting. If they ever forgave me, they never told me so.

General Coutts reminded me of that debacle when we met at the Chalk Farm Band centenary celebrations in November 1982. I respectfully apologised.

That afternoon at Sandwich the band, by now 'dried out', marched through the narrow, winding, crowded, lined streets to the Guildhall to receive a civic reception on behalf of the mayor who was absent through illness.

Some of my pub friends attended their first Army meeting that afternoon and the band's visit became a talking point in the town. On the Monday morning, when I changed the copper and silver from my 'paper round' at the nearby baker's shop – as was my weekly custom – Mrs Franklin, the baker's wife, opened the conversation with the question, 'Exactly where is Chalk Farm?' Before I could produce a map of the London Underground she provided the answer. 'I say it's the farm on the left just before you get into Minster,' she volunteered. Such is fame!

Finance was a problem as it has always been in small corps. Our first week's salary was six shillings and eightpence (34p in modern currency). Much would depend on the self-denial centage. From the well-kept brief I found that our target for 1951 was £167. I gathered that this figure would not be easy to come by.

Door to door, shop to shop and farm to farm, collecting was a personal matter. On a borrowed bicycle my coverage of the 36 villages in our district began the third week in January and, with a break over the Easter weekend, lasted until the third week in April. My wife collected in the town.

We managed to smash our target in time for the ingathering, at which our family presented a topical elocutionary threesome, 'Pounds, Shillings and Pence'.

When, in April 1951, Charles Terrot's television play, *Shout Aloud Salvation*, was shown, Bandmaster and Mrs Sole invited us, with a number of corps comrades, to their home to see it. This was the first time we had seen 'domestic' television. Nina and I had witnessed an experimental presentation from the *Daily Mail* Ideal Home Exhibition at Olympia before the war when a live show on a stage was shown on a small screen round the corner, but this was different.

The script of *Shout Aloud Salvation* was written after much research and gave an authentic account of Salvation Army activity in the last two decades of the 19th century. Hailed by critics as the television play of the year, it told the story of Janine Mayhew, a beautiful Yorkshire girl who became one of William Booth's first 'Hallelujah Lasses' and, as an officer, went with her lieutenant, Maud Harding, to commence Army work at a town in the north of England.

The climax of our stay was a corps outing to London, including a tour of the training college and culminating in a festival by our band and songster brigade at Camberwell Citadel. Commissioner John Bladin presided and the sections 'did us proud'.

That morning we had received farewell orders and there was much speculation as to what our next appointment might be. Our thoughtful corps treasurer was certain it would be Chartham, 'where money grows on trees', a prospect which immediately excited our inquisitive young son.

After a week, which seemed longer, marching orders gave us the news that we were to return to International Headquarters. I was to join the *War Cry* staff.

Our feelings were decidedly mixed. We felt it had been a happy, fruitful and character-building year, and we would miss the unique opportunities presented by a corps officer's life. We would like to have stayed on at Sandwich for a longer period, to build upon the lessons we had learned from the previous 12 months.

Looking back, our big regret is that there is no longer a corps in that town. Its closure has left a gap in our lives and those of other officers privileged to be stationed there. But we are grateful for every memory and thank God for every blessing.

Chapter 17

With Notebook and Biro

MY first reporting assignment as a member of the *War Cry* team was carried out before I had officially joined the staff or even presented myself at Denmark Hill, where the Editorial Department was still situated. A letter from the editor arrived while we were still at Sandwich asking me to cover the opening of the new Army exhibition at Clapton on the afternoon of Monday 4 June.

Other instructions were received before we left Sandwich. A letter from the Staff Secretary at IHQ regretted that quarters for us in London would not be available and requested us to make our own arrangements for temporary accommodation. Another from the Assistant Staff Secretary asked me to report at her office at 9 am on that Monday. This initial appointment now had to wait until the Tuesday.

My parents, still living at Willesden Green, made room for us in their home and it was from here that I made my way to Clapton to begin my new life as an officer-journalist.

The museum was mounted and made available mainly for Salvationist visitors to London during the Festival of Britain, celebrations convened to mark the centenary of the Great Exhibition erected in Hyde Park under the patronage of the Prince Consort in 1851. The massive glass building created for the purpose was later reconstructed as the Crystal Palace at Sydenham. The Clapton Institute was the Army's festival centre.

As *The War Cry* was going to press while the opening was taking place, I was required to phone my report through to The Campfield Press. The next day I saw it in print in an advanced copy of that week's issue, and thought the whole operation rather marvellous.

I had, however, by no means exhausted the subject in the 100 words allocated to my report. I examined the exhibits minutely for the best part of an hour, filling my handy notebook with all sorts of data. By the end of that month this information had found its way into an article for the magazine page. Knowing that as a member of the staff I could not be accredited with the feature I thought up a nom de plume, settling for my second and third Christian names – John Railton. That has been retained to this day.

There was much at the museum to intrigue and inspire. High on the list was the bottle buried by William Booth at the stone-laying of the Poplar Christian Mission station in 1872. This contained three copies of *The Christian Mission Magazine* and a preachers' plan. The historic bottle, with its contents, was discovered among the debris left by the Second World War.

Then there was the flag hoisted by the Founder at Calvary; the bonnet that was with Consul Emma Booth-Tucker at the time of her fatal railway accident in the USA; the application for officership completed by Commissioner Edward Higgins (father of General Edward J. Higgins and grandfather of Mrs General Orsborn) in 1881; and the autograph album containing the signatures of officers who attended the international Staff Councils of 1904. In this last-named showpiece I was interested to discover the signatures of my grandparents.

Many of those 1951 exhibits are now in the keeping of the Heritage Centre.

I became the fifth member of the *War Cry* team. There had been little change among the personnel of the department since I had left it to enter training college two years before – the stalwarts were still there.

My first Sunday in the department was spent reporting the meetings led at Regent Hall by Commissioner Wilfred Kitching, who a few days before had arrived in London to become the British Commissioner.

In the afternoon the commissioner produced William Booth's original handwritten teenaged resolve, which was read meaningfully to the assembled company. I was to witness this kind of dramatic, telling effect repeated time and time again during the next 12 years.

Another reporting assignment that summer took me to Clapton Congress Hall for a Sunday morning meeting addressed by Mrs General Bramwell Booth. Erect and firm of voice, despite her nearly 90 years, Mrs Booth thrilled the congregation with the story of her beginnings in the Christian faith.

Her memories of the Army Mother's teaching, of the moment when she herself stood up in the Steinway Hall in London's West End and said, 'I have never seen it like that before', of how she went home quoting the words of 'O When Shall My Soul Find Rest' (newly written by Mr Bramwell Booth) and surrendered to God in her room and how she went to the mercy seat in the Whitechapel hall thrilled her hearers.

Stirring testimonies were a feature of the powerful meeting. A man who had come from Switzerland said he wanted publicly to thank The Salvation Army for sending its officers to his land. A woman told Salvationists that when she was in Holloway Prison it was Mrs Booth who befriended her and led her to Christ. This historic visit was part of a day's meetings led by Commissioner Catherine Bramwell-Booth.

About this time a quarters became vacant at Shirley, close to where the counties of Kent and Surrey meet, and we became soldiers at Croydon Citadel. Apart from the time we served in Canada we have remained linked with the Army's 'No 9' corps ever since.

Before the end of the year I accompanied the British Commissioner to South Croydon, at which corps he and Mrs Kitching had been welcomed as soldiers. At one point in the meeting the commissioner left the leadership in the hands of the Divisional Commander (Lieut-Colonel William Grottick) and, with nine other campaign 'spies', swooped upon the immediate vicinity of the hall.

'The War Cry is coming with me,' announced the commissioner and, duly armed with Army booklets and periodicals, we approached 'contacts' and asked three questions: 'When did you last attend a place of worship?' 'Did you go to Sunday school when you were a child?' and 'Have you ever attended a Salvation Army meeting?' The 200-yard stretch of Brighton Road immediately on the coast side of the Swan and Sugar Loaf, in those days so uneventful after nightfall, sprang to life for a few moments.

Among those put 'on the spot' in this forthright way were a bus driver who had attended the 'juniors' in Shropshire years ago, a newspaper reporter on her way from a meeting, a shopkeeper, an agnostic and a woman waiting at a phone kiosk. Returning to the hall the 'spies' recounted their experiences.

I was to hear '*The War Cry* is coming with me' many times during the next three years.

On the morning of Wednesday 6 February 1952 we had been in the office about an hour when the departmental head received a telephone message requesting the entire IHQ staff at Denmark Hill to assemble in Room M of the training college. This was most unusual and there was much speculation as to what could be afoot as we made our way across to the main building.

When we arrived, the Chief of the Staff had already taken his place on the small platform and lost no time in announcing that King George VI had passed away during the night. He had received the news from the American Embassy, even before the British public had been informed over the radio. We were stunned.

Speaking with deep emotion and as an American who keenly felt the loss of 'a wonderful person, a wonderful example and a wonderful Christian', the Chief went on: 'The things he did during your great trial, especially during the blitz, made a great impression upon my heart. We in the United States just loved the man. He was a good man, a man who loved his people. My people will feel that they have lost one of their own. He was a man who turned his handicaps into strength.'

The next issue of *The War Cry*, which went to press five days later, carried a photograph of His Majesty on the front page and, on page three, a full-length tribute by the General concluding with a four-verse poem he had specially written to accompany the feature.

General Orsborn lost no time in calling upon Salvationists to hold their own memorial service. This was held on Sunday afternoon 17 February, two days after the funeral, in the Royal Festival Hall and led by the General. Timed for 3 pm it was preceded by a procession of witness – it was termed a 'memorial march' I believe – which formed up on the Embankment near Westminster Bridge 75 minutes before that hour and proceeded to the hall.

Major Eric Coward and I were detailed respectively to cover the two historic events, and after an early lunch I made my way through the rain to the rallying point near the Horse Guards Parade. As a nearby clock chime struck two the procession moved off, headed by the Union Jack proudly borne by Colonel William Charles, tall and straight, who ten years before had led the International Staff Band through the gateway of Buckingham Palace to play to his late majesty.

Among the various departmental changes which occurred about this time was the appointment of Major Bernard McCarthy as editor-in-chief for South Africa. Owing to an outbreak of chickenpox among their four children, Major and Mrs McCarthy's departure was delayed by many weeks, but eventually, after Christmas, we all gathered at a London terminus to wish them 'God speed' as they boarded the boat train. These were always harrowing experiences.

One of my recognised duties, after prayer by the editor-in-chief or an overseas department representative, was to strike up a suitable chorus to be sung as the final whistle sounded, doors were closed and the train drew out of the platform. This time it was 'We'll Never Let The Old Flag Fall'.

In the excitement of taking leave of our popular colleague and his family I started the singing much too high, with what devastating results can be well imagined. Fortunately our gallant, if fruitless, efforts to negotiate the heights of tonal shrillness were swallowed up in the prolonged, deafening comment of the faithful old steam engine as it coerced its precious cargo of emigrating passengers into the smoke-filled tunnel. The train out of sight, we dissolved into a bundle of laughter, which reaction happily eased the tension. Not every station farewell ended so hilariously.

During this period, the General's Christmas party for officers' children living in the London area was a regular new-year feature. A number of rooms of the International Training College were suitably decorated to create a Christmas atmosphere and various games were organised according to the respective age groups.

For some years I was required to serve as a benign Father Christmas and to arrive in a variety of ways. One year I descended from the roof – just how, I cannot now imagine – and on another occasion multitudinous noises created the impression that I was coming by spaceship. My main function was to distribute presents to those attending the party for the first time.

In all these endeavours my faithful henchman was colleague Will Pratt, whose fertile mind could always be relied upon to produce some new approach to the old Santa Claus legend.

On the last day of January 1953 we heard of the disastrous floods which had devastated east and south-east England during the night. For many corps in this area a Sunday of normal activity was changed into a day of social service.

The next morning, at the press, the *War Cry* team worked non-stop recording the news as it was telephoned by officers and correspondents on the spot. Half-a-dozen telephones would not have been enough to cope with the reports. A sympathetic Campfield Press director made an extra line available to us.

Brigadier George Higgins, divisional commander for East London, told of travelling to Rayleigh and Hadleigh, where rest centres, including Army halls, had been opened for the evacuated people of Canvey Island, one of the worst-hit areas. On the island itself the hall was flooded to the doors. The commanding officer, Second-Lieutenant John Nesbitt, and the local Baptist minister, the Rev Mr Hodgson – who earlier had helped with the mass evacuation – built an emergency bridge from the hall to the road bank and rescued many from flooded dwellings. Between 400 and 500 Canvey residents were unaccounted for.

Senior-Major George Ferguson, the divisional chancellor, arrived at Canvey to lead Sunday meetings but, realising the situation and being unable to contact the lieutenant, he linked up with Lieut-Colonel George R. Bell, manager of the Hadleigh Land and Industrial Colony, who, with local comrades, provided refreshments throughout the day for police, firemen and other rescue workers.

The divisional young people's secretary (Major William Fenwick) left for the Thames-side area as soon as the news was received and with Senior-Captain Denis Hunter, young people's secretary in the Central London Division, and Major James Sanderson, the Poplar commanding officer, worked continuously in the Plaistow, Canning Town and Poplar districts. Major Sanderson made a raft of boards and barrels in order to rescue people from the upstairs windows of their homes. When this sank he managed to secure an unattended dinghy which was used to deliver tea to the marooned.

From Grays, Senior-Captain Ronald Topley reported that, when the flood waters necessitated evacuation at Tilbury, the Army's offer of help was quickly accepted. Bandsmen and songsters of the corps left the platform for duty at rest centres, where they worked throughout the night. The men used their cars to convey people to billets and to transport quantities of clothing. Much of this came from Salvationists who ransacked their own homes to meet the need, and also gave accommodation to some of the evacuees, among them a mother and three children, one of them a baby in arms.

The reports continued to arrive. At Louth, the corps officers had spent the Sunday serving refreshments to the more than 1,200 evacuees at a reception centre set up in the town hall. At Alford, a second reception centre was set up to cope with refugees from Mablethorpe and Sutton-on-Sea.

The Governor of the Men's Social Work (Lieut-Commissioner Owen Culshaw) arranged for a large consignment of beds, blankets, clothes and food to be sent to Whitstable, where Senior-Major Adeline Jones opened her quarters to supply 300 cups of tea to relief workers. Neighbours brought food and rendered untiring assistance until the arrival of Brigadier Leonard Walker, of the British Red Shield Services, who continued to provide meals from a mobile canteen stationed in the high street. Salvationists also assisted in relief work at Herne Bay and Margate.

Aided by our efficient liaison man at Denmark Hill, we worked feverishly, taking down all the information, sifting it and shaping it into some kind of coherent, comprehensive story before handing it to the linotype operators. Lunchtime was staggered that day and it was well into the late evening before we could catch a train from St Albans.

We were fortunate to find an empty carriage and on the way to London discussed the emergency and held an informal editorial conference. The assistant editor felt that next week's issue, already mapped out, should be rehashed in the worthy cause of topicality. We pooled ideas and decided to get to the office earlier than usual the next morning to search for suitable material already in hand. We were warned that it could mean our having to provide articles ourselves.

Much midnight oil was burned that week, but when the issue for 14 February came off the presses we felt that it had been worth it all. My main contribution was a front-page feature, 'I Remember Canvey Island'. Major Coward gave it this arresting title, which was far more pungent than the original one.

My article was accompanied by a page-width agency picture of a Salvation Army officer at Whitstable bringing comfort to an elderly, bedridden woman stranded in her first-floor room by the floods. A narrow plank fixed from the roadway to the front-window porch added drama to the scene.

I was delegated to report the Canvey Island memorial service on the Sunday and was required to cancel a 'specialing' appointment at Luton Citadel. I travelled down with the divisional commander. As the Army hall was flooded and severely damaged by the rising water, Lieutenant Nesbitt arranged for the island's only remembrance service to take place in the Baptist church.

Among the 40 who attended were those who had lost loved ones in the disaster, a local Salvationist who had cycled from Rayleigh, where he had been evacuated, and a group of bandsmen from Southend Citadel who, with their commanding officer (Major Marcus Brown), had come to assist.

Major Brown led the meeting, Brigadier Higgins gave the address and the commanding officer, while the congregation stood in remembrance, read the names of those who had lost their lives. One man remained seated, stunned and gazing into space. On his knee he balanced his three-year-old daughter. They were the survivors of a family of six.

It was a far happier occasion, three months later, which took me to RAF Station Abingdon, to await the Hastings passenger plane bringing Lieut-Commissioner Herbert Lord and his six compatriots from captivity in North Korea. The 11,000 miles' journey had made headlines in the national press and anxious relatives and friends were gathered on the airfield to catch a first glimpse of their loved ones.

After RAF and Foreign Office officials boarded the plane and the crew disembarked, there was a period of nervous waiting. The Chief of the Staff broke the silence by inviting the crowd to sing 'Praise God From Whom All Blessings Flow'. Recorded and broadcast later that day, the singing of the familiar doxology found an echo in a million hearts. The seven men heard it as they waited in the plane.

As a battery of press cameras trained upon the open doorway the men came down the gangway. The third man, bronzed and smiling radiantly, was our own Herbert Lord. We were surprised to see him with a beard and wearing a grey suit. As if sensing our surprise, he pointed to his clothes and told us how the British air force men in Berlin, where the plane stopped over on its journey from Moscow, would not allow him and his companions to return to England in the rough attire in which they had been travelling. The men took up a collection, called in a Naafi representative and had the former internees fitted with completely new outfits.

At Clapton a 'Welcome Home' banner streamed across the street, Army flags flew from most houses and life-saving guards from Lanark House formed a guard of honour. That evening the Congress Hall Band left its practice to play outside the quarters. Relatives and neighbours joined in singing the well-known songs, which included 'Jesus, The Very Thought Of Thee', one of 60 hymns compiled from memory by the commissioner and his colleagues during the years of internment.

The next day the Chief of the Staff led a 'Welcome Home' meeting at Clapton Congress Hall. The commissioner's epic return from North

Korea had been greatly publicised and the old building was packed. His strong, vibrant voice rang through the hall as he declared: 'Time soft-pedals the harsh things,' and added, 'I am not one who likes to keep his nose where the stinks are!'

Only a passing reference was made to the much-publicised 'death march' and the 'birdseed' (he called it millet). Instead, he gave an enthralling testimony to the grace of God which enabled him to know his Bible better when he had no Bible to refer to – which helped him in his relations with his fellow-captives, which gave him courage to witness to a baiting prison guard, which helped him to regard a meal of poor food and water as a sacrament.

Standing by the penitent form at which he had knelt as a boy and on the platform where he had been commissioned as an officer and dedicated for service in Korea 43 years earlier, the commissioner pledged himself to engage in that 'fanatical, apostolic Christianity' which he had learned from experience to be the only weapon against the militant, atheistic, materialistic religion which had captured so many hearts in the east.

The Chief read a message from the General expressing his relief and welcoming the commissioner back to the Army's fighting line. This also gave an opportunity for the Chief to announce that the General had promoted the returning warrior to the full rank of commissioner.

When the meeting commenced Commissioner Lord, at the behest of the Chief of the Staff, appeared in the civilian suit he had worn at the aerodrome arrival. He later left the platform, reappearing to present himself in Salvation Army uniform for the first time in nearly three years.

After a period of recuperative furlough the commissioner was appointed territorial commander for South Africa and after some years as international travelling commissioner he, with Mrs Lord, retired from active service and settled in the Shirley district of Croydon, where he was greatly respected by his fellow soldiers.

* * * * *

It was typical of British Commissioner Kitching that he should decide to conduct an open-air meeting outside The Blind Beggar public house on the evening of Founders' Day (2 July). At the meeting Commissioner Kitching announced that he and First-Lieutenant Stuart Booth (great-grandson of the 'first Salvationist') would enter The Blind Beggar to press the claims of God as William Booth had done 88 years before them. Once again he invited *The War Cry* to accompany him. Once again I was *The War Cry*.

We entered in a blaze of publicity, to find that the only customers were an elderly couple, the man extremely hard of hearing. The commissioner, like the good evangelist he undoubtedly was, lost no time in introducing the Army and speaking freely with our 'congregation'. The landlord quickly appeared and objected to our 'invasion'. If the opposition encountered was not as demonstrative or vocal as in 1865, it was none the less real and in no uncertain terms we were ordered to leave. The request was respectfully complied with, but not before the objector had heard of a living Saviour to meet the need of every man.

On 28 November *The War Cry* announced that, for the first time, an assistant editor had been appointed to *The Musician* and that, after two-and-a-half years as a member of the *War Cry* staff, First-Lieutenant Brindley Boon would take up his new post at the end of the year.

I returned to serve on *The War Cry* but not for another 18 years when, on 1 April 1972, I succeeded Lieut-Colonel Bernard McCarthy as editor. In addition, I became assistant editor-in-chief, which appointment brought me into close contact with my old *Musician* editor, Colonel Sidney Williams, whom I was to succeed as editor-in-chief a year later when he too retired.

This dual assignment was retained until May 1976 when my appointment as chief executive officer for the 1978 International Congress was announced.

I remained as editor-in-chief, while getting the congress plans 'off the ground', until the end of that year.

An enjoyable sideline for me was involvement in 'Christmas At The Manor', an upstairs-downstairs musical presentation – with Ray

Fensom as a benevolent squire-compère – which for two years replaced the traditional carol service at Westminster Central Hall.

This new-look production relied for its appeal on the merger of two old ideas – the Christmas pantomime and the carol concert. Below stairs, Major Joy Webb led a chorus of kitchen maids. The National Bandmaster (Captain Trevor Davis) was the piano-playing butler. Farmer Leslie Condon conducted the village orchestra.

Brigadier Leslie Pull was the policeman and Rupert Hanson the postman. High-quality seasonable music was provided by Little Rustic Temple Band (Woking bandsmen in disguise) and the programme was rounded off with a mime play presented by the village players (Chelmsford Drama Group, directed by Mrs Major Marian Howe, whose versatile husband was the 'oldest inhabitant').

There was plenty of good music, good acting and good fun. How we succeeded in converting the awkward Central Hall platform into a two-storey manor house with a barn thrown in I shall never know, but somehow the illusion 'came off'. In devising, writing and producing this 'something with a difference' I appreciated once again the invaluable support and practical help of Lieut-Colonel Will Pratt, as he was then.

Brindley and Nina on their wedding day

Brindley and Nina in training

Brindley and Nina being commissioned by Training Principal Commissioner John Bladin

Brindley conducting Sheffield Citadel Band and massed songsters in a broadcast from Leeds (picture: Yorkshire Television)

Chapter 18

My Worlds Converge

THE best apprenticeship a Salvation Army journalist can have is to serve for a time on *The War Cry*. Training on that paper consists of quick-thinking reporting, preparing concise paragraphs of latest news for press day, shaping up other people's copy, reading proof galleys and making up pages of type for the printer, to be read in proof form later. Each responsibility requires skill and is a vital part of the urgent necessity of meeting the weekly deadlines.

In my days on the staff of the parent periodical a reporter accompanied the General and Chief of the Staff on all their appointments in the British Isles and on the continent of Europe, and the British Commissioner on his within the four London divisions (there were five for a time). A Monday press day demanded that no time could be lost in writing up weekend, Sunday or weeknight activities.

Early in my officership, New Year's gatherings in Scotland, led by the Chief of the Staff, provided excellent experience. Leaving King's Cross on the Thursday, New Year's Eve, I was in Edinburgh in time to be whisked away by my good friend Bandmaster Alex Thain to a Gorgie Corps social before conducting a watchnight service. After this, I was introduced to the delightful tradition of first-footing, being generously supplied with pieces of coal and boxes of chocolates for distribution.

New Year's Day meetings were held in the ancient Assembly Hall of the Church of Scotland and the next morning we travelled on to Glasgow where, after a devotional meeting at Anderston Citadel, festivals were held in St Andrew's Hall. Salvationists of the city also gathered in another hall for Sunday meetings led by the Chief.

At the end of all this, after partaking of hurried refreshments at Glasgow Central Station, I boarded the night train for London, writing my report of three full days of meetings and seeking to do justice to three marches of witness from the confines of a top bunk in a four-berth sleeping compartment, a minimum of illumination ensuring that my travelling companions (all strangers) would not be withheld from slumber.

There was no time for second thoughts. My arrival in London after a brief sleep, when my scribbling was over, was followed by a cold train journey to St Albans and a brisk walk from the station through 'the fields' in the invigorating morning air. This jolted me back to normality. The enthusiastic Scottish crowds, the old friends, the exhilarating music and the seasonable north Britain snowstorms and icy streets seemed miles away, which they were, of course. My independent comments for *The Musician* would come later, in time for that paper's press day the following Friday.

Most days of the week we were at the office until a late hour. The editor was there too, coping with the administrative demands of his appointment during office hours and attending to his journalistic responsibilities in the comparative quietness of evening. But those Denmark Hill offices were not too separated, which meant that with our doors open, as they invariably were, mutual advisory sessions of free-flowing banter and a sudden outburst of song enlivened the passing hours.

This then was the kind of apprenticeship I was privileged to serve. I have cherished the memory of it all my life.

When I returned to *The Musician* as an assistant editor, my two worlds converged. My cup of happiness was overflowing. I was an officer, a journalist and was able to use my musical interest, especially as I had already been a member of the International Staff Band for two years.

My craze for anniversaries soon became apparent. With the 40th anniversary of the *Empress Of Ireland* tragedy coming up, I wrote to Toronto, asking Colonel George Atwell, one of the survivors of the Canadian Staff Band, to recall the event for the benefit of *Musician* readers. The colonel's graphic article made compelling reading.

The farewell of General and Mrs Orsborn from international leadership took place during a day's meetings in the Royal Festival Hall. This modern building, but three years old, had gained a special place in the General's affection. In the early days of the Festival of Britain he led a stirring Sunday morning salvation meeting there and later the same year presided over the International Staff Band's diamond jubilee celebrations festival. The Army's memorial service for the late king had been held there and the General had conducted 'A Crowning Day' to commemorate the coronation of the new monarch.

It was natural, therefore, that this orator-leader, songwriter and music-lover, who promised at his election to give the Army wings – and had kept his word – should come back to Britain's newest home of the arts for his public farewell. The day had a rewarding, joyous conclusion, perhaps summed up in the final paragraph of my report: 'General Orsborn will carry many memories of his London farewell into retirement, aided, as he himself said, by a tape recording of the proceedings, but on Thursday night there was no mechanical invention to record his joy as scores of seekers made their deliberate way to the mercy seat. That will be his most hallowed recollection.'

And so 'A.O.', poet and evangelist – he will feature again in this story – passed from the scene of action in the 50th year of his officership, the first IHQ junior to become General, but not before due editorial honour had been paid to him and he had been persuaded to write out his favourite chorus in his own hand for the interest of *Musician* readers. This was 'Except I Am Moved With Compassion', to which he added, 'Written in 1923 and still the cry of my heart.'

* * * * *

The leadership of the new General began dramatically. In the early hours of the morning after he had assumed office – Founders' Day – Wilfred Kitching heard a voice, the voice of the Spirit, saying, 'Go down this day to Mile End Waste. Walk along Mile End Road and remember that it was 89 years ago to the day that William Booth went that way. Try to imagine how he might have felt even though the area has changed and the circumstances are different.'

Without saying anything to his wife or those around him in the office, at one o'clock that afternoon he called for ten copies of *The War Cry* and bade his driver, Senior-Captain Sydney Woodall, to drive him to the beginning of Mile End Road. Once there he said he would be back in an hour.

No Army journalist accompanied the General on that trip, but we are grateful to General Kitching for his own account of that historic walk, published in his autobiography, *A Goodly Heritage*. He says, 'Leaving my Army cap in the car and turning up my collar so as not to be identified as a Salvationist, I walked with brisk step toward the point where stands the statue of William Booth. I approached one man and asked if he could tell me anything about the statue and what it represented.'

There follows a graphic account of a number of encounters and some of it makes sad, disturbing reading as the General describes the conversations with the youth whose mind was as dark as a jungle and the old man sitting on the kerb outside the London Hospital waiting to die because he had come to the point in life where there was no further use for him in the world.

Says the General: 'It was well on into the afternoon when I again took my place at the desk of my office at Denmark Hill, sobered in my spirit, not elated, knowing full well that "people matter", and the people who matter in the estimate of every Salvationist, whether he be General or soldier, are first of all people who are away from the Kingdom of Christ and who need the strong arm of the world's only Saviour.'

The 80th birthday of Retired Bandmaster Herbert Twitchin was marked by a celebration festival at Regent Hall presided over by Retired Bandmaster Fred Cobb, of Hendon. Among messages received on this milestone was one from Her Majesty the Queen, sent from Balmoral. Other congratulatory letters were read at the festival from the General, the newly-appointed British Commissioner (Commissioner Joshua James), Sir Jack Hobbs and Mr Harry Mortimer.

Less than a month later the 'happy Salvationist of Oxford Street' was promoted to Glory, only a week after presiding over a festival given by Folkestone Songster Brigade at Shepherd's Bush. It was not difficult to write a worthy tribute or to find words to describe the funeral service, held, of course, at Regent Hall.

At a time when London's lunch hour was at its height, policemen signalled Oxford Street's stream of traffic to a standstill as, headed by the band with which he had been associated for 72 years, 'Bert' Twitchin made his last journey. Crowds stood in a solid mass as the procession passed. On the coffin rested the bandmaster's baton, cap and cornet.

The first appearance of the renowned conductor, Sir Adrian Boult, at a Salvation Army gathering was considered of sufficient news value to merit a 'staff report'. For this purpose I duly attended the South London 'Trumpet and Voice' Festival in an impressive building which was then known as the Lewisham Town Hall.

Introduced by Bandmaster William Overton, who for so long served as principal trumpet in the BBC Symphony Orchestra when Sir Adrian was the principal conductor, I was privileged to interview the eminent and gracious musician informally over a cup of coffee. He was generous in his praise of Army music-makers, a respect which began when, as a boy in Liverpool, he saw and heard the bands of that city engaged in their gospel ministry. I discovered Sir Adrian to be a man of high Christian principles – a Quaker – and a teetotaller and non-smoker. He stayed long after the programme, signing autograph albums and chatting with young admirers.

Four evenings later – on a Sunday – I unexpectedly met Sir Adrian Boult again. It was at Southend-on-Sea, where I was leading meetings in connection with the retirement of Songster Leader Victor Newman. We were holding our open-air meeting on a deserted corner in Arctic weather conditions. Suddenly I was aware of the presence of some interested listeners on the pavement. In the centre of the group, his coat collar turned up in protection against the elements and his ample trilby hat pulled down over his face, was Sir Adrian himself.

I felt that a personal contacting would not go amiss and walked towards our welcome congregation. Surprisingly Sir Adrian recognised me, reiterated his enjoyment of the Lewisham programme and introduced me to his colleagues, gentlemen of the Royal Philharmonic Orchestra, which was scheduled to give a concert in the town later that night. They were enjoying a 'necessary stroll' before returning for the performance.

In the August of 1955 Brigadier Albert Kenyon was announced to be editor of *The War Cry*, and I was to succeed the brigadier as editor of *The Musician*.

The General himself broke the news to me. In that traditional playful way that leaders of those days had of imparting good tidings, he lost no time in announcing, as I entered his office at Denmark Hill, 'I'm giving you farewell orders.' I almost collapsed in the waiting chair. He speedily explained: 'I'm taking you out of one chair and putting you in another. I'm making you editor of *The Musician*.' Shades of William Bramwell Booth and even his own father, Commissioner Theodore Kitching. That was a method of appointment 'W. K.' had inherited.

After barely a month in the appointment I had to lay aside pen, typewriter, scissors and paste to attend the editorial and literary session at the International College for Officers, but not before I had reported the national songster festival, at which a Lincoln electronic organ (played by Deputy Songster Leader Michael Kenyon of Ilford) was used for the first time both for solo and united singing items and Erik Leidzén, on his first visit from the USA for 21 years, was a welcome guest.

Rather reluctantly, I admit, I made my way to The Cedars ('the house on the hill'). I had passed my precious *Musician* into safe keeping. The editor-in-chief, a former editor, was to take over in my absence. I am sure Colonel Wiggins relished the prospect.

The War Cry announced: 'Something new in Army history is the first prolonged international editorial course which opens at the International College for Officers on Thursday 6 October, and is to continue until 14 December. All aspects of the writers' craft as it is used by Salvation Army editorial and literary workers will have consideration. A visit to mills which supply newsprint, copy-hunting expeditions and lectures form part of the curriculum.'

This unique gathering of specialists became known as the editors and writers session. Major Will Burrows, Captain Will Pratt and I represented IHQ. Other Britishers, Lieut-Colonel George B. Smith (Territorial Youth Secretary, Scotland) and Major Jean Trainer (Women's Social Work Headquarters), were there as contributors to Army periodicals. Seventeen territories were represented, five editors-in-chief among them.

The ICO Principal (Lieut-Commissioner Alfred Gilliard) was the editorial doyen of us all and the official seal was placed upon the session by the promotion of the editor-in-chief at International Headquarters, Lieut-Commissioner Arch Wiggins, to that rank on the opening day.

In those pre-chalet days at the ICO, dormitory accommodation was the order of the day. I seem to remember four or five of the male comrades sharing a bedroom, although one of the party, finding it impossible to sleep in such an unaccustomed situation, would venture forth with his pillows to find an alternative billet. The staff, on its early morning rounds, wondered in which cubbyhole they would find him next!

My room-mate for most of the session was Major Jonah Munyi, who edited the East Africa *War Cry* in both English and Swahili. We shared lots of fun during those six weeks. I was so saddened when, some time later as a brigadier and general secretary for East Africa, he met his death in a car accident.

Leslie Fossey, whose devotion and loyalty to *The Musician* in the days of my editorship never ceased to amaze me, spared neither time nor money as he travelled extensively in the interest of the paper. The numerous interviews with personalities through the medium of his tape recorder – something new in Army journalism – enabled readers to meet emerging music leaders and soloists as well as catching new glimpses of established favourites.

The drawing of Leslie holding a cumbersome tape recorder became a familiar page heading, but wore rather thin after a while. When

Leslie himself commented, 'They'll begin to feel sorry for my tired arms,' I decided on a change of illustration and a new heading was prepared.

The most homely of these interviews must have occurred early in 1956. On the morning of Saturday 14 January I was at headquarters, about to board the ISB coach for Ipswich, where the band was to conduct weekend meetings, when a telephone message gave us the news that Bandmaster George Marshall had been promoted to Glory. Having gone to press with *The Musician* the day before, I realised that almost a week would pass before we could announce the passing.

I immediately put through a phone call to The Campfield Press and, although the issue was already running, I was in time to stop the press for a four-line insertion: 'News has been received of the promotion to Glory of Bandmaster George Marshall, OF.' Printed in bold type, it was headed simply 'STOP PRESS NEWS'. Only the date, 14.1.56, was added.

This preliminary announcement meant that, the following week, we could pay a worthy tribute to our promoted comrade. A front-page article gave a synopsis of the bandmaster's life. Page two carried a report of the funeral at South Shields, conducted by the British Commissioner, and the General's tribute. The editorial, devoted to the bandmaster's gifts, concluded, 'The Army treasury of lovely melodies and exquisite harmony will be the poorer for George Marshall's passing; but the hallelujahs of Heaven will be enriched by his gracious spirit and fighting faith,' words which Lieut-Commissioner Wiggins did me the honour of quoting in *Triumph Of Faith*, his biography of Bandmaster Marshall.

But it was Leslie Fossey's interviews with George and Jenny Marshall, hitherto unpublished, which created the most interest and caught our imagination.

Two weeks after George Marshall's passing I attended my first councils as editor. These were for bandsmen of the Northern, Durham and Tees Divisions (three separate commands in those days) and held in Gateshead Town Hall. Jenny Marshall, by special invitation, attended the night session. The 750 men spontaneously stood in silent respect as the short, slight figure moved to the front of the platform to address them. In a clear voice she gave a message that those present will never forget.

'I am proud to be Jenny Smith Marshall,' she said. 'My husband was six feet a Christian gentleman and his influence on my life can never be estimated.' Taking as her text the words of Paul that her husband had, at the request of the General, sent to the bandmasters and songster leaders councils some months earlier, Mrs Marshall appealed for a fuller consecration to God's service on the part of every age group represented. 'Is your motto "Excelsior"?' she asked the young men. 'God wants your remaining years,' she told their fathers.

Inter-divisional councils for bandsmen and songsters took me to such centres as Birmingham (citadel and later town hall), Manchester (Star Hall and then Bell Vue), Southampton, Newcastle, Bristol and Glasgow. I was privileged to take part in the sessions, either with a practical talk aided by one or other of the sections; or by a male voice party; a paper on programme building; or a 'commercial' on *The Musician*. I always welcomed the last-named assignment, for I believed in 'Our Own' and wanted all Army music-makers to share my devotion.

Between sessions I tried to find a small unoccupied room where I could meet *Musician* correspondents. I reserved a large part of my heart for these faithful reporters whom I regarded as our outside staff. They belonged to us and it was a joy to greet them in this way, thank them and give them an opportunity to fire away with their complaints. I could not answer them all, but at least we got to know each other and came to realise that our end product was the same.

* * * * *

In April 1957 *The Musician* celebrated its golden jubilee and we could not allow the anniversary to pass unnoticed. We went to town to make the 6 April issue a worthy one.

Congratulatory messages were received from the General, the Chief of the Staff (Commissioner Edgar Dibden), the British Commissioner

(Commissioner Joshua James), the National Secretary for Bands and Songster Brigades (Lieut-Colonel Ernest Rance) and former editors and associates – including a tribute to the first editor, Colonel Arthur Goldsmith, paid by Henry Hall, once his office boy.

In October of that year it was announced that, after 35 years in editorial work, the editor-in-chief, Lieut-Commissioner Wiggins, was to farewell from that appointment to take up special literary work on behalf of the General, including the compilation of Volumes IV and V of *The History Of The Salvation Army*. He would be succeeded by Lieut-Commissioner Reginald Woods, who had already been appointed literary secretary upon the retirement of Colonel Catherine Baird. Thus the two departments were brought together again under one head.

We took our leave of 'A.R.W.' at a two-day departmental gathering at Rosehill, Reading, the first time such a concession had been granted. It was a memorable occasion, with the farewelling commissioner the life and soul of the party, permitting the years to roll away and treating us to some of his imperishable memories. Apart from the fun and the fellowship, there were many high moments of spiritual inspiration. I believe that event still remains unique in the history of the department.

We began to extend our overseas news about this time. This development encouraged correspondents from around the world to dispatch reports of musical happenings in their territories. A report of a festival in Kitchener (Ontario), sent from Toronto, arrived at the *Musician* office five days after the event and was in time to go to press the next day. In less than a week readers in Canada were reading of the festival in their airmail copies from London.

Another indication of the vast improvements in worldwide communications in the late 1950s was shown by a letter that arrived on my desk at headquarters on 13 November 1957. It had been written in Calcutta five days before and was from General Wilfred Kitching, then in the midst of a great Indian campaign.

We have General Kitching to thank for the development of the healthy, controversial correspondence columns of *The Musician*.

Mind you, the General was no 'pushover'. Army music had been his lifelong hobby and he did not want to see its cause hurt or retarded. Quite frequently I would be asked to go to his office – usually on a Thursday morning. When I saw *The Musician* proof pages on his desk I knew the reason for my being summoned.

Examining the pages of letters in front of him he would say, 'This first letter. Does it carry your judgment?' I would confirm that it did, or it would not have reached the printed page stage. Other questions might follow. Did I know the writer? Was he sincere in his comments? Was he a good bandsman? If my explanation met with his approval, he would take his 'WK' circled rubber stamp and impress it carefully at the top of the page.

Not all the letters passed his eagle gaze so easily. Some needed to be rephrased before he would pass them for publication. He possessed a good literary sense as well as a keen interest in the paper.

All good things must come to an end, and I was genuinely sorry to leave *The Musician*, although a few years later I was reappointed editor for a year, which period covered the centenary celebrations of 1965.

They were exciting days. My colleagues on the paper joined me in round-the-clock reporting of ten days of non-stop events. On the first day, for instance, I hurried from Buckingham Palace, where I had stood in the forecourt with the International Staff Band and Earlscourt Band from Canada, across to the Royal Albert Hall for the royal opening of the celebrations by Her Majesty the Queen and then dashed to Clapton Congress Hall for a welcome meeting and pageant – all by public transport. I remember pausing at a small café near Stepney Green underground station to partake of a cup of tea and a bun before continuing my journey.

In addition to all the reporting, I was co-opted as an associate conductor to relieve Major Dean Goffin and Captain Norman Bearcroft, who were on permanent duty at the Albert Hall. I was also required to lead united songster brigades at Clapton and Westminster Central Hall. This entailed travelling extensively in London and the home counties for rehearsals, a foretaste of wider experience to come.

Shortly before returning to *The Musician* I had accepted the bandmastership at Croydon Citadel and with that section being involved in the centenary field day at Crystal Palace my congress plate became full to overflowing. The band had the honour of opening the series of programmes in the idyllic setting of the concert bowl, where hundreds could relax in deckchairs and hear the notes wafted across the water from the spacious, eye-pleasing semi-dome. It was a mixed blessing, though, for the bowl, outside the grounds, was not very easy to find and so only a small audience gathered at this early hour.

We were later among the 18 bands which played together in the arena for the march past, at which General Frederick Coutts took the salute. So many bands functioning at the same time could have been complete chaos, but this possibility was avoided by a hurried word of command carried by Major Goffin along the ranks, requesting the respective bandmasters to take up the beat from the staff bandmaster. Soon the spectators were treated to an unrehearsed drill of waving batons, and brilliant precision was assured as the bands twice played a round of marches non-stop!

It was good to be back at Crystal Palace after 31 years, even if it had taken on a new look.

Chapter 19

Reporter At Large

THE life of a Salvation Army journalist in London was many-sided. There were routine duties which tied one to an office desk. There were frequent reporting assignments demanding travelling to all parts of the British Isles. Occasionally an opportunity arose for an overseas trip. This was a distinct privilege that every member of the editorial staff appreciated and never took for granted – one of the perks of the job.

An officer-journalist is required to serve a reasonable apprenticeship before being entrusted with such a responsibility. My big moment came early in 1953 when the editor-in-chief broke the news to me that the General had approved the suggestion that I should accompany him and Mrs Orsborn to The Netherlands for an Easter campaign. This was the first I knew of such a possibility. It was part of a wise, established policy. Should the General not have agreed to the proposal, I would have been none the wiser and therefore not disappointed.

An overseas visit by a *Salvationist* reporter was regarded as an investment. In 1953 flying to such an appointment was still years away. Overland train travel, as well as Channel crossings, was considered to be a vital part of one's education, especially with frontier hold-ups and the examination of papers and passports involved.

It was not merely a question of covering, for *The War Cry*, meetings led by the General or Chief of the Staff and then returning to prepare copy for the next press day. The reporter was required to travel in advance, perhaps to visit another country en route, gather stories from Army establishments, carry out interviews with interesting personalities and generally fill one's notebook with potential material for all the Army periodicals. *The War Cry, The Musician, All The World* and *The Deliverer* were all expected to benefit from the financial outlay involved.

It was arranged, therefore, that I should call in at Belgium for a few days before travelling on to link up with the international leaders in Amsterdam. My route took me from Dover to Ostend and thence by train to Brussels. I never found such journeyings lonely or irksome. Armed with a couple of books on local colour borrowed from the library, I would while away the hours committing many of the facts to memory and noting information which might prove useful as a background to the reports.

An interesting programme had been planned for me, and soon after becoming orientated in my comfortable little room at the billet, and finding my bearings in a strange city, I was sitting in on the activities of a woman goodwill sergeant who had a record of distinguished service in the then Belgian Congo. There followed visits to a mothers and babies home – at the terminal of a tram track just outside the city, I remember – and a thriving men's industrial centre where both furniture and lives were being repaired. There was no shortage of copy.

Sunday was spent at Jumet, a mining community 90 minutes' bus ride from Brussels. The route took me past the battlefields of Waterloo, to which historic town I returned at leisure a few days later to examine the exhibits of the impressive museum and the breathtaking larger-than-life diorama in a nearby building.

At Jumet I was greeted by the Commanding Officer, First-Lieutenant Samuel Vanderkam, whom I had met in London when he was a 'Peacemaker' at Denmark Hill. I was to be his 'special'. He was to translate my messages.

There were 11 corps in the Belgium Command, which limited the scope for officers' appointments. The lieutenant had been stationed at Jumet as a single officer. His wife had also been stationed there. Now they were there again as a married couple.

On the train journey to Holland my travelling companions were two couples who had interesting Salvation Army links. An elderly Dutch husband and his wife were returning to their home at The Hague following a holiday in France.

220

Their daughter, whose husband had been in the consular service in Indonesia at the outbreak of war in the Far East, was left homeless and helpless when he was taken off to internment. She thought of the Army and in a social home found shelter and comfort. Her parents were deeply moved as they expressed their appreciation to me.

The other couple were an American soldier and his wife. Their home was in Los Angeles and the bronzed young man told me that it was after switching on his radio early the previous Easter morning (1952) and hearing again the message of a risen Saviour that he decided to renew his church membership and attend a place of worship with his wife. He did not know that the speaker at that Hollywood Bowl sunrise service had been General Orsborn.

By tradition Good Friday meetings in Amsterdam were held on the ground floor of the fashionable Krasnapolsky Hotel and this spacious area was filled three times for 'Day at the Cross' meetings led by General and Mrs Orsborn.

Easter Sunday was spent at Rotterdam, a city rebuilt since I was there with the International Staff Band in 1949. On the Monday the General led meetings at Gröningen, in the north, and the following day presided at the opening of a new main building at the Army's farm at Lunteren. Saturday was a day free from public events. So that every possible moment might be utilised in the most beneficial way, my editorial escort, Senior-Captain Dirk Lissenberg, suggested that we should visit an institution at Haarlem, where an enterprising work was going on and many incidents of helpful rehabilitation could be recounted. I readily agreed and we duly caught the train from Amsterdam.

On the way my memory began to work overtime. The name of Haarlem rang a distinct bell in my mind. At school, in a book with large print, suitably illustrated, I had read the account of how this town had been saved from flooding by the bravery of a Dutch boy who put a finger through a hole in the dyke. It was a story well known to children of my era. I had also read, far more recently, that a memorial had been erected to the memory of that national hero.

221

I expressed my thoughts to my travelling companion and sought his confirmation that Haarlem was indeed the scene of the famous exploit. The captain looked blank. He had never heard of the incident. Nor had our officer friends in Haarlem. I must have been wrong. Perhaps it was another boy in another place.

Our business concluded, we made our way to the station for the return journey. The captain had a brainwave. He approached a bus conductor standing by his vehicle in the station yard. There was an animated conversation and then the captain beckoned me.

Yes, there was such a memorial at Spaarndam, some six miles away on the coast. The bus went there. The next journey was the last of the day. Did I still want to go? Of course I did. I might never be in Haarlem again. It was too good a chance to miss. So we boarded the bus.

On the way the knowledgeable conductor sat with us, kindly offering further information. My good friend faithfully interpreted so that I might get the complete picture.

It was all a myth. There never was such a boy. Had there been it would have been physically impossible for him to withstand the full onslaught of the floods against such overwhelming odds. So many British and American servicemen had visited the place during the war and afterwards, expecting to find some evidence of the story on which they had been nurtured, that the Dutch Tourist Association decided to erect a monument to the boy who never existed, so that 'pilgrims' would have something to see.

Spaarndam was a small fishing village and the bus terminus. The conductor informed us that we had ten minutes before the bus returned and that we would find the memorial in the second sluice on the right.

There it was, a bronze statue of a kneeling boy with his finger stopping the dyke leak. It was unveiled by Princess Margriet of The Netherlands on 7 June 1950, in the presence of Queen Juliana and Dutch dignitaries.

Closer inspection revealed that the inscription, in Dutch and English, read: 'Dedicated to our youth to honour the boy who symbolises the perpetual struggle of Holland against the water.'

There was sufficient time to take a photograph and run for the bus, but yet another British visitor went away satisfied, even if the inhabitants of Spaarndam did go about their Saturday afternoon business quite oblivious of his presence, or that of the statue, it seemed.

I have a special souvenir of that initial reporting assignment. It is a handwritten note, which General Orsborn handed to me when he arrived at Schiphol Airport. It said: 'Just a little to give to or buy something for your wife as a token of thanks for letting you come with me at Easter. A. O.'

A cheque for two guineas went a long way in 1953!

In 1955 I made my first visit to Scandinavia for the annual congress in Stockholm. I had read many reports of this great event and heard many accounts from senior colleagues. Now it was my turn.

Anxious that these early journeys to and from the continent should be as varied and interesting as possible, I arranged to travel by way of Harwich, Esbjerg, by train across Denmark to Copenhagen, ferry to Malmö and then on to Stockholm. The return was to be via Copenhagen and the long European route to the Hook of Holland, passing through Denmark, Germany and The Netherlands. A day was spent in Copenhagen with the Territorial Commander (Lieut-Commissioner William Cooper). The congress leaders were General and Mrs Wilfred Kitching.

Swedish Salvationists gave a worthy welcome. An additional attraction was the presence of Erik Leidzén, returning from New York to the land of his birth after 19 years.

I spent the eve of the congress (Thursday) visiting a number of corps halls in the city, where delegates, in divisions, were holding their 'preliminary' to the great weekend. Seasons of prayer were intermingled with songs and testimonies. The congress itself began on the Friday evening with the traditional march from territorial headquarters through the wide thoroughfares of Stockholm's west-end to the Royal Tennis Hall.

At Blasieholm's Church, on the Saturday afternoon, I caught my first sight and sound of Tranås Band on its native soil, with the familiar figure of Maestro Leidzén in the middle. I had heard the band some eight years before when it took England by storm. It had been my pleasurable responsibility to report the final festival at Clapton before I had even joined the staff of *The Musician*. I was an instant devotee. I am sure that it was the inspiration and efficiency of that band which gave British bands – those of London in particular – the impetus to rise from their knees after the long war years and to face the future with new heart and hope.

In that Stockholm church the acoustic properties were perfect. The sonorous sound made its way seemingly with sheer delight to every available aid provided by the architect's artistic workmanship.

As I made my way to the Royal Music Academy after the Saturday night meeting scores of Salvationists were leaving the Academy. I looked at my programme to confirm the advertised time. Yes, 10.30 pm! There were ten minutes to go. This great crowd moving in the opposite direction had been unable to gain admittance to the all-ticket festival advertised to be given by Erik Leidzén and Tranås Band. Seats had been booked months before.

The setting of that midnight Academy event will live in my memory: the old concert hall, intimate and regal; the soft lighting and comfortable seating of the auditorium, contrasting sharply with the straight-backed wooden chairs and ultra-modern illumination on the platform; the Salvation Army blue mingling with the lighter hue of military service uniform scattered here and there, while holidaymakers, relishing the glorious summer weather, wore suitable attire to add even greater colour to the scene.

For Erik Leidzén it was a homecoming, a domestic occasion in which I felt something of an intruder. In this city he was born – some months after his officer-father's promotion to Glory. In this academy he studied music and in the gallery, he told the crowd, indicating the spot, he sat for many an hour to hear the orchestra, a full score open in his hand as he followed the music.

'Tranås is my band,' he told the audience. 'There are four Eriks in it and I make the fifth.' Earlier in the day I heard him address a private gathering of bandsmen in Stockholm Temple. Although this event took place between the afternoon and evening meetings some 600 bandsmen were present to benefit from the composer's words.

Three years later I was again in Stockholm at congress time – with the Chief of the Staff (Commissioner William Dray) and Mrs Dray. On this occasion I decided to take the long sea route from Tilbury to Gothenburg – all two-and-a-half days of it. This proved a wise decision. It was a restful voyage, with comfortable cabin accommodation, congenial company and plenty of sunshine to boost one's physical wellbeing.

The train journey from Gothenburg to Stockholm was a tremendous experience. At every stop uniformed Salvationists joined us, in large or small numbers according to the size of the township. The whole scene had a touch of 'going up to Jerusalem' about it.

Within a short time of arriving in Stockholm I was guest of honour at a Thursday pre-congress meeting at Stockholm 7, where the commanding officer was Senior-Captain Berth Anderson, composer of the march 'Looking Heavenward' and a number of other instrumental and vocal pieces published in Sweden. When requested to 'perform' at the piano, I invited the captain to go into a side hall, write a short original melody, bring it back and I would attempt to 'paint a picture' around it. He sportingly obliged and while I played a 'party piece' he duly invented eight bars of melody which was then presented as an *air varié*.

I was privileged to take a musical part in the Saturday afternoon's bandsmen's gathering and to address the fine representation. In this meeting Tranås Band gave its first public rendering of 'Lord Of The Sea'.

Again the midnight festival proved a great attraction. Three years earlier I had fallen in love with the distinctive singing and playing of the string bands, which I described in *The Musician* as 'the music of Heaven'. In 1958 I noticed that a change was taking place in such presentations. One of the three contributions from Stockholm 3 String Band, 'We Hear Our Leader Calling', was presented as a three-part song in which the familiar guitars were discarded for an unusual accompaniment of three cornets and a piano.

225

The words were by the late Commissioner James Toft and the programme note gave the information that the composer of the music was unknown. Imagine my surprise, therefore, when, after the first few bars, I recognised Ivor Novello's First World War hit 'Keep The Home Fires Burning'.

I had looked forward to the all-night crossing from Stockholm to Helsinki. Eighteen meetings in a full weekend of exciting congress events, plus the preliminaries on the Thursday and Friday, had taken toll of my physical and mental resources. Now that my press telegram report was winging its way through the night to London, the invigorating northern air, swallowed in gulps from the passenger deck, followed by a good sleep, would provide welcome relaxation before my arrival in Finland and another round of congress gatherings with the Chief of the Staff and Mrs Dray.

The myriad lights of the city were shining brightly as we left the shelter of Stockholm and headed for the open sea. This brilliant panorama gave way to a series of spasmodic twinkling beacons in the distance. These were lighthouses thoughtfully erected on a number of hazardous miniature islands of rock, there to guide the Baltic traffic to the sea and safety.

This was a beautiful spectacle at first but, as the zigzag trail of the sizeable vessel became more pronounced, the voyage became less agreeable. Rather than encourage further discomfort I decided to retire early to my cabin, in the hope that the sensation pulsating through my head and stomach would quickly pass off.

I was grateful for a single cabin. A horizontal posture brought a measure of relief and a little sleep. Suddenly I was brought fully to my senses by an urgent knock on the door. 'Come in!' I dreamily invited. A smartly dressed ship's officer entered. He said something, in Finnish I presumed. I looked blank. He said something else, in Swedish I concluded. I still looked blank and started to apologise, regretting that I did not understand what he was saying.

In perfect English the officer courteously informed me that my lifeboat was number one, then stiffened, clicked his heels, bowed his head and made towards the door. It always helps to know one's lifeboat number! My peculiar sense of English humour got the better of me. Before he could make his exit I asked naively, 'When?'

The man halted, turned in my direction, again clicked his heels and bowed, and said unsmilingly, 'Sir! It is not *when*, it is *if.*' In that strange, unexpected way I received one of my most effective lessons in the English language.

I immediately fell in love with the Finnish Salvationists. In a week with them I learned to respect their indomitable spirit and happy determination. My first contact provided ample evidence of these qualities. On the Friday, the beginning of congress meetings, they formed up eagerly in the railway square and, with Helsinki Temple Band leading the way at a brisk pace, marched along the cobbled streets to the attractive Exhibition Hall a mile distant.

When the procession had barely reached the halfway mark torrential rain began to fall and continued until the end of the journey. Many were without coats, but still they marched. Those who had been wise enough to bring umbrellas hastened to share them with less-prepared comrades.

From my place with representative overseas officers I followed hard upon the band, which gained my admiration in the 'monsoon' crisis. They played their marches joyously, despite the conditions. The drummer especially commanded my attention. Coatless, he was soaked within seconds but continued to give the rallying beat with perfect precision and power. No fair-weather drummer this. When the drumskin became saturated, still it stood up bravely to its ceaseless rhythmic beating. Only when the head of the bulbous stick flew off to fall with a resounding splash in the flooded roadway was it silent. But only for a minute. After the drummer, who was a prominent territorial headquarters officer, had waded ankle-deep in water to rescue what remained of the stick-top he returned to the task, applying his fist to the patient and ever-responding skin.

After 30 congress meetings in Finland I returned to London via Sweden and Norway. On the night train to Bergen sleep did not come easily. That journey has to be experienced to be believed. While I slept most of the way I was sufficiently awake at times to appreciate the beautiful landscape, the fir forests vying with the majestic mountain ranges for prior claim upon my early-morning viewing.

The train went on and on, tunnelling its way through the giant woodlands, climbing slowly but surely towards the high peaks, snow-capped even in midsummer. At one wayside station snow lay on the platform – and still it was not cold.

At Bergen, I was met by First-Lieutenant Edward Hannevik. I knew that this was the city of Edward Grieg and Ole Bull and expressed a wish to see the statues erected to these great Norwegian musicians. Although it was a murky Sunday morning and there was not a great deal of time to spare, the lieutenant guided me along the street to a patch of green where stand the memorials. I had time merely to take a hurried photograph of each.

At Bergen 2, where the Hanneviks were the corps officers, I took part in the holiness meeting, which had a familiar ring about it. Commissioner Emma Davis, on furlough, gave the address, borrowing a colonel's tunic and major's bonnet for the occasion. She had been touring the northern fjords and had not anticipated any Army activity.

* * * * *

Although I had visited Switzerland with three British bands – the ISB (1954), Nottingham Memorial Halls (1965) and Chalk Farm (1967) – I had not been to the lovely land of mountains and lakes solely in the interests of the Army's press. My opportunity came in May 1973 when I accompanied General and Mrs Erik Wickberg for Ascension Day meetings.

For an hour in the morning Salvationists took over Bahnhofstrasse, Zürich's street of wealth and home of the famous 'gnomes' whose financial influence is a European byword. The banks and business houses were closed even on a Thursday – this day in the Christian calendar is recognised and respected in Switzerland and public and private transport was diverted to enable the traditional Army parade to spread itself impressively and unhindered.

Loudspeakers in trams acquainted passengers with the altered routes and added their own appreciation of the marching forces. General Wickberg, with the Territorial Commander (Commissioner Francis Evans) by his side, took the salute as German-speaking Swiss officers and soldiers marched proudly past.

That is one vivid memory I brought home with me. Another was of the end of the final meeting of the day – begun at 4.30 in the afternoon to enable the Salvationists to return to their distant homes in reasonable time. As the crowd spilled out of Zürich's lovely congress hall on to the lakeside, holidaymakers in the glow of the setting sun gathered to hear what was happening at an open-air meeting conducted by Zürich Central Band in a nearby bandstand. The background of snow-capped mountain ranges made a peaceful setting.

Before that year (1973) was out I was again on the Continent – this time in Berlin for Repentance Day meetings, led by General Erik Wickberg. The three traditional gatherings were held in the Ernst Reuter Haus – named after the city's first post-war mayor. An outstanding feature was the first presentation in Berlin of the mini-musical from *Hosea*, directed by Divisional Bandmaster Karl-Heinz Reck, of Stuttgart. The near-professional production became a vehicle of blessing and challenge.

The General was very much at home in Berlin. There he had gone to school, served as a young officer and later as the territorial commander.

One of the highlights of my journalistic life was the visit with General Wickberg to Austria. It was the first visit by an international leader in the 47-year history of Army work in that country.

Despite this unbroken record of service, including the period of the Second World War, it was obvious that Army work was still largely unknown in Austria. Upon our arrival at Vienna Airport the official examining our passports asked to see the permits for us to wear 'that uniform'. This unexpected challenge required an explanation and the General, with his knowledge of German, became our spokesman. It was confirmed that the official did not recognise the Army uniform, nor had he heard of *Die Heilsarmee*. After further interrogation and assistance from a second official, we were allowed into the country – for four days.

After a hurried meal in the men's social centre, the dining room of which was afterwards transformed into a television studio in preparation for an interview to be broadcast three days later, a two-hour train journey to Linz, a noted industrial town, provided the General with the opportunity to converse in French with a woman traveller who, while vaguely aware of Army work, had never before seen a male Salvationist.

The opening of a new industrial home in Linz was enlivened by the Swiss Officers' Band, which the previous day had made a 700-mile coach journey to support the events. Speakers seized upon the centre's location – Bethlehemstrasse – as a symbol of new birth and new hope that would cause 'even the angels to applaud', as one of them aptly suggested.

Although there was no corps in Linz, where Adolf Hitler had spent much of his boyhood, there was no doubt that the work of the Army in the town was greatly respected. The many friends who gathered to identify themselves with the launching of the new social centre (including the deputy burgomaster) were loud in their praise for the officer-in-charge, Captain Edwin Gut, who had directed social work in the area for ten years.

I was interested to learn that members of the officers' band had spent some time in carrying out manual work on the hostel to prepare it for the General's visit. Captain Gut himself had carried out the electrical installations and much of the renovating, including building cupboards.

The festival that evening was held in the council chamber of a political party. Set out like a magistrates' court, the hall required the General and his party to occupy the high-backed chairs on the 'bench', with the band and congregation seated below, facing the 'platform' from three directions. The small but appreciative audience was drawn, in the main, from the Protestant community, and the programme proceeded undisturbed by a witches' coven being held in a lower hall! I quickly learned that spiritism had a firm grip upon the people of Austria.

After a meeting on the Sunday morning, which was virtually the religious inauguration of the centre and in which six speakers from the many denominations took part, and an early lunch, the Swiss musicians boarded their coach for Vienna, which took them on the swift-moving autobahn in dazzling wintry sunshine and within awesome sight of the snow-packed Austrian Alps. We followed by train two hours later, but not before I learned that Beethoven was often in Linz, to see his brother who was a chemist. This mundane but profound thought reminded me that I was not far from the musical heart of the world. A little to the west was the romantic *Sound Of Music* country. To the east was Vienna, home of lovely melodies and capital of the one-time proud Austro-Hungarian Empire.

The band was most anxious to make the most of its time in Vienna and soon after arriving was on its way to a series of open-air gatherings in the centre of the city. In Austria the Army is not recognised as a church but as *Verein der Heilsarmee* (the Association of The Salvation Army). This ensures police protection for its activity, including open-air meetings for which special permits are issued.

This means that application to hold open-air meetings must be made well in advance, the exact time and place being required to be given. It is the normal procedure for a policeman, on seeing an Army gathering, to examine the certificate of authority before permitting it to continue.

The desire of the Swiss bandsmen, therefore, was a spontaneous decision and, as there had not been time to notify the authorities, their activity was limited to a series of musical stops on a brief march through the streets. There was no speaking or religious propaganda, but handbills advertising the evening meeting were freely distributed.

The evening meeting in the Albert Schweitzer Hall took the form of a musical programme with a strong salvation appeal. The cosmopolitan congregation included embassy diplomats, representatives from all the churches, a few uniformed Salvationists and a number of observers attracted by the afternoon invitation of the band.

General Wickberg spent his final day in Vienna meeting state, local government and diplomatic leaders. The first appointment was with the Federal Chancellor (Herr Bruno Kreisky) – the first time that an Austrian head of state had so honoured The Salvation Army.

In an unhurried audience the chancellor, quite relaxed and with courteous interest, discussed world affairs with the knowledge of an expert and was well aware of global social conditions. Our uniform, which had caused so much bewilderment on the streets of the city, was not unknown to him. He had seen Salvationists at work in Finland and had stayed at the Army's hotel in Stockholm.

A welcome feature of the historic weekend occurred on the Monday evening when a film on Army work was screened on TV, the first time such recognition had been given to Salvationists in Austria.

One of the outstanding events of Army history in Austria before the Second World War was the visit of Chalk Farm Band in the summer of 1936. This was Bandmaster A. W. Punchard's last tour with the band and it took in six countries – The Netherlands, Germany, Czechoslovakia, Austria, Switzerland and France. Quite an undertaking in that pre-flying era.

As a former 'Chalk Farmer' I wanted to see the scene of the band's triumphant open-air festival of nearly 40 years earlier, when thousands on a Saturday afternoon greeted the first – and only – British band to play in the Austrian capital.

The state buildings were still there, as were the 900 parks, greens and spacious squares. In a quiet, secluded, well-kept garden I came across Mozart's memorial. The beautifully carved instruments at his feet denoted his craft while his batonless hand was conducting from the score spread out on a music stand in front of him.

This was the master in action. Cherubim adorning the memorial had instruments in their hands, as if giving heavenly approval to his genius and delighting in the divine sounds.

I remembered that Mozart died penniless and was buried in a pauper's grave in this city with only the undertaker and his men present. They searched for his coffin years later, but it was never located. But you do not really need a grave to honour such a musician. His music, living and pure, is his greatest epitaph, but I am glad the people of Vienna remembered to erect a monument.

A walk towards the old city took me past the magnificent opera house where Johann Strauss's *Die Fledermaus* is performed each New

Year's Eve and near to Praterstrasse, where 'The Blue Danube' was composed. If the river which gave the famous waltz its title, and runs through the eastern part of the city, was ever blue, pollution has long since given it a brown tint, but its romance is not lost.

I spent some time in St Stephen's Cathedral, where Joseph Haydn was a choirboy. When Haydn was dying in 1809 the French were bombarding the city. His servants were terrified, but Haydn took it all very calmly. He asked to be lifted from his bed to the piano and when he had been comfortably placed he played his Austrian Hymn three times over, while the guns were thundering outside.

At that moment there was another composer in Vienna, crouching in a cellar, with cotton wool stuffed in his ears. That was Beethoven. His hearing had begun to go and he was frightened that the sound of the explosions would still further endanger it. He lived another 18 years and it is said that Vienna had never seen a funeral like his. Beethoven's monument is flanked by nine angels, one for each of his symphonies.

Franz Schubert, another son of Vienna, died in the city at the age of 32. The inscription on his tomb reads: 'Music buried here a rich possession and yet fairer hopes.'

Before leaving for the airport I walked across the city to the Army's women's home. This pillar-frontaged building is impressive. During the Second World War it was a Gestapo headquarters and was later occupied by Russian forces. I was shown horseshoe indents on the polished oak floor of the wide entrance hall made, I was told, by the animals as, mounted by their Russian masters, they were ridden through the massive doorway and up the stairway.

At the top of the stairway, and close to the door leading to Austria's only corps hall, was a filled-in frame that had once contained a full-length portrait of Adolf Hitler.

Five months later I was in Stockholm reporting my third congress there. It was fitting that the final weekend of active service for General and Mrs Erik Wickberg should be spent in this way and that Swedish Salvationists should be given the privilege of bidding farewell to the international leaders before they entered retirement.

The Territorial Commander (Commissioner Harry Tyndal) spoke for them all when, in introducing visitors, he said, 'They belong to us.' The General replied, 'Although I have given my life to an international movement my heart and passport have always been Swedish.' Thirty-two of his 40 years of officership had been spent outside his native land.

At Skansen, the great open-air cultural and entertainment centre high above the city, the great congress ended with thanksgiving and praise to God for nearly 700 seekers during the weekend. The General's brief message had to do with two words which prove difficult to say in the Swedish language: not because of any problem of pronunciation, but because of the meaning involved in honestly saying them. In English the phrases are equally difficult to say: 'Thank you!' and 'Forgive me!'

A week later I was in London, reporting the retirement salute to General and Mrs Wickberg in the Royal Festival Hall. Salvationists from four nations participated.

In the spring of 1975 I did some more personal pioneering, this time in Portugal with General and Mrs Wiseman.

With a confident declaration, 'We're going to turn the world upside down', ringing from tuneful, vigorous voices, the then three-year-old Salvation Army in Portugal – some 60 strong – greeted General and Mrs Wiseman on the airport concourse as they arrived for the command's first congress.

On the Sunday, in a dockside restaurant overlooking the River Tagus, with a clear view of Lisbon's seven hills wreathed in glorious sunlight and close to where stands the huge statue of Christ with a hand outstretched as if in compassion towards the city, Major Carl Eliason pointed out the spot where he, with his wife and family, had arrived three years earlier to take charge of Army work in a strange land, without a hall or a Salvationist in the city.

They were thrilling days in Lisbon. For once there was no brass band to help swell the congress singing, but so much was there an air of pioneering about the place that I was not aware of the missing ingredient. The major was an able accordionist and I could imagine how valuable his playing had proved in the early days in Portugal. My assistance on the organ of various churches and at the piano in the Army hall during the weekend, released him to give full leadership of the meetings and translation duties.

A year later, and after I had embarked upon my International Congress duties on a part-time basis, I was privileged to accompany General and Mrs Wiseman to Hanover for Germany's 90th anniversary congress.

This important event concluded, it was on to Amsterdam to attend a five-day conference of European leaders. During this I was privileged to address the august assembly on matters relating to the forthcoming International Congress, discussing planning and putting them in the picture regarding each territory's involvement.

Thus ended my overseas reporting where it had begun – in The Netherlands. Some 27 years had passed since that first trip with the International Staff Band in 1949. Altogether 14 countries had been visited – two of them on five occasions. The experience proved to be of untold value.

Chapter 20

Some Special Assignments

ONE of my official duties was to make periodic visits to one of our much-loved 'retireds'. She was Brigadier Ruth Tracy, then in residence at Sunset Lodge, Tunbridge Wells. My instructions were to 'cheer her up'. Inevitably she did that for me.

We never seemed lost for conversation. Songwriting was our common interest and I always had many questions to ask about her songs, nine of which were included in the 1953 edition of *The Song Book Of The Salvation Army*.

I had first met Brigadier Tracy when I was the songster leader at Child's Hill. When my first song was published she took the trouble to drop me a note of congratulations and best wishes for 'future creations'.

I last visited the brigadier a week after she had celebrated her 86th birthday. Once more discussing her songs, I confessed that my favourite was 'Send Out Thy Light And Thy Truth, Lord', especially when used, on very rare occasions, to the tune for which it was written, immortalised as the cornet solo in the Goldsmith selection, 'My Light'. (I believe the secular words are 'True as the stars that are shining'.)

We differed in our choice of 'favourites'. The brigadier revealed that hers was 'Where are now those doubts that hindered all his will from being done?'. She meaningfully quoted the first verse and when the refrain was reached lifted her hand in witness as she repeated, 'I have pleasure in his service, more than all.'

She was a gracious lady, one of our first notable songwriters. My memories of those visits proved helpful when I came to write *Sing The Happy Song!*

Not all good copy needs to be chased, although a reporter has always to be on the lookout for material. Some equally good material arrives unexpectedly at one's office door. This was the case when, on a day in July 1960, I was privileged to spend a little while in the company of the Rev Sidney E. Cox.

Mr Cox – once a brigadier in The Salvation Army – and I had met briefly when the ISB visited Miami, Florida, during its 1957 tour in the USA, and it was beneficial to have this further association.

In speaking of the more than 300 songs from his pen, my guest expressed surprise that some of his earliest compositions were still very much alive in Army circles, among them 'You Can Tell Out The Sweet Story' (his first song published in 1915), 'I Was Wandering In The Wilderness' and 'I Love Him Better Every Day'. One has only to recall some of the songs bearing his name in the Army songbook to realise the writer's gift for effective composition, both words and music. Such favourites as 'God's Love Is Wonderful', 'The Saviour Sought And Found Me' and 'This One Thing I Know' will never die.

This gracious and interesting personality had attended the Keswick Convention and was on his way to Northampton, his birthplace, when I met him. He had left this town for Canada some 53 years before, as a lad of 19, and this was his first return to England. The previous day, in the company of Senior-Major Charles Skinner, the Rev and Mrs Cox had attended the holiness meeting at Penge, where Mrs Cox had knelt at the mercy seat as a girl. To see the same spot in the same hall provided her with a moving experience.

* * * * *

One of my most memorable assignments was to interview Commissioner Catherine Bramwell-Booth on the eve of her 90th birthday. I had met the commissioner once before. On a cold wintry night in 1947 I boarded a tram outside International Headquarters (then at Denmark Hill) bound for the Oval Underground Station where I would change for a train for home.

238

She was seated on one of the side seats inside the door of the lower deck. I nodded politely as I passed and found a seat halfway along the tramcar. As I fumbled for the threepence required for my fare I was aware that someone had occupied the vacant seat beside me. It was the commissioner. 'May as well let people know we belong to the same Army,' was her whimsical comment. 'Who are you?' She was International Secretary for Europe at that time and I was a recently arrived addition to the *Musician* editorial staff. Haltingly I introduced myself and soon we were exchanging experiences and chatting like old friends.

The memory of the brief but indelible encounter was vividly with me as 26 years later I travelled through the Royal Berkshire countryside to interview the Army's 'grand old lady'.

As I waited at the door of the home the commissioner shared with her two sisters, Lieut-Colonel Olive and Senior-Major Dora, I could not avoid noticing through the large glass panelling an Army drum with the old-style big-headed stick attached. Above this symbol of service, at a dignified angle, was the familiar Army flag forming the centrepiece of a setting completed by an impressive bust of General Bramwell Booth, father of the three sisters.

In preparing for the visit it had been agreed that I should be granted a 90-minute interview – one minute for each year of the veteran leader's life. Promptly I was escorted up the staircase and shown into the commissioner's study. Despite her age she rose to greet me, her upright carriage and alert eyes belying her years. She was wearing her uniform, the ribbons of her Commander of the Order of the British Empire and Salvation Army long-service medals proudly displayed.

An exchange of pleasantries, some welcome refreshment, one or two forthright opinions about the Army's press in general and *The War Cry* in particular, and then we were down to business.

'How does it feel on the eve of one's 90th birthday?' I asked. Commissioner Catherine hesitated slightly, as though the thought of such a milestone had not entered her head. But she was soon speaking in her strong, vibrant voice.

'To be quite honest, I don't relish it at all. I pray that the Lord will let me live a little longer and perhaps – perhaps – be of some use. Who knows?'

As the grandfather clock chimed midday I took my leave of this remarkable woman leader whose roots went deep into Salvation Army history, but whose fertile mind was conversant with every latest innovation and newest shocking headline of 1973.

A few days after the interview a carefully wrapped parcel arrived at my home. It was a copy of Commissioner Catherine's biography of her grandmother, the Army Mother. The autographed inscription read:

> *To my fellow Salvationist, Colonel Brindley Boon,*
> *recalling his visit and with prayer that now and always*
> *we may be 'looking unto Jesus the author and finisher*
> *of our faith'.*
>
> *Hebrews, 12:2*

> *from Catherine Bramwell-Booth 1973*
> *'The Salvation Army is love for souls.'*
>
> *W. Bramwell Booth.*

* * * * *

A month later another special assignment took me to the retirement home of General and Mrs Wilfred Kitching, delightfully situated in the charming Sussex countryside and within easy reach of the sea. I was instantly aware of a peaceful atmosphere that was not entirely to do with the quiet, select bungalow community in which they lived. Rather had it to do with the spiritual contentment that had always made their salvationism such a strong, influential quality. It was the eve of the General's 80th birthday.

I was intrigued by all the souvenirs. They adorned the walls of the lounge, overspilt into the conservatory and rather unexpectedly turned up again in the General's 'den'. There, among other treasured documents, was the framed copy of his Certificate of Appointment signed by the members of the 1954 High Council which elected him to the Army's supreme office. He was the first General to receive such a certificate.

The Army was only 28 years old when the General was born. He was dedicated to God under the flag by Commissioner Railton. Knowing that this 'soldier-saint' had often stayed at the Kitching home when the General was a boy, I asked him to describe the effect that the commissioner had had upon his young life.

'I was always impressed by the fact that he was very zealous,' he said. 'He would often share a room with me – my mother never knew when my father was going to bring him home – and I would wake up in the night and hear him praying.'

He commented on the original 'mixed bag' of Army leaders, singling out Oliphant, the London clergyman, and Cadman, the Rugby chimney sweep, as typical 'opposites' who were welded into the unique fellowship of those early-day apostles. He referred warmly to his days as national young people's secretary in war-torn Britain. I also learned of the ministry of prayer and letter-writing in which he and Mrs Kitching were engaged in retirement.

The afternoon went all too quickly. A tastefully prepared meal with vegetables from the 'Kitching garden', followed by delicious fruits cultivated in the same way; a text from the musical promise box which, when the lid was opened, played 'Standing On The Promises Of God'; a prayer along personal lines and for the wider world of Salvation Army life beyond the trees, lanes and enchanting coastline, and I was off. Clutched in my hand was an autographed book he had given me with the prayer that it might prove useful to me in my work.

During my more than ten years on *The Musician* I travelled many miles in the British Isles. Much of this had to do with the reporting of national and inter-divisional councils and festivals. At other times my journey was to follow up a story which had caught our ear and to prepare a full-length feature amplifying the brief item of news that had reached us.

There were scores of such thrilling experiences. There is room only for a few.

When, in the summer of 1957, it was announced that Abergavenny Band was to take part in the bandmasters councils festival at the Royal Albert Hall in the October, I felt that this section of nine bandsmen should be featured. The corps officers, Captain and Mrs John Parker, and their comrades heartily agreed. This resulted in the photographer, Stan Chapman, and I spending a weekend in that border town, known as the 'Gateway of Wales'. There had never been more than 14 members of Abergavenny Band. As soon as it struck up the march 'Exultation' in the Saturday night meeting I sat up and took notice. My immediate reaction was 'tuneful and musicianly' and this impression remained with me throughout the weekend. In the three minutes that the march took to play I glanced at the men, one by one. Each was complete master of the situation. Some were using more than one book, for they were trained to fill in the gaps caused by missing parts. The deputy bandmaster was playing a medium Bb bass with an Eb bass copy as well. When he was resting on his own part, it seemed easy for him to carry on playing the other, even if this meant quick thinking in the matter of transposition.

All nine were local officers. All but one, the songster leader, were products of the corps.

We stayed over on the Monday to visit the men at their places of employment. The photos with brief captions made an interesting middle-page spread and served as a good introduction to the London festival. Stan 'snapped' them at work: the engine driver, the railway guard, window cleaner, shopkeeper, production foreman at a nylon spinning factory, progress records clerk at a mechanical joint factory, Ministry of Supply training officer – it takes all sorts to make up an Army band.

On the big night the gallant nine from the 'shadow' of the 'Sugar Loaf mountain' acquitted themselves with glory, the staff band moving for the Welsh musicians to take the centre position for their items. It was necessary for Bandmaster William Davies to play cornet. His brother Harold, the deputy bandmaster, took over as conductor, his bombardon slung over his shoulder and resting on a knee balanced on a chair. They spent the Sunday at Sutton, the home corps of their officers.

In March 1957 I was invited to accompany Regent Hall Band to Buckingham Palace in celebration of that corps's 75th anniversary. Several times I had watched and listened from the other side of the railings, and now, for the first time, I marched through the famous centre gateway into the forecourt. As the band played, suddenly a curly head was spotted in the corner of a second-floor window above the main entrance. A face then appeared and the crowd's intake of breath denoted that five-year-old Princess Anne had been recognised. She had left her lunch (by permission, the Queen later revealed) to see the Army band.

I stood next to Band Reservist Jack Merrick, ex-pugilist, ex-Covent Garden porter and trophy of grace. The tune 'Aurelia', featured in the final meditation 'The Light Of The World', brought back memories to him. He was the only one present who had taken part in that first march to the palace in 1910. It was while Bandmaster Herbert Twitchin was leading his band in the playing of that tune that Queen Alexandra, so recently widowed, appeared on the balcony and acknowledged with a hand wave the bandsmen in the courtyard below.

'I was the colour sergeant then,' Jack confided in me, 'complete with turn-up trousers and buttonhole boots.' The veteran was thoroughly enjoying his seventh visit to the royal residence.

Towards the end of 1960 I realised an ambition – to publish George Bernard Shaw's candid impression of what he saw and heard when he attended a Salvation Army band festival at Clapton Congress Hall in 1905.

Then a noted music critic, he had been invited by Bramwell Booth, then Chief of the Staff, to provide the comments. I had come into possession of a copy of the document some years before and now, 55 years after the event and ten years after the author's death, General Kitching had given permission for it to appear in print.

Shaw's comments were interesting and enlightening but one wonders how much of his writing was done with tongue in cheek.

An immediate reaction was received from Colonel Bertram Rodda, a former chief secretary in the British Territory and by then living in retirement in California. He remembered, as a young captain serving in the Chief of the Staff's office at International Headquarters, being shown the sealed file with the whisper that George Bernard Shaw had been asked to give a candid opinion of a massed festival but his findings would be so disturbing that it was decided to keep the matter *sub rosa*.

The colonel added: 'I had to wait 45 years to be allowed to know what was in the sealed file handled those years ago on the second floor of the old IHQ.'

On Christmas Eve 1956 I was at Regent Hall to report the first meeting to be televised from a Salvation Army hall in Britain. It was an ITA carol service. An announcement, a camera close-up shot of the familiar crest at the back of the platform and the strains of 'Christmas Joy' played by the 'Rink' Band conducted by Kenneth Cook, and the Army was on the air and on the screen.

For half an hour viewers at their firesides heard the carols sung by united songster brigades selected from the London area and conducted by Lieut-Colonel Ernest Rance, and interspersed with solo verses by Mrs Captain June Mingay and Deputy Songster Leader Ron Badnall, of Kingston-upon-Thames. Brigadier Fred Grant was at the electronic organ.

To get a complete picture I went behind the scenes. Outside in Princes Street stood six mobile vehicles. A generator could be heard pumping its power while layers of cable led from the units through the open door along the passageway to the hall itself. The youth centre next door was converted into a transmitter.

Inside Regent Hall the transformation was remarkable. The gallery space immediately above the clock had been built into a stage on which stood two giant cameras. Substantial scaffolding lent its necessary support. More scaffolding was erected in the 'boxes' then situated either side of the platform and a mammoth light occupied the position opposite. Other powerful lights shone from vantage points throughout the hall and microphones hung from many parts of the building.

Another Army TV feature took me to Woking, in the summer of 1960. This was for Associated-Rediffusion's series *Pursuit Of Happiness*, in which the interviewer, Daniel Farson, was 'rather like a man with a butterfly net trying to capture and for a moment pin down the elusive quality of happiness'.

The Army's contribution to the series did not consist only of a casual shot or two of a Sunday afternoon open-air meeting and the march to the hall. The cameras, with the efficient technical team, visited the home of a bandsman who was a postman and was 'caught' teaching his two sons to play brass instruments; a public house in which another bandsman regularly distributed Army periodicals; and the weekly band practice.

When the lights fused and there was a temporary halt in the filming, I asked Daniel Farson if this was his first professional contact with The Salvation Army. He said it was, but quickly added, 'I have always wanted to work with your people and this gives me an opportunity. I was anxious to include a small, dedicated group in this series and believed that this band, with its colourful setting and enthusiasm, could provide the answer.'

On Maundy Thursday 1965 a phone call sent me hurrying to Broadcasting House for a recorded interview on Jack de Manio's popular early-morning radio programme, *Today*. It was the era of rhythm groups, and 'modern music' was very much with us. I had been persuaded to write a three-article series on the subject for *The War Cry*, and the first of the contributions had caught the eye. The BBC sensed a story.

As I walked along Upper Regent Street towards Langham Place and the huge structure which, to me, always resembled a half-finished ocean liner, I thought of my last visit to the home of the BBC. That was more than 30 years earlier. I was out of work and had seen an advert for a junior clerk in the Purchases and Accounts Department of the corporation. I did not get the job, but at least it had given me my first awe-inspiring glimpse of Broadcasting House.

Quite recently I unexpectedly discovered who did get the job. It was Robert Dougall, who 'graduated' to become a top-quality newscaster. In his autobiography he reveals how he came to fill the vacancy without even applying for it!

Jack de Manio received me in the entrance hall with charm and courtesy and escorted me to his office on the third floor. He had read my article and wanted me to tell listeners, in the interview, how and why the Army rhythm groups had begun to take the place of brass bands. I respectfully pointed out that I had not said that; furthermore I did not believe it. To me it was not a matter of rhythm groups or brass bands. It was rhythm groups *and* brass bands. There was room for them both.

The interviewer latched on to that thought and asked me to enlarge upon it, switching on the recording equipment as he did so. When the interview went out on Easter Monday I was surprised to find that Jack de Manio's questions were quite different from those asked four days before. He had obviously rephrased them to bring them into line with my impromptu discourse on modern Army music and its function. I considered this to be a masterpiece of technical juggling quite unknown to me in those days.

It was fitting that Nottingham Memorial Halls Band, from the city of the Founder's birth, should be invited to undertake an overseas campaign in the Army's centenary year. I was happy to be appointed to accompany the band as International Headquarters representative, again providing a day-to-day report for *The Musician*.

At 2 am on Friday 27 August 1965 the band flew out of London Airport bound for Switzerland. An hour later we were passing over Paris and 40 minutes after that the plane landed at Basle. The journey had taken 100 minutes, a little more than half the time it had taken the band to travel from Nottingham to Heathrow.

Five o'clock in the morning is an unusual hour to be picked up by billeters, but this was the hour the Nottingham bandsmen met their hosts and were conveyed to homes for little more than two hours' rest. At 9.30 the band was at the recording studio for a session which lasted six hours.

There was much to attract in the band's presentation. The programmes were wisely constructed by Bandmaster Ralph Bristow;

the singing of the male chorus, under the leadership of Deputy Bandmaster Ken Buxton, was balanced and appealing; the drumming displays by the percussionists never failed to create something of a sensation; and at the performance of Graham Woodcock on the xylophone the crowds erupted.

This instrument was quite new to Army audiences in Switzerland. It was known in secular circles and had been seen on television, but not in a Salvationist setting. After Graham's debut in this role in Zürich, the acclamation would have put even a BBC applausemeter out of action. There were whistles and cries of 'Encore!' The German-speaking chief secretary, who was presiding, was well aware of the Army regulation which forbade a repeat performance. He was also acquainted with 'an old English custom', as he called it, when such a unanimous request was met with a presentation of 'a second verse', thus evading the official ruling.

When the excitement had at last died down the colonel turned to the bandmaster and asked innocently, 'Have you another werse?' Quick as lightning Ralph Bristow replied, 'No we haven't another worse, but we have one just as bad!' The bandsmen enjoyed the joke even if the audience may have been rather dubious. The encore was equally well received.

A free afternoon in the sunshine at Biel-Bienne was divided between a trip on the lake – at its roughest for some years – and a cable ascent to the city's lofty peak. The lake trippers landed at beautiful St Peter's Island, where Jean-Jacques Rousseau, the French-Swiss philosopher, lived for some time. In his room, now part of a hotel, we were interested to see that the last English tourists to sign the visitors' book were the Beatles, but suspicions were aroused when it was noted that one of the group, 'Georges Harrison', had 'Liverpoll' as his town of residence. Or was he fooling?

Those who made the other excursion were 'treated' to a concert by a village band, which was evidently put off its stroke by the unexpected presence of the much-advertised Salvationist visitors.

Chapter 21

Behind a Baritone

MY first weekend away as a member of the International Staff Band was at Torquay in October 1952. The 'Indian summer' weather was perfect and the popular Devonshire holiday resort was crowded with the late season visitors.

We travelled from London by train and, as was customary in those days, marched from the station to the point of official reception, the Pavilion. Police diverted traffic and crowds lined the pavements to form a human avenue through the main thoroughfares.

One frightening memory lingers from that first weekend. After the Sunday afternoon programme, Senior-Captain Harold Wright, one of the 'double Bs', asked me if I would read a Scripture portion in the evening open-air meeting, for which he was responsible. He handed me a piece of paper with the verses duly noted.

I duly read my parable from the New Testament and was on my way back to my second baritone position when Harold Wright made it clear that I had not finished my stint of duty. 'Just a minute,' he said, and then proceeded to tell the huge crowd that I was a journalist who was used to looking for the salient points in other people's copy, and that he was one of those who had 'suffered' from the generous application of my blue pencil.

'I am going to ask the lieutenant,' he went on, 'to tell us what the salient points are in the story he has just read.'

What would you have done? I hurriedly opened my Bible at that passage, beginning to address the congregation as I quickly alerted my eyes to roam hopefully from line to line in search of some inspiration, at the same time praying that divine deliverance would not be long in arriving. I heard myself saying slowly and deliberately, playing for time as I progressed, 'As... I... read... that... passage... of... Scripture... it... occurred... to... me... that...'

I cannot claim that the ordeal resulted in success.

Upon joining the ISB one could reckon upon being issued with a new cap and a new pair of trousers. The blue tunic, festival tunic and model 'C' overcoat were usually from stock. My blue tunic and coat had previously been worn by Brian Cooper, who had entered the band as a youth, made quite a name for himself as a pianoforte soloist on the programmes and was now undertaking national service. As there was no suitable red tunic available it was necessary for me to be measured for a new one.

The festival tunics were kept in a large wicker basket permanently stocked in a corner of the band room. They were loaded on to a van, coach or train with the instruments for engagements and allocated with the traditional ritual before a meeting or festival. The names, written in large letters in the linings, were ceremoniously read out and the tunics claimed. If the claimant was missing when his name was called he had to wait for the next time round, rather like collecting one's baggage from an airport baggage-claim conveyor belt.

Some of the uniforms had been around a long time and the linings bore a fascinating catalogue of names. At times these were added to the names of the present wearers. This meant that often the recital included 'Coxhead', 'Samuels' and 'Colley'. Sometimes a wag in historically festive mood would add such personalities as 'Goldsmith', 'Drage' and 'Hurren' or 'Cadman' and 'Dowdle'. All that ended a long time ago and now all band members are responsible for the safety and cleanliness of their own tunics. Much more hygienic! Much less fun!

In April 1953 in the Dorking Halls, Surrey, and sponsored by First-Lieutenant and Mrs Edward Cotterill and local Salvationists, a festival was given for which the chairman and guest of honour was Dr Ralph Vaughan Williams, OM. Although the great composer had had an earlier contact with the corps – a wartime event when he presided over a meeting in which the then divisional commander (Major Edgar Grinsted) recounted some of his flying experiences in the First World War – this was his first encounter with the staff band.

I was one of those who proudly obtained the great man's autograph on the front page of my programme. It is now Army musical history that the outcome of that Dorking link-up was 'Prelude On Three Welsh Hymn Tunes', written as a tribute to the band.

The ISB spent the weekend before Her Majesty's coronation (2 June 1953) at St Ives. The commanding officer (Captain Ken Nutty) went to town to organise a visit that would be remembered and talked about for years to come.

We travelled by all-night train from Paddington on the Friday, arriving somewhere about six o'clock on the Saturday morning. Captain Nutty had succeeded in interesting the café proprietors along the seafront in our visit, the result of such publicity being an invitation to breakfast from all of them! This news was broken to us as we alighted from the train. We dared not offend the good people, we were informed, and would therefore be required to partake of the repast provided in each of the restaurants in turn. We must not eat too much at any one place. What breakfasts they prepared! We did our best to oblige. Never was so much eaten by so few in so little time!

It was a wonderful weekend. Gaily decorated streets were thronged. Festivals and meetings were packed to capacity limits, with disappointed hundreds unable to gain admittance. The crowd that attended the Sunday evening community hymn-singing from the slipway, characteristically led by Captain Nutty, was estimated at 3,000.

The peak moment of the outdoor witness was the Sunday afternoon parade when the band headed contingents of forces personnel and civic organisations past the base where a famous rear-admiral took the salute. St Ives's first woman mayor attended all the gatherings.

Looking back over the years, each campaign of those days seems to have been eventful. There are far too many to be remembered in detail and I am able only to select a few campaign highlights of my eight-year membership.

In the summer of 1959, in keeping with many other bands in the British Territory which pledged themselves to undertake the extra mile to render unusual evangelical service in the Mission To The Family Year, the ISB conducted a Sunday campaign in the Sussex countryside.

Following 'knee-drill' at Brighton Congress Hall, where a festival had been given the previous night, we travelled by coach to Henfield. Soon after 9.30 am we marched from the village green through the main street to the strains of 'Victors Acclaimed'. A Christian friend was waiting for us and happily joined us in the two open-air meetings.

At Cowfold we played on the village green while cottagers, who had not witnessed such a sight for 20 years, stood at their doors. One of the bass players left the ring to contact a number of young men engaged in preparing a nearby cricket pitch for the afternoon match. Others spoke to interested bystanders. The final open-air meeting of the morning was conducted in the welcome shade of a giant tree at Lower Beeding, with the century-old church a colourful background.

After an alfresco lunch, provided I seem to remember by our kindly Brighton hosts, the afternoon was spent on the Langley Green and Ifield housing estates, adjacent to Crawley New Town. In the brilliant sunshine, which illuminated the day's activities, several open-air meetings were held and many families received Army literature and an invitation to attend meetings at the local corps.

To cater for the crowds of children sitting on the grass, Staff Bandsman Bert Thompson's Dormobile, used for some years to convey the percussion instruments, became a puppet theatre. Will Pratt and Alf Holmes became chief actors in the presentation of the parable of the unjust steward (remembered from training college days) and Messrs Cobb, Jenkins, Boon and Condon were left behind to accompany chorus singing, while our amused colleagues, led by a somewhat startled bandmaster, marched off across the green to another point of contact.

The day ended with a salvation meeting in the packed hall of a new school at Crawley. Many in the congregation were attending their first Army gathering.

Staff Band weekends at Regent Hall were always traumatic occasions. The Saturday evening audience was quite different from any other gathering of Salvationist brass band fans. They were eager to hear the new music to compare it with the contributions of Hawkes, Goldsmith, Coles and Marshall in their prime, and to assess its potential publication value.

Just to sit and play one's part in the band was bad enough. To have to make some platform offering was even more formidable. On my first visit with the band I was required to testify in the Sunday salvation meeting. The next year, with General Albert Orsborn in the chair a few weeks before his retirement, I was entrusted with the Saturday festival Bible reading and exhortation.

Afterwards, as we were disrobing in the 'Rink' band room, a former high-ranking Army leader made a beeline for me, pressing through the throng with his hand outstretched. I eagerly took it, thinking that here was a word of commendation on my public speaking debut with the band that would encourage me to even greater endeavour. What he actually said was, 'Your tunic's too short. Ask them to get you another one.' Deflation was steep that night.

Centenaries were beginning to emerge. On a Friday evening in June 1955 we were at Stockwell Green Congregational Church for the 100th anniversary of the marriage of William Booth and Catherine Mumford. Commissioner Catherine Bramwell-Booth gave the address and General Kitching unveiled a plaque to mark the occasion. The following year we were at Regent Hall to celebrate the centenary of the birth of their firstborn, William Bramwell Booth.

There were international congresses too. In the summer of 1956 the corps cadets of the world met in London to commemorate the diamond jubilee of the movement. The next year the golden jubilee of the home league was observed with an international congress in London.

The only Abney Park funeral I attended during my period in the band was that of Mrs General Bramwell Booth in June 1957. We headed the procession from the Stoke Newington hall (the service had been held at Clapton Congress Hall the night before).

For that afternoon a touch of old-time Army pageantry was recaptured. To the strains of 'Promoted To Glory', the long march began and traffic was halted as a host of Salvationists – officers, local officers, bandsmen, songsters and colour sergeants proudly bearing the flags of London corps – followed the earthly remains of the 95-year-old warrior to their last resting place.

Another memorable highlight was when we met at Judd Street to provide Dr Ralph Vaughan Williams with his first hearing of 'Prelude On Three Welsh Hymn Tunes'. Seated between General Wilfred Kitching and Colonel Albert Jakeway (Head of the International Music Editorial Department) in the conference room, the eminent British composer, a copy of the score before him, listened to his first work for brass band. The piece had been passed for presentation and publication by the International Music Board a few days earlier.

During the initial run-through the great man spotted a wrong note by the second trombone and stopped the band. Closer scrutiny revealed that an accidental was missing from the manuscript. What discernment at 82 years of age!

A month later Vaughan Williams was an eager listener in the Maida Vale studio of the BBC when 'Prelude On Three Welsh Hymn Tunes' received its public premiere in a *Listen To The Band* broadcast. He followed the playing from the proof pages of the full score on a music stand. As the final majestic chord died away Bandmaster Adams showed his acknowledgement to the composer who, with a happy wave of the hand, indicated his approbation.

My outstanding memory of the visit to London by Emil Söderström, the noted Danish-American composer, is of his arriving the night before at the small hotel in King's Cross where he was staying. He had taken a 'constitutional' around the city streets and he could not remember the address of the hotel, even though he knew the street. Eventually he made the right decision as to where he was staying by recalling that the scraper at the entrance when utilised responded with the note of Gb! What perfect pitch!

For a time our small basement band room in Upper Thames Street – at the back of what remained of IHQ – was out of commission because of long-overdue renovations. All rehearsals were held at Judd Street. For those bandsmen still in residence at Denmark Hill – Captain Pratt and myself – this meant a midday trip three days a week and a similar journey on Wednesday evenings.

On the former occasions we were required to down pens or abandon typewriters at 11.45 am, take a hurried lunch in the top avenue canteen and make sure of catching the train from Denmark Hill to Holborn Viaduct. This journey took 12 minutes. A 20-minute service did not allow the 12.32 pm to be missed. The link-up between British Rail and the London Transport (Metropolitan) line at Farringdon Street necessitated a jog through Smithfield Market and a last-minute sprint if the train was approaching the platform. Another brisk walk from King's Cross Station to Salvationist Publishing and Supplies completed the post-lunch dash. We were usually there in time to commence playing at 1 pm.

The return journey was the same in reverse and we could generally be depended upon to be back at our desks by 2.30 pm!

There was a particular day when Tom Rive's symphonic variations, 'I Know A Fount', was receiving meticulous attention. Sections G, H and part of I were being treated to detailed concentration. Arriving rather breathless, I took my place and prepared to perform, only to discover that throughout those movements my part indicated 54 bars' rest. I never played a note. It was an exhausting and expensive interlude. But not entirely fruitless. I was able to improve my faculty as a listener.

There were informal, more relaxed engagements as well. Two family outings to Whipsnade Zoo were both spoiled by incessant rain, but a third trip, by coach to Windsor and thence by river steamer to Maidenhead, ended with a festival presided over by Senior-Major Arnold Brown, in London from Toronto to explore the possibility of a television series in which the ISB later appeared.

On a Thursday afternoon in the late summer of 1954 the ISB left Victoria Station for its fourth post-war campaign and its first visit to Switzerland for 43 years. The sun was shining and the weather experts were smiling. The tour was to last for 14 days. An innovation was that we wore epauletted raincoats for the first time. After the crossing from Folkestone to Calais, the journey to Basle was carried out by trans-European night express. The comfort of sleepers was denied us. We crowded into four reserved compartments, sitting bolt upright and whiling away the hours with stimulating conversation.

Upon our arrival in Basle we were welcomed by the Territorial Commander (Lieut-Commissioner Norman Duggins), our old leader, Mrs Duggins and representative officers.

That afternoon's journey to Aarau gave us a foretaste of things to come. The road took our coach along the bank of the Rhine, fast moving and swollen by recent heavy rainfall. Across the river the lovely woodland of Germany presented an irresistible attraction for the band's many amateur photographers.

For the first four days of the campaign Brigadier Walter Zahnd, who travelled with us throughout, sat in the front of the coach and at intervals would point forlornly to one way or another and solemnly declare, 'Gentlemen, if it were a clear day we would see the Alps.' After a while this monologue became a united choral chant. We even reached the stage of doubting if there were in fact any Alps!

We had proof enough on the Monday. As, with special permission, we led a procession of Salvationists through the streets of Geneva a curtain of mist lifted to reveal Mont Blanc in all its majesty and beauty, the radiant sunlight crowning its white-cloud peak with a halo of pink and gold. Europe's highest mountain had appeared at the psychological moment to add its welcome and provide us with a never-to-be-forgotten first glimpse of the Alps.

After three days in French Switzerland we left for a long ride to Adelboden, a mountain village situated nearly 6,000 feet up in the Bernese Oberland. The journey took us through breathtaking scenery which defied description. We were conscious of having the privilege to be the first British band to tour Switzerland by motor coach.

An incident which happened on the last day in Liestal is worth recording. As our coaches drew up at the door of the beautiful church in which we were to give our final programme a crowd of children playing in the cobbled square ceased their activity to discover the reason for this 'invasion' at four o'clock on a quiet September afternoon.

A Swiss lieutenant travelling with us called a boy from the crowd and introduced us to 'one of the most famous organists in Switzerland'. We would have had no difficulty in picking him out in a crowd. His curly head, high forehead, fine features and aesthetic countenance marked him as distinctive and, even without hearing him play a note, the mere look of the boy convinced us that we were in the presence of a genius.

But we did hear him play. When he was asked to let us have that privilege, his eyes lit up. He was off as fast as his 11-year-old legs could carry him, across the square, through the ancient doorway of the church, down the aisle and up the winding stairway to the organ loft.

The organ was not strange to him. He had permission to practise on it every day. While the electric motor was warming up he was adroitly preparing for his recital. And then he began to play. What he was playing was photographed in his mind and, with gifts far beyond his years, his long, sensitive fingers found their easy way from chord to chord while his nimble feet, scarcely long enough, worked the pedals with intelligence and artistry.

We asked his name. It was Florenz Jenny. We made a note of it. His father, Pierre, was the village organist. The boy had given his first organ recital at the age of eight.

As he played I was told that Florenz was already known in most of the capital cities on the continent of Europe. He had just returned from a tour of France, Belgium and Holland, where thousands had listened to his music. I was assured that it was not difficult to fill any cathedral in Switzerland for his recitals and his listeners paid handsomely for the privilege.

I was rather moved when told that it was the boy's wish that any profits from his playing should be sent to Dr Albert Schweitzer's hospital at Lamberéné.

We saw Florenz again. He was at the night festival, seated with members of his family in the front row of the gallery. His appearance was 'picture book'. In his green velvet suit with lace collar and looking for all the world like 'Bubbles' of the famous painting, he sat with his head resting on his linked hands. Nothing on the programme escaped him. 'Gems From *Messiah*', 'Treasures From Tchaikovsky' and the rest held his rigid attention. Only when a piece was completed would he relax with a heavy sigh, to give a significant smile to his father.

I visited Liestal twice again – with Nottingham Memorial Halls Band in 1965 and Chalk Farm Band two years later. I spoke of my young friend on each occasion. He was not present but news of my references reached him all right, for after both visits I received a note of thanks, written in delightful 'English' and addressed to me at headquarters, thanking me for remembering him and bringing me up to date with his musical interest and activity.

The second note gave me the news that he was in the final stages of his medical studies and hoped soon to qualify as a doctor. He informed me, too, that although music was so important to him it must remain as a hobby. That is why he took up additional studies. Shades of Schweitzer!

A period of hectic preparation preceded the ISB's first campaign in the United States of America in the spring of 1957. Additional rehearsals were the last of our worries. Visits to the American Embassy for questioning, fingerprint taking and the issuing of visas were relieved by the taping of material to be released as a tour LP record 'over there', the allocation of new festival tunics and the band's first set of blazers and late work in anticipation of a month's absence from the 'hub'.

These original blazers bore an all-white pocket 'ISB' monogram, the intertwined lettering looking for all the world like an elaborate dollar sign.

There was an air of mild excitement as we met outside the weed-overgrown ruins of what once had been the Army's International Headquarters in Queen Victoria Street to board the KLM coach which was to take us to Heathrow. The departure 'lounge' of London Heathrow Airport consisted of a number of huts situated on the Great West Road. From one of these we were taken by airport bus to our DC4 Edam Flying Dutchman airliner. It took 21 hours' flying time, with two stops en route, for us to reach New York!

The journey was one of sharp contrasts. We left London in glorious sunshine with excellent visibility. An hour later we saw Blackpool Tower far below us on our port side and some five hours later, after continuous sunshine, we made our first stop at Keflavik (Iceland).

Here we were greeted by a group of Salvationists who had travelled from Reykjavik to make the contact.

Airborne again, we began the long flight across the Atlantic. The glorious sunset gave way to inky blackness as we flew through the night. It was a cold trip. When the wings of the plane became iced up it was necessary for the heat from the cabin to be transferred to the wings. As the lumps of ice became dislodged they crashed against the body of the plane with a frightening thud which tossed our chartered aircraft about like a woodwork model.

That was all a long time ago. Today super-pressurised cabins and modern de-icing facilities are part of the recognised equipment.

After seven hours of adventurous flying we touched down, at the third attempt, at Gander (Newfoundland), where a blizzard was raging. A way was made for us through the snow so that we could hurry in single file to the well-heated airport accommodation. After a hurried meal we were taken to the airport's theatre where two songs were recorded for a future local broadcast.

After a number of attempts, we eventually took off again in a snowstorm. The weather had improved by the time the cold, grey light of dawn pierced the monotonous darkness to bring the first signs of a new day. Far below we could see the huge areas of Canadian woodland and then signs of life as we passed over Halifax (Nova Scotia). But soon the fascinating coastline was lost to view as the weather deteriorated. Mist and rain quickly followed and we were deprived of the eagerly awaited thrill of seeing the magical New York skyline from the air. After the inevitable period of circling we came out of the low cloud to make a perfect landing on the runway of the city's international airport (now the John F. Kennedy), still in course of construction. It was 8.30 am on Friday 5 April.

It was not easy to get into the United States. We were led to isolated boxes for close interrogation, the bandmaster more than the rest of us. The officials could not believe that we would not be earning money while in their country and that our purpose for being there was purely evangelistic with no commercial interest. Eventually our explanations were accepted, although further suspicions were aroused when Major Harold Orton was sought out and requested to open his luggage. Calm reigned once more when it was discovered that the ticking coming from his suitcase was no more than the mechanism of an uncooperative alarm clock.

Our good friends Erik and Maria Leidzén were among the first to greet us. They had been waiting for two hours in case the plane arrived ahead of schedule. Within an hour we were playing on the steps of the city hall. In cordial terms the president of the city council greeted us, wishing the band well for its great tour, as did the Mayor of São Paulo, Brazil, on an official visit to the city.

A welcome festival in the famous, impressive Carnegie Hall, scene of so much of the city's musical history, was followed by a congress festival. This, divided into four parts, was a marathon affair. It began at 7.30 pm. Three hours later we took the platform for the final items. The programme ended at 11.20!

Music congress events continued on the Sunday with a holiness meeting and an afternoon final festival, at the end of which the audience spontaneously rose to acclaim the band.

'We have waited 65 years for the International Staff Band to visit America,' said Commissioner Norman Marshall, 'and now at last you have come and conquered.'

That night we conducted the meeting at the New York Central Scandinavian Corps, where the Leidzéns were soldiers. As on the Swiss tour, I was committed to reporting the campaign for *The Musician*. This meant writing up each day's happenings before I went to bed and regularly dispatching cables or air letters according to the urgency dictated by the next press day. By this means readers back home were able to share the thrills of the great adventure while we were still in the United States.

The next morning we had time to view New York from the top of the Empire State Building before taking to the road and making our way westward. Our first stop was Allentown and the Tuesday brought us to Washington, DC, capital city of wide boulevards and monumental classical buildings, in cherry blossom time. The journey to Philadelphia was made by train. A posse of policemen on motorcycles was waiting and acted as our escort throughout the day.

The fact that it was the anniversary of William Booth's birth added significantly to the occasion when we visited the sacred spot where Eliza Shirley commenced the Army's work in the USA a year before the Railton 'invasion'. As we stood with bowed heads the Deputy Bandmaster (Major Charles Skinner) gave thanks to God for that history-making event and its tremendous outcome.

Next day we flew down to Miami, Florida, fabulous city of white villas, palm-lined avenues, coconut groves, dazzling sunlight and penetrating, health-giving warmth – a sub-tropical paradise. After landing in a fierce electrical storm we stepped from a plane into a temperature of 80 degrees to be greeted by a seemingly endless host of cheering Salvationists headed by the Territorial Commander (Commissioner William Dray). A cardboard box, addressed and presented to each bandsman, contained a colourful cabana two-piece suit. These were immediately pressed into service when a few hours' appreciated relaxation provided us with the wonderful experience of a swim in the warm waters of Florida, a steamboat trip around this man-made 'millionaires' playground' and a memorable view of Miami by night from a high-up hotel balcony.

From the sweltering heat of Miami to the blinding snow of Pittsburgh! It sounds fantastic, but that was the climatic change we experienced after covering a distance of 1,500 miles in less than five hours in the ultra-comfort of a Golden Falcon Super Constellation airliner.

As the plane came to a halt we saw waving Salvationists, two of whom were holding a banner: in giant letters was printed 'Welcome to the International Staff Band'. Then we heard music and recognised the familiar figure of Bandmaster Phil Catelinet as he conducted Pittsburgh Temple Band in 'Under Two Flags'.

While we were conveyed to the divisional headquarters by a fleet of cars driven by local Salvationists, Colonel Frank Fairbank and Brigadier Bernard Adams were transported by helicopter from the airport to the centre of the city. There was, as ever, a tremendous

261

interest in our visit. The police and fire departments of the city disposed of 20,000 tickets for the weekend events. To meet this excessive demand we were persuaded to put on an additional Saturday afternoon programme.

We continued westward; to Akron, Ohio, world-famed as the 'rubber city'; Columbus, where our old 'chief', Commissioner John J. Allan, presided over the festival; and Cincinnati, the city with the fascinating rhythmic name. One of the first things we noticed was that the car driven by the divisional commander was numbered 'SA1'.

Following an all-night train journey we drew into Chicago Grand Central Station a few minutes before seven o'clock on Good Friday morning. Among the reception committee was Captain Gordon Coles, of the Chicago editorial department, who handed me a cable received from London giving the distressing news that one of my reports, airmailed from Philadelphia, had not arrived. This meant sacrificing a morning rest period to shut myself away in a cubbyhole off the hotel lounge allocated to us to make good the deficiency. As I had not kept a copy of the report I had to recapture in my mind the happenings of five full days, and this while the 'music' of my typewriter was required to compete with the 'music' of Emil Söderström's voice as, through the thin separating wall, he regaled my colleagues with his inimitable fund of stories. My cable was transmitted without delay. My original report, unexplainably sent by surface mail, turned up some time later.

On our way to participate in the impressive third session of the non-stop 'Three Hours at the Cross' service we passed along the notorious 'Skid Row' and past the Harbour Light Corps. Seasonable music played a special part in the evening programme presented in the Great Orchestral Hall.

For the second night running there were no comfortable billets. We left Chicago at midnight and I never will forget the sight of the myriad lights of that great city becoming smaller yet brighter as we gained height and headed for the West Coast. Although this scheduled flight was normally non-stop, the pilot, over the loudspeaker, explained that because of the excessive load of instruments the plane would stop for refuelling at Omaha, Nebraska.

Airborne again, the first light of dawn gave a glimpse of the Rockies far below and later a bird's-eye view of Las Vegas, which looked like a toy town assembled by hand in the midst of a vast desert. The delightful journey continued until we touched down in Los Angeles, where the Territorial Commander (Lieut-Commissioner Holland French) came aboard to extend 'a thousand welcomes'.

Soon we were speeding through the beautifully laid-out streets of this lovely symmetrical city, oil derricks vying with orange groves for priority viewing. The festival that night was given at Long Beach.

The next morning (Easter Sunday) we were called at 3.30, after barely three hours' sleep. We were bound for Hollywood Bowl and the famous sunrise service. As we approached, worshippers in their hundreds were alighting from parked cars and making their way in the darkness to layers of terraces which stretched away to wooded hills in the distance.

Our position in the front of a gigantic flower-decked stage in the massive shell provided a wonderful view. At the first streak of dawn across the darkened sky, white-clad trumpeters standing before a huge cross high on a green-clad mound heralded the break of Easter Day. At the same time the massive choir behind us shed their black cloaks to reveal a white-clothed host in the shape of a cross. Hollywood was living up to its reputation.

The soloists were two noted filmland personalities, Jeanette MacDonald and Howard Keel. That sunrise service, attended by 20,000 people, went out to a television and radio audience of a hundred million.

That afternoon, in the Pasadena Municipal Auditorium, the chairman was Dr Meredith Willson, composer of 'Banners And Bonnets'. His wife featured this song in the festival as a solo, with her husband at the piano.

There was no bed for us again that night. We were required to take the long all-night flight back to Chicago and then left immediately by coach for Kalamazoo. Here the sound of British dialects, predominately Scottish, brought a welcome touch of home.

We had been looking forward to a good night's rest after four nights, but for most of us it was not to be. Being billeted with friends

263

from the Old Country, there was so much news to catch up on and so many topics of mutual interest to discuss.

Arthur Rolls and I stayed at the home of old training college colleagues, Jim and Eva Pattison. We never did get to bed, but managed to devour pints of good English tea! The next night, crowds flocked across the nearby Canadian border into Detroit. At the get-together after the festival an iced cake suitably inscribed and depicting the Atlantic crossing was a considerable attraction.

Before leaving for Cleveland early the next morning we heard the radio announcer predict a warm day beginning with a temperature of 62 degrees and rising to 81 degrees. He was right. It was Miami all over again. Within a short while of arriving we were in the KYW TV studio appearing in the *Open Camera* feature.

The programme was interrupted by the announcement of a tornado warning. The danger was heading for that area and the inhabitants were advised to stay in their homes to await periodic weather bulletins. Civil defence units were instantly alerted.

Despite this dramatic announcement, darkening skies and the intense humid atmosphere, more than 2,000 people filled the Masonic Temple for the evening festival. Halfway through, news that the danger had passed was greeted with relieved applause. The citizens remembered only too well the devastation caused by a tornado in 1951.

On the Thursday we continued our journey towards Canada in heatwave conditions, halting for a short stop in Buffalo before proceeding to Niagara Falls. By this time torrential rain had taken the place of glorious sunshine, and we learned afterwards that we had just made it; the roads from Buffalo were impassable, due to floods, and some 200 Salvationists from there were unable to get through for the festival.

A complete day off beside the impressive, awe-inspiring falls enabled us to relax and recuperate some energy before the strenuous Canadian weekend. Some were privileged to view the great wonder of the world by plane or helicopter. Major Charles Skinner and I travelled on in advance to Toronto, where we were guests of Danforth Songster Brigade. It was good for us to meet this renowned brigade for the first time, to share fellowship over refreshments and conduct them in some of our own compositions.

On the Saturday evening, in Toronto's massive Varsity Arena, the Territorial Commander (Commissioner Wycliffe Booth) presided and an item of special interest was the first presentation of 'The King's Musicians', a march by Colonel Bramwell Coles, then living in retirement in the city, written to commemorate his golden jubilee as a composer.

And so from Toronto the triumphant campaign continued into the fourth week with a memorable stop in Montreal, where Mayor Jean Drapeau welcomed us to the magnificent city hall, the first Salvationists to be received there for 28 years. Then it was back into the United States (a 90-minute hold-up at the border because of customs regulations affecting the instruments delayed us considerably), with engagements in Schenectady, Boston, Hartford and Newark. A day's rest in New York preceded our return journey across the Atlantic, with a stop at Gander, where a handful of Salvationists again greeted us, and then straight to London. We slept all the way!

In my early days in the International Staff Band visits to the EMI St John's Wood recording studios were fairly frequent, as were radio broadcasts. It was certainly a leap forward in '78' productions when 'The King Of Kings' was available, in the summer of 1953.

This was advertised as a 'masterpiece' and, as if desirous of adding further inducement to buy, the magic words, 'Recorded for you on Regal-Zonophone MF 370-371 (in automatic sequence)' were thrown in. Issued at the same time were the 'Dovercourt Citadel' and 'Exultation' marches and Parry's 'Jerusalem'. Each record was priced 3s 4d (17p today). 'Prelude On Three Welsh Hymn Tunes' and 'Concertino For Band And Trombone' (featuring Maisie Wiggins) was a further three-record release.

With modern 'dubbing' devices not then in vogue, a recording session could take a long time, one section often being required to be repeated time and time again until producer, technicians and bandmaster were satisfied.

265

The ISB's first LP was pressed in the USA and issued there in connection with the 1957 American tour. The music was taped in London and sent out. At first it was thought that the programme would be recorded in the old band room in Upper Thames Street, but early experiments were spoiled by extraneous traffic noise. Blankets were brought in to drape across the windows and doors in an attempt to deaden the sound, all to no avail. In the end the platform of Regent Hall was considered to be the most suitable 'studio'.

It should be put on record, however (please excuse the pun!), that one of the blanket-deadened pieces was retained on the LP, for what purpose I cannot remember.

The staff band's first official LP was not cut until 1960. This was the first of many and marked a new era of brass band recording within the Army's ranks.

Tape recording was virtually unknown in the early 1950s. It was an historic moment when, in 1954, such equipment was installed in the corner of the small band room and was placed in the tender care of Ken Percy. In my mind's eye I can still visualise the clumsy, double-tiered, wooden structure standing some three feet from the ground. But it denoted technical progress and made us feel remarkably 'with it'.

Broadcasts at that time were from a variety of BBC studios. A one-time church in Farringdon Road, the Playhouse – a former theatre situated beneath Waterloo railway bridge – disused film studios in Maida Vale and above a Piccadilly restaurant were all frequent venues.

On an early occasion at the Playhouse – it must have been 1953 – Harry Mortimer, responsible for brass and military band broadcasts with the corporation, introduced us to a young announcer, a recent addition to the staff, who was about to present his first programme. His name was Richard Baker. It was my regular duty to 'fill in' the announcers with information concerning the music we were to play. As I sought to be helpful to the 'new boy' I noticed that he was as nervous as we were!

I wonder if the confident, self-possessed, charming personality of today remembers that first announcing assignment in the company of a Salvation Army band?

In 1953 we became film stars. The International Public Relations Department thought it would be a good idea for a 16mm sound film of the band to be produced, featuring the staff band presenting the *air varié*, 'Go Down, Moses', then awaiting publication. A professional company was engaged and the filming took place one evening in the women's dining room of the International Training College at Denmark Hill.

It was not the most enjoyable of occasions and there were many problems, mostly technical, associated with the bold experiment. Without a break the shooting and recording went on and on until, as the hour of midnight approached, the usual high standard of disciplined deportment was forgotten as those of us without private transport left our instruments and stands where they were to make a beeline for the last train from Denmark Hill. We were just in time. Where it was going we hadn't a clue but managed to clamber aboard.

After a few changes – Elmers End comes particularly to mind – I eventually found myself at Woodside and briskly set out for Shirley, where I lived. Those with any knowledge of that part of London will realise that such a journey on foot is a tidy step by any standard of physical fitness.

The film was not a success. The playing was reasonable, and the close-up shots of the various sections were good. But the synchronisation left much to be desired. When viewers listening to Roland Cobb's enchanting cornet *obbligato* in the slow movement would have welcomed a camera study of his handsome features, they had to be content with admiring trombonist Cyril Brisley's profile.

The cost of the film, which ran to 300 feet, was five guineas, with spool and container. Postage was in addition. I never knew how many copies were sold but I was sharply reminded of the sad debacle when some years later I saw an advertisement in *The Musician* offering one such film for sale. I hope the Londonderry reader disposed of it! This historic piece by the ISB of 30 years ago is well worth seeing – and having in one's archives.

Our next excursion into the realm of film-making was more successful. It was to do with the popular *Living Word* series shown throughout the USA and Canada and took place in the spring of 1958. We spent a week (Monday to Friday) in a hired studio in Merton, South London, and were required to return to complete the five sessions two weeks later.

The inspiration behind the whole venture was Senior-Major Arnold Brown, who served as executive producer for the series. With typical forthright challenge the major talked to us in a rehearsal break in the band room.

'It is no longer a matter of reaching merely the 60s around the open-air line or the 600s in our halls,' he said. 'It is the staggering challenge of communicating, face to face, with 60 million televiewers. If opportunities to reach people in public places decline, we must seize these new opportunities to meet them in their parlours.'

Our day started in the make-up chair at 8 am. It was not until 10.30 pm that we left for home. The experience was unique. The thrills were many.

To be seated under the melting glare of a battery of giant lights totalling some 100,000 kilowatts – necessary because of colour photography – was not a pleasant experience. The blinding pencil ray of the spotlights dazzled the eyes for minutes after they had been switched off, but so efficient was the running of the studio that we were not required to suffer those discomforts for long at a time.

We soon became accustomed to the trade jargon. 'Rehearsal bells' meant more than a double ring. The two words, clearly spoken by the assistant director, denoted that silence was required and none would think of whispering after such an order. Instructions were never lengthy, most consisting of 'Lights on', 'Doors closed', 'Fans off, 'Roll 'em', 'Action cut' and 'Two bells'.

Although the music was to be incidental to the main feature it was evident that Senior-Major Brown, who directed the sequences, was desirous of obtaining the best results. This made it necessary for some of the shots to be repeated – some more than once. On one occasion the flight of a bumblebee across the set suspended operations.

Extracts from no fewer than 52 marches, selections and other types of composition were recorded while the cameras operated. That would cover 26 instalments of the new series of programmes.

At last, after more than 26 hours had been spent in the studio and something like 16,000 feet of film had passed through the cameras, the tiring and exacting task was completed. This was one small part of the comprehensive feature. Across the Atlantic the film needed to be edited and some superimposing arranged which would allow for the band and voices to be heard together in the final production.

We felt that if the International Staff Band could play some small part in such spiritual endeavour in the future we would feel well repaid for the hours of extra duty and grateful for the opportunity to help propagate the gospel through this powerful medium of mass communication.

Three years later, in Toronto, watching the series in our quarters after the Sunday morning meeting became a weekly feature of our personal television viewing.

Chapter 22

New World Interlude

ON a Monday in November 1960 I returned from conducting songster weekend meetings at Long Eaton to learn that the Chief of the Staff wanted to see me.

Commissioner William Dray was a man of few words. After inquiring about my health and that of my wife he came straight to the point. He took it that we would not be averse to an overseas appointment. I agreed. We had indicated this when completing our candidates' papers.

There was silence. I mustered sufficient courage, despite the 'butterflies' in my stomach, to ask if this was a hypothetical question or was such a move likely. The Chief hesitated, as if anxious not to give too much away, and then intimated that there was something 'in the offing'.

'When?' I wanted to know.

'February,' was the decisive reply. I had three months to get used to the idea.

My next question was inevitable: 'Where?' The Chief smiled knowingly, as if to suggest I was asking too much. He provided three clues. My appointment would be of an editorial nature. It would be in an English-speaking country. It would be a 'congenial climate'. It did not take long for me to conclude that such a threefold description would apply to at least five territorial centres around the world. Perhaps I should not have asked.

I was requested to treat the matter as confidential, although permission was granted for me to discuss the subject with my wife and John, who, at 17, would need to be included in our plans. In the agonising weeks that followed we shared many 'family conferences',

271

as our son called them. Whether he would come with us would depend on our destination. For reasons best known to himself he eliminated all but two possible destinations from his future plans.

We went about our busy life as normally as possible. Christmas came and went. We spent two days with my parents and other members of the family, sensing that it could be the last Yuletide we would spend together. The new year dawned. We were due to go in a month. Surely we would be hearing soon.

On the third day of 1961 we were put out of our misery. The Chief of the Staff sent for me. This was it.

'We're sending you to Canada,' he calmly stated, 'but not until April. The St Lawrence River will be clear of ice by then and you will be able to sail right up to Montreal.' I sensed a touch of excitement in his voice. He was Canadian and knew the country. Captains did not fly to appointments in those days.

April! Another three months to go. We were relieved to know that Canada was one of the two countries to which John would be happy to accompany us!

To an English schoolboy of my generation Canada was something of a utopian El Dorado. Magical thoughts continued to fill my mind as we packed to leave for a new life in a new world. I had already visited the country with the International Staff Band but was sensible enough to know that the glamour of such a tour would be quite different from arriving as settlers, as Canada House insisted on calling us.

There was no let-up on engagements. As editor of *The Musician* I was on duty when General Wilfred Kitching met bandsmen at Clapton Congress Hall and when the British Commissioner (Commissioner Edgar Grinsted) led similar inter-divisional councils in Newcastle and Birmingham.

My good friend Captain Dean Goffin, National Secretary for Bands and Songster Brigades, generously arranged a farewell festival and musical salute in our honour at Camberwell and we took our leave of editorial colleagues at a departmental gathering at Denmark Hill on Monday 20 March. Since that important interview of four months before, Commissioner Dray had retired from active service and returned to Canada, and now, at my farewell, the Staff Secretary (Colonel William Ware) read a letter of appreciation and good wishes from his successor as Chief of the Staff (Commissioner Norman Duggins). The occasion was made more poignant by the fact that the Chief, after barely two months in office, had been promoted to Glory from a Glasgow hospital early that morning. His letter, dated the 20th, must have been one of the last he signed. I still have it to remind me of my first band leader whom God saw fit to call Home at the height of his powers and in the prime of his life.

After a seemingly never-ending series of farewells, we left Euston Station on Tuesday 4 April after spending Easter weekend with my parents at the home of my sister and brother-in-law, Thelma and Gordon Pinchbeck, at Worthing.

Just before the boat train was due to pull away for Liverpool, editorial colleagues and other friends closed ranks for prayer and to sing 'I know the Lord will make a way for me', led by the Under-Secretary for the Americas, Colonel John Atkinson, a former departmental comrade. I had attended many such departures before but this was different.

There were many delays that day. We arrived in Liverpool very late but were cheered by the sight of the Divisional Commander (Lieut-Colonel George Coxhead) and Divisional Young People's Secretary (Brigadier William Davidson), who had courteously waited several hours to share a brief greeting and handshake.

We boarded the liner alone and made our way to the cabins. Someone had beaten us to it. A Croydon Citadel comrade soldier, Lucy Riches, in Liverpool on holiday, had made it her business to find out the number of our cabin and to decorate it with choice flowers. She remained with us until the boat sailed and our last view of England was of Lucy on the dockside waving and becoming smaller and smaller as we sailed out to sea.

It was this kind of 'extra mile' service that earned Lucy Riches membership of the Order of the Founder from General Clarence Wiseman in 1976.

We sailed from Liverpool on the *Empress Of England*. It was not a pleasant journey. We were confined to our cabins for most of the Atlantic crossing. Being the first boat up the St Lawrence following the long winter freeze-up brought its own problems. One morning we were awakened at about three o'clock by an unfamiliar grinding sound. I dressed hurriedly and made my way on deck. With a first glimpse of the fantastic sight that confronted me I returned to fetch Nina. This was a sight she must not miss.

We were, in fact, stuck hard in pack ice, with hungry seals poking their heads through every available opening while they performed a slithering ballet. From then on our progress was slow as the *Empress* moved in circles to extend the narrow channel of water before us. After a brief stop in Quebec we eventually arrived in Montreal two days late.

That first night was spent in a social services establishment near the central station and we woke the next morning to hear the announcement over the radio that Yuri Gagarin, a major in the Russian army, had become the first man in space. It was the beginning of a new era.

The rough seas played havoc with our luggage. My wife had been advised to take her best china with us. Most of it constituted wedding gifts. Practically all of it was found to be smashed on arrival. The iron supports of her faithful old sewing machine had snapped like matchsticks. As I came down the gangway of the boat at Montreal I was horrified to see some of my precious books scattered over the dockside. One of our boxes seemed to have been dropped from a height and had literally burst its sides. All this was not a good beginning.

After an eight-hour train journey to Toronto we were greeted by a number of old and new friends, among them our former corps officers, Lieut-Colonel and Mrs Wesley Rich, and bandmasters from five corps in the city area, each anxious to enlist the services of our son. More than one had brought a cornet with him. John eventually decided on Earlscourt, where he played solo cornet during his stay in Toronto.

The Editorial Department was domiciled in an old property in (or 'on' as North Americans say) Jarvis Street, some two miles from territorial headquarters. The editor-in-chief, Lieut-Colonel Herbert Wood, whose family emigrated from Dover in 1910, had been a colleague in the editors and writers session at the ICO.

Canada is a great sandwich-eating country. Most city workers carry their lunches in telltale brown paper bags. There is no attempt at camouflage. As one holds the neat bundle in the subway, along the street or on the streetcar or bus, all the world will know that one is 'eating out'.

Those lunchtimes in the library at Jarvis Street, when we gathered around the huge table to enjoy our repast, became informative interludes as we swapped experiences and learned from each other. Only the sound of celery being munched obliterated the sound of healthy conversation.

That fellowship was not allowed to remain intact for long. Soon I had the editorship of *The Crest* added to my duties as assistant editor of *The War Cry* and I later became editor of the parent paper.

No time was lost in welcoming me to the Toronto Salvationist musical fraternity; an annual informal gathering of 'musical males' was organised by Bandsman Will Creighton, of East Toronto, at the home of Bandsman and Mrs Jack Jerrett, of West Toronto. The tape recorder was put to good and useful purpose.

It was a moving experience to hear extracts from the previous year's meeting, held the night before Colonel Bramwell Coles left for a holiday in England, a journey from which he was not to return. The colonel had been persuaded to tell the company how he came to write his first march, and in the silence of that room, a year later, we were privileged to listen to the voice of the composer recalling the happenings of those days 55 years earlier.

Plenty happened during the first few weeks of our residence. Within two months of arriving we were at the Varsity Arena for the spring festival. The guests of honour were Winnipeg Citadel Band. Something of the vast distances covered by the Canada and Bermuda Territory was immediately appreciated when I learnt that this famous section from Western Canada was paying only its second visit to Toronto in 40 years and the first for 23 years. The band had travelled the 1,000 miles by plane.

The delight of the Salvationists of Eastern Canada to see their musical comrades was expressed in no uncertain manner as, headed by the Union Jack and the familiar Army tricolour, the Winnipeg bandsmen, in single file, marched across the great arena to take their places on the raised platform that has for so long been a position of honour for visiting sections participating in this popular event.

When the New York Metropolitan Opera Company was in town its bass soloist, Jerome Hines, spent all his off-duty periods at the Harbour Light Corps and Centre, playing table tennis with the men and chatting to them informally about spiritual things. The officer in charge, Brigadier Joshua Monk, invited him to take part in a meeting. I reported the visit for the Army's press and had the pleasure of accompanying the distinguished guest at the piano.

Jerome sang about 20 songs, testified and made a mercy seat appeal. He was on his feet for 90 minutes. The response was wonderful. My wife and I had supper with him afterwards and found him great company.

This noted vocalist first met the Army when he heard an officer speak about its work in the Bowery district at a fashionable Park Avenue church in New York. Impressed, he promised to sing at a social institution. Weeks passed and he had almost forgotten his pledge until one night when, in the vicinity of Hyde Park, London, he heard a Salvation Army band.

With a twinge of conscience he consulted a telephone directory and was led to contact Senior-Major Stanley Burton at Paddington Goodwill Centre. His offer to 'do anything' to help was readily accepted. Too embarrassed to take a taxi to The Salvation Army, he walked the five miles.

The six feet six inches tall opera singer found himself helping to collect a pile of bedding, then practising 'Onward, Christian Soldiers' for three hours in his hotel bedroom, before singing it that night to an open-mouthed audience of men at Victoria Home Men's Social Work

Centre, Whitechapel, at a meeting addressed by Brother Hugh Redwood. When Jerome Hines returned to New York he at once linked up with the Army there and later both he and his wife knelt at the mercy seat.

On another visit to London the singer again visited the Paddington Goodwill Centre and gave a one-man programme to aid a Czech refugee whose legs had been amputated and who was feeling seriously depressed. Colonel Albert Jakeway and Erik Leidzén were among the guests on that occasion.

In his autobiography, *This Is My Story, This Is My Song*, Mr Hines recalls incidents and pays tribute to the dedication and caring of Senior-Major Burton and his helpers, particularly mentioning Captain Lilian Wrigley. His respect for the captain shines through this part of his story with impressive transparency. His conversations with her are remembered in detail and it was she who stumbled on the discovery that the tall, handsome American who wanted to help at Paddington was, in fact, a star of the New York Opera Company, then in town.

My wife and I became soldiers at North Toronto Corps and I have many happy memories of the corps, among them my association with the band and songster brigade and their respective leaders; my wife's leadership of the home league fellowship; the faithful ministry of notable corps officers; the brisk walk through the winter snow to the meetings; and the appreciated comradeship of officer-soldiers of the corps.

Canada is by nature a great camping country. This characteristic naturally spilled over into Army life. Each division had its own lakeside camp where delegates to various events were billeted in cabins and communal facilities made for good fun and enriching fellowship. My first experience of this took me to the Quebec and Eastern Ontario Divisional Camp for participation in a territorial music leaders institute. This venue was delightfully situated at Lac L'Achigan, some 50 miles from Montreal, nestling beneath the lovely Laurentian Mountains.

The following month I was at Jackson's Point, situated on Lake Simcoe some 70 miles from Toronto, for the Metropolitan Toronto

Division's music camp. Honoured with the music directorship, I had my first taste of these renowned North American events and was able to compare them with similar activities in Britain.

An encouraging feature of the camp was the abundance of youthful composers among the delegates. These entered for the 'Original Melody' competition which required them to write a tune either to words in the songbook or written especially for the occasion. After a process of elimination the remaining melodies were heard in turn. One was presented on the piano. Another was sung as a vocal trio. Two were played as soprano cornet solos.

A band weekend retreat was something new to me. That is why I did not hesitate to accept the invitation to be the guest at West Toronto Band's fourth event of this kind, held at a delightful summer cottage at Hall's Lake, in the Halliburton Highlands of Ontario.

In such ideal surroundings Bandmaster Douglas Pugh and his men entered wholeheartedly into the varied programme – a series of spiritual meetings, an afternoon of recreational pursuits, discussion groups and instrumental and vocal rehearsals which lasted from Friday night to Sunday evening. In an off-duty interlude I was introduced into the pleasant intricacies of volleyball and horseshoes.

My first tour of Eastern Canada took me first of all to Moncton, New Brunswick, to report congress meetings led by the Territorial Commander (Commissioner Wycliffe Booth). It was the first time that the Eastern Canada Congress had been held there and the city was stirred by the 'invasion'.

The Saturday morning parade through the streets by hundreds of uniformed Salvationists was headed by Montreal Citadel Band, which had flown in the night before. It was a joy to be in such close proximity to this famous section, then under the leadership of Morley Calvert.

In the festivals the band excelled in 'The Victory Of Love' and 'Army Of The Brave' and made a tremendous impression with unaccompanied singing under the direction of Songster Leader Edley Selwood, whom I remembered as bandmaster at Worthing.

It was not until we lived in Toronto that I discovered that no point in Britain is more than 80 miles from the sea, as the crow flies. In

Toronto the coast was 1,300 miles away in one direction and 3,000 miles in the other. We missed the ozone. In Halifax it was so different. I spent longer than I intended just looking out to sea and taking deep breaths of the bracing air. It did me a world of good.

On my way back to Toronto I 'touched down' in Montreal for songster weekend at the Citadel. This enabled me to meet brigades from Point St Charles and Verdun at the Saturday united festival. It was an inspiration to find my old friend, Bram Allington, playing solo cornet in Montreal Citadel Band.

I accompanied the band to a hospital on the Sunday morning and visited a veteran retired officer, Major Alfred Smith, in his ward. The major gained fame as a vocalist in the International Staff Songsters in the days of Colonel Herbert Jackson and was bandmaster at Thornton Heath before transferring to Canada in 1929. He was also well known at Nunhead.

Then aged 81, Major Smith had been an active bandsman at Montreal Citadel until a short while before my visit. I was amazed at his up-to-date knowledge of worldwide Army musical affairs.

The Ontario Congress, held for the first time in Hamilton and led by the Territorial Commander of the USA Eastern Territory (Commissioner Holland French), erstwhile member of three staff bands, provided an opportunity for me to hear more Canadian bands. In the Sunday afternoon's congress festival, in the city's great ice rink forum, bands from Toronto Temple, Hamilton Argyle, Kitchener and Danforth took part and the songster brigades of Danforth, Windsor Citadel and Brantford performed as individual sections. I was particularly impressed by the pianoforte soloist, 11-year-old Leonard Ballantine of Windsor Citadel, who played an original composition, 'The River Speaks'. He won the hearts of the audience as his nimble fingers careered across the keyboard. In my *Canadian Clippings* regularly supplied to *The Musician*, I commented: 'This was an outstanding achievement, the boy's piano technique matching the skill of his creation.' I felt certain I would hear of him again.

Like the Salvationists who remember William Booth, the number of English people who can recall the far-off days when snow at

Christmas could be relied upon as a regular feature of the seasonal calendar is dwindling. When Irving Berlin's 'I'm Dreaming Of A White Christmas', with Bing Crosby as the crooning star, avalanched on to the hit parade of its day, it was more than a pleasant disc of a sentimental song feelingly presented. The Englishman regarded it as a nostalgic lament for a bygone age – and went on dreaming!

Not so the Canadian. Snow, snow and more snow is a hardy annual and one cannot even begin to dream of a Christmas that isn't white. At least, that is what we were told as we were preparing for our first Christmas away from home.

Our advisers were right. Falling true to form, the snow began to descend during one night and continued its fascinating performance for two days, thus ensuring that the streets of Toronto would be well covered for the Christmas season. Two days' snow cemented by a near-zero temperature meant that most of Canada would be in this icy grip for months.

Although signs of Christmas began to appear in various guises from September onward, it was not until the end of November that the tension was stepped up. North Americans go for parades in a big way and, at the slightest provocation, will celebrate thus. So it was that, on a Saturday morning, practically all Toronto turned out for the traditional Santa Claus Parade, sponsored by a large store in honour of the old gentleman who is quite unknown as Father Christmas, except to recent immigrants from the Old Country.

This is one of the occasions of the year when Torontonians brave the severe elements and forsake their centrally heated homes and warm cars or public vehicles. My wife and I preferred a 'ringside' seat at the television set and had an excellent view of the show. All the fun of the circus was let loose along Yonge Street, the famous thoroughfare separating the east of the city from the west and along which Evangeline Booth, nearly 60 years earlier, travelled on horseback to her office in Albert Street when she commanded the Canada Territory.

Marching at a tempo that would send an International Staff bandsman packing for a pair of roller skates, a number of American trumpet bands blared their way to a breathless finale. Headed by a smartly clad group of female drum majors, performing acrobatic gymnastics with their wands, corps of 'majorettes' added colour to the occasion. Brass bands, the majority of them playing 'Santa Claus has come to town', were dotted at intervals throughout the procession to prevent any kind of lag in the entertainment; floats portraying nursery rhymes rolled majestically by; and bringing up the rear was Santa Claus himself, standing up in his reindeer-drawn sleigh, thundering his greetings to his young and not-so-young patrons through the powerful microphone secreted in his generous flow of whiskers.

December was not many days old before the television commercials began to take on a seasonable look. When one has 14 channels to choose from there is plenty of variety and, with most of the adverts featuring a Christmas carol, it was easy to catch the North American spirit. We quickly noticed that merely singing the traditional songs was not enough. The participants had to be suitably clad and in this respect were more English than the English. Most of the men carollers were dressed in the familiar grey toppers and tails, with cravats to match. Their ladies wore poke bonnets and crinolines. All could have stepped right out of Quality Street.

Many of the carols were new to us. 'Deck The Halls' was a great favourite and the one we heard most of all, 'Joy To The World', was a close second. 'Jingle Bells' and 'Holy Night' were also heard a great deal.

It was interesting to discover that, when it came to Christmas decoration, it was the outside of the house that received special attention. Inside the homes festive embellishments were sparingly displayed, but the householders vied with each other for the best outdoor show.

In downtown Toronto the Christmas kettle, manned by headquarters officers and cadets, was a familiar sight. One evening a casual glance at the television provided me with the thrill of seeing the New York Staff Band appearing on the popular *I've Got A Secret* programme from an American station. There were other Army features televised during the season.

With the snow freezing layer upon layer, the streets soon became treacherous. One day, just before Christmas, I was sliding to the editorial offices across a busy intersection when, not for the first time that morning, my legs involuntarily cut a rhythmic caper in the air and I found myself on my back gasping for much-needed breath. A fellow traveller who, in more normal times, might have stopped and requested money for a streetcar ticket, calmly commented: 'Pick yerself up, brother,' and hurried on leaving me to manoeuvre myself into a sitting position before realising that the traffic lights had changed to green and I had no alternative!

Distances in North America take some getting used to. It took a long time for me to understand that 500 miles' travelling from Toronto could bring me to Montreal, Chicago or New York. Admittedly that is further than London is from Edinburgh, but the superb motorways made the journey so much quicker and easier, even with the national state and provincial borders to be crossed. That is why the presence of the Chicago Staff Songsters with Major Carl Lindstrom as conductor, in Toronto for the territorial songster festival, was not considered to be unusual. This applied to the frequent interchange of American and Canadian corps sections.

My first tour of Western Canada was carried out in the spring of 1962. It lasted ten days. Flying the 1,300 miles from Toronto, with one stop in Windsor, I arrived in Winnipeg in time for the Friday night rehearsals at the citadel. This enabled me to make an early contact with the efficient young people's band and to rehearse the brigade in one or two pieces for the weekend.

Saturday afternoon councils for YP band and singing company members provided an opportunity to meet the fine Salvationist youth of a city which bears an honoured name in Army history.

While in the 'prairie capital' I was shown the site of the old THQ, a reminder of the days between 1915 and 1932 when Canada was divided into two territories and Winnipeg vied with Toronto for pride of place.

From the snows of Winnipeg I travelled to the even deeper snow of Regina, Saskatchewan. Here the handful of instrumentalists were conscious of the great exodus which, over the years, had taken their comrades to swell the ranks of Salvationist musicians in British Columbia or Ontario.

Bandsmen and bandswomen from Moose Jaw and Weyburn joined us for a band practice. All wore full uniform, even if the visitors did have 50 miles to travel. We shared a season of spiritual fellowship before parting company.

During an afternoon break I was taken by the commanding officer to a session of the Provincial Parliament of Saskatchewan and listened to a heated discussion centred upon the rising cost of wheat transportation. Seeing me admiring some of the flags in the large marbled hall, a uniformed attendant explained that they were relics from the First World War, with the exception of the white ensign, which had hung at the cenotaph in *Trafalgar Square*, London, England, for some years. How could I tell him that the cenotaph was in Whitehall?

But I had difficulty in remaining silent when he went on to add: 'So saturated is it with the smoke, rain and fog of London that the ensign would fall to pieces at the slightest touch.' Such is the legend that had grown in Canada around London's alleged weather, just as the English schoolboy's picture of Canadians is mainly sleighs, huskies and blinding blizzards.

At Edmonton Airport, Alberta, I was met by a former ISB colleague, Major William Hosty. Although this was officially the first day of spring it was still delightful winter, with a hot sun shining gloriously on piled snowdrifts and a treacherous surface.

Thanks to the discovery of rich oilfields in Alberta, in scarcely more than 50 years Edmonton had passed from a sprawling little pioneer frontier town in the wilderness to a bustling metropolis. Bill Hosty showed me the newly erected Golden Jubilee Auditorium. It was his responsibility, as public relations officer, to fill this lovely hall of 2,700 seats for the forthcoming visit of the International Staff Band.

Edmonton was for some years the home of Gustav Grozinsky, composer and author of 'Neath Our Standard, We're Engaging' ('I'll Be True'), and in his memory I played an impromptu arrangement of this familiar melody as a pianoforte solo. There were those present who remembered the 'little old gentleman' who used to sit at the end

283

of the fourth row back on the left-hand side of the hall, but few linked him with his fine old song.

In announcing the item I produced a treasured souvenir. When we were stationed at Sandwich my harvest collecting one day took me to the village of Wingham, on the main road to Canterbury. In the window of one of the few shops in the only street, I noticed standing behind a variety of junk, a document headed by the Army crest and eight colourful international flags. The words 'The Salvation Army' and 'The World for Christ' completed my first impression.

A closer scrutiny revealed that this was a captain's commission issued by the Home Office, International Headquarters, Queen Victoria Street, London, and dated 30 October 1894. It was appointing Captain Grozinsky to the command of Wingham Corps and was signed 'on behalf of the General' by T. Henry Howard, Territorial Commissioner.

The telltale tinkling of a bell, worked by a string set in motion by opening the door of the shop, denoted my presence and brought a cheerful, elderly proprietor from his living room at the back of the premises to the entrance which was hidden by a heavy curtain. My excited enquiry did not bring forth an enlightening response. He did not know how long the commission had been there, or whence it came. It had, in fact, been there for as long as he could remember. I could have it for sixpence.

The historic commission, mounted on cardboard, had been well preserved. That night in Edmonton, thousands of miles away from the Kent countryside, people queued to examine it and to tell me of 'old Gus'.

After my memorable evening at Edmonton Citadel, a further heavy snowstorm during the night covered the countryside with yet another white blanket, but the elements were braved early the next morning as Major Hosty drove me the 200 miles to Calgary. The roads were treacherous for a while, reducing the speed to a crawl, but suddenly the conditions improved and patches of grey grass appeared amid the islands of ice. On the outskirts of Calgary the outline of the Rocky Mountains could be seen through the mist and an hour or two to spare gave me the chance of making the additional journey to Banff.

This is one of the beauty spots of Canada and the great towering pinnacles of white majesty presented a thrilling sight, even in the 'off season' – 'When It's Springtime In The Rockies' kept coming to me in flashes of melodic inspiration.

Back in Calgary I was captivated by the 'western' atmosphere, with inhabitants of the nearby Indian reserves mingling with the cosmopolitan crowds in the busy railway station and farmers, wearing the familiar stetsons, discussing important business deals in the city's many restaurants.

The next morning a jet plane took me high above the Rockies and on to Vancouver, British Columbia. The weather was really springlike when I arrived, even to the extent of refreshing rain. But the daffodils, crocuses and narcissi were in glorious bloom, reminding me so much of England at that time.

My first engagement was a Friday evening council for bandsmen and songster groups of the city. Composite groups from Vancouver Temple and Mount Pleasant were on hand for demonstration purposes. Visitors for the Saturday divisional festival were Seattle Songster Brigade from the nearby USA Western Territory. Singing with Vancouver Temple Songster Brigade was Jenty Fairbank (younger daughter of Commissioner and Mrs Frank Fairbank), who was about to return to London and to enter the training college after a happy stay in Western Canada.

A memorable tour at an end, I returned non-stop to Toronto by *Silver Dart* jet in five minutes under four hours. When, some months later, I covered the same journey by train, through the Rockies and across the prairies, it took three days and three nights.

There was an air of excitement in our home as the 1962 visit of the International Staff Band approached. We were at Malton International Airport when they arrived from the USA and it was good to be with them for their busy weekend in Toronto, in London, Ontario, for the territory's 80th anniversary celebrations, and in Montreal.

In Toronto at the same time as the staff band was Britain's Prime Minister Harold Macmillan. When he received the freedom of the city outside the city hall the band supplied a half-hour programme before the premier arrived and also played during the ceremony. As the Prime Minister left his car and passed through the military guard of honour on his way to the specially erected platform the ISB's fanfare trumpets heralded his approach. They were later heard, with brilliant clarity that thrilled the witnessing crowds, in the introduction of the national anthem.

That summer I was invited to be the international guest at the annual USA Central Music Institute at Camp Wonderland, Wisconsin. As it was necessary for us to make this a part of our annual furlough, my wife and I spent a few days in New York (travelling by all-night Greyhound bus), where we attended Sunday meetings at Times Square Corps and at the Bowery, and then journeyed on by the famous *20th Century* night express train to Chicago. Here we were made welcome at the home of Captain and Mrs Gordon Coles who, after a few delightful days, drove us through the lovely mid-American countryside to the camp. They were ten memorable days.

When the Chief of the Staff (Commissioner Erik Wickberg) paid his first visit to Canada I reported his campaigns in Calgary and Winnipeg. The night journey to Winnipeg took me through Medicine Hat and equally romantic stations, the Indian names of which had been my companions since boyhood. It was quite 'unreal'.

Memories of our stay in Canada come crowding into my mind after all these years: visits to numerous corps for musical weekends; councils for bandsmen and songsters, particularly those held at North Bay; accompanying Earlscourt Band to Plain Fields, New Jersey, for a weekend of spiritual and cultural success; sharing the platform at Danforth with Erik Leidzén for a Sunday campaign; hearing over the phone the news of Erik's passing; listening enthralled to such soloists as Rita Green and Will Overton 3,000 miles from home; serving on the territorial planning and music boards; being 'in' on the first reports of the Army's pioneer work among uranium diggers of Labrador – there are so many.

It is no exaggeration to say that we left a part of our hearts in Canada.

The International Staff Band in 1959 (Brindley is 3rd from right, second row)

Brindley gives Pope Paul VI a Chalk Farm Band banner to commemorate the band's visit to the Vatican. Also pictured are Bandmaster Michael Clack, Lieut-Colonel Jean Bordas (Officer Commanding, Italy) and General Secretary Brigadier Raymond Yarde

Brindley in the Royal Box at Wembley Stadium (1978 International Congress)

Brindley on his 95th birthday, with Major June Kitchen, son John, granddaughter Georgia and sister Thelma

Chapter 23

The Salt of the Earth

IT was the Chief of the Staff (Commissioner Erik Wickberg) who gave me the news. Major Dean Goffin was to return to New Zealand as a divisional commander and I was to succeed him as National Secretary for Bands and Songster Brigades in the British Territory.

In that quaint way that departmental heads had of imparting information without giving anything away, the editor-in-chief, Commissioner Alfred Gilliard, had entered my office and calmly advised me to 'brush your tunic and go to see the Chief of the Staff'. That could mean only one thing: big news!

I was sad to leave the editorial fold. Since my return from Canada I had served happily as editor of *Vanguard* and then was given the unexpected privilege of having a second bite of the *Musician* cherry.

When we came back to London, Commissioner William Grottick was editor-in-chief and literary secretary and it was a pleasure to serve under his direction for two years. The commissioner did not claim to be 'editorial' or 'literary' in the traditional sense, but he proved himself an administrator of outstanding quality and gave us the benefit of his long years of responsibilities in the British Territory and his territorial leadership in Scotland and South Africa. He was devoted to his staff and earned our respect and affection. He was upright in stature and character.

As I moved from IHQ to NHQ – from the fifth floor to the fourth floor of the new '101' – the prospect of my appointment thrilled yet humbled me. The names and faces of my illustrious predecessors haunted me: Alfred Braine, Wilfred Kitching, Charles Durman, Edward Saywell, Ernest Rance and Dean Goffin. I had known them all. They were personalities to be reckoned with. In my moments of rededication I prayed that I might prove worthy to serve Britain's fine Salvationist-musicians as well as they had done. The bandsmen and songsters in the Army's homeland were, I decided, the salt of the earth and worth serving.

When I took up my duties in September 1966, Captain Norman Bearcroft was in his sixth year as national bandmaster and Captain June Kitchen had joined the staff some time before. To have the support of such enthusiasts gave me an ideal start.

I was soon in action. Within days of taking over I was sending a representative diamond wedding greeting to Colonel and Mrs Railton Howard and an 80th birthday message to General Albert Orsborn. My first public engagement in my new capacity was an event at Hendon organised by my former banding colleague, Major Ken Nutty. This, in the main, took the form of a 'fireside interview', the major putting me 'on the spot' regarding the future of Army music and the recent innovation of rhythm group music. The meeting culminated in my presenting a new flag to the band.

For me this was a happy occasion, for Bandmaster Fred Cobb had gone out of his way to encourage me since my earliest beginnings at nearby Child's Hill Corps and many long-established friends were still Hendon bandsmen and songsters. In addition, many in the congregation had known me from boyhood.

It was a hectic last quarter of the year. The national songster festival at Clapton Congress Hall gave me my first taste of such organisation and of carrying out rehearsals with brigades for several weeks beforehand, in readiness for the great evening. The all-London songsters councils the next day were the last to be held in that historic building. The provision of meals was proving a problem, especially with the old Temple now out of commission and, that year, we experimented with a buffet lunch and tea. It was all very tasty and more-ish, but the delegates missed the sit-down hot repasts which had been a feature of former gatherings. Milling around with a chicken leg, sausage on a stick and a variety of sandwiches balanced precariously on a plastic plate wasn't quite the same.

When Dr Barnardo's Homes celebrated their centenary in October 1966 at the Royal Albert Hall it was a compliment to The Salvation Army that one of our 'choirs' should be asked to take part. This was not surprising; it was a conversation between William Booth and Thomas Barnardo, then a student at the London Hospital, after a Friday evening holiness meeting in the Whitechapel hall that led to the doctor embarking upon his life's work for homeless children.

The medical student was a regular attender at Christian Mission meetings and suggested to the General Superintendent that he should do something for the boys Barnardo had discovered sleeping under railway arches, on straw and in carts because they had no homes to go to.

Perhaps William Booth was in dyspeptic mood when he replied: 'We've got as much on our plate as we can possibly manage at the moment; but there's a job that *you* could do.'

Frederick J. Coxhead, pioneer Christian Missioner, builder and later corps sergeant-major at Leyton 1, claimed to have overheard the conversation and more than 60 years ago recalled the incident for the benefit of *War Cry* readers. Other versions of the story are given in *The History Of The Salvation Army*, volume 1, and *Words Of William Booth*. One thing is common to all three: Booth was undoubtedly the inspiration behind Barnardo's decision to rent a house in Hope Place, Hull Lane, Stepney, at 12 shillings a week to accommodate his first group of homeless boys.

The centenary celebrations were held on a Thursday afternoon and took the form of a pageant devised and produced by Ralph Reader, of *Gang Show* fame. Historical scenes and musical items were skilfully woven into the professionally conceived pattern of presentation and the London Chorus (as we called it), consisting of songsters from London corps, contributed 'Shout Aloud Salvation', 'All In The April Evening' and the 'Hallelujah' Chorus. Russ Conway, performing his brilliant pianoforte technique again after a prolonged absence from the concert platform because of illness, was particularly charming to the Salvationists and insisted at the climax of his second number that

I should step forward to conduct the great audience in 'Land Of Hope And Glory'.

Ralph Reader was a genial, efficient and experienced master of ceremonies. In an interval during rehearsal we chatted about his earliest memories of the Army, in his native Somerset town of Crewkerne, and of the days when his father was the bandmaster at the corps there. He never forgot his Salvationist background.

To secure a chorus of 500 mixed voices on a Thursday afternoon was to me something of a miracle, but I was soon to learn that there was no limit to the sacrificial service given regularly in this way by Army musicians. After the festival, I had the honour of being presented to Her Royal Highness Princess Margaret, Patron of Dr Barnardo's, who spoke in glowing terms of the 'choir's' singing and was interested to learn of its total amateur status.

Another early commitment took me to the Manchester Granada TV studios for an intensive day's recording of background music for a documentary on the Army's function in contemporary Britain. This was called *The Warmongers*, and featured Lieutenant Sylvia Gair, formerly of the Joystrings.

The musical score of this 45-minute film had been written by Arthur Butterworth, noted North Country composer, and I was required to conduct this work with Stockport Citadel Band and Manchester Openshaw Songster Brigade. Neither section was seen in the finished production. It was a fascinating, complicated score, and it was good to have the composer's guiding presence throughout the day. There were many memorable melodies, I remember, but the extract that stands out in my mind was a stirring movement – what we would call a festival march – entitled 'Reclamation'.

Sylvia's co-star was an actor-vocalist named Gerald Hely, who was deeply affected by the impact of the production. I saw him again some years later, on the stairs of the Westminster Central Hall during an interval in a day's meetings. He confirmed the spiritual impact of that earlier encounter.

I have another memory of that recording session. In another studio the cast of *Coronation Street*, under the bright lights and energetic

290

cameras, were preparing another episode in the popular soap opera. Some of us were smuggled in and, in a break in shooting, were introduced. We met again at lunch, when we found ourselves next to the familiar characters in the canteen queue. I sat at a table with 'Jack Walker' and Ben Kingsley, later to become really famous in the title role of *Gandhi*.

Not only did I inherit 23,000 songsters and 18,000 bandsmen when I took charge of the Bands Department, but also a number of rhythm groups as well; there were many more than 100 of them, the Joystrings leading the way.

Captain Joy Webb was a member of the staff and the members of this famous group were attached to the department as well. When the captain was taken ill on the eve of a campaign in East Anglia the British Commissioner (Commissioner William Cooper) decided that I should accompany the group for the weekend. In no way did I attempt to take Joy's place, I hasten to add!

This assignment gave me an appreciated opportunity to witness the activity of those dedicated young Salvationists at close quarters and to assess the effectiveness of their ministry. I helped them load, unload and reload their instruments and equipment in the compact utility vehicle provided and travelled with them by wedging myself into a limited space normally reserved for the streamlined Captain Webb. It was not easy, but lots of fun.

It was a pleasure to be with them and to take part in their so original presentation of the gospel message – in the Grand Theatre, Great Yarmouth; a Saturday afternoon visit to Norwich Prison; a crowded youth crush; a midnight sortie on a night club of doubtful reputation; three crowded meetings at Norwich Citadel (with many seekers at night); and a final musical spiritual challenge to a packed schoolroom in Sheringham.

That weekend confirmed me as a Joystrings fan. Their music was not of my vintage or idiom, but their fearless attack upon the stronghold of Satan, their efficient approach to music-making and their concern for the Kingdom left me in no doubt as to their place in the ministry of Army music.

The first councils festival in the Albert Hall in which I was organisationally involved lingers prominently in my memory. The Festival of Gospel Song (1963) and Century of Song (1965) had reached a high standard. We called the 1967 event the Festival of Sounding Praise, taking this from a verse in Isaac Watts's hymn 'Before Jehovah's Aweful Throne':

> We'll crowd thy gates with thankful songs,
> High as the heavens our voices raise;
> And earth, with her ten thousand tongues,
> Shall fill thy courts with sounding praise.

The National Songsters gave a premiere performance of Edward Gregson's cantata, 'In The Beginning'. Bandsman Ken Weston of Brighton Congress Hall, a professional musician released from a Glyndbourne engagement to take part in the festival, thrilled us with his violin solos, accompanied by Marjorie Ringham, and tastefully supplied an *obbligato* in the chorus's singing of 'Ye Must Be Born Again'. Songster Mrs Ann Ross, of Upper Norwood, was the vocal soloist. Lieut-Colonel Charles Skinner conducted his setting, 'Sounding Praise', composed for the occasion for the 1,000 voices to feature. Two Leidzén numbers – 'Lay Thy Load Of Sorrow' and 'Homeward Bound' – were effectively revived under Norman Bearcroft's baton. The Joystrings performed from a specially erected podium in the arena.

At one point in the proceedings the National Songsters were required to make their way hurriedly from the platform and climb via a series of stairs, doorways and corridors to the topmost gallery, there to provide an 'echo choir' for Joy Webb's 'The Shepherd's Song'. I learned afterwards that a mild state of panic existed when some of the doors were found to be locked and alternative routes were required to be explored. As it was I was relieved no end when, at the appropriate part of the song, the distant angelic voices came soaring through the lovely hall. This item, together with 'There Will Be God' with which it was linked (this had Bill Davidson as soloist with full chorus backing), was accompanied by a string ensemble.

Another success that night was the male chorus singing of 'What Shall The Answer Be?'. In his arrangement, Norman introduced a solo French horn (Peter Clack), whose plaintive tone added a unique quality to the singing and gave the old gospel song a touch of revived beauty. A quartet of French horns drawn from the Red Shield Band also featured in other chorus items, even those supported by the ISB. My arrangement of Evangeline Booth's 'Fling Wide The Gates' benefited from this added quality of tone, particularly in the angelic 'trumpeting' effects. Bandmaster Michael Clack was at the organ, of course.

Highlights of that (for me) memorable occasion were captured on a successful LP recording, 'With A Thousand Voices'.

At the conclusion of the following day's songster leaders councils in the Assembly Hall of the International Training College, led by General Frederick Coutts, we moved, almost without a break, into a *Sunday Half-Hour* radio broadcast. I had felt for a long time that some of the best singing in the Army was heard when provided by a company of music leaders in councils and that it was worthy of a broadcast. On 11 June 1967 my dream came true.

The staff band accompanied; Lieut-Colonel Adams conducted; the ISB male chorus and the National Songsters contributed 'solo' items; Ronald Allison introduced the programme. After the broadcast the producer, the Rev W. Kennedy-Ball, commented upon the rich content of the 'full-throated yet controlled' congregational singing and, a few days later, a letter received from the Rev John Lang, Head of Religious Programmes (Sound), said: 'The whole occasion had a splendour which we do not often manage to achieve.'

Praise indeed! Another chapter of Army musical history had been opened.

It was with joy that I learned that I was to accompany my old band, Chalk Farm, on its 1967 European campaign as headquarters representative. BBC *Town And Around* television cameras were at the hall early on the Friday morning, 26 May, to see the band leave for Southend Airport.

The hour-long flight brought us to Ostend, then we were conveyed by coach to Brussels. The Officer Commanding, Belgium (Colonel

Adolf Dürig), met us with the news that, because of a tragic fire at L'Innovation, a department store, a royal reception at the city hall had been cancelled out of respect for the feelings of the population – stunned by reports of 400 dead. Later in the day we visited the scene of the tragedy and saw the demolition squads still at work searching for bodies.

The evening festival, held in the central hall of the Belgian Evangelistic Mission, was marked by a musical tribute to the memory of the victims.

The next morning saw an early start and a six-and-a-half-hour train journey to Strasbourg, France. We gave an evening festival in this Alsatian hometown of Albert Schweitzer and conducted the holiness meeting the following morning. This was the start of a long, tough day that continued, after a further 90-minute train journey, at the Mennonite chapel at Kirkenhof, some 30 miles outside Belfort. Later, after an alfresco meal and a car journey into Belfort, the band marched through the town before presenting in the Army hall its second two-hour festival of the day.

On the Monday we left for Switzerland, our third country in four days. After a march through the town and a festival in the quaint village church at Liestal, a day-long train journey took us across the Swiss-Italian border to Turin, there to be received by the General Secretary (Brigadier Raymond Yarde) and the nine bandsmen of the local corps – the only Salvation Army band in the country.

Prior to the programme – recorded by Radio Turin and broadcast the next day – I was invited to rehearse the Turin bandsmen in the *Triumph Series* meditation 'My Faith Looks Up To Thee'. That night I was able to congratulate Bandmaster Michael Clack and his men on being the first British corps band to visit Italy and upon campaigning in their 12th European country.

And on to Rome! This was another hot and sticky day-long train ride and, on arrival, we were welcomed by the Officer Commanding (Lieut-Colonel Jean Bordas). As I alighted from the train the colonel greeted me warmly, took my arm and, as we walked along the platform, broke the news that an invitation had been received from the Pope for the band to play at the Vatican during the three-day stay in the city.

This was startling news. Such an ecumenical link-up had not been envisaged. I felt that the acceptance, or courteous decline, of the summons could not be my responsibility. After a delightful meal in heatwave conditions in the Army's *Albergo del Popolo*, and while the band played in the famous Pincio bandstand in the leafy Villa Borghese, with the lights of the city twinkling far below in the gathering dusk, I put a phone call through to London to seek the advice of General Frederick Coutts. The General felt he could not give his answer at once, but needed time to consider the matter and to consult international advisers. I could expect a reply at nine o'clock the next morning.

I took Bandmaster Clack into my confidence, but to this day I am convinced that none of the bandsmen was aware of the behind-the-scenes drama being enacted. The situation was delicate.

The next morning a phone call from International Headquarters, dead on time, gave the information that the visit to the Vatican had been approved. The General made two requests, that we should make the occasion as 'Army' as possible and that every attempt should be made to sing 'O Boundless Salvation!' in the presence of the Pope. I promised to do my best on both counts.

The decision was made known to the papal authorities, but in reply to our request for the band to play inside the Vatican the answer was non-committal – 'Possibly one tune!'

When the bandsmen returned from a sightseeing tour I met them in the hall of the Rome 1 Corps and broke the news, stressing the implications of such an historic happening and praying that the opportunity might be used to God's glory. We then enjoyed a period of relaxation at Ostia, Rome's silver-sand playground, which took the sting out of the tension and brought us refreshed to the evening programme in the Protestant Waldensian Church. 'The Holy War' brought the crowd to its feet, I remember.

The next day, Friday 2 June, was a public holiday and we left by private bus in good time for our Vatican appointment. Crowds were already gathering in the open streets. We had no idea what form our 'appointment' would take, or what kind of reception we would receive. All we knew was that we would not be permitted to march or play before entering the Vatican. This did not mean that we would approach the entrance as a nondescript group of casual sightseers. Carrying their instruments, the bandsmen formed up behind the colour sergeant who, the flag at 'shoulder arms', led us across St Peter's Square towards a door indicated. The brightly garbed Vatican Guard sprang to attention as we passed.

Shown into the Benedictine Chapel, the bandsmen were allocated pews on the right-hand side of the lovely, artistically designed building. Soon afterwards the first of the 1,500 pilgrims invited to attend the annual service of blessing began to arrive. The audience that day was representative of certain industries, communities and cultural and recreational pursuits. Forty selected from these groups were escorted to specially reserved seats near the Pope's throne. They would be personally presented to His Holiness. Included in this number were members of the Italian international soccer team. Lieut-Colonel Bordas, Brigadier Yarde, Bandmaster Clack and I were also recognised with a place of honour.

Contrary to expectation the band was asked to play some 'suitable music' soon after its arrival. Deputy Bandmaster Ray Todd duly conducted the playing of a number of hymn tunes loved by all denominations. For half an hour it went on, until the vast chapel was packed.

As the time of the Pope's arrival drew near, Bandmaster Clack was asked, 'Will the band play some happy music as the Pope is brought in?' 'Why not a march?' I whispered. A march it was and Pope Paul VI was carried in with due ancient ceremony to the strains of 'The Invincible Army'. It was an emotional moment.

The playing ceased. The platform was lowered. The Pope dismounted and climbed the steps of his throne. The preliminary rituals over, he spoke informal words of welcome, in the course of which, in excellent English, he welcomed the band, remembered the wives and families and thanked them for letting the bandsmen come to Rome to impart its 'soul-lifting music'. Later in the impressive service he gave what my interpreter assured me was a good old-fashioned holiness address.

At the conclusion of the proceedings the Pope left his elevated place to return to ground level and, as he did so, the voices of the Chalk Farm bandsmen began to sing William Booth's immortal song 'O Boundless Salvation!', with its moving sentiment, 'Now flowing for all men'. The Londoners again took up their instruments to play more inspiring music at the prompting of a nearby chapel authority.

It came to the turn of Michael Clack and me to be presented. I handed the Pope an Army pennant bearing the name of the band and the bandmaster gave him a copy of the LP recording prepared for the tour. His Holiness, in return, presented us each with a medallion to mark the occasion, spoke in eulogistic terms of the band's playing, thanked us for coming and hoped we would come again. He shook hands a second time and moved on, but then, as if becoming conscious of 'Hursley', which the band was then playing, came back again. 'That is how music should be played,' he said.

The music continued as the Pope was borne along the aisle towards the door. He paused to acknowledge the band on his way out and the band went on playing while the great crowds of pilgrims left the chapel.

Inspired and encouraged by our reception inside the Vatican it was decided that we would make our exit from the building across St Peter's Square with flag flying, drums beating and instruments sounding forth in rejoicing. It had to be a repeat of 'The Invincible Army'. As we marched away, the Vatican Guard sprang to attention in salute, sightseers pressed forward to take photographs and a party of English visitors, hardly able to believe their eyes, cheered.

That afternoon I phoned the General, gave him a brief résumé of the momentous happenings and assured him that the visit had been 'real Army' from our standpoint and that we had indeed sung the Founder's song in Vatican City, in the presence of the Pope.

Before leaving for Switzerland that night – this meant an overnight train journey – we visited the Colosseum, scene of the martyrdom of so many early Christians. Near the cross marking the spot where the last Christian to die there met his death, we sang 'When I Survey The Wondrous Cross' and prayed. It was a moving moment.

The weekend in the French-speaking part of Switzerland could have been an anticlimax but this was certainly not the case. After a Saturday festival in the lovely lakeside resort of Vevey – the band had hoped to play to Charlie Chaplin at his nearby home – we travelled the next morning by train to Lausanne, where baggage was required to be transferred across 12 platforms in as many minutes in order to catch the connection to Paris. The baggage party, directed by the efficient deputy bandmaster, began its task briskly enough as the men disappeared towards the slope leading to an underground network of tunnels – and then went missing. The Lausanne-Paris express arrived and still the 'baggage carriers' had not shown up. One imagined sinister undertones. What a plot for a spy story!

The Swiss railway authorities were kind, even if our explanation was difficult to accept. After a delay of 20 minutes the missing men and instruments reappeared, to the relief and cheers of their anxious comrades. As the baggage party entered the chasm below the tracks the complex electrical system had decided upon a power cut. It had taken all that time, stumbling about in the pitch darkness, to discover the exit. The joys of touring with a famous band!

By the time Paris was reached most of the bandsmen were in the grip of a mild epidemic, but the evening festival in the Paris Central Hall went through as scheduled, even if some of the victims slept through the afternoon three-hour sightseeing coach tour of city landmarks. Upon our arrival in the capital placards outside the station were giving news of the latest international crisis – the beginning of the six-day war in the Middle East.

A communal billet on the lower deck of the Army's barge, *Louise Catherine*, on the Seine was not conducive to a 'good night's rest', but a jet-hop into Heathrow got us home for breakfast.

Tony Peagam, one of the trombonists, concluded his series of reports for *The Musician* with:

Can ever a tour have been so happy, so successful, so history-making? Can ever modern-day Salvation Army bandsmen – amateur music-makers and evangelists all – have had such an opportunity to taste the heady wine of early-day pioneering? Who would have thought it possible to turn back the years and capture once again the true spirit of 'Punchard' trailblazing?

* * * * *

At the conclusion of the second Holiday Plus Fellowship Week at Butlin's, Clacton-on-Sea, officers of the British Territory moved in for annual councils. Not for many years had a British Commissioner been able to meet all the officers under his command at the same place at the same time. Commissioner William Cooper relished the innovation.

One of my outstanding memories of that weekend is the premiere performance of *Take-Over Bid* on the Sunday afternoon. The two Johns were then corps officers in the West London Division – Captain Gowans at Kingston-upon-Thames and Captain Larsson at Hillingdon. Members of the cast were recruited from the division. They could not have had a more searching baptism of fire. How would this new idiom, inspired and energetically supported by the British Commissioner and National Youth Secretary (Brigadier Denis Hunter), be accepted?

They need not have worried. The officers, veterans and youngsters alike sat through 18 songs, lapping up the humour, prayerfully accepting the challenge of the more sombre scenes and taking readily to this new means of reaching the masses with the gospel. As the last exciting chord of the final chorus lingered in the air the huge audience jumped to its feet, its applause revealing approval, its tears expressing the mighty moving of the Spirit. Musicals had come to stay.

The first public presentation was in Reading Town Hall on Saturday 14 October 1967 and the second in Acton Town Hall a week later.

No one was more delighted than I at this emergence of the Army's own Gilbert and Sullivan – or Rodgers and Hammerstein if you prefer.

I remembered my own attempts to write and produce this kind of creation at Child's Hill and Chalk Farm and the severe rebuffs I had received, even to the extent of threatening to relieve me of my songster leader's commission. Times had changed. All credit to our leaders in 1967!

Instead of the traditional *Messiah* night at Clapton Congress Hall in aid of the Army's goodwill work, we handed over to the Joystrings for what they called a 'Christmas Package'. It was an original and fascinating presentation. Captain Joy Webb never did things by half measures.

The Joystrings themselves were ensconced on a huge, three-tier tubular stand, drummer Wycliffe Noble being seated on the summit at the level of the top stalls and looking festive behind his multicoloured lighted drums and effects. Bill Davidson, on the next level, surrounded by balloons and tinsel, plucked his electric guitar. Peter and Sylvia Dalziel (I had attended their wedding at New Addington earlier in the year) were at floor level, as also was Joy Webb, seated behind an electric organ.

There were microphones everywhere, tall and short, movable and fixed, and the spotlighting was captivating: coloured, revolving, as well as the fierce glare of a white star.

The charming, relaxed compère was television personality Polly Elwes, and other friends of the group who took part were David Kossoff, with his Old Testament readings, and Jack de Manio, who made the financial appeal.

On paper perhaps our plans for 1968 looked too ambitious. Internationally we were to celebrate the 90th anniversary of Salvation Army bands and the 70th anniversary of songster brigades. In the British Territory it was Youth Year.

The first anniversary occasion came at the end of March with a Festival of Praise at Clapton Congress Hall. This was mainly a London and Home Counties event with bands from Gillingham (Alfred Springate), Hadleigh Temple (Michael Kenyon), Staines (Brian Bowen), Wood Green (Gordon Jewkes) and Worthing (Leslie Tickner) taking part. Older music was represented by the playing by the massed bands of Colonel Arthur Goldsmith's selection 'The Banner Of Liberty'.

The next day's councils for bandsmen of the North, South, East and West London and Canterbury Divisions, Brighton Area and Regent Hall Corps constituted three 'firsts'. It was the first time such an event had been held in the Fairfield Halls, Croydon; it was the first time the International Staff Band had participated in such gatherings (at least in living memory); and it was the first time General Frederick Coutts had led them. Two thousand delegates attended, most of them taking meals at the nearby technical college. Many restaurants in the town opened at our request especially for the occasion.

Little Hythe Band shared the afternoon platform with the International Staff Band.

On a Saturday in May, bands from Croydon Citadel, Penge, Plumstead, Sutton and Walthamstow marched from Trafalgar Square along the Strand, Fleet Street and Ludgate Hill with a mounted escort to St Paul's Cathedral for a festival of praise and thanksgiving for 90 years of Army banding. As the Lord Mayor of London, two high sheriffs and the city marshal entered the cathedral the grand organ sounded out 'I've Found A Friend In Jesus', written by Charles Fry, the Army's first bandmaster. Similar recognition to the anniversary was given later in the year in Westminster Abbey and Westminster Cathedral. Brother David Hughes, of Regent Hall, was the inspiration behind these three occasions.

In the summer, a mammoth Congress Cavalcade was held at the Crystal Palace. We of the Bands Department shared the planning of the day with the Youth Department and the division of interest worked splendidly. Brigadier Hunter and I, with other members of the planning council headed by Lieut-Colonel Leslie Pender, made many visits to the venue and found the Crystal Palace authorities delighted to welcome us back to the scene of so many historic Army events.

From the flag break at 10.30 am it was a non-stop programme. Taking part was a chorus of 2,000 songsters (probably the largest group ever to participate in an Army event), 1,000 bandsmen (representing 36 bands, one from each division and area in the territory), overseas youth groups, torchbearers, corps cadets, scouts, guides and brownie guides, plus 600 delegates to the British Youth Congress.

Six bandstands were established in various parts of the grounds. They were named after noted composers of a bygone era: Slater, Hawkes, Goldsmith, Coles, Marshall and Leidzén. With clockwork precision the bands marched to and from the various bandstands, each section making the most of their two spots allocated during the day.

A popular feature was the marching competition, the winners, Tottenham Citadel Band, being awarded a cup donated and presented by George and Lily Crooks, Regent Hall stalwarts.

In the great march past the parading hosts took their places on the grass arena where the congress chorus, accompanied by the International Staff Band, sang the 'Hallelujah' Chorus. The General took the salute and addressed the estimated 40,000 people who had gathered.

There were other 90th anniversary commemorations, notably a service of thanksgiving held in Croydon Parish Church and addressed by the General. This was the first Salvation Army meeting to be held in this ancient church and was the borough's tribute. I had an honoured place in the procession, walking with the staff bandmaster, Lieut-Colonel Bernard Adams. Major Leslie Condon (who had been appointed National Bandmaster when Major Norman Bearcroft farewelled for Canada) conducted the united bands of Thornton Heath, Upper Norwood and Croydon Citadel. All three of us were citizens of the Borough of Croydon.

No fewer than four overseas bands visited Britain that year. At Eastertide we welcomed Örebro from Sweden and Oslo 3 from Norway. I travelled with the former section. Both bands made a marked impression.

The presence of the New York Staff Band and Wellington Citadel Band helped to step up interest in the Bandmasters Councils Festival. The American visitors had concluded a European tour which took in The Netherlands, Switzerland and Germany, and the first band from New Zealand to visit the Army's homeland came from a successful campaign in North America.

The New Yorkers took part in the following day's bandmasters councils at Denmark Hill before returning home. The New Zealanders remained to complete an 18-day tour which included England, Scotland, Ireland and Wales. Great crowds greeted the band at every centre, the neat traditional form of crisp tonguing appealing especially to veteran band enthusiasts.

On the final day of the tour, Wellington Citadel Band accompanied Regent Hall Band to play in the forecourt of Buckingham Palace. In this way royal recognition was given to the anniversary celebrations.

Three other happenings that year are worthy of mention. At the bandmasters councils the General announced the reintroduction of divisional bandmasters in the British Territory and handed commissions to the first three to be appointed. In July the Joystrings, their mission completed (to quote their leader), passed into Salvation Army musical history from the stage of the Fairfield Halls. The national songster festival marked the 70th anniversary of songster brigades and included a flashback to 1898.

In addition to national events, councils had been held in Plymouth, Cardiff and Leeds and there had been an abundance of weekend 'specialing' and other official commitments.

It is inevitable that members of the Bands Department should spend a great deal of time in travelling to and from engagements throughout the territory. I took my life in my hands – and threatened other people's as well – when I decided to learn to drive.

Major Leslie Condon should have received the Order of St Christopher, or some such motoring award, for his patience and bravery during that period. What a good job he was gifted with an iron-nerve temperament! At the same time I realise that our many outings provided excellent opportunity for me to gain the necessary experience to give me a reasonable chance to pass my test – eventually.

When an inter-divisional festival was due at such centres as Leeds, Liverpool, Manchester, Newcastle, Blackburn, Sheffield, Birmingham, Bristol or Cardiff, we would leave London on the Monday and spend the week in the respective divisions, separating for rehearsals each night and coming together for the united final run-through at the chosen venue on the Saturday afternoon. Many such journeys were made.

The evenings were thrilling. I always enjoyed meeting our musicians and their leaders. Many became personally known to me. The daytime sometimes dragged. There was always work to be done in the mornings with pen and paper. This was often carried out in a comfortable billet, the genial hosts having left for work and shown me the way to the food cupboard. If this was not convenient the local library was utilised.

Major June Kitchen (we all three held that rank at the same time and irreverently called ourselves the Magi) and my wife would arrive on the Saturday morning by train for duties in connection with the weekend, and after partaking of kindly prepared refreshments after the final session on the Sunday night we would return to London, travelling through the night. This was excellent experience for a learner-driver preparing for his test. The good Major Condon insisted that we travelled by a route that avoided the motorways, so that I could drive all the way. I, on the other hand, was most happy for him to relieve me at the wheel whenever a motorway was signposted.

We were a happy carload. It was tremendous fun. We sang to keep the driver awake. Les gave some of his marvellous Suffolk and Norfolk impressions. My wife remembered some Welsh words and phrases she had learned at school in Gorseinon. June treated us to a touch of Devon, where she had been evacuated as a schoolgirl during the war. I just kept my eyes on the road, looked out for the tail lights of the vehicle in front and enjoyed the entertainment.

On one trip, when we had preferred the Al on our ride from the north, so intent was I on my wheelcraft that I forgot to keep an eye on the petrol gauge. The entertainment abruptly stopped when I announced that the needle was on 'Empty'. It is not easy to find a garage open in Baldock at four o'clock in the morning, but at last, when we thought all was lost, we were successful. We were doubly successful, for next to the petrol pump was an all-night café where I was able to partake of my favourite refreshment in such circumstances – pork pie and orangeade – and Les enjoyed a grapefruit and a glass of milk. The ladies were far more circumspect.

I passed my driving test the morning after Londoners had welcomed members of the seventh High Council, summoned to elect a successor to General Frederick Coutts.

One day the telephone rang. The voice at the other end said: 'Winston Churchill here.' Thinking it was a former editorial colleague in leg-pulling mood, I replied, 'Really? Lord Nelson here.' It took only a second or two to convince me that it *was* Winston Churchill at the other end: the grandson of the great man.

He was seeking the services of a Salvation Army band for the following day, a Friday. It was at the time of the Biafra crisis and there was to be an all-night vigil on the steps of St Paul's Cathedral that night and a protest march through the streets of London the next morning. The organisers wished an Army band to head the procession behind a draped empty coffin.

I courteously explained that our bands were not permitted to take part in political demonstrations. Mr Churchill seemed surprised and expressed the thought that he had always been of the opinion that The Salvation Army existed to help people. I confirmed that such a code of policy was still observed but there were necessary exceptions.

'Are you the highest authority?' he asked. I assured him that I did not have the last word, but felt certain that permission would not be given for any such participation.

'I asked to speak to General Booth,' he said. How disappointed he must have been to ask for General Booth and be put through to Major Boon!

* * * * *

United singing featured prominently in the farewell of General Coutts at the Royal Albert Hall in 1969. Memories of the centenary celebrations were revived with 'Worthy Is The Lamb', 'Storm The Forts' and 'Happy Song', while the General's final charge to his officers and soldiers was prefaced by the singing of 'O Save Me, Dear Lord', the solo part being taken by Songster Mrs Mary Miller, of Wellingborough, who had sung it in the same hall at the centenary. Dear Mary! How her passing a few years later affected her many friends.

The national songster festival at Clapton Congress Hall proved to be the last event of its kind to be held in that historic building. Exactly 40 years before, the first national songster festival had been held there and now the brigades of Manchester Openshaw, Croydon Citadel, Tunbridge Wells and Hillingdon, together with Tottenham Citadel Band and the Southsea Joybelles, had the honour of being present at the swansong.

The next day the British Commissioner conducted the first councils to be held for all-London songsters in the Fairfield Halls, following the lead set by the bandsmen the previous year. After a curtailed break for lunch, delegates were back in their places an hour before the afternoon session to rehearse for a recording to be broadcast in the *Sunday Half-Hour* series. The actual recording was made after a shortened tea interval, immediately prior to the evening session, the songs being introduced by Major Will Pratt. Sutton Band provided the accompaniments and I was privileged to conduct.

The programme was broadcast on the BBC Radio 2 network (and on the World Service) three weeks later and reached faraway places. Messages of appreciation were received from such centres as Germany and Malta, and the British Commissioner heard from a Salvationist in Melbourne, Australia, who had not only listened to the broadcast at 6.30 on the Monday morning but had also taped it and sent a copy to the commissioner.

Our busy programme was carried over into the new year. New-style uniforms were introduced, united songsters sang 'Shout Aloud Salvation' and 'Cleansing For Me' at the valedictory meeting at Clapton Congress Hall; the first divisional bandmasters conference was held at Sunbury Court; and the national songster festival, taken away from London for the first time, was held in Sheffield City Hall.

In Wilfred Pickles's 'Have a go' parlance, my most embarrassing moment was during the bandmasters councils festival at the Royal Albert Hall when, just as I was to conduct the chorus in 'Soldiers Of

Christ', General Erik Wickberg promoted me to the rank of brigadier. The General was thoughtful enough to present me with a set of stars to be worn on my tunic at councils the next day!

The international visitors that year were Box Hill Band, from Australia. They took part in the Royal Albert Hall festival and in the later annual event in Fairfield Halls before spending a Sunday with us at Croydon. It was a pleasure to tour with them. They were popular everywhere they went.

There is space to tell of only one incident. I thought that on its way from Blackpool to Leeds it would be interesting for the band to stop for lunch at the famous Ilkley Moor, so, in planning the route, arrangements were made accordingly. Arriving at the restaurant, Bandmaster Keith MacPherson suggested to me that we should sing grace to the tune of 'Cranbrook' ('On Ilkley Moor Baht 'At'). I thought it a good idea and, as the men stood by the tables in readiness for the meal, I duly struck up 'Be present at our table, Lord' to the proposed tune.

Either because they didn't know the tune or had been prompted otherwise, the bandsmen remained silent and, to my horror, I discovered I had embarked upon what turned out to be 20 bars of sheer agony. There could be no retreat. That was my last solo in public. My 'friends' at least had the good 'grace' to afford me deafening applause at the conclusion of my ordeal.

* * * * *

The ITV network series, *Stars On Sunday*, was an immediate success. The idea of the programme, produced by the religious broadcast department of Yorkshire Television, was that viewers should request their favourite religious songs, ballads, hymns and readings.

The first programme was transmitted on 17 August 1969. Six weeks later the Southsea Joybelles made the first of several appearances in the feature, which ran for 15 weeks. When the series was resumed, Jess Yates, the executive producer, thought a Salvation Army chorus and brass band should take part. This led to my assembling the

307

Northern Chorus, which had done so well for us at the national songster festival in Sheffield, with Sheffield Citadel Band.

We met for a full day of tele-recording in the Leeds studios of Yorkshire Television on Monday 30 November 1970. The brigades came from Doncaster, Gainsborough, Leeds Central, Leeds West Hunslet, Shaw, Sheffield Citadel and York. For many it meant the loss of a day's employment. It was a 12-hour stint.

The first programme featuring the chorus and band was shown early in the new year and the regular appearance for some weeks after that earned the Army many new friends. I received some most interesting letters: from school friends, former RAF colleagues, people with whom I had worked in my first job and many housebound Salvationists to whom the feature meant so much.

Some months later the 'stars' assembled again for another day in the Leeds studios to film and record a second series. Again seven brigades and the same band took part, and a 'bevy' of timbrelists was added in the complement to great effect. A memory is of production having to be delayed while some of the younger songsters queued to obtain Michael Parkinson's autograph. I had never heard of him at that time and could not understand the fuss.

The songster leaders councils festival at the Royal Albert Hall carried a new look in 1971. Gone was the 1,000-strong chorus, which, for years, had adorned the platform and the programme. Birmingham Citadel Songster Brigade alone represented the vocalists of the British Territory. The visual and musical colour was supplied by string bands from Örebro (Sweden), Copenhagen Temple (Denmark) and Oslo 3 (Norway), each of which undertook an individual tour afterwards.

For some years the organisers of these events had come in for considerable criticism because of the alleged excessive length of the programme. Particularly the previous year had I been taken to task, even to the extent of being called upon to explain in the open forum session in the afternoon of bandmasters councils. I decided, therefore, to do away with the announcing of items as such. The General and Chief of the Staff 'played ball' and the items were introduced by the lowering and raising of lights, both white and a variety of colours.

The Chief spoke briefly at the beginning of the evening and returned to the platform just before the end to introduce the special Children's Year epilogue. In his report for *The Musician* Captain John Larsson said:

'The emotion of the moment was heightened when young Jonathan Byfield, young people's singing company member from Croydon Citadel, stepped forward into the spotlight and recited words from the Scriptures, words of Jesus regarding children, whilst the ISB male chorus hummed quietly in the background... As the lights slowly, so slowly faded on the boy at the end of the item no heart could have remained unmoved. Continuing the epilogue, the ISB played Ray Steadman-Allen's "Young In Heart", finishing on a hushed note, before the Chief pronounced the benediction.

'The lights came on. The magic was gone. It was time to go home. It had been a good evening, with something for the eye as well as the ear, for the heart as well as the mind. And when we got outside it was still light. It was only 9 pm!'

From the first Butlin's Holiday Plus Fellowship Week at Clacton in 1966 members of the Bands Department bore the brunt of the responsibility for the evening entertainment. At first the programmes were divided, two separate performances going on at the same time – in the Gaiety and Playhouse Theatres. Norman Bearcroft and his team were responsible for one and I and my cronies for the other. After half an hour we were required to change houses, each group passing the other in the grounds as we ran in costumes to save as much time as possible.

When the event was transferred to Bognor in 1969 things were easier, the Gaiety Theatre in those days being large enough to seat the entire camping community. By this time Leslie Condon had joined me, as had Brigadier Edgar Grinsted, George and Lily Crooks and Peter and Sylvia Dalziel. We could afford to be more ambitious with our nightly spectaculars, although our planning could not begin until we arrived.

Such a programme meant conceiving ideas (usually at the morning conference) and writing sketches and songs each day. Time had to be found for rehearsing, as well. It was the discovery of some life-size

'Daleks' in the props room backstage that led to the science fiction scenes of that era. I became Dr Who, possessed of the power to send the cast anywhere I wished, and remained as that character for the rest of my time at Butlin's.

What fun we had the night we sent them to the moon! Corrugated cardboard 'uniform' was all very well – until Les Condon tried to bend over to lift his accordion. The weightless sausages were most lifelike as they floated in space, always just out of reach of ravenous astronauts. On another occasion, 26 bandsmen, hidden under a mammoth green curtain with just their legs showing, served as the Loch Ness monster, the bell of George Crooks's sousaphone making an admirable head for 'Nessie'. Britain's entry into the Common Market was celebrated with a round-up of European countries and their musical people.

There are more serious memories. The late-night community singing sessions which became prayer meetings as many knelt in dedication. The private counselling of needy campers that was never publicised. The thrill as 200 bandsmen, many from small bands, played such masterpieces as 'Treasures From Tchaikovsky' under the baton of the national bandmaster.

Butlin's in 1971 included a BBC *Sunday Half-Hour* broadcast for the first time. The dawn of the tape cassette era has made such happenings far more common.

The early part of 1972 was taken up with planning for the British Congress. This was to last for six days and it was decided to take the vast Wembley Arena (at that time still known as the Pool) for all the meetings. Music was to play a leading part in the celebrations, of course, and Major Condon and I made several visits to Wembley in preparation for the participation of a congress chorus and several representative bands, including the Chicago Staff Band. These contacts with the Wembley authorities stood me in good stead when, six years later, I came to make links in connection with organising the International Congress.

The congress was a tremendous success, the arena, seating 10,000, being filled for each of the Sunday meetings led by the General, as well as the Saturday festivals and other events.

In the midst of the preparations I received farewell orders and handed over to Major Condon. Captain Trevor Davis was appointed national bandmaster in the major's place. However, I was requested to share the conducting at Wembley, leading the chorus in such pieces as 'Stand Up For Jesus', the sessional song, 'Victorious', and 'When Jesus looked o'er Galilee' ('Fewster'), this by unaccompanied male voices.

As a songster leader, one of my favourite pieces had been 'Behold Us Now Repentant', with words by Lieut-Commissioner Arch R. Wiggins to Colonel Arthur Goldsmith's arrangement of one of Mendelssohn's *Songs Without Words*. All through the six years I was in the Bands Department I dreamed of using this overlooked gem on a national occasion with a large chorus. At Wembley my dream was realised. The commissioner was there to hear it. He considered this to be one of his best sets of verses, and up till then he had never heard it sung. Commissioner Ernest Fewster was also present to hear the male voices so tenderly sing his lovely tune.

In this dramatic and emotional way I took my leave of the musicians of the British Territory. I shall always treasure the memory of having the honour to serve them, for I do indeed regard them as the salt of the earth. I learned to love them for themselves and for the very work's sake.

Chapter 24

Keyboard Reflections

THERE have been so many notable soloists with whom I am privileged to have had happy association as accompanist over the years that I cannot mention more than a few. The first was not a Salvationist. He was, in fact, Ernest Lough, a boy chorister of the Temple Choir, London, who had become an overnight sensation with an His Master's Voice recording of Mendelssohn's 'Hear My Prayer' and 'O For The Wings Of A Dove' on the reverse side. It soared to the top of the 'charts' of 1927.

David Barrett, son of our Sunday school superintendent at Cricklewood Wesleyan Church, attended the City of London School, where Ernest was also a scholar, and succeeded in persuading him to take part in one of our periodic Wesley Guild concerts. I was deputed to play for him and so met for the only time this silver-voiced, dreamy-eyed, sad-faced youth whose fame we so much envied.

He sang 'O For The Wings Of A Dove', 'Where'er You Walk' and other classical gems. It was, I seem to remember, a non-stop recital lasting some 45 minutes. Certainly a sight-reading test for a 13-year-old novice pianist! Many years later I heard a recording of Ernest Lough, by then a mature baritone, singing duets with his former soprano self. A masterpiece of superimposing! When Commissioner Catherine Bramwell-Booth was featured on *Desert Island Discs* some years ago I was interested to discover that Master Ernest Lough's singing of 'Hear My Prayer', with the Temple Choir backing, was one of the records she had chosen to take with her on her predetermined shipwreck adventure.

In May 1933, Captain and Mrs Percy Pugmire were appointed to Child's Hill. It was not long before the captain persuaded his father, the legendary Colonel Joseph, to visit us and I was entrusted with the organ accompaniments to his vocal solos.

Joseph Pugmire was the natural successor to John Lawley as a singing evangelist. He is remembered mainly as the leader of prayer meetings in the great gatherings conducted by the Army's Generals. His skilful intermingling of songs, solos and prayers made him a master in the art of soul-winning. When Edward Higgins became General he appointed Colonel Pugmire to be his ADC and, as such, he travelled the world. It was a rare let-up in his busy schedule that left the colonel free to spend a Sunday at his son's corps.

In the afternoon he lectured on 'Songs that reach the heart' and introduced plenty of vocal illustrations to aid his talk. He was difficult to accompany. He was unpredictable in time, tempo and rhythmic observance. Singing with all the passion of his soul, he would suddenly stop in his tracks to reiterate the words and the message and then, equally without warning, continue the song where he had left it – and he was always dead on key.

Colonel Pugmire sang all the favourites that day – 'I Heard A Voice So Gently Calling', 'I Have Pleasure In His Service', 'Sunshine On The Hill', the lot. How the congregations enjoyed him – and how honoured and humbled I felt as I tried to catch him up or to alight on the right key when he struck up a chorus without waiting for any mechanical aid!

When Ensign Alfred Gilliard became editor of *The War Cry*, he asked his brother-in-law, Songster Leader Vickery, to write a song for the paper's midsummer issue. The result was 'Let The Sunshine In'. The following year it was suggested that the special number would be geared to hikers. Alf Vickery obliged with 'Don't Miss Your Way To Heaven'.

This became an annual assignment until the outbreak of war. The songs came seemingly without effort: 'The Land Of God's Sunshine And Love', 'Travel Along In The Sunshine', 'Face The Sunshine' and 'On The Road Of Happiness'. He also grouped together a number of other popular sunshine songs and choruses, not all his own compositions, as a vocal medley and these were later arranged for bands by Eric Ball. This 'Rays Of Sunshine' was played a great deal on the International Staff Band's 1954 tour of Switzerland. The choruses of Vickery's songs are easy to learn. The fact that the sunshine collection had its first publication in *The War Cry* assured the songs and choruses of immediate success. What an opportunity it was for corps officers stationed at seaside towns, on an August holiday Sunday, to be able to teach the crowds at beach meetings an up-to-date chorus! Typical of hundreds of such instances was the letter sent to *The War Cry* on 20 July 1938 by the commanding officer at Bangor (Northern Ireland). He told the editor: 'We received our *War Crys* on Thursday afternoon and were so pleased with "Face The Sunshine" that we learned it ourselves and then taught it to a vast crowd which gathered around our "open-air" that evening. They took it up well and sang heartily as a holiday crowd on the promenade can sing. Consequently we sold a large number of *War Crys*. C. S. Church, Major.'

Major Church became greatly loved by servicemen in the war that was so soon to come.

Whenever I hear a 'Vickery' chorus I have a vision of the songwriter facing an audience of several hundred at Broadmoor, Parkhurst, Wormwood Scrubs, Strangeways or Durham. He tried his latest creation out on the prisoners and they, ever quick on the uptake, roared with laughter at such lines as 'Don't stay grumbling, shut behind your door', 'Take away the barrier and let the sunshine through' or 'Don't stay grumbling, planning, scheming'. But they got the message! They sang heartily. It was a pleasure to assist him at the piano and to help launch some of his popular songs.

My music-moulding apprenticeship continued on the headquarters building when I was called upon to accompany such soloists as Arthur Rolls (trombone), Bram Allington (who as a young Wombwell bandsman had taken part in that last Crystal Palace festival in 1934), Dennis Smith (euphonium) and Jack Taylor (soprano).

Dennis gave my solo, 'A Starry Crown', its first public airing – at a Sunday afternoon united orderlies meeting at Victoria Homes, Whitechapel, with pianoforte accompaniment. Some 18 years later Arthur presented my trombone solo, 'Count Your Blessings', to a meeting of the International Music Board.

* * * * *

315

Although I did not play for Major Leslie Condon on many public occasions I must refer to the numerous informal programmes – mostly at Sunbury Court – when we joined forces. These were mainly during music leaders courses when, on one evening in the week, we 'let our hair down' and relaxed with good, healthy fun.

After performing expertly on the hosepipe – always with apologies to Mozart – and acceding to a serious request to sing something, Les would introduce a touch of novelty by requesting a favourite chorus or verse melody which he promised to feature as an E♭ bass solo. His prowess on this instrument was universally recognised and the gathered company always seemed to relish his ability simultaneously to think music and transfer those thoughts into impressive sound.

In a more limited manner I was expected to act similarly, providing an extempore accompaniment to his composition and performance. Not all the melodies requested suited the familiar theme-and-variation treatment, but we usually managed to overcome the difficulty. The item was always a riot and the admiring listeners worthily recognised the Condon genius with prolonged applause at the conclusion of the item.

Of course, we had worked out an overall scheme long before, based on the old Wright and Round formula. After someone had shouted for 'Annie Laurie', 'Land Beyond The Blue' or 'Travel Along In The Sunshine', we took a minute or two to decide upon the key – and then we were away. After eight bars of introduction Les would embark upon a dazzling cadenza, planned to take one's breath away at the first encounter. Then some thematic music from the piano would follow in this order: first variation in triple time; flourishing second movement with masses of running about, covering as many octaves as physically possible; melody in the relative minor; triple-tonguing final movement with plenty of 'smash and grab', finishing with a note high in the heavens against a series of crashing chords passing through a chasm of changing keys until daylight safely materialised. The ruse never failed. Les was always the master.

Chapter 25

Words and Music

SOMEONE once asked me if I was the son of the Songster Leader Boon who used to write music. I have obviously been travelling along the road of Army songwriting for a long time.

It really began at the funeral of Commissioner John Lawley. I was nine years of age and, as was usual when big Army events took place, my mother had kept me away from school to attend.

As they carried the coffin into Clapton Congress Hall I was intrigued to see that, in addition to Lawley's cap, his Bible and songbook were prominently on view among the flowers. The presence of the Bible, if unusual, I could understand, but why the songbook? My mother explained that the commissioner had been a great singer and had written many songs, some of them included in that very book. I was impressed.

That afternoon the congregation sang for the first time a song by John Lawley, written during his last long illness and found among his papers following his promotion to Glory. It was 'Though thunders roll and darkened be the sky, I'll trust in thee'. The tune, 'Sandon', was well known because of its association with the words 'Lead, Kindly Light', and we sang heartily. In a moving tribute, General Bramwell Booth said: 'He sang his way through life and he will sing his way through eternity. His was a ministry of song.'

I remember reading the words printed on the order of service and thinking how wonderful it must be to write a song like that, to see it in print and hear it sung in public. That funeral service programme dated 14 September 1922 is among my prized possessions. The words still leap out of the page at me.

I did nothing about the ambition born that day until, some five years later, our Sunday school superintendent at the Wesleyan church

317

announced a competition in which scholars were invited to write a children's hymn for the forthcoming anniversary. The successful entry would be sung on that day. Words and melody were required and the church organist would harmonise the prize-winning effort.

With heart-searching zeal and much enthusiasm I set about the task – and could not stop. After I had written 36 verses I decided that I had gone sadly astray and tore up the copy. Remembering the sad fiasco afterwards I realised that I had attempted to set the Bible in verse, paraphrasing in rhyme as many incidents as possible. What a mix-up it all was! My first attempt at hymn writing was not a success.

Some time passed before I again tried my hand. By this time I was a Salvationist and a teenaged songster leader. One day the singing company leader – a charming young lady of my own age – asked me to write a song for her girls and boys to sing at the anniversary that summer. I blushed – as I always did when young ladies spoke to me, and still do – and began stammering an apology, explaining that I felt I would not be much good at that kind of thing. She smiled and simply said that she would like me to try.

That did it. The truth was that I rather liked the singing company leader and that made all the difference in the world. I went home and started strumming on the piano, adding words as I went along until 'A Song Of Happiness' was completed. The singing company sang it at the young people's anniversary; it was submitted for publication; Colonel Frederick Hawkes, in his reply, kindly commented that it had made 'a favourable impression on my mind'; and the song was published in the YP Supplement of *The Musical Salvationist* in the October of that year, 1933, barely six months after it had been put on paper.

And so, my 'Lawley' dream came true and I saw my name in print as a songwriter for the first time, having written words and music. Nearly 30 years later I perpetuated my indebtedness to John Lawley's inspiration in a *Unity Series* selection which I was surprisingly permitted to call 'Lawley's Songs'. This was later transcribed as a vocal piece.

In my own beginnings as a songwriter I was fortunate to know Adjutant Doris Rendell. Her output was prolific and she was a source of constant encouragement as she kept sending verses to me. I was not alone in this. Ernest Rance, Fred Grant, Charles Skinner and others had good reason to be grateful to Doris Rendell.

Adjutant Rendell and I collaborated in two young people's songs, 'Hear Us, We Pray', and 'Such A Lovely World He Made'; a wartime selection, 'Our King Cometh'; a vocal solo, 'Sunshine Of Love', made popular by her friend, Adjutant Eva Fouracre; and other songs, including 'Let Peace Reign In Your Heart' from a Coronation pageant in which Adjutant Fouracre sang this song, 'Immortal Love' and 'Joy In Service'.

At one time Colonel Mrs Ivy Mawby was always on hand as an office colleague to join me in producing a song for a special occasion. These included the classical arrangements 'If Thou Art Near', 'Seeking For Thee' and 'When Hearts Are Young'; 'The Kingdoms' (not to be confused with the songster selection of almost the same name), written for the Festival of Britain national rally in 1951; and 'Singing We Go'.

In an earlier chapter I spoke of the more than 80 wartime songs I had written for camp concerts and musical plays, mostly in a fairyland setting for the benefit of patients of a children's hospital in St Bride's Bay, Pembrokeshire, who had been evacuated to that idyllic setting from bomb-ravaged Cardiff. It is natural that the music of some of these should have found its way into Salvation Army usage, with suitable words aiding the 'conversion'.

Earlier, at RAF Sopley, it may be remembered, I obtained the permission of Patience Strong to set her words, 'The Men Who Fight For England', to music. They had appeared in the *Daily Mirror*. This was arranged for a male voice octet. For a long time after the war I thought about making this available for Army purposes but in my numerous attempts to write words could not get the original poem out of my mind. My good friend Miriam Richards came to the rescue and 'Triumphant In The Combat' came into being as a mixed-voice setting. It is in *Gems No 6*, but never really caught on.

Another song written at that time was 'England Is A Garden'. As I also wrote the words there was no author's permission to be sought on this occasion. It was first sung by a lad from the Manchester area with a pleasing light baritone voice. I believe he lost his life as a radar operator in an invasion operation in Normandy. I sent a copy to Raymond Allen, a noted resident singer at a summer show at the Bournemouth Pavilion (not to be confused with the two young Salvationists then earning reputations in Army circles or the later ventriloquist, all of the same name). He gratefully accepted it and immediately included it in his repertoire in Bournemouth and on his subsequent wartime tours.

'England Is A Garden' has never been amended for Salvation Army use, but when Croydon Citadel Home League Fellowship Singers presented 'The Glory Of The Garden' as a spectacular item at a national home league rally at Westminster Central Hall, at a similar event at Butlin's Holiday Plus Fellowship Week and various other centres, permission was granted for the song, with its original words, to be included. The lovely old-world costumes and rustic setting added to the atmosphere.

Two songs written for a musical fairy story, *The Enchanted Castle*, became well known in their new guise. 'One Happy Day', sung by a princess imprisoned by her mentally unbalanced father in the tower of a royal castle as she awaited rescue by her handsome prince, became: 'Singing we go, our joy to show, we want to fill the world with music.' Ivy Mawby caught the spirit of my original intention and it became the camp chorus of the first national singing company camp at Sunbury Court in 1948.

The other song, 'Enchanted Castle Of My Heart', was featured as a duet by the princess and her prince. The prince was Pilot Officer Pip Marsden, a Tynesider who in the early days of post-war television had his own children's programme as an expert on bird life. The romantic little song was an immediate success. How the hospital patients – many of them physically handicapped and lying on their backs – to whom the first performance was presented loved hearing the hero tell the heroine:

> *I have been dreaming of someone,*
> *Someone to cherish and hold:*

Just like the fairy book story,
Sweeter one never was told.
Now I have found that someone,
You have dropped out of the blue:
Such a beautiful someone,
And that someone is you.

and the climax of the refrain when the prince and princess join voices in singing:

Open the door and let my love come in;
Enchanted castle,
Enchanted castle of my heart.

When I was a cadet and Colonel Gordon Mitchell asked me to write a song for our session's dedication ceremony in connection with commissioning events, that love song came to mind and, placing myself in the way of inspiration, I prayed that something worthy might be the outcome. I was led to blend the music of 'Enchanted Castle Of My Heart' with my deep spiritual longings of that moment. In this unexpected way, and without premeditation, 'I have been dreaming of someone' became 'I would be thy holy temple' and 'Enchanted Castle Of My Heart' was transformed into 'I Dedicate Myself To Thee'.

I never dreamed that my words would find a place in so permanent a treasury as *The Song Book Of The Salvation Army*. I was not aware, in fact, that they would fit any other tune. It must have been a member of the Song Book Revision Council of 1950-52 who suggested 'Showers Of Blessing'. It is no secret that I was never very happy with this 'marriage' and, in the absence of the original melody, would have preferred 'Jesus Is Looking For Thee', with necessary adjustments to the words of the refrain. It is, I feel, more in keeping with the rhythm and sentiment of the words and allows for two eight-line verses instead of four of four lines – as shown in the original 'I Dedicate Myself To Thee'.

There may be those who would criticise me for giving spiritual emphasis to secular music. For myself I have no regrets and would remind such critics of our traditional heritage. Charles Fry, Enoch Kent, William Pearson and Albert Orsborn are surely worth imitating.

My early years as a youthful songster leader coincided with the emergence and development of the vocal selection form of composition. This could have greatly influenced my own launching out in that direction. When I took Child's Hill Songster Brigade on its first 'specialing' engagement under my leadership – to St Albans in March 1932 – 'Wonderful Promises', a prize-winning number in a national competition written by Bandmaster and Mrs Herbert Mountain, was all the rage. This was included on the programme. Another popular selection was 'Trust In The Lord', a Bible setting by Bandmaster Herbert Twitchin. The Assurance Songsters had made these and other vocal compositions popular and I quickly became intrigued by this form of writing.

Ernest Rance was undoubtedly my hero in this realm. His versatility impressed me. I had seen him as 'end trombonist' with the Men's Social Work Headquarters Band at big festivals; heard his brilliantly-chorded concertina solos and his accompaniments to leading Army soloists as he deftly manipulated the keys of what sounded like an electronic organ. It was, in fact, very much a pedal-controlled instrument with a variety of effective stops. A number of these unique organs had been donated to London hostels.

The first impact of Adjutant Rance, the composer and songwriter, upon me was when he gained a first prize in the International Music Competition of 1932 with the words and music of 'Song Of Songs'. This was so different in structure, harmony and rhythmic effect, and arrested the attention from the moment it was introduced by Leyton 2 Songster Brigade when sung from manuscript at the National Songster Festival in January 1933. The next year Ernest Rance gained another 'first' with 'Our Glorious Heritage' (words by Doris Rendell). Other similar works followed, among them 'Melody Makers' (again with words by Doris Rendell) and 'Trumpeter, Sound', with his own words.

All these won my admiration and fired me with determination to emulate his style, if I could. When he seemed to abandon this extended 'through setting' form of composition and turned his gifts and attention to creating melodic gems to familiar words I fancied myself as his successor. May I be forgiven!

The first was 'Into The Presence Of The King', of which I wrote in the opening chapter of these memoirs. From the moment this piece was presented to the International Music Board it found a champion in Colonel Railton Howard. As soon as it was published (September 1938) the Assurance Songsters took it up and featured it at the last Associated Headquarters Festival, held at Clapton Congress Hall the following January.

This was followed by 'Our King Cometh' (words by Doris Rendell) which, like so many wartime publications, was 'lost' because of its untimely appearance in *The Musical Salvationist*; 'Hosanna In The Highest' (a setting of the Palm Sunday story from Mark's Gospel); 'Beautiful Zion' ('Glorious things of thee are spoken'); 'The Beatitudes' (words by Arch R. Wiggins); and 'New Jerusalem' (verses selected from Revelation 21).

In the last-named selection I experimented with a section of choral speaking. I had been interested in this art form at school and had been reminded of its potential effectiveness at the first post-war songster festival at Clapton, in January 1946. The united brigades, under the leadership of Major Edward Saywell, in featuring James McGrahanan's song 'By Grace Are Ye Saved By Faith', introduced a repeat of that familiar Scripture text *spoken* by the entire chorus. This was the major's own initiative, to introduce variety, but I decided to write it into 'New Jerusalem'.

The idea was not a success. The majority of songster leaders were not acquainted with choral speaking and thought it unnecessary if they possessed an able elocutionist who could put it over in solo voice. In this way, generally speaking, the whole point was missed. Mind you, there is an excellent '78' recording of Harlesden Songster Brigade featuring it in this way with June Dermott (née Martin) as the delightful elocutionist, but I am pleased that for the LP of the mammoth chorus singing it during the Centenary Celebrations in the Royal Albert Hall Major Dean Goffin insisted on all the voices taking part, as was intended.

Early in the war I jotted down a melody which had been in my head for a long time. Words, however, would not come. On New Year's Eve 1940 I came off duty at our radar station at Foreness Point, Cliftonville, and, glancing out to sea in the direction I knew unfriendly hordes were massing, I wondered what the new year would bring and lifted up my heart in prayer for peace. Just then a horrific far-away flash illuminated the blackened sky, but only for a second. There was no accompanying explosion, just silence. I never knew what caused the flash. But I do know that in that unexpected experience an enlightening phrase flashed into my mind, 'A light came out of darkness'. It literally happened. I thought instantly of the melody awaiting words.

Returning to my billet, I did not go to bed until I had retrieved my precious Army songbook from my kitbag and turned to the familiar song, which was number 229 in the 1930 edition. I read through the verses and discovered that my melody fitted them perfectly. I would need to search no longer.

The music, with the first verse, became the initial movement of a vocal selection and I duly forwarded the completed work to Colonel Bramwell Coles, Head of the International Music Editorial Department, for his consideration. The colonel, as ever, was most frank and expressed the opinion that the remainder of the piece did not reach the quality of the first verse. With my approval he would like to publish it as a verse and chorus song. He was right. Envoy William Hawley's words, to my music, were published in September 1941 and reprinted in *Gems No 5*.

I suppose 'New Jerusalem' was the last vocal selection I felt the urge to write. As I became more and more immersed in editorial duties the opportunities for musical composition seemed to become fewer and fewer. This is not really surprising when one contemplates the similarity in the two creative interests. For me Army journalism was a 24-hour-a-day pursuit, but I was always grateful for the occasional prompting of special requests which sent me searching for manuscript paper and appropriate passages of Scripture.

When we were stationed at Sandwich a letter arrived one morning from Colonel Coles. 'It is about time we heard from you again,' he began and immediately continued with, 'It is two years since "New Jerusalem" was published. Another selection is due.' I admit that I thrive on such encouragement, but I replied to the colonel thanking him for his interest and reminding him that I was now in the throes of harvest festival district collecting in the town and its nearby 36 villages, which left little time for the luxury of writing music. That was that, I thought.

Not a bit of it. In a day or two another letter from the music editor arrived, hoping that we would have a successful conclusion to our harvest effort and 'if there are any crumbs of inspiration left over, please remember us'. What else could I do but once again place myself in the way of inspiration? As I cycled day after day around the Kentish countryside I looked for ideas, all in vain. On the last day of collecting, I came to a picturesque cottage with a beautiful garden. The occupier was resting on his spade after a work session.

I commented upon his lovely garden, to which he whimsically replied: 'You should have seen it when I first came here. It was a wilderness of a place.' Like a flash came the words from Isaiah, 'The wilderness and the solitary place shall be glad for them, and the desert shall rejoice and blossom as the rose.' And so 'The Kingdom' was born. The music began to form in my mind as I travelled the six miles back to the town and was mentally completed before I arrived. That night I played it through on the hall piano and next day celebrated the end of our harvest effort by putting it all on paper and forwarding it to Colonel Coles as 'a crumb of inspiration'.

'Born To Be King' was written following a request from Colonel Coles (then living in retirement in Canada) and Major Arnold Brown that I should compose something for a coronation festival in Toronto. 'The Morning Star' was composed in response to a suggestion by Colonel Albert Mingay (then Chief Secretary for the Australia Southern Territory) that I should write such an anthem for the chorus to sing in annual congress gatherings in Melbourne. When the Sydney Salvation Singers were invited to participate in the International Congress of 1978 I was asked to provide something special for them to sing in the Monday Royal Albert Hall festival. The result was 'Lord

Of The Nations', a setting of verses taken from Moffatt's translation of the Bible. I never heard the selection sung. I was presiding over a similar programme at Wembley that night.

It is an honour to have been asked to write seven sessional songs. For four of these – 'The Heralds', 'Soldiers Of The Cross', 'Victorious' and 'Servants Of God' – I provided my own words. Authors of the other three are Mrs Commissioner Mona Westergaard ('Pioneers'), General Frederick Coutts ('Swordbearers') and Lieut-Colonel Miriam Richards ('Greathearts'). It should be explained that 'Greathearts' was written for the session of that name in Canada, but was published in *The Musical Salvationist* as 'Greathearts For God'. 'My All For Thee' was written as the Soul Winners' dedication song, and was intended as a companion to 'I Dedicate Myself To Thee'.

I am aware that the anthem type of composition belongs to a bygone generation of Army music-makers and is as remote today as 'Cry Out And Shout', 'The Great Review' and 'Jesus said "I Am The Resurrection And The Life"' were in my young days. We are living in a more scholarly and more sophisticated age in which gifted musical students are given opportunity to express themselves in the idiom of modern invention. Is it wrong of me to hope, however, that some of the compositions I have mentioned may have helped to bridge the gap between the ancient and the modern and played some small part in the development of Army vocal music?

Let us not become too sophisticated. Hawkes's 'Bless The Lord, O My Soul', published in 1922, and Marshall's 'The Lord Is My Shepherd', published four years later, were undoubtedly ahead of their time. Both are worthy of revival by enterprising leaders. There may be other pieces.

* * * * *

It took 14 years for me to write *Play The Music, Play!* including the long period of research. *Sing The Happy Song!* was required to be completed in 28 days. The 1978 International Congress was already approaching when it was decided that a new paperback version of the history of Army bands should be produced, together with a companion volume covering the story of Army vocal music. Both were required to be available for sale at Wembley and other congress centres.

Research into all aspects of our music over many years had provided me with plenty of material. It was a matter of collating the information into chapters and dashing it all off on the typewriter. For *Sing The Happy Song!* to be ready for the end of June The Campfield Press would need to have the copy by the end of January.

Amid all the congress planning, on which I had been working full time for a year, I commenced my formidable task on 5 January 1978 and worked solidly through weekends (Friday to Sunday) and each night of the week. As each chapter was finished the rough page of type was passed to the literary secretary who arranged for copies to be prepared and sent to the printer.

I would not wish to live through another month like it.

For the National Drama Council's participation in the Wembley subsidiary programme I wrote a full-length play, *Miss Duff*, based on the early life of Commissioner Mildred Duff. The play was afterwards presented at other centres, notably Stratford Goodwill Centre, Croydon Citadel and North Walsham, the home corps of Commissioner Duff. The party visited the ancestral home of the gracious lady.

One of my most rewarding assignments was to provide music for a play written by my esteemed editorial colleague, Lieut-Colonel Bernard Watson. This was a biblical presentation entitled *Song Of The Hills* and contained an abundance of sensitive well-conceived blank verse, as well as rhyming prose which became the 16 songs included. This, I seem to remember, was performed at Chalk Farm, Wimbledon and Thornton Heath.

The 'orchestra' consisted of Susan Handscombe (flute), Miriam Broom (violin) and myself doubling on organ and piano, according to the requirement of the particular scene. The National Songsters did effective work as the angelic chorus, producing a tape recording which, when presented in the performance, gave the right ethereal impression.

Somewhere there is a tape of the music of the play, but I shall always regret not having made time to transfer the full score to paper. Other musicals in which I have happily been involved are *The Happy Warrior* (script, lyrics and music), based upon the earlier life of Bandmaster Herbert Twitchin and written as part of Regent Hall Band's centenary celebrations in 1982, and *The Man With The Lamp* (script and lyrics), a life of Commissioner John Carleton commissioned for the Penge Corps centenary in 1983. Captain Diane Lillicrap wrote excellent music for the latter production.

My first excursion into Army musical presentation had taken place soon after my appointment as a songster leader when, in collaboration with the singing company leader (who later became my wife), I wrote a little item featuring the singing company members as flowers in a garden. Our corps officers' younger daughter, three-year-old June Peach, was too young to sing in the singing company but we found her a part which brought responsibility for waking the flowers to morning glory after the long slumber of the night. In her crinoline dress and poke bonnet she was a pretty sight.

June, although showing early promise, had not then blossomed into the soloist we were to know in after years, but I do remember her concern for her elder sister when she volunteered the advice, 'I think that's too high for Coral, don't you?'

* * * * *

As a small boy I was captivated by the titles of marches our band played. When I discovered that a march was named after a corps or town I was not satisfied until I had located the place on the map. This led me, I have been told, to taking an atlas, as well as star card and songbook, to the meetings. It was certainly a way of interesting a restless youngster, even if my father was required frequently to give me a clue as to the area in which the various places were situated.

By this means I came to know the whereabouts of Seaham Harbour, Blackpool, Bridgwater, Nunhead and Wearmouth. The last one took some grasping. It was not really surprising that, when I came to write band music, I should want to compose a march named after our corps.

In this respect 'Child's Hill' did not appeal. I decided against it and alighted upon the more attractive 'Hillside' and so, under this title, my first band piece was published in June 1940. The title had a double connotation. I hoped its link with the corps was obvious. In addition, I looked for a chorus which might amplify the meaning of the name and decided to use for the trio a tuneful melody which, with the accompanying words, was extremely popular for some years. This was:

> *Don't stay in the valley*
> *Where the shadows fall,*
> *Climb up to the mountain top,*
> *'Tis the sweetest place of all.*
> *Catch the heavenly breezes,*
> *Live in God's sunshine;*
> *Doubts and fears will flee away,*
> *You'll be happy all the time.*

Some 16 years later I wrote a *Triumph Series* march, 'Sandwich', to commemorate our happy year spent at that corps. The bass solo in that is 'O Jesus, My Saviour, Will Welcome Sinners Home', reminding us of a remarkable case of spiritual restoration we experienced in our midst when a notorious drunkard (a former Salvationist) returned to the fold.

Another march, 'Lift Up The Flag', came into being after Colonel Bramwell Coles asked me to write a simple march that wartime depleted bands could play. 'Croydon Citadel' was written for that corps's 90th anniversary celebrations in 1959. Yet another, 'North Toronto Young People', is a tribute to the youth band of that corps, at which we were soldiers during our stay in Canada. Band Leader Herb Dowding requested it and the band brought it to England when it represented the Dominion at the 1965 Centenary Celebrations. I had the joy of conducting the march during the band's lunchtime programme on the steps of St Paul's Cathedral.

The prize-winning *Triumph Series* meditation, 'Still With Thee', owes its origin to Holden Beaumont, a Men's Social Work Band colleague and personal friend. It was he, when he was in charge of singing in the band, who showed me Harriet Beecher Stowe's words to Ira D. Sankey's music and asked me to arrange it for the octet party to feature. The song was new to me but I immediately fell a victim to its charm and content. It became a popular item on band programmes. Despite its publication in *The Musical Salvationist* as long ago as 1922, the song was not then in Army use.

When the 1939 international competition was announced I thought of this song and decided to use it as the basis of my meditation. A transcription of the male voice setting forms the middle movement, with a cornet *obbligato* added to provide colour. I was most happy when the tune became generally available to our bands.

As a lad at Willesden Green I was greatly affected by lovely melodies, especially when they were joined with deeply stirring words. A song that falls into this category is 'Beautiful Land, So Bright, So Fair, Untold Glories Linger There' to the tune of 'Beautiful Star'. I first heard this sung as a solo by Songster Leader Arthur Kimpton when he returned from service in the First World War. I have a feeling he was deputy bandmaster as well at that time.

The song made an indelible impression upon me, especially the chorus, with the sentiment, 'Home of the soldier, beautiful home'. As the soloist was a soldier recently come home from the war, my thoughts became somewhat confused and I quite imagined the 'beautiful land' he was singing about to be England. Anyway, I liked the song and remembered it sufficiently to include it as a tenor horn solo in a selection which I called 'Home Of The Soldier'.

Another flashback to those infant days resulted in my choosing one of the first songs I remember, 'You Can Tell Out The Sweet Story', as the theme of an *air varié*, 'The Sweet Story'. Another memory of boyhood provided the theme for the euphonium solo, 'A Starry Crown'. When I wrote the solo, in the early 1930s, the refrain of 'Ten Thousand Souls' (then TB 115) was:

Then come, O come, and go with me,
Where pleasures never die;
And you shall wear a starry crown
And reign above the sky.

Hence the title. When a new songbook was published in 1953 I was amazed to see that the third and fourth lines of the refrain had been changed to:

And you shall gain the crown of life,
The soul's eternal prize.

This made my title redundant. But I still prefer the original words!

A lack of inspiration in the choice of a title can sometimes 'hold up the works'. Before starting on a new composition I would consult Colonel Coles regarding the material I wished to use. His advice was always most helpful, for he knew what songs were being used currently in various journal numbers and would give his opinion if he thought a particular melody had been overworked.

This happened with a *Triumph Series* selection I had in mind. I told him which three songs I wished to use and he saw no problem with any of these. What was my title? I quietly explained that I had not thought of one. He noted again the songs I planned to include and then turned to a foolscap book. In this, he told me, he wrote any likely titles that he stumbled upon or which came to mind. Such entries were mainly for his own use and as he completed a work he would cross out the original idea. No wonder he had been able to alight upon such inspired titles as 'Undaunted', 'The Glory Of The Combat', 'In The Firing Line', 'The Flag Of Freedom', 'Bravest Of The Brave', 'Warrior Grit' and 'The Divine Pursuit'.

With me sitting opposite him he began to go through his titles and paused at 'Streams Of Mercy'. 'That's it,' he said. 'I'll give you that one, free, *gratis*,' methodically taking his pen to delete it. It was a good, all-embracing title, for the songs to be incorporated were 'O Have You Not Heard Of The Beautiful Stream?', 'O Far Whiter Than The Snow' and 'There Flows A Stream From My Riven Side', with the refrain 'The precious blood is flowing over me'.

I spoke of that generous spirit in the tribute I was honoured to pay at Bramwell Coles's funeral service. I came to musical maturity under his influence and guidance.

When, one summer, I reported congresses in Norway, Denmark, Sweden and Finland in unbroken succession I heard some songs and choruses over and over again in all four territories. The haunting melodies became embedded in my mind, only to surface at most inconvenient times. Some of these were afterwards collated and put into a selection, 'Memories Of Finland', written for Croydon Citadel Band's tour of that country in 1960. The music editor, by then Brigadier Charles Skinner, felt that the selection would have a wider appeal if renamed 'Scandinavian Congress', and as such it was published.

I am indebted to so many people for either supplying words to be set to music or providing ideas upon which a new song could be based. Some songs have come unaided and unsought with momentary flashes of inspiration. For such experiences I am eternally grateful and still regard it as a miracle.

'Spirit Divine' came to me one wartime Whit Sunday morning when I was on duty in a radar cabin in the heart of the New Forest with eyes glued to a tube waiting for something to 'turn up'. I thought of my Salvationist comrades gathered at Boscombe enjoying the holiness meeting and felt a sense of loneliness as my one-man vigil continued.

Words came easily to me as I imagined the congregation a few miles away:

Come, great Spirit, come,
Make each heart Thy home;
Enter every longing soul
Come, great Spirit, come.

A melody came with the words and the verses were merely an amplification of the refrain. The song was complete – in my mind – before one o'clock came and I went off duty.

I believe it was Major Dean Goffin and Captain Norman Bearcroft who gave this song the boost it needed when they included it in the 1965 Centenary Celebrations.

With typical courtesy Major Leslie Condon sought my approval to write a meditation on this song, as a reminder of our years together in the Bands Department. This moved me greatly and there was no hesitation in my agreement.

It was at the request of Commissioner William Cooper, then British Commissioner, that I wrote 'Weaver Divine'. I was editor of *The Musician* (for the second time) and he wanted a song based upon the subject of his theme for that year's field officers councils. His subject was 'The Divine Weaver'. The first session was held at Regent Hall and I was invited to launch the song, which I had written to the tune 'Saved By Grace'.

Some time later it was published in *The Musical Salvationist* to original music I had prepared for it and was included in *Keep Singing!* to 'Harton Lea', without the chorus.

Commissioner Cooper also asked me to write a theme song for another series of councils, this time held at Butlin's, Clacton. By this time I was National Secretary for Bands and Songster Brigades and part of the National Headquarters family. His topic was 'Mission', which explains why this particular word appears so frequently in 'Thou Hast Called Me From The Byway', married to the tune of 'South Shields'.

This was intended to be a sequel, not necessarily a companion to 'I Would Be Thy Holy Temple!'. The first song represented a dedication made at the beginning of one's spiritual career. The other was intended as a song for 'mid-career'. The song was used with telling effect as part of the call to renewal in those Butlin's councils.

'Thou Art Holy, Lord Of Glory' was inspired by a festival of thanksgiving held in Croydon Parish Church celebrating the 90th anniversary of Army bands. As I processed along the aisle at the beginning of the service I became caught up in the ritual of the ceremony and with a clear glimpse of the altar was sharply reminded of Isaiah's experience in the Temple. My unworthiness seemed to be compatible with that of the ancient prophet and, unexpectedly, a song was born.

I certainly had the incident of Isaiah in mind when I wrote:

> *Thou art holy, Lord of Glory,*
> *From thy altar blessings flow;*
> *I, unworthy, kneel before thee,*
> *Cleanse from sin and peace bestow.*
> *Come, O Lord, with tender healing,*
> *Touch my lips with living coal;*
> *Sanctify each human feeling,*
> *Speak and make me fully whole.*

It was set to the tune 'Denmark Hill', one of my favourites, and when I was again asked to provide a song for officers councils, there was one ready, without necessarily fitting into any special theme. For those coming to seek spiritual refreshment the second verse had special meaning:

> *If my strength is at its weakest*
> *And my weariness brings pain,*
> *With my spirit at its meekest,*
> *Thou canst lift me up again.*

Many friends during those councils thanked me for that verse, their hand outstretched to grasp mine in Christian fellowship.

History has proved that the most popular congregational songs have been those launched successfully by songster brigades years before. We seem to forget that 'Jesus, Thou Art Everything To Me', 'All Your Anxiety', 'O Man Of Galilee', 'God's Love Is Wonderful' and 'O What A Wonderful Day' – among many others – were popular songster pieces a quarter of a century before they appeared in *The Song Book Of The Salvation Army* and corresponding tune books.

One of the greatest experiences of my life occurred during a 15-day visit to Israel. Six days were spent in Jerusalem and nine in Galilee. In

Jerusalem I was invited to be the speaker at the traditional Sunday morning service at the Garden Tomb. As a Salvationist, in my uniform, I accepted. Seven hundred pilgrims were present in the glorious August sunshine.

Later that week, having a couple of hours to spare in the busy tourist programme, I called upon two old friends, Arthur and Wyn Holliday, then in charge of the Christ Church Hospice, within the walls of the old city and near the Jaffa Gate. We talked together, caught up on home news and shared some refreshments.

'Before you go,' said Arthur, 'will you come into the church with us and play something on the piano?' I readily agreed. The request was for 'Beautiful Zion'. I sat down at the lovely grand piano and began to play 'Glorious things of thee are spoken, Zion, city of our God'. The words took on new meaning. This was the place which inspired the vision of the New Jerusalem. I was there. Those words had inspired me to write the tune without my being fully aware of the physical link. I finished playing and closed the instrument with loving care. None of us could speak for some time.

I had a similar feeling a few days later when we travelled through the bleak, desolate Judean desert and came suddenly upon the lush living greenery of Jericho. The wilderness and the solitary place... the desert shall rejoice and blossom as the rose. It all made sense.

Chapter 26

Where We Came In

THE 1978 International Congress was the fifth event under that title to he held in Salvation Army history. There were the centenary celebrations of 1965, to commemorate the founding of The Christian Mission, from which our beginnings are dated, and those gatherings must take their place with the International Congresses of 1886, 1894, 1904 and 1914 as anniversary landmarks in the Army's story.

It must not be imagined that the idea of such another congress had not been mooted during the intervening 64 years. Soon after her election as General, Evangeline Booth, in 1935, had a vision of Salvationists from all parts of the world again meeting in the city of the Army's birth, and a suitable announcement was made. It was to have taken place in 1937. In 1936, however, a brief paragraph in *The War Cry* informed the Army world that the proposed event had been cancelled. No explanation was given.

General Albert Orsborn had a similar dream. 'On taking office in 1946,' he writes in his autobiography, 'I immediately initiated inquiries as to the possibility of a fifth International Congress, remembering personally the immeasurable benefits of the 1904 and 1914 events. I was troubled by the tragic spiritual losses to us and to the world from the fact that 32 years had passed since Salvationists crossed the boundaries of kin, coast and language and met together within the supernational Kingdom of God on earth. I strove to overcome difficulties of transport, accommodation, finance – not to mention the shortage of officers. I failed, and I shall always mourn the fact.'

There is no doubt that the 1965 celebrations created such a tremendous interest and were such an outstanding success that almost immediately plans were set in motion to organise another

337

international gathering of Salvationists as soon as practically possible. It was, in fact, announced that it had been decided to hold similar worldwide gatherings every ten years and that plans would be made for an International Congress to take place in London in 1975.

This information was not widely circulated and in the early 1970s the situation was reviewed. It was agreed that 1978 would be a more appropriate year in which to celebrate, that date having special significance in Salvation Army history, marking as it did the important change of name which overnight turned a 'mission' into an 'army'.

The postponement of the international event enabled British Commissioner Albert Mingay to call for a British Congress in 1972. As National Secretary for Bands and Songster Brigades I wholeheartedly supported his proposal and with the National Bandmaster (Major Leslie Condon) became responsible for planning the musical side of that five-day event held at Wembley Arena. Little did I realise that I would be so vitally involved six years later.

A main council to plan the 1978 congress was formed early in 1975, with Commissioner Harry Williams as chairman. This was divided into sub-councils, each responsible for discussing in more detail the various aspects of the celebrations – mainly in the matters of programme content, finance, publicity and organisation.

A further subdivision of responsibility led to the formation of working parties for the various events. While a member of the main council presided over each of these groups, officers and laypeople with specialised knowledge and experience were included in the personnel. All such appointments were made by the Chief of the Staff. The recommendations of the working parties were passed on to the sub-councils and then to the main council with amended proposals if necessary.

In March 1976 an interview with the Chief of the Staff (Commissioner Arthur Carr) resulted in my appointment as chief executive officer for the congress, this, for the time being, in addition to my editorial responsibilities.

My first organisational priority became threefold: 1. Booking halls for public gatherings; 2. Reserving hotel and other accommodation for official delegates and others requiring this facility; 3. Inviting representative overseas music sections and groups, so that maximum warning could be given.

Two things became clear. London was to be invaded by more overseas Salvationists and friends than ever before in the Army's history; there was no indoor hall in the city or suburbs which could house such a number for one single event. For various reasons such well-known venues as Olympia, Earl's Court, Alexandra Palace and the Crystal Palace were ruled out, and even the beloved Royal Albert Hall would be inadequate except in a subsidiary capacity.

The answer was found in Wembley. On this world-famous site, 14 miles out of the city, four buildings would be available for the ten-day programme. The Empire Pool (as it was then called), built just before the Second World War, was the largest covered arena in Europe and seated 10,000 people. That was a good start. A new mammoth conference centre alongside was in course of construction.

When, in faith, a tentative booking was made, the new £17 million complex was being erected and, crawling between the scaffolding wearing protective helmets, Mr Ralph Miller, the conference centre manager, Lieut-Colonel Richard Foale, then National Secretary for Special Efforts, and I found it difficult to visualise this area being taken over by a teeming mass of worldwide Salvationists as they made their way to and from the various meetings.

The new complex would consist of an auditorium with accommodation for 2,700 and the Avon and Severn Theatres, with seating for 600 and 300 respectively. In addition the Royal Albert Hall would be used for the first Saturday, Sunday and Monday so that twin festivals and meetings could be held at the same time. This would mean that 20,000 people could attend during the first weekend. Even that was inadequate and, as is now well known, three other congress centres were added to the programme that first weekend, bringing the total to eight.

The first discussion with Wembley authorities took place there on 11 May 1976 and from that moment onwards we received nothing but the utmost courtesy and co-operation from all members of the organisation. By this time it was possible to outline the day-to-day programme envisaged and I mustered sufficient additional courage to press the likelihood of the Empire Stadium, accommodating 100,000, being used for a Field Day during the congress. This would be known as the Congress Spectacular and would include the march past of the delegates and a short service of thanksgiving.

At about this time a tentative booking of 4,000 hotel rooms in London was made. The 1978 International Congress was well and truly launched.

The congress office, consisting at first of three small rooms on the fourth floor of International Headquarters, was opened in January 1977, when I farewelled from the Editorial Department to give full-time attention to the task entrusted to me. This coincided with the appointment of Lieut-Colonel Ronald Topley, whose long experience in the Army's travel services fitted him for the responsibility for transport arrangements. With the important matter of accommodation added to his duties, I knew that this aspect of our multifarious planning was in safe and capable hands. I was not mistaken.

The third member of that early staff was Lieut-Colonel Margery Joy. As secretary to the editor-in-chief, the colonel had been 'in' on the congress from the preliminary stages of planning and I was naturally relieved when the Chief of the Staff acceded to my request that she might be permitted to continue her valued assistance in the congress office.

In her secretarial capacity Margery Joy evolved an efficient filing system and was able to draw upon her long knowledge of IHQ procedure and protocol. Later, when work in the office developed and more help was enlisted, she successfully took a large measure of staff management under her wing.

Visits to Wembley became more than a weekly outing for Lieut-Colonel Topley and me. It was necessary because of the many-sided structure of the set-up there. They were watertight compartments and, with so many halls being required at the same time, more than one authority was required to be consulted.

340

Thus we struck up a happy working relationship with John Lord and his assistant Pippa Cross at the conference centre; Tony Rudge and Brian Sladen at the arena; David Price-Smith and Bob Moore at the box office; and John Evans and his staff at the stadium. They all good-naturedly marvelled at the magnitude of our undertaking and confessed that it was the biggest event that they together had embarked upon. It was probably this mutual respect which led to the box office seconding six of its staff permanently to issue tickets for the congress events. That was in February 1978. Four months later the orders were still being dealt with. The small staff remained calm and courteous, dealing with the many telephone inquiries as efficiently as possible.

It was General Arnold Brown, soon after he succeeded General Clarence Wiseman in the summer of 1977, who thought of adding a series of commemoration services to the extensive programme of congress events already prepared. He felt that Sunday 2 July – Founders' Day – presented a unique opportunity for the established church to pay its own tribute to The Salvation Army. With this in mind he wrote to the Dean of Westminster (Dr Edward Carpenter) and the Dean of St Paul's (Dr Martyn Sullivan). The response was immediate and friendly and an interview was immediately arranged.

Interviews with officials at the abbey and cathedral resulted in both authorities agreeing to hold a service in the morning and evening respectively of the first Sunday of the congress, bearing in mind the special significance of the day. I sought to make it clear that the General's idea was that the service should basically be recognised as the Church's tribute to the Army and would not be a case of the Army conducting a service in hired premises.

The internationalism of the occasion was immediately respected and it was agreed that some 200 delegates, mostly from overseas, would attend each service and that the New York Staff Band and Soweto Songsters would participate in Westminster Abbey and Melbourne Staff Band and Agincourt Temple Songster Brigade in St Paul's. A Salvationist would be invited to read one of the lessons in each building and the flag of International Headquarters would be received and 'laid up' at the high altar. The respective deans would preach the sermon. Members of the public would be encouraged to attend.

It was later arranged for the delegates selected for these services to march to the respective rendezvous. Those attending Westminster Abbey, headed by the Seoul Boys' Home Band, paraded from Buckingham Gate along Victoria Street. The St Paul's service delegates, with Melbourne Staff Band, marched from International Headquarters through adjacent city streets. Tickets for the public were rapidly disposed of and both buildings were packed out, in addition to the vast crowds present for simultaneous Founders' Day meetings at the Royal Albert Hall and in the four halls at Wembley. The abbey service was televised over the ITV national network.

After proudly leading the Westminster contingent and being prominently picked up by TV cameras high above the roadway, the boys from Korea, not being required for musical duty in the abbey, were permitted to leave their instruments in Jerusalem Chamber while they took their place in the congregation. When I learned, during a visit to the Receiver-General, that this historic small room off the cloisters was to be reserved for this purpose my memory became alerted.

I remembered, when studying Shakespeare's *Richard II* at school, stumbling on the fact that, when King Henry IV came to the throne, having supplanted Richard, his cousin, a gypsy foretold that he would die in Jerusalem. As he never visited the Holy Land there seemed little chance of the warning coming true. One day in 1413, however, he was taken ill while at prayer in Westminster Abbey and was carried into nearby Jerusalem Chamber where he died, partly fulfilling the gypsy's forecast.

This was also the scene, in 1870, of the first meeting of the committee for the revision of the Bible and of later work on this controversial translation. A set of brass instruments can now be added to the historic data!

Following the announcement in the Army's press of the two services referred to, it was suggested to the General that the

Nonconformist Church should not be excluded from the celebrations and that the City Temple, Holborn Viaduct, would prove a fitting setting. It was also pointed out that it was from the pulpit of this noted church that Catherine Booth, the Army Mother, delivered her last public address just 90 years before, on 21 June 1888.

The General approved of the proposal and wrote to the resident minister, Dr Brian Johanson. Again immediate agreement was expressed and this resulted in my calling upon Dr Johanson and his assistant, Dr Robert Norris. Both received me with charm and courtesy and took time to conduct me on a tour of their lovely rebuilt church, reminding me of the occasional visits I made there before the war to hear Dr Leslie Weatherhead.

Dr Norris, from South Wales, revealed that his boyhood had been spent in the corps at Aberdare and that he invariably attended meetings when visiting relatives who still lived there.

It was agreed that Salvationists should read the lessons and that Oslo 3 Band and Sydney Salvation Singers would also take part. To match the other services, 200 official delegates would be present.

Dr Johanson immediately saw the effective potential of the service and suggested that, if the entire force could march from International Headquarters to the City Temple, the band might play outside the church for 15 minutes before the service was due to begin. Both these suggestions materialised.

With preliminary arrangements decided upon, it was left to us to work out the detailed plans: on that first Sunday to get the New York Staff Band from its West London hotel to Westminster Abbey by 8.30 for the balance test and then, after the service and lunch, to transport it to tea at Wembley where it was the duty section in the night meeting in the arena; to convey Melbourne Staff Band after the morning meeting in the Wembley Arena and lunch to IHQ in time for a hurried tea and march to St Paul's; to bring Soweto Songsters from their billet at the International College for Officers, Sydenham, to Westminster and transport them to another centre for the salvation meeting; to ensure Agincourt Temple Songster Brigade travelled from morning duty at the Royal Albert Hall to the evening cathedral service.

343

Such a mammoth operation had to be repeated 100 times during those eventful ten days.

On numerous occasions during main council meetings, it was urged by some members that Salvationists should be seen on the streets of London in some strength during the period of the congress. The possibility was explored and although there were problems created by the widely-scattered venues for events and an already crowded programme, a mammoth rally in Trafalgar Square (as in 1965) and the church commemoration services could provide opportunity for massed marches to be organised.

It was apparent that several different authorities were involved in this connection, and Mr Bernard Gibbs of the Parks Division of the Department of the Environment was most helpful in supplying names of responsible bodies. He was the liaison officer for the use of Horse Guards Parade and promised to bring the matter to the notice of his committee upon receiving a written request. The letter was written and the committee acceded to our request – in principle. There were many conditions of acceptance to be observed.

Permission to hold the rally itself was given by another branch of the department. In normal circumstances such permission is withheld until a month before the proposed date. When I explained that we would need to know long before that time so that our overseas delegates might be alerted, a special meeting of the council was held and an exception was made regarding our application.

Then there was the march itself. This was a matter for the Metropolitan Police. My call at Cannon Row Police Station, by arrangement, was met with courtesy and immediate helpful co-operation. The proposal that the march should move off from Horse Guards Parade and proceed via Parliament Square and Whitehall was approved, together with the recommendation that coaches might be permitted to park near Trafalgar Square to convey the International Staff Band and overseas music sections to Wembley or the Royal Albert Hall in time for rehearsals for the evening events.

At Cannon Row I received the congenial undivided attention of Sergeant George Garnham, who interrupted his work of mapping out a route for a royal occasion to hear my request. Of the old school of London 'bobbies', George was the son of a policeman and, as a boy, lived in a block of flats in Judd Street, overlooking SP&S, Ltd. He had been brought up on the sight of uniformed Salvationists hurrying to enter or leave the buildings.

After an opening gambit the sergeant took over. He could visualise it all. Ideas just poured from his alert mind and details that had never entered my head seemed to rush to his brain with lightning rapidity. He knew his London and reeled off the side streets and open spaces that we could use for parking coaches waiting to convey the official delegates to their evening venues. His enthusiasm mounted even as we talked.

I raised the subject of traffic control. His reply was to ask: 'Do you know Alan Rushforth?' Of course I knew the Regent Hall corps sergeant-major. 'He's your man,' went on the sergeant. 'We have him to contend with every Sunday. He directs your marches down Oxford Street and Regent Street and through Piccadilly Circus. Takes over our job as well. He's a headache to us, but we love him. Put him in charge and he, with our men, will see you through.'

Let me here confess that I had already earmarked Corps Sergeant-Major Alan Rushforth as our traffic controller and parade marshal and on the eventful day, as the clock on Horse Guards Parade struck two and the stationary Regent Hall Band began to play a familiar march, Alan, having called the mass to attention, stepped off, with the International Staff Band following him, at the head of 3,000 Salvationists. Traffic in Whitehall was held up for an hour to allow the procession to move unhindered. Police in strength were on duty on the mustering ground, along the route, in the march and at Trafalgar Square.

Good as his word, George Garnham had taken care of every detail of the planning.

While at Cannon Row Police Station I obtained permission for the delegates attending the Westminster Abbey commemoration service to march from Buckingham Gate, but for the corresponding events at St Paul's Cathedral and the City Temple permission had to be given by the City of London Police. In all instances the police authorities acted with courtesy, geniality and a tremendous respect for the Army.

Further evidence of this respect was shown on Monday afternoon, 3 July, when the Lord Mayor of London granted a civic reception to General and Mrs Brown, the Chief of the Staff and Mrs Cottrill, other Army leaders, representative delegates and auxiliary friends. This was held at the Guildhall.

The fact that the General had received the Freedom of the City of London a few days before added to the occasion and marked the historic recognition – the first General to be so honoured since the Founder.

In April 1978 our pressurised small staff was augmented by the appointment of Major Alan Coles as assistant to the executive officer. He quickly adjusted to the many demands made upon him.

At about the same time Major Raymond Caddy joined us and soon sensed what was required of him. He did a noteworthy job in leading the team responsible for the allocation of official delegates' tickets and related tasks. This was a tiring and painstaking task but seemed to suit his calm and thorough temperament. Major Caddy supervised the filling of delegates' kits, in which a number of officer-wives were involved.

As the pace hotted up and 'D-Day' approached further assistance was enlisted and we were delighted to have the services of Major and Mrs David Napier, of Scotland Territorial Headquarters.

Following the acceptance of the General's invitation for His Royal Highness the Prince of Wales to perform the congress opening ceremony on Friday 30 June, I was requested to contact the prince's equerry to discuss detailed planning. This resulted in an invitation for me to go to Buckingham Palace.

This appointment with Captain Tim Ward, Equerry to the Prince of Wales, was arranged for Monday 17 April. In the waiting room of the comptroller's office I was welcomed and put at ease by a smart, young footman who introduced himself as Salvationist Andrew Renouf.

A copy of the proposed programme was submitted and Prince Charles's participation discussed. I also left a copy of the 1965 opening ceremony by Her Majesty the Queen. Later a draft copy of the programme was forwarded to the palace for the Prince's approval. This was received over the phone, with the information that His Royal Highness would be accompanied by his assistant private secretary and a private detective.

Not unreasonably we spent a lot of time planning that opening. So much depended upon its success, we felt. From the beginning it was obvious that the 10,000-capacity Wembley Arena would not accommodate all those wishing to be present, especially with the more than 2,000 official delegates receiving priority consideration. The problem was partially overcome by hiring a closed-circuit television system that would enable an overflow audience in the hall of the conference centre to share the main gathering.

As the great day drew nearer, visits to Wembley became more frequent. Planning the march in of the delegates demanded our careful attention. With the eye of memory I can still see Alan Coles, with a stopwatch in hand, pacing out the distance from the rear of the arena to where the various delegations would be seated, while I hummed march after march. Able statistician that he is, he worked it out to the second. He reckoned that the entry of delegates from 50 territories and commands would take exactly 45 minutes. That was dependent upon the ISB maintaining its usual steady tempo.

On the eve of the congress my wife and I took up residence close to the Wembley complex. This became our home for 12 days and nights. We were first on the scene in the morning and the last to leave at night. The only occasions we left the site were for the Saturday march and rally and, on the Thursday afternoon, for the Symphony of Praise three-staff-band festival in the Royal Albert Hall.

We took our places on the platform for the opening ceremony not knowing if all the delegates had reached Wembley, or even arrived in England. Two o'clock eventually came. A signal was flashed to Major Ray Bowes, the staff bandmaster. Drummers Thompson and Symonds beat and rolled the familiar introduction. The International Staff Band embarked upon a sparkling march. All heads in the congregation turned towards the doors. The congress was under way.

Responding to the rhythm of the band and the welcoming applause of the eager spectators, the delegates entered, territorial and command name boards identifying them. In alphabetical order they proudly marched: Australia Eastern, Australia Southern, Belgium, Brazil, Canada, Caribbean, Congo, Denmark.

I was mesmerised by it all. The dream of years had come true. Was I quietly weeping amid the tumult of excited sound?

Major Coles's calculations had been accurate. At 2.44 precisely the last of the delegations had moved to their places and we had planned that, without a break, the Prince of Wales, escorted by the General, would enter and walk the length of the arena to take his place at the specially prepared rostrum in the centre of the stage.

I panicked. The guest of honour was not there. Not even the General was in sight. The crowd looked anxiously towards the door. I hurriedly suggested to the Chief of the Staff, who had taken the salute as the delegations passed before him, that the audience should be seated. This was done and the relaxed atmosphere and quiet chatter relieved the tension. Not many could have been aware that something had gone wrong.

Then the panic was over. With a signal from the rear of the arena the staff band's trumpeters triggered a rousing fanfare and the Prince of Wales and the General entered.

I could not understand the delay. Timing details had been worked out. The prince was to land by helicopter on the playing fields of a local school, having travelled from an earlier function at Wells Cathedral. There a car would be waiting to transport him to the Wembley Arena.

We had not, however, allowed for the school pupils parading on the landing field to cheer His Royal Highness's arrival. This led to an official reception and a personal walkabout by the prince.

After the opening meeting the royal visitor received 30 representative Salvationists and friends who were presented to him by the General. My wife and I were privileged to be among the number, as were such distinguished guests as the Archbishop of York (Dr Stuart Blanch), Lord Armstrong of Sanderstead and Mrs Margaret Thatcher, then leader of Her Majesty's opposition. The General introduced us.

In a relaxed conversation the prince revealed his interest in music, asking about the composers of the various songs and band pieces featured that afternoon, and asked a number of questions relating to the organising of such an international event. It was obvious, too, that he wanted to know more about the Army, confirming the impression of our Movement so poignantly expressed in his speech. 'To my mind, the example set by The Salvation Army is Christianity at its most essential, simple and effective level.'

'When it is all over,' he told me, 'you must have a wonderful holiday.' Perhaps I should give serious thought to the prince's advice.

This concludes the extracts from the series of articles published in *The Musician* between 1981 and 1984 and used by permission.

Chapter 27

And Now, Hallelujah…!

OFFICIAL retirement for Nina and me came on 1 March 1979 after a six-month extension of active service which enabled me to complete the mammoth task of bringing the congress matters to a satisfactory conclusion and also to complete some special writing assignments that I had undertaken. A state of nervous exhaustion did not, however, prevent my commencing work immediately as a member of the *Musician* team at the request of the then editor-in-chief, Lieut-Colonel William Clark. This brought me great pleasure and satisfaction and I soon became caught up in the week-to-week publication of the paper and sought to make the features for which I was responsible – mostly personality paragraphs – as interesting and attractive as they had been in my more active days.

An event in which I quickly became involved was the 'Salute to *The War Cry*' festival held to mark the centenary of the first issue of the paper in 1879. This important event was held in a crowded Regent Hall and presided over by General Arnold Brown, who was supported by the Chief of the Staff (Commissioner Stanley Cottrill) and other leading officers. My main contribution, I suppose, was to write a new song for the occasion which I called 'The Joyous Proclamation'. This was sung by my old brigade, Chalk Farm Songsters. My good friend Ray Steadman-Allen wrote a march with the same motive in mind, which he entitled 'Our "War Cry"' and this was played by Regent Hall Band.

The following year, 1980, I was finally able to keep the promise I had made to the Prince of Wales and, incidentally, also to myself, to take that 'wonderful holiday'. And so, in the autumn of that year, Nina and I decided it would be nice to revisit our old stamping ground

351

of Canada and soak up the 'autumn gold' which Canadians delight in calling 'the Fall'. Two weeks in the Toronto area were followed by a further fortnight in Victoria on lovely Vancouver Island. The period in Toronto was taken up with festivals, mainly a weekend at Agincourt where we enjoyed fellowship with many good friends we had made during our stay in that area some 20 years before.

Victoria was a unique experience. They say that it is more 'British' out there than Britain itself. It was so strange, for instance, to see London buses on the streets with their familiar destination boards. One had 'Marble Arch' on it as its terminus while another declared it was heading for 'London Bridge'! It was a thrill to climb up the back staircase as we used to on the old London omnibuses and view the delightful surroundings of Victoria in that way. In the shops I saw 'sherbet fountains' for sale and felt sure these had disappeared from the London scene well before the Second World War.

The musicians of Victoria feel very isolated and so I was glad to bring some encouragement and inspiration to them while I was there.

The following year provided a thrill of a lifetime and one that I will certainly never forget. One afternoon, while sitting in the office at IHQ, I received an unexpected telephone call from the music director of the New York Metropolitan Division inviting me out to a 'Friday Night at the Temple' event of which I had heard so much. It was to take the form of a composer's festival and I was to be honoured by the presentation of my band and vocal works – or, at least, some of them. They called it a 'Profile' festival and there had already been two of these events in past years. Firstly, Eric Ball and then Albert Jakeway (then in his 80s) had been invited out to participate in a programme of their music provided by the New York Staff Band and the New York 'Friday Night at the Temple' Chorus.

And so I went out for three days (left on the Thursday and returned on the Monday). The Saturday night festival was held in a packed Centennial Temple. It was a great occasion. To say that I was thrilled to hear no fewer than 14 of my pieces would be the understatement of the century, let alone the year! The items ranged from my very first march, 'Hillside', named in honour of Child's Hill Corps where I spent my youth, to the *Festival Series* tone poem, 'Altar Of Praise'. I was particularly pleased with the way in which the New York Staff Band responded to my baton in my selection 'Scandinavian Congress' and was grateful to Bandmaster Derek Smith for the courtesy of that honour.

After the Saturday night festival I went on tour, covering three states. This was a wonderful experience, albeit a very tiring one as well!

Meanwhile, my busy life of 'specialing' continued. I accepted invitations to conduct band and songster weekend meetings while, at the same time, quite a number of invitations also came in for radio interviews. I remember being with Roger Royle on a programme about Victorian hymns in which I was able to say one or two things about the history of some of our Salvation Army songs and of the music hall ditties from which they were 'converted'. By this means I was able to keep 'with it' to some extent and keep the Army's point of view well before the public.

It was a big disappointment, however, when on my 70th birthday I was informed I could no longer work for my beloved Editorial Department, regulations stating that 'retirement' must be brought strictly in line on the occasion of such a milestone. It was not a nice thought to feel that, after all the years, my services were no longer required (officially, at any rate).

However, to my great surprise, the day following my 70th birthday I received a telephone call from my friend Lieut-Colonel Ray Bowes inviting me to take responsibility for the copyrights relative to the new songbook and new tune book. I informed the dear colonel that I did not think this would be possible, as I was now 'over age' for the task. He said he would bring the matter to the Chief of the Staff and, to my amazement, the Chief gave permission for me to work for the Music Editorial Department on this assignment (which was then, I gathered, a little in arrears!) from home.

This, then, started a period of what I considered to be great usefulness in negotiating with the copyright owners and securing their permission for their songs to be used. Then, the respective fees having been quoted, I was able to inform the songbook council of the progress that was being made. It would take too long for me to record here details of all the experiences I had but I did have a personal conversation on the telephone with Stuart K. Hine who translated Carl Boberg's wonderful hymn 'How Great Thou Art!' I discovered he was living at Frinton-on-Sea and, although he was then well over 90 years of age, we had a most coherent conversation about his masterpiece and, after much negotiation and not a little 'bartering', we came to an arrangement whereby we could use his song without any great cost to ourselves, apart from the usual copyright fee.

Another experience that comes to mind is to do with the songs of Sidney Cox. Unfortunately, Sidney Cox, who wanted all his songs to come to the Army, was, towards the end of his days, persuaded to hand over many of his copyrights to Singspiration Inc Ltd. This presented great problems for us when we came to consider his songs for inclusion in the new songbook and tune book. We discovered there was a very significant copyright which would have caused us to be heavily involved, financially, in gaining permission to use them.

The songbook council felt the cost would be too great and so I was asked to contact Singspiration in America and this I did. Eventually, after much correspondence to and fro, they kindly agreed that they would waive the cost of the copyright on any of Sidney Cox's songs that we wanted to use, but they would not hand over the copyright. That is why we have the acknowledgement at the beginning of the songbook indicating that the copyright of Sidney Cox's songs is held by Singspiration Inc although, happily, they were published without any cost to The Salvation Army.

At the end of 1983 the Salvation Army musical world and particularly that associated with Croydon Citadel was shattered by the news of the sudden death of Major Leslie Condon, who had served as bandmaster at that corps for some years. His promotion to Glory occurred on Christmas Eve, just as he was about to commence carolling with the band. The bandsmen were devastated, not only by the passing of their beloved leader, but also because they were preparing for a tour of Denmark and Sweden the following Easter. In the circumstances I was invited to accompany the band on its tour, not as bandmaster I hasten to assure you, but to keep a 'fatherly' eye on things and help maintain morale among the bandsmen. In spite of the sadness which surrounded the occasion we had a great tour, although we were all very conscious of Leslie's absence.

The year 1985 was an important one for me for three very good reasons. Firstly, my book *ISB* was launched in the summer; secondly I was recalled from retirement to serve as Chairman of the Planning Council for the International Youth Congress to be held in America; and thirdly my granddaughter, Georgia, was born.

In 1952, General Albert Orsborn had given me the task of writing the history of Salvation Army bands. It was then that I started on my work which became *Play The Music, Play!*

At that time most of the original staff bandsmen were still alive. I remembered Commissioner Samuel Hurren had been in the Junior Staff Band before the International Staff Band was formed. I spent a day with him at Broadstairs where he lived in retirement, wandering round the coastal area chatting and sitting down here and there before he took me back to his home for a drink of tea served in a little basin without a handle! (He always believed in drinking tea out of such a receptacle!)

I collected a lot of material from him and had, in previous years, also interviewed a number of former bandsmen such as Colonel Arthur Goldsmith and A. W. Punchard, who had been in the junior staff band with Commissioner Hurren years previously. There was so much copy that when I came to write *Play The Music, Play!* I found there was far too much information about the Staff Band to be accommodated into a single chapter in that book. I did manage to abridge some of the material into one chapter (and this does appear in *Play The Music Play!*) and left all the rest 'on hold', as it were.

It was Staff Bandsman Cyril Brisley who, one day, had the idea that someone ought to write the history of the Staff Band. I said, 'Well, I have it!' As it was felt to be too long to wait until the band's centenary in 1991, it was suggested that I should prepare it for the 90th anniversary in 1981. And so in 1980 I set about writing the story of the Staff Band which became my volume of history – just 30 years after I had initially started collecting the material. It was eventually published in the summer of 1985.

I suppose it was my experience with the 1978 International Congress that prompted the powers that be to appoint me as a member – and later chairman – of the Planning Council for the International Youth Congress of 1985 to be held at the Western Illinois University, USA. This involved going backwards and forwards across the Atlantic for planning meetings in America and returning to International Headquarters to handle all the applications that came from all around the Army world. The university campus at Western Illinois was a tremendous place, catering for 6,000 people, and they all turned up for this the first international congress held outside of London, all previous events having been held in the UK capital.

The third great experience of 1985 was the birth of my beloved granddaughter, Georgia, who was born in September of that year. She brought great joy to my wife and me, particularly in Nina's latter years when she was far from well and for some considerable time I was unable to leave her side. After many years of failing health and our 57 years of happy married life, my dear wife was promoted to Glory on 6 September 1995. During that difficult time Georgia brought great comfort to us both and on the occasion of Nina's funeral paid a lovely tribute to her grandma.

Two experiences of 1990 come to mind, particularly as they were the last occasions on which I did certain things. I was invited to be the guest speaker at the quarterly meeting of the Bournemouth Retired Officers' Fellowship. The event was held at Sopley Park where, years before, I had been stationed with the RAF. It is now a Bible College. It was a very nostalgic experience to revisit the old surroundings where, in a very different setting, I think I had been able to do some good and write some songs which have since been 'converted' by my penning Army words to the original music.

My final 'specialing' engagement was to conduct band weekend meetings at Winton Corps in May of that year. It was particularly memorable for me because I was invited to stay over for Monday night and recount some of the more hilarious moments – the lighter side – of my varied career.

It was a great thrill in November 1991 when I was invited to take part at the centenary festival of the International Staff Band, held in the Fairfield Halls, Croydon. I was given a spot in the middle of the programme and was able to recall several names and characters of bygone years. This led to my being invited to participate, more recently, in the latest miracle of modern technology – the CD-Rom (don't ask me what it means!). In this I was able to contribute some facts about the history of the band, again mentioning some of the personalities of the past and the things they had done.

Although my memory goes back to the first band to fly to an appointment – in December 1933 – my latest recollection is of the first CD-Rom to be used by a brass band anywhere in the world, so I feel rather proud of that record.

Reflecting, as one does in retirement, on all the days of my pilgrimage, I can only thank God for every experience that has been mine, for his guidance and strengthening presence over the years and for the very real privilege of enjoying 'The Best Of Both Worlds'.

Chapter 28

Epilogue

IN July 1996 I received a coloured picture postcard from General Paul Rader posted from the Holy Land. In it he told me that he and a party of seven had met for worship in the Garden of Gethsemane where, within sight of the Temple of Jerusalem across the Valley of Kidron, they sang 'I Would Be Thy Holy Temple' 'with great blessing'.

That one of my songs should have been sung in such a holy place and that the international leader of The Salvation Army should take the time and trouble to write a handwritten card to tell me of the occasion made me feel very humble indeed.

No composer could ask for a greater accolade.

Index

A

Abergavenny Band 242
Abney Park Cemetery 21, 28, 56, 253
Adams, Bernard 154, 159, 254, 261, 293, 302
Adelboden 256
Agincourt 73, 341, 343, 352
Akron, Ohio 262
Albert Schweitzer Hall 231
Alexandra, Queen 44, 243
Alford 201
All The World 149, 219
Allan, John J. 154, 172, 262
Allen, Raymond 320
Allentown 260
Allington, Bram 102, 279, 315
Allison, Ronald 293
Almelo 160
'Altar Of Praise' 353
Ambassadors Session 191
Amsterdam 175, 220, 221, 235
Anderson, Berth 225
Anderston Citadel 207
Andre, Eric 103
Andrews, George 117
Anne, Princess 243
Armstrong, William 110
Arnhem 160
Ash 187
Associated Headquarters 65, 78, 83, 100, 323
Assurance Songsters 101, 107, 322, 323
Atkinson, John 150, 273
Attlee, Clement 128

Atwell, George 208
Australia 42, 45, 147, 149, 172, 306, 307, 325, 348
Austria 94, 183, 229, 230, 231, 232, 233
Avon Theatre 1, 339

B

Badnall, Ron 244
Baird, Catherine 149, 216
Baldock 304
Baldwin, Stanley 55
Ball, Eric 2, 3, 64, 65, 91, 96, 314, 352
Ballantine, Leonard 279
Bands Department 145, 291, 301, 303, 309, 311, 333
Bandsman And Songster, The 34, 37, 57, 59, 65, 66, 87, 144
Barking 79
Barnado, Thomas 289
Barnet 22
Barnett, Alfred 92
Barrett, David 313
Basle 246, 255, 256
Battle of Britain 121, 122, 155
Bax, Bernard 57
Bearcroft, Bramwell 112
Bearcroft, Norman 112, 217, 288, 292, 302, 309, 333
'Beatitudes, The' 323
Beaumont, Stuart Holden 78, 330
'Beautiful Land, So Bright, So Fair, Untold Glories Linger There' 330

361

'Beautiful Star' 330
'Beautiful Zion' 323, 335
Belfort 294
Belgian Evangelistic Mission 294
Belgium 220, 257, 293, 348
Bell, George Robert 105, 200
Bellamy, Corporal 118, 119
Belsize Park 133
Bergen 227, 228
Berlin 203, 229
Bermondsey 75, 141
Bernese Oberland 256
Best, Arthur 94, 95
Birmingham 102, 137, 146, 147, 160,
  215, 272, 303, 308
Bishop's Stortford 66
Blackburn 303
Blackfriars 18, 56, 75, 82, 84
Blackpool 307, 328
Blackwell, Ben 148, 149, 151, 152, 153,
  159, 161, 178
Blackwell, David 154
Bladin, John 172, 193
Blanch, Dr Stuart (Archbishop of York)
  348
Blasieholm's Church 223
Blind Beggar, The 205
Blood Of The Lamb, The 1
Bloomfield, Leonard 71, 75, 87, 113
Bloomfield, SL Tom 33
Boberg, Carl 354
Bognor 309
Boon, Alfred Railton, 22
Boon, Annis (née Fielding) 15, 20, 22
Boon, Brindley vii, viii, ix, 8, 20, 28, 68,
  115, 120, 153, 158, 205, 240, 305,
  317
Boon, Georgia 355, 356
Boon, Herbert 28, 66
Boon, John Brindley (Brindley Boon's
  son) 35, 134, 138, 167, 181, 189,
  271, 272, 274

Boon, John Brindley 14, 134
Boon, Nina (née Hart) 59, 69, 92, 108,
  110, 119, 124, 125, 126, 131, 132,
  134, 138, 158, 166, 168, 179, 186,
  191, 193, 274, 351, 356
Boon, William Brindley 14, 15, 16, 17,
  18, 19, 20, 21, 23
Booth, Bramwell 2, 18, 19, 20, 21, 22,
  50, 56, 197, 212, 239, 240, 243, 253,
  317
Booth, Catherine (née Mumford, Army
  Mother) 28, 69, 75, 179, 197, 240,
  253, 343
Booth, Dora 239
Booth, Evangeline 49, 50, 55, 72, 81, 83,
  84, 85, 90, 96, 97, 102, 185, 187,
  280, 293, 337
Booth, Fleur 179
Booth, Herbert 18, 27
Booth, Lucy 55
Booth, Mrs (Florence) 2, 197, 253
Booth, Olive 239
Booth, Stuart 205
Booth, William (The Founder) vii, 15,
  16, 19, 55, 56, 61, 69, 75, 101, 159,
  179, 193, 196, 205, 209, 210, 246,
  253, 261, 279, 289, 297, 305, 346
Booth, Wycliffe 265, 278
Booth-Tucker, Emma 196
Bordas, Jean 294, 296
'Born To Be King' 325
Boscombe 132, 133, 161, 162, 332
Boston 265
Boult, Sir Adrian 211, 212
Bournemouth 55, 77, 126, 130, 131,
  320, 356
Bowen, Brian 300
Bowes, Ray 4, 160, 347, 353
Box Hill Band 307
Boxmoor, Hertfordshire 84
Bradlaugh, Charles 17
Brain, Russell 70

Braine, Alfred 287
Bramwell-Booth, Catherine 197, 238,
239, 240, 253, 313
Branksome 55
Brantford 279
Brengle, (Samuel Logan) 50
Bridgwater 328
Brighton 101, 155, 252, 292, 301
Brindley, James 13
Brindley, Sarah 134
Brisley, Cyril 133, 267, 355
Bristol 60, 77, 154, 215, 303
Bristow, BM Ralph 246, 247
British Airborne Cemetery 160
British Columbia 282, 285
British Congress 310, 338
British Empire Exhibition 41, 42
British Red Shield Services 201
British Territory viii, 4, 18, 38, 60, 108,
147, 161, 244, 251, 287, 299, 300,
303, 308, 311
British Youth Congress 302
Broadmoor 79, 141, 315
Broadstairs 189, 355
Brockman, Leslie 124, 185
Bromley 9, 34
Broom, Miriam 327
Brown, Arnold 2, 81, 255, 268, 325, 341,
346, 351
Brown, Arthur 107
Brown, Marcus 202
Brussels 220, 293
Buckingham Gate 145, 342, 345
Buckingham Palace 3, 10, 145, 146, 199,
217, 243, 303, 346
Buffalo 264
Buntingford, Hertfordshire 57
Burgess, Caleb 91
Burrows, William (Will) 149, 152, 153,
154, 161, 213
Burslem, Staffordshire 14
Burton, Stanley 276

Butler, Jack 25, 26, 27, 29, 30, 31, 32
Butler, 'Mick' 25
Butler, Sara 23
Butler, Sarah (née Verrinder) 25
Butlin's 110, 299, 309, 310, 320, 333
Butterworth, Arthur 290
Button, Charles and Annie 127
Buxton, Ken 247
Byfield, Jonathan 309

C

Caddy, Raymond 346
Cadman, (Elijah) 241, 250
Calais 94, 255
Calderwood, Jimmy 142, 143
Calgary 284, 285, 286
California 244
Calne, Wiltshire 121
Calvary 111, 196
Calvert, Morley 278
Camberwell 168, 170, 171, 177, 180,
193, 272
Cambridge Heath 2, 162
Camp Wonderland, Wisconsin 286
Campfield Press, The 104, 159, 162, 195,
200, 214, 327
Camphill Borstal 71
Camsey, Terry 4
Canada viii, 33, 42, 50, 91, 190, 197,
216, 217, 238, 264, 268, 272, 273,
275, 276, 277, 278, 279, 280, 282,
283, 285, 286, 287, 302, 325, 326,
329, 348, 352
Canadian Clippings 279
Cannon Row Police Station 344, 345
Canterbury 123, 180, 181, 191, 284, 301
Canvey Island 200, 202
Cardiff 135, 139, 160, 303, 319
Cardington 113, 115, 117, 137
Carleton, John 19, 328

363

Carnegie Hall 260
Carpenter, Dr Edward (Dean of
    Westminster) 341
Carpenter, George 136, 153
Carr, Arthur 338
Cartwright, William 185
Casson, Lewis 96
Catelinet, Philip (Phil) 56, 91, 96, 146,
    261
Catford 107, 121, 180
Caversham 101
Celebes 162
Centenary Celebrations (1965) 329,
    333
Century of Song 292
Chalk Farm vii, 2, 37, 91, 93, 95, 97, 99,
    100, 102, 103, 108, 110, 111, 112,
    133, 134, 146, 147, 158, 161, 168,
    189, 191, 192, 228, 232, 258, 293,
    297, 300, 327, 351
Chamberlain, Neville 100
Champion Park 168, 170
Chapman, Stanley 150, 151, 162, 242
Charing Cross Road 17, 138, 140
Charles, Prince of Wales 346, 348, 351
Charles, William 199
Chartham 194
Chatham 124
Chelmsford 79, 206
Chesham 28
Chicago 262, 263, 282, 286, 310
Children Of The Empire 109, 110
Child's Hill 51, 52, 53, 54, 59, 64, 65, 92,
    109, 110, 124, 134, 237, 288, 300,
    313, 322, 329, 352
'Child's Prayer, A' 157
Chippenham 76
Chipping Norton 54
Christ Church Hospice 335
Christchurch 126
Christian Mission, The 196, 289, 337
Christian Mission Magazine, The 196

'Christmas At The Manor' 205
Christmas Carol, A 43, 79, 80
Church, George 154
Church, C. S. 315
Churchill, Winston (grandson of the
    below) 305
Churchill, Winston 128
Cincinnati 262
Cinderella 135
City of London 4, 346
City Temple 3, 343, 345
Clack, BM Michael 293, 294, 295, 296,
    297
Clack, Peter 293
Clapton 23, 52, 58, 60, 89, 144, 147,
    189, 195, 203, 217, 224
Clapton Congress Hall 1, 2, 49, 50, 58,
    69, 75, 95, 154, 160, 179, 197, 203,
    217, 243, 253, 272, 288, 300, 306,
    317, 323
Clark, William 351
Clark's College 47, 57
Cleaver, Arthur 109
Cleckheaton 14, 15, 16
Cleveland 264
Cliftonville 122
Clydebank Band 154
Coates, June and Carl 141
Coates, Richard 141
    Mrs 141, 142
Cobb, BM Fred 210, 288
Cobb, Roland 252, 267
Cobley, Winnie 107
Cole, Mrs 190
Coles, Alan 346, 347, 348
Coles, Bramwell 3, 37, 91, 155, 253, 265,
    275, 302, 324, 325, 329, 331, 332
Coles, Gordon 262, 286
Coller, Charles 49
Colley, (Alfred) 250
Columbus (Ohio) 262
Comrade Of The Cross, A 111

364

Condon, Leslie 206, 252, 302, 303, 304, 309, 310, 311, 316, 333, 338, 354, 355
Cook, Kenneth 244
Cooke, Oliver 107, 108
Cooper, Brian 250
Cooper, William 173, 223, 291, 299, 333
Copenhagen 223, 308
Cork, Teddy 184
Cornelius, Doris 186
Cornelius, Sid 186
Cossar, Lily 107
Cotterill, Edward and Mrs 250
Cottrill, Walter Stanley 80, 81, 346, 351
Coutts, Frederick viii, 147, 150, 191, 192, 218, 293, 295, 301, 305, 326
Covent Garden 243
Coventry 125, 137, 161
Coward, Eric 199, 202
Cowfold 252
Cox, Gordon 173, 174, 175, 176
Cox, Rev Sidney E. 238
Cox, Sidney 33, 354
Coxhead, Frederick J. 289
Coxhead, George 273
Crawley New Town 252
Creighton, Will 275
Crest, The 275
Crewkerne 290
Cricklewood 21, 47, 48, 313
Crooks, George 302, 309, 310
Crooks, Lily 302, 309
Cross, Pippa 341
Croydon 135, 177, 204, 301, 302, 307, 333, 357
'Croydon Citadel' 329
Croydon Citadel vii, 197, 218, 273, 301, 302, 306, 309, 320, 327, 332, 354
Crystal Palace 26, 49, 55, 70, 195, 218, 301, 315, 339

Cuell, Edgar 102, 103
Culshaw, Owen 201
Czechoslovakia 232

D

'Daddy's Deputy' 34
Dalziel, Geoffrey 173, 178, 190
Dalziel, Peter 300, 309
Dalziel, Sylvia (née Gair) 290, 300, 309
Dalziel, William 156, 158, 189
Danforth 73, 264, 279, 286
Darlington 143
Davey, Booth 111
Davey, Maureen 157
Davidson, Bill 292, 300
Davidson, William 273
Davies, William 242
Davis, Emma 228
Davis, Trevor 206, 311
Deal 185, 188
Deliverer, The 220
Denmark 112, 223, 308, 332, 348, 354
Denmark Hill 100, 101, 149, 151, 153, 163, 168, 176, 180, 195, 198, 201, 208, 210, 212, 220, 238, 254, 255, 267, 272, 303
Dennis, Thomas 86
Derby 19, 22
Dermott, June 323
Detroit 264
Dibden, Edgar 215
Dickens, Dorothy 133
Dilloway, George 85
Ditmer, Stanley 4
'Divine Weaver, The' 333
Dollis Hill 7, 35
Doncaster 308
Dorking 250, 251
Dover 20, 22, 125, 184, 220, 275
Dowding, BL Herb 329

Dowdle, James 21, 250
Downham Market, Norfolk 100
Drage, (Thomas) 250
Drapeau, Jean 265
Dray, William 225, 226, 261, 271, 273
Drury Lane 108, 109, 110, 135
Duff, Mildred 327
Duggins, Norman 256, 273
Dunkirk (near Canterbury) 123
Dunkirk 112
Durham 214, 315
Dürig, Adolf 294
Durman, Charles 287
Dye, Bobby and Lily 44

E

Earl's Court 97, 339
Earlscourt Band 217, 274, 286
Early, Sidney 117
East Africa *War Cry* 213
East Finchley 20, 22
East Grinstead 174
East London Chorus 69
Eastry 187
Ebbs, William Alex 22
Ebbsfleet 183
Edinburgh 157, 207, 282
Editorial Department 20, 148, 149, 195,
   275, 340
Edmonton (Alberta) 283, 284
Edmonton (Greater London) 51
Edward VII, (King) 44
Edward VIII, (King) 44
Edwin, Onslow 64
Eli Beckett and Company 25
Eliason, Carl 234
Elizabeth II, (Her Majesty) Queen 210,
   217, 243, 251, 347
Elizabeth, Queen (Queen Mother,
   Duchess of York) 1, 2, 71, 109, 146

Elmers End 267
Elwes, Polly 300
EMI St Johns Wood 265
Empire Day 42, 43
Empire Pool (Wembley) 310, 339
Empire Stadium 340
Empress Of England 274
Empress Of Ireland 21, 208
En Avant! 94
'Enchanted Castle Of My Heart' 321
Enchanted Castle, The 135, 320
'England Is A Garden' 319, 320
Ernst Reuter Haus 229
Esson, BM William 26, 28
Evangeline Booth Youth Centre 101
Evans, Francis 94, 229
Evans, Idwal 154
Evans, John 341
Evans, Wesley 157, 177
Everett, Handel 177
Everett, Lily 178
'Except I Am Moved With Compassion'
   209

F

Fairbank, Frank 261, 285
Fairbank, Jenty 285
Fairfield Halls (Croydon) 301, 303, 306,
   307, 357
Farson, Daniel 245
Fensom, Ray 205
Fenwick, William 201
Ferguson, George 200
Festival of Britain 195, 209, 319
Festival of Gospel Song 292
Festival of Sounding Praise 292
Fewster, Ernest 311
Finland 226, 227, 232, 332
First World War 7, 10, 33, 103, 108, 115,
   125, 126, 130, 226, 250, 283, 330

366

Flanders 125
Fleet Street 46, 301
Foale, Richard 339
Folkestone 211, 255
Foreign Office (Salvation Army) 23
Foreness Point, Cliftonville 122, 324
Fossey, Leslie 213, 214
Fouracre, Eva 92, 95, 109, 319
Fowler, Brenda 157
France 25, 95, 111, 183, 186, 220, 232, 257, 294
Francis Street Hostel 77, 78
Freeman, Gerald 68, 75, 76, 79, 81
French, Holland 263, 279
Frinton-on-Sea 354
Fry, Charles 301, 322
Fry, Fred W. 60, 91
Fuller, George 84, 85, 155

G

Gaiety Theatre (Clacton) 309
Gainsborough 308
Galilee 111, 334
Gander (Newfoundland) 259, 265
Garnham, George 344, 345
Gateshead 214
Gauntlett, S. Carvosso 149
Geary, George 45
Geneva 256
George V, King 42, 56
George VI, King (Duke of York) 1, 3, 71, 109, 128, 198
Germany 94, 112, 149, 223, 232, 235, 256, 302, 306
Gethsemane 359
Gibbs, Bernard 344
Gilliard, Alfred 95, 149, 213, 287, 314
Gillingham 38, 173, 300
Gladstone Park 7

Glasgow 101, 157, 207, 208, 215, 273
Godfrey, Sir Dan 77
Goffin, Dean 148, 177, 217, 218, 272, 287, 323, 333
Golders Green 124
Goldsmith, Albert 177
Goldsmith, Arthur 37, 66, 69, 71, 87, 92, 93, 95, 121, 134, 155, 216, 237, 250, 253, 301, 302, 311, 355
Gorgie Corps 207
Gothenburg 225
Gowans, John 110, 299
Grant, Fred 244, 319
Grays 201
Great Exhibition 195
Great Orchestral Hall (Chicago) 262
Great Western Hall 18, 82
Great Western Hostel 82
Great Yarmouth 291
'Greathearts' 326
'Greathearts For God' 326
Green, Rita 286
Greet, Sir Ben 43
Gregson, Edward 292
Griffiths, Archie 107
Grinsted, Edgar 97, 250, 272, 309
Gröningen 160, 221
Grottick, William 177, 197, 287
Grove Lane 170
Grove Park 9
Grozinsky, Gustav 283, 284
Guilford, Earl of 187
Gullidge, BM 35
Gut, Edwin 230
Guy's Hospital 93
Gypsy Nell 34

H

Haarlem 221, 222
Hackney 101

Hadleigh (Essex) 89, 154, 156, 157, 163, 187, 200, 300
Hadley Wood 101
Hague, The 220
'Hail To The King!' 3
'Hail, Britannia!' 110
Haines, Cliff 107
Haines, William 50
Halifax (Nova Scotia) 259, 279
Halifax 56
Hall, Henry 107, 108, 216
Hall's Lake 278
Hamilton 279
Hammersmith 18
Hammond, Walter 45, 46
Hampstead 189
Handscombe, Susan 327
Hannam, Stanley 89
Hannevik, Edward 228
Hanover 235
Hanson, Rupert 206
Happy Warrior, The 328
Harding, Maud 193
Harker, Clifford 138
Harlesden 23, 65, 133, 154, 188, 323
Harris, Catherine 119
Harris, William G. 149, 167
Harrow 35, 41, 91
Harrow-on-the-Hill 36
Hartford (Connecticut) 265
Harwich 160, 223
Hatfield 159
Hawkes, Frederick 91, 155, 253, 302, 318, 326
Hawley, William 324
'Hear Us, We Pray' 319
Heckmondwike 15, 16
Heilsarmee, Die 229
Helsinki 226, 227
Hely, Gerald 290
Hemel Hempstead 93
Hendon 54, 157, 210, 288

Henfield 252
Henning, Sylvester 132
'Heralds, The' 326
Herne Bay 201
Higgins, Edward 21, 22, 50, 55, 58, 70, 152, 196, 314
    Mrs (Catherine) 36, 70
Higgins, George 200, 202
Higgins, Ruth 177
High Council (1929) 50
    (1946) 146
    (1954) 241
    (1963) 305
High Wycombe 70
Highgate 160
Hill, Edward 37
Hill, Ernest 85
Hillingdon 299, 306
'Hillside' 329, 352
Hilversum 160
Hine, Stuart K. 354
Hines, Jerome 276, 277
History Of The Salvation Army, The 216, 289
Hobbs, Sir Jack 46, 47, 210
Hodgson, Rev Mr 200
Holborn 46, 135
Hold Fast Session 101
Holden, Rev Stuart 78
Holland 160, 161, 220, 222, 257
Holliday, Arthur and Wyn 335
Holloway 93, 197
Hollywood Bowl 221, 263
Holmes, Alf 252
Holz, Richard 4
'Home Of The Soldier' 330
Home Office (IHQ) 18, 284
Homefield Park 76
Hooper, Sam 65
Hope Place, Hull Lane, Stepney, 289
Horse Guards Parade 199, 344, 345
Horsham St Faith 119, 120

368

'Hosanna In The Highest' 323
Hosty, William 283, 284
Household Troops Band 91, 184
Howard, Railton 64, 83, 288, 323
Howard, T. Henry 284
Howe, Marian 206
Hoxton 168, 169, 170
Hughes, David 301
Hunsworth 14
Hunter, Denis 177, 201, 299, 301
Hurren, Samuel 50, 55, 250, 355
Hyde Park 9, 171, 172, 195, 276

I

'I Dedicate Myself To Thee' 179, 321,
    326
'I Would Be Thy Holy Temple' viii, 178,
    321, 333, 359
'If Thou Art Near' 157, 319
Ifield 252
Ilford 212
'Immortal Love' 319
India 16, 45, 132
Inglis, 'Jock' 133
International Band Music Competition
    (1934) 78
International College for Officers (ICO)
    212, 213, 275, 343
International Congress (1886) 18, 337
    (1894) 337
    (1904) 22, 337
    (1914) 33, 337
    (1978) 1, 2, 42, 205, 235, 310, 325,
    326, 337, 338, 340, 356
International Headquarters (IHQ) viii, ix,
    3, 16, 18, 20, 22, 56, 63, 64, 84, 100,
    106, 148, 150, 153, 194, 195, 198,
    209, 213, 238, 244, 246, 254, 258,
    284, 287, 295, 340, 341, 342, 343,
    352, 356

International Music Board 21, 110, 121,
    177, 254, 315, 323
International Music Editorial
    Department 3, 56, 91, 254, 324, 353
International Public Relations
    Department 267
International Staff Band (ISB) 2, 4, 55,
    60, 66, 78, 82, 91, 94, 101, 144, 154,
    160, 161, 177, 199, 208, 209, 214,
    217, 221, 228, 235, 238, 249, 250,
    251, 252, 255, 258, 260, 261, 265,
    266, 267, 269, 272, 283, 285, 286,
    293, 301, 302, 309, 314, 344, 345,
    347, 355, 357
International Staff Songsters 279
International Trade Department 19
International Training College (ITC) 100,
    148, 150, 159, 167, 168, 172, 176,
    199, 267, 293
International Training Garrison 2
International Youth Congress (1985) 356
'Into The Presence Of The King' 5, 323
Ipswich 214
Ireland 67, 303
ISB 355
Isle of Thanet 182
Isle of Wight 71, 77, 87
Israel 334
Italy 294

J

Jackson, Herbert 279
Jackson's Point 277
Jakeway, Albert 69, 254, 277, 352
James, Joshua 210, 216
James, Will 93
Japan 50, 94
Jarvis Street 275
Jenkins, (William) 252
Jenny, Florenz 257

369

Jenny, Pierre 257
Jericho 335
Jerrett, Jack and Mrs 275
Jerusalem 334, 335, 342, 359
Jerusalem Chamber 342
Jewkes, Gordon 300
Jewkes, Thomas 177
Johanson, Dr Brian 343
Jones, Adeline 201
Jones, Mai 139
Jones, Tom 188
'Joy In Service' 319
Joy, Margery 340
Joyce, C. A. 71
'Joyous Proclamation, The' 351
Joystrings 290, 291, 292, 300, 303
Judd Street 49, 64, 67, 101, 153, 168, 254, 345
Juliana, Queen 160, 222
Jumet 220
Junior Staff Band 66, 355

K

Kalamazoo 263
Keep Singing! 333
Keflavik (Iceland) 258
Keith Prowse and Co, Ltd 81
Kenley, Surrey 154, 155, 156
Kennedy-Ball, Rev W. 293
Kensington 138
Kent 52, 122, 161, 183, 191, 197, 284
Kent Street Baths 160
Kent, Enoch 322
Kent, Robert 39
Kentish Town 102
Kenton, SL Stanley 184
Kenyon, Albert 150, 161, 212
Kenyon, Michael 212, 300
Kettering 149, 154
Kilburn 107, 166

Kimpton, SL Arthur 330
'Kingdom, The' 325
'Kingdoms, The' 319
Kingston upon Thames 90, 157, 244, 299
Kirkenhof 294
Kitchen, June 288, 304
Kitchener (Ontario) 216, 279
Kitching, Mrs (Kathleen) 197, 223, 240, 241
Kitching, Theodore 212
Kitching, Wilfred 33, 35, 97, 196, 205, 209, 210, 216, 223, 240, 243, 253, 254, 272, 287
Kitley, Walter and Lilian 131
Kniveton, Harry 95, 188
Korea 203, 204, 342
Korumburra, Australia 172
Kreisky, Bruno 231

L

Labrador 286
Lanark House 203
Lane, Andrew 127
Lang, Rev John 293
Langdon, George 67
Langham Place 60, 245
Langley Green 252
Larsson, (Karl) 50
Larsson, John 110, 299, 309
Larwood, Harold 45, 46
Las Vegas 263
Lausanne 298
Lawley, John 50, 314, 317, 318
Leeds 101, 118, 303, 307, 308
Leicester 79, 101
Leidzén, Erik 52, 72, 73, 212, 223, 224, 260, 277, 286, 292, 302
Leidzén, Maria 260
'Let Peace Reign In Your Heart' 119, 319
Lewis, John 94, 113

370

Lewisham 211, 212
Leyton 289, 322
Liestal 256, 258, 294
Life Of Brindley 13
'Lift Up The Flag' 329
Lillicrap, Diane 328
Lindstrom, Carl 282
Linz 230, 231
Lisbon 234
Lissenberg, Dirk 221
Listen To The Band 254
Literary Department 150
Little Hythe Band 301
Little, Herbert 93
Liverpool 101, 211, 273, 274, 303
Liverpool House 105, 106
Liverpool Street 119
Living Word 268
Local Officer 20
Lockyer, Alfred 78, 160
Lomond Grove 171
London Chorus 289
London Girl Singers 157
London Hospital 69, 210, 289
London, Ontario 285
Londonderry 267
Long Beach 263
Long Eaton 271
Lord, Herbert 203, 204
Lord, John 341
'Lord Of The Nations' 325
Lord's 4, 46, 47, 68
Los Angeles 221, 263
Lough, Ernest 313
Louth 201
Lower Beeding 252
Ludgate Hill 301
Lunteren 221
Lupton, Ellen 123
Luton Citadel 202
Luxembourg Gardens 94
Lyon-Shaw, Bill 129

M

Mablethorpe 201
Mackenzie, Wing Commander S. 155
Macmillan, Harold 285
MacPherson, BM Keith 307
Macpherson, Sandy 169
'Mahlah' 150
Maida Vale 254, 266
'Maiden Tribute' 18
Maidenhead 255
Maidstone 79
Major Barbara 96
Malmö 223
Man With The Lamp, The 328
Manchester 14, 77, 78, 97, 101, 178,
    215, 290, 303, 306, 319
Mandarin, The 43
Manio, Jack de 245, 246, 300
Manners, Lord and Lady 131
Manston 122
Mare Street 153
Maréchale, (La) 69, 179
Margaret, Princess 290
Margate 122, 123, 124, 125, 126, 201
Margriet, Princess 222
Marriott, Bertram 34
Marsden, Pip 320
Marshall, George 85, 155, 214, 253, 302,
    326
Marshall, Jenny Smith 85, 214, 215
Marshall, Norman 260
Martin, John and Mrs 89
Marylebone 82, 85
Maud, Queen (Norway) 44
Mawby, Ivy 150, 157, 319, 320
Maxwell, (William) 50
Mayhew, Janine 193
McCarthy, Bernard 199, 205
McGrahanan, James 323
McLean, Percy 104
Melbourne 306, 325, 341, 342, 343

'Memories Of Finland' 332
'Men Who Fight For England, The' 129, 319
Men's Social Work (MSW) Headquarters Band 55, 66, 71, 72, 75, 79, 81, 87, 89, 90, 92, 93, 110, 112. 113, 322, 330
Men's Social Work (MSW) 66, 67, 82, 90, 94, 99, 104, 113, 140, 141, 144, 147, 201
Merrick, Jack 243
Merton 268
Metropolitan Music Hall (Edgware Road) 43, 79
Metropolitan Police 344
Miami (Florida) 238, 261, 264
Middle East 138, 139, 298
Middle Wallop 130
Middlesbrough 85
Middlesex 45, 90, 158
Middlesex House 106
Middlesex Street 66, 77, 92, 105, 153
Mildmay 52, 58, 161
Mile End Road 209, 210
Mile End Waste 179, 209
Milford Haven 136
Miller, Mary 306
Miller, Ralph 339
Miller, Rankin 136
Mingay, Albert 325, 338
Mingay, June 244
Minster 193
Miss Duff 327
Mitchell, Gordon 178, 321
Moncton, New Brunswick 278
Monk, Joshua 276
Montreal 265, 272, 274, 277, 278, 279, 282, 285
Moon, Gladys 144, 149
Moore, Bob 341
Moore, Frances 123
Morecambe 118, 119

Morfonde 94
'Morning Star, The' 325
Mortimer, Harry 210, 266
Mount Pleasant 285
Mountain, BM Herbert and Mrs 322
Moyler, John Thomas 150
Moyse, John 173
Muir, Hugh 140, 147
Munich 90
Munyi, Jonah 213
Musical Salvationist, The 3, 33, 110, 132, 147, 318, 323, 326, 330, 333
Musical Troopers 60
Musician, The vii, viii, 37, 101, 108, 121, 144, 145, 147, 148, 149, 152, 154, 160, 161, 163, 168, 205, 208, 209, 212, 213, 214, 215, 216, 217, 218, 219, 224, 225, 239, 241, 246, 260, 267, 272, 279, 287, 298, 309, 333, 349, 351
'My All For Thee' 326

N

Napier, David 346
National Headquarters (NHQ) 18, 84, 145, 154, 156, 287, 333
National Secretary for Bands and Songster Brigades viii, 216, 272, 287, 333, 338
National Secretary for Special Efforts 339
National Songsters 292, 293, 327
National Young People's Department 156
Neald Hall 76
Neath 161
Nelson 156, 158
Nelson, Victor 65
Nesbitt, John 200, 202
Netherlands, The 219, 222, 223, 232, 235, 302

New Addington 300
New Forest 126, 131, 332
'New Jerusalem' 15, 323, 324, 325
New York 163, 223, 258, 259, 260, 265,
   276, 277, 281, 282, 286, 302, 341,
   343, 352, 353
New Zealand 55, 80, 81, 130, 148, 182,
   287, 302
Newark 265
Newcastle 75, 85, 92, 215, 272, 303
Newman, Victor 211
Newport, Isle of Wight 77
Niagara Falls 264
Nicholson, Joe 51, 52, 53, 55, 166
Noble, Wycliffe 300
Norfolk 100, 120, 304
Normandy 320
Norris, Dr Robert 343
North Shields 85
'North Toronto Young People' 329
North Walsham 327
North, Michael 139
Northampton 101, 238
Northern Chorus 308
Northern Ireland 315
Northwood, Eric 154
Norway 44, 50, 112, 227, 302, 308, 332
Norwich 119, 120, 291
Notintone Place 101
Nottingham 101, 228, 246, 258
Nunhead 108, 170, 279, 328
Nutty, Ken 133, 251, 288

O

'O Far Whiter Than The Snow' 331
'O Have You Not Heard Of The Beautiful
   Stream?' 331
'O Jesus, My Saviour, Will Welcome
   Sinners Home' 329
'O Save Me, Dear Lord' 305

Officer, The 19, 20, 150
Olaf, Crown Prince 44
Old Compton Street 138
Oliphant, (W. Elwin) 241
Olympia 193, 339
Omaha, Nebraska 262
'Omnia Vincit Amor' 97
'One Happy Day' 320
Ontario 216, 277, 278, 279, 282, 285
Örebro 302, 308
Orsborn, Albert 20, 22, 33, 36, 38, 121,
   146, 153, 163, 188, 198, 209, 221,
   223, 253, 288, 322, 337, 355
Orsborn, Mrs (Phillis) (Taylor) 36, 196,
   209, 219, 221
Orton, Harold 260
Oslo 302, 308, 343
Östby, (Klaus) 155
Ostend 220, 293
Ouchterlony, Hanna 16
'Our King Cometh' 319, 323
Out Of The Blue 129
Overton, William 211, 286

P

Paddington Goodwill Centre 276, 277
Pageant of Army Progress 55
Paisley Citadel 174, 176
Palmerston North Band 80
Paris 93, 94, 246, 298
Parker, John and Mrs 242
Parkhurst 71, 79, 315
Parry, (Hubert) 265
Parry, Dr Joseph 39, 69
Pasadena Municipal Auditorium 263
Pascal, Gabriel 96
Pattison, Jim and Eva 264
Paul VI, Pope vii, viii, 295, 296, 297
Peabody Buildings 171
Peach, Coral 328

Peach, June 328
Peagam, Tony 298
Pearson, William 322
Pembrokeshire 136, 319
Pender, Dinsdale 154
Pender, Leslie 301
Penge 2, 147, 238, 301, 328
Percy, Ken 266
Perry, Sam 162
Philadelphia 261, 262
Phillips, George 60
Piccadilly 10, 77, 266, 345
Pinchbeck, Gordon 273
Pinchbeck, Thelma (née Boon) 34, 35, 273
'Pioneers' 326
Pittsburgh Temple Band 261
Plain Fields, New Jersey 286
Plaistow 201
Play The Music, Play! 326, 355
Plumstead 301
Plymouth 43, 303
Point St Charles 279
Pontefract 92
Pontypridd 101
Poole Arts Centre 65
Poplar 179, 196, 201
Portsmouth 71, 102
Portugal 234, 235
Poste Parisien 94
Potter, David 78
Pratt, Will 161, 200, 206, 213, 252, 254, 306
Price, BM Neil 119
Price-Smith, David 341
Pugh, BM Douglas 278
Pugmire, Joseph 314
Pugmire, Percy and Mrs 313
Pull, Leslie 206
Punchard, A. W. (A.W.P.) 37, 91, 93, 103, 108, 113, 133, 147, 168, 189, 232, 355
Pursuit Of Happiness 245

Q

Quebec 274, 277
Queen Victoria Street 18, 56, 63, 84, 106, 153, 258, 284
Queen's Hall, Langham Place 60, 61, 112

R

Rader, Paul 359
RAF Honiley 137
RAF Station Abingdon 203
RAF Uxbridge 136
Railton, George Scott 22, 241, 261
Railton, John 196
Ramsgate 184, 185
Rance, Ernest 69, 71, 75, 78, 87, 163, 216, 244, 287, 319, 322
Raper, Frances 59
Rawbone, Frank 146, 191
Rayleigh 200, 202
Reading 101, 107, 117, 133, 216, 299
Reck, Karl-Heinz 229
Red Shield Band 293
Red Shield House 145
Redcar 85
Redwood, Hugh 277
Rees, David 21
Regent Hall (Rink) 2, 9, 10, 38, 49, 56, 58, 61, 65, 75, 76, 85, 91, 93, 94, 96, 97, 101, 104, 107, 108, 144, 145, 146, 147, 154, 157, 161, 170, 187, 188, 190, 196, 210, 211, 243, 244, 252, 253, 266, 301, 302, 303, 328, 333, 345, 351
Regina, Saskatchewan 282
Rendell, Doris 92, 119, 318, 319, 322, 323
Renouf, Andrew 346
Reykjavik 259
Rich, Charles 50, 83
Rich, Wesley 100, 111, 113, 146, 274

Richards, Miriam 319, 326
Richborough 183
Riches, Lucy 273
Rickmansworth 35
Ringham, Marjorie 292
Ripperston 134
Rive, Tom 255
Robinson, William and Mrs 181
Rochdale 16
Rodda, Bertram 244
Rolls, Arthur 264, 315
Rolls, Bertie 188
'Romance Of The Salvation Army, The' 82
Rome vii, 111, 294, 295, 297
Rookstone 101
Root, Fred 45
'Rosehill' 101, 216
Rosehill Band 133, 154
Ross, Ann 292
Rotterdam 160, 221
Royal Albert Hall 53, 55, 70, 71, 72, 75,
 82, 95, 96, 143, 146, 161, 188, 217,
 242, 289, 292, 305, 306, 307, 308,
 323, 325, 339, 342, 343, 344, 347
Royal Army Service Corps 9, 34
Royal Exchange 56
Royal Festival Hall 198, 209, 234
Royal Tennis Hall (Stockholm) 223
Royle, Roger 353
Royston, Yorkshire 92
Rudge, Tony 341
Rugby 158, 241
Rushforth, Alan 345
Russell, Eric 107
Ryde 71

S

Salisbury 130
Salvation Army Assurance Society, The
 51, 55, 64, 95, 100

Salvation Army Fire Insurance
 Corporation, The 101
Salvation Army Halt 159, 160
Salvation Army Year Book, The 150
Salvationist Publishing and Supplies,
 Limited (SP&S) 64, 82, 101, 121, 255,
 345
SP&S Band 101
Salvationist vii, 219
Sampson, Lily 150
Samuels, (Albert) 250
Sanderson, James 201
Sanderstead, Lord Armstrong of 348
Sandringham 44
'Sandwich' 329
Sandwich 53, 54, 125, 179, 181, 182,
 183, 184, 185, 186, 187, 188, 191,
 192, 194, 195, 284, 324
Sankey, Ira D. 330
Saskatchewan 282, 283
Saywell, BM Edward 38, 145, 148, 161,
 287, 323
Scandinavia 177, 223
'Scandinavian Congress' 353
Schenectady 265
Scotland 160, 207, 213, 287, 303, 346
Scotland Yard 4
Scott, Clement 81
Seaham Harbour 328
Seattle Songster Brigade 285
Second World War 61, 79, 81, 167, 184,
 196, 229, 232, 233, 339, 352
'See The Colours Go Passing By' 179
'Seeking For Thee' 319
Selwood, Edley 278
Seoul Boys' Home Band 342
'Servants Of God' 326
Severn Theatre 1, 339
Sharp, Richard 130
Shaw 308
Shaw, George Bernard 96, 243, 244
Sheard, Arthur 60, 61

Sheerness Corps 161
Sheffield 303, 306, 308
Shepherd's Bush 211
Sheringham 291
Shirley 197, 204, 267
Shirley, Eliza 261
Shout Aloud Salvation 193
Silfverberg, Erik 4
Sing The Happy Song! 237, 326, 327
Singapore 177
'Singing We Go' 157, 158, 319
Singspiration Inc Ltd 354
Sizeland, Eddie 191
Skinner, Charles 66, 68, 75, 78, 90, 121, 238, 261, 264, 292, 319, 332
Sladen, Brian 341
Slater, Richard 104, 155, 302
Smith, Alfred 279
Smith, BM Derek 353
Smith, Dennis 315
Smith, Frank 17
Smith, George B. 154, 155, 213
Smith, John Evan 22
Smith, Joseph 22
Snook, John 177
Söderström, Emil 254, 262
'Soldiers Of The Cross' 326
Sole, BM Roland 184, 193
Song Book Of The Salvation Army, The 237, 321, 334
Song Book Revision Council (1950-52) 321
'Song Of Happiness, A' 318
Song Of The Hills 327
Sopley 126, 127, 128, 129, 130, 131, 133, 319, 356
Soul Winners Session 326
Souter, Edward 93
South Africa 199, 204, 287
South Croydon 168, 197
'South Shields' 333
South Shields 85, 214

Southall Songsters 65
Southampton 215
Southend 95, 202, 211
Southsea 20, 22
Southsea Joybelles 306, 307
Soweto Songsters 341, 343
Sowton, George 96
Spa Home 141
Spa Road 75, 81, 141, 142, 143, 144
Spaarndam 222, 223
Spencer, BM Herbert 51, 54, 56
Spicer, Stanley 185
'Spirit Divine' 332
Springate, Alfred 300
St Albans 22, 101, 159, 174, 202, 208, 322
St Andrew's Hall (Glasgow) 207
St Andrew's, Willesden 39, 44
St David's (Pembrokeshire) 136
St Ives (Cornwall) 251
St Mildred's Eventide Home, Westgate 186
St Paul's Cathedral 3, 56, 301, 305, 329, 341, 342, 343, 345
St Paul's, Portman Square 78
St Peter's Church, Sandwich 183
St Stephen's Cathedral (Vienna) 233
Staff Councils (1904) 196
Staff Department 20, 23
Staines 157, 300
Standard Bearers Session 163, 178, 180
Standing, Michael 139
'Starry Crown, A' 315, 330
Stars On Sunday 307
Stead, W. T. 18
Steadman-Allen, Ray 4, 133, 171, 179, 309, 351
Steinway Hall (London) 197
Stepney Green 217
'Still With Thee' 121, 330
Stockholm 223, 224, 225, 226, 232, 233
Stockport Citadel Band 290

Stockton 143
Stockwell Green Congregational Church
  253
Strangeways Prison 78, 315
Strasbourg 294
Stratford Goodwill Centre 327
Straughan, Will 52, 54, 55, 125
'Streams Of Mercy' 331
Sturgess, Catherine 150
Stuttgart 229
Sullivan, Dr Martyn (Dean of St Paul's)
  341
Sunbury 157, 158, 163, 187
Sunbury Court 50, 90, 101, 306, 316,
  320
Sunday Half-Hour 177, 293, 306, 310
Sunderland Citadel 85
Sunset Lodge, Tunbridge Wells 237
'Sunshine Of Love' 319
Surrey 47, 144, 154, 155, 197, 250
Sussex 76, 155, 174, 240, 252
Sutcliffe, Herbert 45
Sutton 243, 301, 306
Sutton-on-Sea 201
Sweden 16, 73, 225, 227, 302, 308, 332,
  354
'Sweet Story, The' 330
Swindon 121, 159
Swiss Officers Band 230
Switzerland 197, 228, 232, 246, 247,
  255, 256, 257, 294, 297, 298, 302,
  314
'Swordbearers' 326
Sydenham 195, 343
Sydney Salvation Singers 325, 343
Symonds, (Ronald) 347

T

Talbenny 134, 135
Tarrant, Frank 44, 45

Tate, Cynthia 8
Tattersall, John 171, 172
Taylor, Bramwell 36
Taylor, Jack 315
Temple Choir (London) 313
Terrot, Charles 193
Thain, BM Alex 207
Thanet 122, 182
Thatcher, Margaret 348
'There's A Challenge Ringing Out Along
  The Highway' 178
Thompson, Bert 252, 347
Thorn, Dennis 107
Thorndike, Dame Sybil 43, 96
Thorndike, Russell 43, 79
Thornsett, Derbyshire 13
Thornton Heath 93, 279, 302, 327
'Thou Art Holy, Lord Of Glory' 333
'Thou Hast Called Me From The Byway'
  333
Tickner, Leslie 300
Tilbury 201, 225
Today 245
Todd, Ray 296
Toft, James 226
Topley, Bernard 93
Topley, Ronald 201, 340
Torchbearers Session 60
Toronto 73, 208, 216, 255, 264, 265,
  269, 274, 275, 276, 277, 278, 279,
  280, 281, 282, 285, 325, 352
Torquay 249
Tottenham Citadel Band 21, 85, 154,
  302, 306
Tottenham Court Road 153
Town And Around 293
Tracy, Ruth 237
Trainer, Jean 213
Tranås Band 223, 224, 225
'Triumphant In The Combat' 319
Tucker, Frederick (Booth) 16
Tunbridge Wells 237, 306

Tunes For Worship 15
Twickenham 157
Twitchin, BM Herbert (Bert) 9, 10, 91,
    101, 104, 145, 210, 211, 243, 322,
    328
Tyndal, Harry 234

U

United States of America (USA) 49, 50,
    72, 102, 149, 154, 196, 198, 212,
    238, 258, 259, 260, 261, 265, 266,
    268, 279, 285, 286, 354, 355, 356
'Unsinkable Boat, The' 179
Unsworth, Isaac 150
Unsworth, Madge 149, 150
Upper Norwood 292, 302
Upper Thames Street 254, 266
Usher, George 76
Utrecht 160

V

Vancouver, British Columbia 285
Vanderkam, Samuel 220
Vandon Street 153
Vanguard viii, 287
Varsity Arena (Toronto) 265, 275
Vatican vii, 295, 296, 297
Vaughan Williams, Dr Ralph 42, 250,
    254
Verdun, Canada 279
Verein der Heilsarmee 231
Vevey 298
Vickery, Alf 314
Victoria, Vancouver Island 352
Victoria Home Men's Social Work Centre
    75, 81, 276
Victoria Homes, Whitechapel 315
Victoria, Queen 28, 143

'Victorious' 311, 326
Vienna 229, 231, 232, 233
Vlaardingen 160, 161

W

'Wake Up, Britannia!' 95
Wales 134, 138, 139, 161, 242, 303,
    343
Walker, Leonard 201
Walker, William 132
Walthamstow Band 301
Wandsworth Band 35
War Cry, The viii, 2, 3, 17, 18, 20, 24, 27,
    94, 95, 103, 107, 149, 159, 160, 194,
    195, 196, 197, 198, 200, 205, 207,
    210, 212, 219, 239, 245, 275, 289,
    314, 315, 337, 351
Ward, Tim 346
Ware, William 273
Warmongers, The 290
Warren, Harry 169, 173, 179
Washington, DC 260
Watson, Bernard 149, 151, 152, 327
Watson, Winnie 157
Watts, Charles 66
Wearmouth 328
Weatherhead, Dr Leslie 48, 343
'Weaver Divine' 333
Webb, Burnal 77
Webb, Joy 206, 291, 292, 300
Wellingborough 306
Wellington Citadel Band 302, 303
Wellman, Ernest 83
Wembley 1, 3, 41, 42, 310, 311, 326,
    327, 338, 339, 340, 342, 343, 344,
    347, 348
Wentworth Street 106
West Newton 44
Westergaard, Kaare 158
Westergaard, Mona 326

378

Western Illinois University, USA 356
Westminster 341, 342
Westminster Abbey 3, 143, 301, 341, 342, 343, 345
Westminster Cathedral 301
Westminster Central Hall 48, 75, 206, 217, 290, 320
Weston, Ken 292
'When Hearts Are Young' 319
Whitechapel 75, 197, 277, 289, 315
Whitechapel Road 69
Whitehall 283, 344, 345
Whitstable 201, 202
Whyteleaf 155
Wickberg, Erik 228, 229, 231, 233, 234, 286, 287, 307
Wielemaker, Johann 175
Wiggins, Arch R. 28, 65, 144, 145, 147, 149, 212, 213, 214, 216, 311, 323
Wilkins, Fred 107
Willesden 23, 25, 26, 39, 43, 45
Willesden Green 7, 20, 22, 26, 28, 32, 33, 82, 195, 330
Williams, Comr Harry 338
Williams, Harry 39, 40, 43
Williams, James 107
Williams, Sidney 149, 152, 160, 161, 205
Willson, Dr Meredith 263
Wimbledon 102, 327
Winchester 71, 88, 89, 133
Windsor (Canada) 279, 282
Windsor 255
Wingham 284
Winney, Ted 133
Winnipeg 275, 276, 282, 286
Winton Corps 356
Wiseman, (Clarence) 234, 235, 273, 341
Woking 206, 245

Wombwell 315
Women's Social Work Headquarters 101, 213
Wood Green Band 36, 300
Wood, Herbert 275
Woodall, Sydney 210
Woodcock, Graham 247
Woodnesborough 187
Woods, Reginald 149, 216
Woodside 267
Woodward, Leonard 162, 163
Wormwood Scrubs 315
Worth 187
Worthing 76, 273, 278, 300
Wright, Harold 249
Wrigley, Lilian 277

Y

Yamamuro, (Gunpei) 50
Yarde, Raymond 294, 296
Yates, Jess 307
Yatesbury 121
Yendell, Muriel (née Wilson) 156, 157, 158
York 308
Yorkshire 14, 92, 185, 193
Young People's Department (National) 154, 156
Youth Department 301

Z

Zahnd, Walter 256
Zealley, Harold 78
Zürich 228, 229, 247